Environmental Fiscal Challenges for Cities and Transport

CRITICAL ISSUES IN ENVIRONMENTAL TAXATION

Series Editors: Mikael Skou Andersen, *Aarhus University, Denmark*, Hope Ashiabor, *Macquarie University, Australia* and Janet E. Milne, *Vermont Law School, USA*

The *Critical Issues in Environmental Taxation* series provides insights and analysis on environmental taxation issues on an international basis and explores detailed theories for achieving environmental goals through fiscal policy. Each book in the series contains pioneering and thought-provoking contributions by the world's leading environmental tax scholars who respond to the diverse challenges posed by environmental sustainability.

Previous volumes in the series:

Original book published by CCH Incorporated

Volumes I–IV published by Richmond Law Publishers

Volumes V–VIII published by Oxford University Press

Volume IX onwards published by Edward Elgar Publishing

Recent titles in the series include:

Volume XIV — Environmental Taxation and Green Fiscal Reform
Theory and Impact
Edited by Larry Kreiser, Soocheol Lee, Kazuhiro Ueta, Janet E. Milne and Hope Ashiabor

Volume XV — Carbon Pricing
Design, Experiences and Issues
Edited by Larry Kreiser, Mikael Skou Andersen, Birgitte Egelund Olsen, Stefan Speck, Janet E. Milne and Hope Ashiabor

Volume XVI — Environmental Pricing
Studies in Policy Choices and Interactions
Edited by Larry Kreiser, Mikael Skou Andersen, Birgitte Egelund Olsen, Stefan Speck, Janet E. Milne and Hope Ashiabor

Volume XVII — Green Fiscal Reform for a Sustainable Future
Reform, Innovation and Renewable Energy
Edited by Natalie P. Stoianoff, Larry Kreiser, Bill Butcher, Janet E. Milne and Hope Ashiabor

Volume XVIII — Market Instruments and the Protection of Natural Resources
Edited by Natalie P. Stoianoff, Larry Kreiser, Bill Butcher, Janet E. Milne and Hope Ashiabor

Volume XIX — The Green Market Transition
Carbon Taxes, Energy Subsidies and Smart Instrument Mixes
Edited by Stefan E. Weishaar, Larry Kreiser, Janet E. Milne, Hope Ashiabor and Michael Mehling

Volume XX — Innovation Addressing Climate Change Challenges
Market-based Perspectives
Edited by Mona Hymel, Larry Kreiser, Janet E. Milne and Hope Ashiabor

Volume XXI — Environmental Fiscal Challenges for Cities and Transport
Edited by Marta Villar Ezcurra, Janet E. Milne, Hope Ashiabor and Mikael Skou Andersen

Environmental Fiscal Challenges for Cities and Transport

Edited by

Marta Villar Ezcurra

Professor of Financial and Tax Law, Faculty of Law, CEU San Pablo University, Spain

Janet E. Milne

Professor of Law and Director of the Environmental Tax Policy Institute, Vermont Law School, USA

Hope Ashiabor

Associate Professor of Law, Faculty of Business and Economics, Macquarie University, Australia

Mikael Skou Andersen

Professor of Environmental Policy Analysis, Aarhus University, Denmark

CRITICAL ISSUES IN ENVIRONMENTAL TAXATION
VOLUME XXI

EE Edward Elgar
PUBLISHING

Cheltenham, UK • Northampton, MA, USA

Published by
Edward Elgar Publishing Limited
The Lypiatts
15 Lansdown Road
Cheltenham
Glos GL50 2JA
UK

Edward Elgar Publishing, Inc.
William Pratt House
9 Dewey Court
Northampton
Massachusetts 01060
USA

A catalogue record for this book
is available from the British Library

Library of Congress Control Number: 2019946155

This book is available electronically in the **Elgar**online
Law subject collection
DOI 10.4337/9781789904185

Printed on elemental chlorine free (ECF)
recycled paper containing 30% Post-Consumer Waste

ISBN 978 1 78990 417 8 (cased)
ISBN 978 1 78990 418 5 (eBook)

Typeset by Servis Filmsetting Ltd, Stockport, Cheshire
Printed and bound in the USA

Contents

Figures

Tables

Editorial review board

The 18 chapters in this book have been brought to publication with the help of an editorial review board dedicated to peer review. The 22 members of the board are committed to the field of environmental taxation and are active participants in environmental taxation events around the world.

Contributors

Acar, Sevil, Bogazici University, Turkey

Akrawi, Emma, Vermont Law School, USA

Araújo Leonetti, Carlos, Federal University of Santa Catarina, Brazil

Ates, Leyla, Altinbas University, Turkey

Aydos, Elena, University of Newcastle, Australia

Bachus, Kris, University of Leuven, Belgium

Braathen, Nils Axel, Organisation for Economic Co-operation and Development (OECD), France

Bourgeois, Marc, University of Liège, Belgium

Burgers, Irene J.J., University of Groningen, Netherlands

Castaldi, Gionata, Italian Ministry of Environment, Land and Sea – Sogesid TA, Italy

Colelli, Francesco, Luigi Bocconi University, Italy

Croci, Edoardo, Luigi Bocconi University, Italy

De Borger, Bruno, University of Antwerp, Belgium

Esteve Pardo, María Luisa, University of Girona, Spain

Gao, Ping, Central University of Finance and Economics, China

Gago, Alberto, University of Vigo; Economics for Energy, Spain

Johnston, Vanessa, Monash University, Australia

Kettner, Claudia, Austrian Institute of Economic Research (WIFO), Austria

Kletzan-Slamanig, Daniela, Austrian Institute of Economic Research (WIFO), Austria

Labandeira, Xavier, University of Vigo; Economics for Energy, Spain

Linares Llamas, Pedro, Pontificia Comillas University, Spain

López-Otero, Xiral, The National University of Distance Education (UNED), Spain

Maillo, Jerónimo, CEU San Pablo University, Spain

Milne, Janet E., Vermont Law School, USA

Molocchi, Andrea, Italian Ministry of Environment, Land and Sea – Sogesid TA, Italy

Oliari, Rafaela Cristina, Federal University of Santa Catarina, Brazil

Peiret García, Clara, IESE Business School, Spain

Ravazzi Douvan, Aldo, Italian Ministry of Environment, Land and Sea – Sogesid TA, Italy

Robinson, David, Oxford Institute for Energy Studies, UK

Rodrigues, Renato, Potsdam Institute for Climate Impact Research, Germany

Teusch, Jonas, Organisation for Economic Co-operation and Development (OECD), France

Vanrykel, Fanny, University of Liège, Belgium

Villar Ezcurra, Marta, CEU San Pablo University, Spain

Villarejo Galende, Helena, University of Valladolid, Spain

Weishaar, Stefan E., University of Groningen, Netherlands

Zachariadis, Theodoros, Cyprus University of Technology, Cyprus

Preface

The concentration of the majority of the world's population in large cities and the ever-increasing transport of people and goods, both internationally and locally, are among the most pressing environmental challenges in the twenty-first century. A United Nations study in 2018 projected that over two-thirds of the world's population will live in urban areas by 2050, compared to just over half today. Urbanization and economic growth, projected by the Organisation for Economic Co-operation and Development to almost quadruple by 2050, will put increasing pressure on cities and transport, heightening the risks of pollution and congestion.

Environmental policies are needed to address the interrelated environmental impacts of urban concentration and transport in the context of growing globalization and the new digital economy. Policy makers face a wide array of issues, including the production, transport and supply of energy, waste treatment, smart city design, different modes of urban transport and the need to develop the fiscal capacity to adequately address these and other challenges. Economic environmental instruments can play a role in shaping behaviour and generating new revenue.

Volume XXI of *Critical Issues in Environmental Taxation* explores specific ways in which environmental taxes and other economic instruments can help to address these issues. It begins with chapters that consider the implications of twenty-first century challenges of the new digital world and fiscal constraints. It then turns to the ways in which economic instruments can encourage urban sustainability in the face of increased urban concentration and how taxation can influence traditional and new forms of transportation. It concludes with chapters that address cross-cutting policies involving the design and evaluation of environmental tax policies.

Although the environmental impacts of urban congestion and transport are multifaceted and complex, we hope that the chapters in this book will offer useful ideas and analysis that can contribute to discussions about the role of environmental economic instruments and reinforce the message that environmental taxation and other economic policies can play a meaningful role in reducing the twenty-first century's environmental footprint.

Marta Villar Ezcurra, Lead Editor
Janet E. Milne, Co-editor
Hope Ashiabor, Co-editor
Mikael Skou Andersen, Co-editor

August 2019

Abbreviations

ANEEL	Brazilian Electricity Regulatory Agency
ARB	Air Resources Board
ATC	Code of Taxes Act with equivalent to income taxes
B2B	Business-to-business
B2C	Business-to-consumer
BEPS	Base Erosion and Profit Shifting
BIA	Business improvement area
BID	Business improvement district
BNDES	Brazilian Development Bank
CATV	Comprehensive Automated Tax on Vehicles
CBA	Cost-benefit analysis
CFC	Chlorofluorocarbon
CHP	Cogeneration
CIDE	Contribution for the Intervention in the Economic Domain
CIF	Cost, Insurance and Freight
CIT	Corporate income tax
c.m.	Cubic metre
CO_2	Carbon dioxide
COMET	Carbon Management Evaluation Tool
EC	European Commission
ECR	Effective carbon rate
EEA	European Environment Agency
EEE	Electrical and electronic equipment
EPR	Extended producer responsibility
ETAAC	Electronic Tax Administration Advisory Committee
ETS	Emissions Trading System
EU	European Union
EUR	Euro
FFS	Fossil Fuel Subsidies
FINEP	Funding Authority for Studies and Projects
FOB	Free on board
GDP	Gross domestic product
GDPR	General Data Protection Regulation

GEM	General equilibrium model
GHG	Greenhouse gas
GPS	Global Positioning System
GWP	Global Warming Potential
HGV	Heavy goods vehicle
IEA	International Energy Agency
ICE	Internal combustion engine
ICSID	International Centre for Settlement of Investment Disputes
ICT	Information and communication technologies
IMF	International Monetary Fund
ISPRA	Italian National Agency for Environmental Protection
ISTAT	Italian National Statistical Institute
ITE	Implicit tax rate on energy
KTOE	Thousand tonnes of oil equivalent
KWh	Kilowatt hour
LCR	Local content requirements
LIDAR	Light Detection and Ranging
MCF	Marginal costs of public funds
MNE	Multinational enterprise
Mt	Megatonne
NACE	Statistical classification of economic activities in the European Community
NAMEA	National Accounting Matrix including Environmental Accounts
OECD	Organisation for Economic Co-operation and Development
P2P	Peer-to-peer
PE	Permanent establishment
PIT	Personal income tax
PoM	Put on the market
PPMC	Paris Process on Mobility and Climate
PPP	Public-private partnership
PPP	Purchasing Power Parity
PPP	Polluter pays principle
PRO	Producer responsibility organizations
PRODCOM	Production Communautaire
R&D	Research and development
SCC	Stockholm Chamber of Commerce
SCM	Subsidies and Countervailing Measures
SCT	Special consumption tax
SDG	Sustainable Development Goals

T	Tonne
TIA	Transport Integration Act
TL	Turkish lira
UK	United Kingdom
UNEP	United Nations Environment Programme
US	United States
USA	United States of America
USDA	US Department of Agriculture
USD	United States dollar
VAT	Value added tax
WDD	Water Development Department
WEEE	Waste electrical and electronic equipment
WTO	World Trade Organization

PART I

Impacts of the Emerging Twenty-First Century Economy

1. Environmental taxation in the digital world

Janet E. Milne*

1. INTRODUCTION

Technological innovation has changed economies from the Industrial Revolution to the new Digital Revolution. Each phase of change generates benefits to society, but also new threats to the environment. Since the mid-twentieth century, environmental protection policies have tried to keep pace, innovating to address ever-evolving challenges. Now the emerging digital economy is bringing swift and significant technological advances. Our daily lives are increasingly digital: wireless email, smart phones, online shopping, Uber, Airbnb, telecommuting, streaming, cloud storage, wearable technology and much more. This digital world is the product of a combination of digital data, analytics that use data and connectivity that allows for the exchange of data on digital platforms, often through the Internet.[1] It has created information highways in the air, revolutionized commerce and transportation, and placed new pressures on the urban landscape.

As one article has noted, "Society's current relationship with the Internet is best described as a blind date."[2] From an environmental perspective, the digital world can reap significant improvements, such as the ability to more effectively integrate renewable energy into the electricity grid and control household energy consumption. But it may also have negative effects, including electronic waste, new demands for energy and accelerated consumerism.[3] The time is right to anticipate how governments might avoid or minimize adverse impacts of the digital economy, before patterns of behavior have solidified.

This chapter explores the potential for environmental pricing to address the digital world's negative environmental externalities. To provide a concrete context, it delves into selected pockets of digital life: the infrastructure that supports the digital world, in particular spectrum and electricity; online retail that digital technology makes possible, with a focus on packaging and drone delivery; major tech headquarters and new forms of transportation that influence the urban landscape; and digital payment systems that change how we pay taxes. Drawing largely on examples from the United States (US), these vignettes provide a partial, introductory glimpse into the implications of the Digital Revolution for the theory and practice of environmental taxes. The pages that follow do not attempt to provide full answers to such a complex, multifaceted topic. They strive instead to highlight the question of whether environmental taxation should innovate alongside the technological changes that increasingly drive economies and society.

2. THE DIGITAL WORLD'S INFRASTRUCTURE

At the heart of the digital world lie the information and communications technologies (ICT) that create data processing and connectivity networks. This digital infrastructure encompasses physical technology such as user devices, data centers and networks. However, it also relies heavily on access to spectrum to transport wireless communications, as well as electricity to power the infrastructure. The following discussion focuses on these intangible elements – spectrum and electricity – as it considers the implications for environmental taxation.

2.1 Spectrum – an Environmental Resource Eligible for Environmental Pricing?

The digital world cannot thrive without access to spectrum. "Spectrum" describes electromagnetic waves operating at various frequencies. Digital technology uses electromagnetic waves to deliver voice, text and video communications.[4] While some data travel by other means, such as through cables, transmission through the air depends upon spectrum. Demands for spectrum are increasing as traffic moves to wireless and mobile devices.[5] According to the International Energy Agency's (IEA) 2017 analysis, the number of mobile phone subscriptions exceeded the number of people on earth.[6] Consumer markets drive demand for data-intensive transmission, in particular video,[7] and projections suggest that 25–50 billion Internet of Things devices will need spectrum access by 2025.[8]

From an environmental taxation perspective, key questions are whether spectrum should be regarded as an environmental asset and, if so, whether environmental pricing theories might apply. One can argue that spectrum is part of the environment because it is a limited natural resource in the commons. The US government and the European Parliamentary Research Service have characterized spectrum as a natural resource.[9]

This classification is consistent with the notion that spectrum is part of the physical, albeit invisible, atmosphere, not unlike oxygen or ozone. Spectrum is also a finite resource. As a Commissioner of the US Federal Communications Commission testified, "The iron laws of physics being what they are, we are simply not making more."[10] Therefore, government needs to use the resource efficiently[11] and ensure that the supply of spectrum can meet growing demand.[12] Access to spectrum may provoke a new generation of environmental justice issues – the justice of who has digital rights of access and on what terms. At the very least, we should consider what constitutes the "environment" for policy purposes and whether environmentalists should have a seat at the table when decisions are made about spectrum's use.

Treating spectrum as an environmental asset opens the door to thinking about how to price this limited natural resource. Governments can allow spectrum use for free by awarding licenses or leaving spectrum bands open to unlicensed use. Free allocation will yield private sector windfalls, but it can also recognize the need to accommodate everyday uses, such as in-home Wi-Fi.[13] Environmental pricing might also play a role. A natural resource tax could allow governments to capture some portion of the economic rent associated with the private sector's use of spectrum.[14] Alternatively, governments could treat rights to use spectrum as property that must be bought from the government or in the marketplace. In 1959, Ronald Coase advocated treating radio and television frequencies as property rights, allowing holders to negotiate to resolve conflicts that cause interference.[15] (This work led to Coase's famous 1960 article, *The Problem of Social Cost.*[16]) Regardless of which pricing instrument governments might use, if any, spectrum represents a financially valuable resource. In the US, one auction for licensed wireless spectrum in 2015 grossed almost $45 billion,[17] and unlicensed spectrum was valued several years ago at more than $220 billion.[18] Revenue from spectrum allocation could fit neatly into theories of environmental fiscal reform.[19] In short, environmental policy would hold a valuable asset.

Much has been written elsewhere about the merits of various approaches to allocating access to spectrum.[20] This chapter serves only as a signal that today's digital world can offer a new lens through which to view the meaning of "environment" and the role of environmental pricing.

2.2 The Digital World's Electricity Consumption – the Continuing Need for Carbon Pricing

ICT forms the essential, vast and ever-growing skeleton of the digital world – data centers that process and store data, networks that transmit the flow of data and connected end user devices from laptops to smart watches. Electricity powers this infrastructure. A report by Greenpeace estimated that the information technology sector, including manufacturing, could account for 12 percent of global electricity demand in 2017, up from 7 percent in 2012.[21] According to the IEA, data centers consumed about 1 percent of global electricity and data networks accounted for another 1 percent. Projections about future energy consumption vary widely: data centers and networks could demand more energy, or advances in efficiency could curb growth in their energy consumption.[22]

The ostensible cleanness of the digital world, which often comes from its ethereal, remote nature, should not cloak its real carbon footprint. For example, Greenpeace maintains a clean energy index for companies that provide a variety of digitally based services.[23] The scores range from highs of 100 percent for Switch and 83 percent for Apple to lows of 2 percent for almost 40 companies. These figures do not account for the electricity consumed by data networks or end users' devices. The carbon profile of that electricity depends on the extent to which local electricity providers rely on clean sources of energy.

The digital context accentuates the need to continue to press vigorously for meaningful prices on carbon dioxide emissions around the globe. Carbon taxes can motivate data centers to find clean sources of energy and encourage end users to focus on the amount and type of electricity their devices consume. Even if new digital applications can conserve energy,[24] it is important to ensure that any benefits do not hide ICT's remaining carbon footprint. This emphasis on carbon pricing is not unique or creative. Using ICT's electricity consumption as just one example, it simply underscores the role of carbon pricing in shaping a clean, new economy.

3. ONLINE RETAIL

The digital world's infrastructure has spurred new lines of business. Online retail provides just one illustration of this consumer revolution. In Europe, online retail grew by 18 percent in 2015 and another 16 percent in 2016.[25] In the US, online retail totaled $389 billion in 2016.[26] McKinsey has observed that technology will disrupt the consumer goods industry in the coming decade.[27] The discussion below focuses on the role of environmental pricing in addressing two consequences of the online retail delivery system: packaging waste and the noise pollution that could arise with drone deliveries.

3.1 Transport Packaging Waste – Who and Where is the Polluter?

As anecdotal evidence indicates, online retail delivers a mounting volume of packages and packaging waste to consumers. Amazon's 36-hour online Prime Day in 2018 generated sales of over 100 million products to consumers in 17 countries.[28] In China, Alibaba's Singles' Day promotion for online buyers in 2017 shipped 331 million packages, up more than 31 percent from the prior year. These sales generate transport packaging waste that must be handled at the purchasers' end. China's 2017 Singles' Day sales alone generated an estimated 160 000 tons of packaging waste.[29]

The rebound effect may contribute to increased levels of consumption and therefore transport packaging waste. The rebound effect is rooted in the notion that gains in energy efficiency may increase energy consumption, but it can apply to efficiencies outside of the energy sector. Analysts have called out the need to assess a range of rebound effects in the digital world.[30] Online retail and associated transport packaging provide a concrete context for considering rebound effects. As it becomes more efficient for consumers to order online, are people are consuming more and generating more packaging waste due to the rebound effect?[31]

Circular economy policy goals seek to avoid waste, reuse it or recycle it.[32] In response to consumers' expressions of "wrap rage"[33] or guilt,[34] online retail platforms may implement voluntary measures to reduce waste or enable recycling.[35] Governments can also set standards. The European Union in 2018 set new minimum targets for Member States to recycle packaging waste, including 85 percent of cardboard by 2020.[36] Fiscal measures can also play a role.

When considering pricing measures for transport packaging waste, fundamental policy questions are whose behavior needs to change and whether a government's tax arm can reach those players. Upstream online retailers make choices about packaging that affect waste downstream, but they are a diffuse group of "polluters" who can be difficult to locate. Online retail platforms may execute sales and shipping arrangements directly or facilitate sales for third parties that ship the goods. For example, Amazon handles approximately half of its sales directly and third-party sellers ship the rest of its orders; eBay operates entirely through third-party sellers.[37] The increasingly international nature of online retail further complicates the ability to influence upstream behavior. Recent surveys of online purchasers in numerous regions of the world found that about half or more purchased outside their own country.[38] Yet governments in the country of destination may have limited legal ability to impose a packaging tax on international shippers beyond their jurisdiction.[39] Governments in both the country of origin and the country of destination need to grapple with the question whether there are ways to influence upstream behavior.

Alternatively, governments in destination countries can focus on downstream consumers. By generating demand for transport packaging, consumers are "polluters". If rebound effects prove real, consumer choices become especially critical. Pricing instruments can directly target consumers by imposing taxes or fees on packaging waste, sensitizing them to the waste associated with their purchases.[40] If the revenue finances local waste treatment, this approach also can shift the cost of waste disposal from local taxpayers or ratepayers to people contributing the waste, drawing on the theory of user fees rather than environmental taxes.[41]

Transportation packaging waste adds urgency, cost, an international dimension and complex new consumer dynamics to the field of waste regulation, already a knotty problem. Still, the polluter pays principle should guide governments, which need to look both upstream and downstream for effective policies within their reach.

3.2 Drones: Noise Taxes or Regulation?

Then there is the matter of how online retail packages reach one's doorstep. The prospect of drone delivery is quickly becoming real.[42] McKinsey projected two years ago that within ten years, drones or autonomous vehicles in developed countries will handle 80 percent of parcel delivery for the proverbial last mile.[43] If used, drones will lift traffic from the streets up into the air. This shift will alter the energy demands of package delivery in still-speculative ways,[44] but drones also generate noise. Studies are starting to assess the degree of annoyance that drone noise generates under various conditions.[45] Noise as an externality puts in sharp focus the choice-of-instrument question. Should government use a pricing instrument or regulation to address noise?

Noise taxes to date have been characterized as "symbolic in practice".[46] Some governments have imposed taxes on aviation noise to help finance mitigation measures around airports.[47] However, drones' pervasiveness, low-flight levels and unaccustomed sound in urban and rural landscapes could ignite a more vigorous discussion of the role of noise taxes. It is important nonetheless to consider whether regulation is better suited to reduce drone noise. Regulation can set noise standards[48] and local land use regulations can influence the location of drone delivery hubs to minimize impacts.

Choice-of-instrument considerations also involve identifying the appropriate level of government with legal power to act, analysis that will vary by country.[49] As a matter of policy, technical design regulation seems better suited to the national level and land-use siting issues more appropriate for local authorities. Tax policies could fall into either domain. Taxes intended to steer design specifications would fit more logically with national taxes. Taxes intended to compensate for specific local externalities could be local in nature.

As a new form of pollution, drone noise presents a fresh opportunity to explore the relationship between regulatory and fiscal policies. Regulation is the right answer if noise pollution at any given level is not an acceptable externality. But if drone regulation would still allow some level of harmful noise pollution due to design limitations or lack of regulatory will, taxes might step in.

4. URBAN CONGESTION

The burgeoning digital economy creates new demands on the urban landscape and transportation systems. This section considers two urban developments that flow directly from the digital economy: large, new urban office complexes that house companies that drive the digital economy; and new transportation systems that operate on digital platforms. Both give rise to the question of whether governments should consider imposing a charge on activities that previously did not lie in the domain of traditional environmental taxation.

4.1 Major Urban Employers – a New Tax Base?

The US stands as a bellwether for considering the influence of large high-tech companies on the metropolitan environment. Tech companies have built major campuses in suburban and urban areas, such as Apple's and Google's headquarters in Silicon Valley, Microsoft's campus outside Seattle, and Amazon's headquarters in downtown Seattle, Washington. Not bound by the traditional infrastructure or natural resource requirements of many "old" industries, tech companies have flexibility to choose locations and employees often want to live or work in cities.[50] And some states compete for their attention. Almost 240 cities responded when Amazon solicited proposals for supplemental headquarters in 2017. New York and Virginia, winning jurisdictions, offered more than $2 billion in tax incentives to attract 50 000 new jobs.[51]

Tech companies can stimulate the local economy, but they can also contribute to traffic congestion and rising costs of housing. The lack of affordable housing in turn can cause people to move further away from their jobs, increasing concerns about environmental justice and carbon footprints. In Seattle, home prices in 2017 rose twice as fast as the next city in the ranking of rising house values.[52] In San Francisco, the median home price in mid-2018 was $1.6 million.[53] In response, several cities have explored taxing employers based on the number of employees to provide funding for transportation and housing needs. These proposals show how environmental pricing might apply to a new kind of tax base – number of employees. Thus, even while some governments offer tax incentives to attract companies, others are seeking ways to shift the cost of negative externalities to companies already on site.

In Mountain View, California, home of Google's headquarters, voters approved a per-employee tax in 2018.[54] At the top end of the progressive tax rate, companies with more than 5000 employees will pay $150 per employee over that threshold.[55] Google, which employs 23000 people in the city,[56] will pay about half of the projected $6 million annual revenue. Revenue will go into the general fund, but can be used to address traffic congestion, bicycle and pedestrian routes, and affordable housing.[57] Cupertino, California, headquarters of Apple, considered a per-employee tax on companies with more than 99 employees in the city, but deferred putting the issue to voters until 2020.[58] The city would have used the revenue, an estimated $10 million per year, to address traffic issues.[59]

In Seattle, home of Starbucks, Amazon and other tech companies, a measure was enacted, then repealed. In May 2018, the City Council imposed tax of $275 per employee on companies with revenue of more than $20 million, which would have generated $50 million per year for affordable housing. The City Council's decision spurred an organized effort to put repeal of the tax on the ballot for voters in November 2018 ("No Tax on Jobs"),[60] supported by Amazon, Starbucks and others. In June 2018, the City Council repealed the tax.[61] In January 2019, Microsoft, headquartered just outside Seattle, voluntarily pledged $500 million to address affordable housing in the region.[62]

From a traditional environmental policy perspective, placing the cost of responding to transportation and housing needs on employers has merit. Employees create externalities by engaging directly in transportation and housing markets, but employers' expansion strategies are the underlying force behind these externalities. There are, of course, other ways that government might address transportation and housing externalities, such as by amending land use regulations, imposing one-time impact fees or exactions at the time of construction, or considering Henry George's theory land value taxation.[63] However, the point here is quite simple. The digital world has created major new economic players that can herald a significant shift in urban patterns. It is time to consider new tax bases that would not have been considered "environmentally related" under traditional twentieth century definitions.[64]

4.2 Curbside Congestion – Fees and New Horizons for Administratively Feasible Tax Bases?

The digital world has created innovative, alternative means of transportation, but those alternatives bring their own style of urban congestion. Private transit options built on digital platforms take many forms. They provide transportation by bus, van, car, bicycle or scooter. They may involve single-use services on a hired basis, such as UberX or bicycle rentals; or they may offer shared transportation, such as Uber Pool, BlaBlaCar and "dollar vans".[65] Employer-operated buses, such as the "tech buses" in Silicon Valley, are not exclusive to the digital economy, but major digital employers have accentuated their visibility.

The focus here is not on whether these services yield a net positive or negative impact on greenhouse gas emissions,[66] but instead whether environmental pricing might play a role in addressing new forms of congestion at the curbside. Ride-hailing services need to pull over to pick up customers at digitally arranged points. Sidewalk bike stations service users and "dockless" bike systems allow riders to pick up and leave bikes anywhere on the sidewalk. Increased bike and electric scooter usage contributes to traffic at the road's edge and generates calls for protected bike lanes. There is now competition for the curbside, long considered a relatively passive public asset.[67]

Some local governments are regulating these adverse effects. In 2018, New York City adopted a one-year ban on issuing new licenses to for-hire cars to gain time to consider how to respond to congestion.[68] Before companies such as Uber entered the market, New York City allowed 13 637 taxicab licenses.[69] In 2018, there were over 100 000 for-hire vehicles on the city's streets.[70] Beverly Hills, California, temporarily banned the use of shared electric scooters in 2018.[71]

Jurisdictions are looking at pricing options as well. When corporate tech buses used municipal bus stops and pullovers that blocked travel or bike lanes, San Francisco responded by negotiating designated stops and administrative fees for each stop.[72] When for-hire electric bikes and scooters in Santa Monica, California, generated concerns about safety and sidewalk and bike path congestion,[73] the city instituted a pilot program. It awarded licenses to four companies to initially operate up to a total of 2000 e-scooters and 1000 e-bikes,[74] and required them to pay an annual fee of $20 000 and $130 for each device in the system to cover the city's cost of operating the program.[75] These fees do not capture the cost of externalities, but under classic fee theory, they move the cost of government administration to the beneficiaries.

These new activities can also lead costly investments in public improvements. For example, a US study estimates that the cost of constructing protected bike lanes can range from about $500000 to $4.3 million per mile.[76] The environmental pricing question is who should pay for public investments in alternative transit: the public that may benefit from reduced pollution or the companies that benefit from using public spaces. If financing for bike and pedestrian measures is a relatively low public priority, a tax or fee can be particularly appealing.[77] Santa Monica's program for e-scooters and e-bikes took a step in this direction. It charges a $1 public right-of-way fee per device per day to fund infrastructure improvements.[78]

The shared transportation community may be open to considering fees. Bird, a dockless e-scooter company, has indicated that it intends to create a fund to help build or maintain bike paths in cities where it operates, financed by $1 per day per scooter.[79] In 2018, a group of companies and organizations around the world signed onto a statement of shared mobility principles that includes a pricing principle: "Every vehicle and mode should pay their fair share for road use, congestion, pollution, and use of curb space. The fair share shall take the operating, maintenance and social costs into account."[80] Over 30 service providers signed on. This principle represents a significant step toward acknowledging pricing as a path forward for shared and other vehicles.

The International Transport Forum, representing 59 countries, went a step further. It has suggested the possibility of "curb-kiss" fees that could help manage traffic and demand for curb access. This option would require the development of new digital infrastructure that would count curb kisses. It could allow for fees that vary depending on time of day, location and type of access.[81] This idea presents an intriguing concept that shows how environmental taxes could reach a new tax base as a result of the digital economy – and how digital technology could make that new tax base administratively feasible. Fiscal policy at the curbs of the future may run the gamut from traditional fees to new tax innovations.

5. DIGITAL PAYMENT – THE NEED TO REVISIT TAX RATE THEORY AND PRACTICE?

Finally, one last inquiry of a more theoretical nature: the effect of digital wallets on the salience of environmental taxes. Does the ease of digital payment make consumers less aware of tax burdens and, therefore, less likely to take tax signals into account in their decision-making? If so, environmental tax rates may need to increase to preserve their behavioral signal.

Forms of payment have shifted over decades from cash to credit cards, and now to digital money and digital wallets. Digital money has been described as value transferred through the digital environment that is backed by cash or a credit card account.[82] Digital wallets, such as PayPal, facilitate these transactions,[83] as do apps on mobile phones. According to a 2016 report, 46 percent of US consumers used mobile payment.[84] Studies have found that payment by credit card increases consumer consumption because it reduces the pain of payment by cash.[85] Although research on the effect of digital payment is still in its early phases, at least one study posits that digital money has the same effect on consumer purchasing as credit cards.[86] As one academic noted in the popular press, "The less friction there is, the easier it becomes to spend . . . Just stand at Starbucks and watch how many people there use their smartphones to buy a latte."[87] Similarly, digital payment may diminish the pain of a tax. A study of highway tolls suggested that the lower salience of electronic collection of tolls allowed government to impose higher toll rates and that elasticity in driving patterns declined in the short run.[88]

If digital payment erodes the salience of environmental taxes, it will be important to revisit the theories underlying environmental tax rates. Under Pigouvian theory, the tax rate should reflect the social cost of negative externalities.[89] However, if the form of payment distorts the rational decision-making that Pigou assumed, the tax rate calculation should be adjusted upward for the "deflation" that might come with digital payment. This would result in an externality-plus tax rate. Under the Baumol-Oates theory of environmental taxation, the tax rate should be set at the level required to reach the desired degree of behavioral change.[90] Therefore, the calculation of a Baumol-Oates tax rate should take into account the behavioral impact of the manner of payment, building in an anti-deflation factor if necessary. Hence, adapting Pigouvian theory to the digital world may require an adjustment in tax rate theory; setting a tax rate under the Baumol-Oates approach only requires an adjustment in how theory is applied.

6. CONCLUSION

This exploration has delved into just a few pockets of the emerging digital world, but it yields several thoughts that may have broader applicability as policies surrounding the Digital Revolution develop. At a fundamental level, the evolution of the digital world should press us to reevaluate how we define the environment. This chapter suggests that the boundaries of the environment could encompass the capacity of the atmosphere to transport the data – the invisible digital highways of spectrum without which the digital world cannot flourish.

Environmental pricing principles should be built into the foundation of the digital world during its relative infancy, not added as a cornice later. The Digital Revolution reinforces the need to continue to apply traditional environmental pricing approaches, such as carbon taxes, to address negative environmental consequences. It also creates new tax bases that demand attention. The inquiry into new taxes, however, requires careful thought about whether environmental goals are best served through pricing measures, regulation or an artful combination. As an enduring principle, environmental taxation is a means to an end, not an end in itself.

The emerging digital world may accentuate the need to consider environmental user fees. Environmental fees sometimes seem rather like environmental taxation's intellectually neglected sibling. Environmental taxes grew from sophisticated economic theories, while environmental fees developed from pragmatic desires to pay for services and often garner less theoretical attention. Yet fees can provide important sources of revenue that governments need to address new demands of the digital economy.

The medium of digital technology can influence the tax base and rate. Digital technology may allow governments to identify and tax activities that previously would have been infeasible. At the same time, new technology may disrupt traditional environmental taxation theory and practice by altering how people pay taxes. Economists, behavioral economists, environmentalists and policymakers need to reconsider assumptions about how to set tax rates.

Finally, perhaps even this preliminary and partial exploration of the intersection of the digital world and environmental pricing can invite others to think about new frontiers for fiscal environmental policies at global, national, and local levels. The digital world knows no national boundaries; nor should the theory and practice of environmental taxation and environmental fees.

NOTES

* The author thanks Emma Akrawi for her invaluable research and editorial suggestions.

1. International Energy Agency [IEA], Digitization & Energy 22 (2017).
2. Daniel Z. Sui and David W. Rejeski, *Environmental Impacts of the Emerging Digital Economy: The E-for-Environment E-Commerce?* 29 Envtl. Mgmt, no. 2, 2002, 155, 159.
3. *See* Klaus Fichter, *E-Commerce: Sorting Out the Environmental Consequences*, 6 J. Indus. Ecology, no. 2, 2003, 25, 27.
4. *See* Congressional Research Service, Spectrum Policy: Provisions in the 2012 Spectrum Act 1 (2015); European Parliamentary Research Service [EPRS], Radio Spectrum 1 (2015).
5. IEA, *supra* note 1, at 109.
6. *Id.* at 15.

7. U.S. Government Accountability Office [GAO], Internet of Things: FCC Should Track Growth to Ensure Sufficient Spectrum Remains Available 17 n. 25, 18 (2017).
8. *Id.* at 1.
9. *Id.* at 4; EPRS, *supra* note 4, at 1. *But see* Milton Mueller, Cato Institute Policy Analysis No. 11: Property Rights in Radio Communication (1982).
10. *Wireless Broadband and the Future of Spectrum Policy, Hearing before the Committee on Commerce, Science, and Transportation, US Senate* (2015) (Prepared Statement of Hon. Jessica Rosenworcel, Commissioner, Federal Communications Commission at 6).
11. Robert Matheson and Adele C. Morris, The Technical Basis for Spectrum Rights: Policy to Enhance Market Efficiency 10–11, 17–19 (2011).
12. *See* Dorothy Robyn, Making Waves: Alternative Paths to Flexible Use Spectrum 1 (2015); GAO, *supra* note 7.
13. *Hearing on Exploring the Value of Spectrum to the U.S. Economy, U.S. Senate Committee on Commerce, Science, and Transportation, Subcommittee on Communications, Technology, Innovation and the Internet* (2017) (statement of Dave Heiner, V.P., Regulatory Affairs, Microsoft Corporation).
14. For discussions of natural resources taxes, see Organisation for Economic Co-operation and Development [OECD] Task Force for the Implementation of the Environmental Action Program for Central and Eastern Europe, The Use of Economic Instruments for Pollution Control and Natural Resource Management in EECCA 51 (2003); H. William Batt, *Taxing Land Rents for Urban Liability and Sustainability*, *in* Environmental Taxation and Climate Change 103–106 (L. Kreiser et al. eds., 2011). A Pigouvian tax that captures the social cost of frequency interference would not seem appropriate if some level of continuing interference would not serve the public interest.
15. R.H. Coase, *The Federal Communications Commission*, II J.L. & Econ. 1 (1959).
16. R.H. Coase, *The Problem of Social Cost*, III J.L. & Econ.1, n.1 (1960).
17. Linda K. Moore, Congressional Research Service, Framing Spectrum Policy: Legislative Initiatives 5 (2016).
18. Doug Brake, Coase and WiFi: The Law and Economics of Unlicensed Spectrum 3 (Information Technology & Innovation Foundation, 2015).
19. S*ee generally* Jean-Philippe Barde and Olivier Godard, *Economic Principles of Environmental Fiscal Reform in* Handbook of Research on Environmental Taxation (J. Milne and M.S. Andersen eds., 2010) 33–58.
20. *See, e.g.*, Moore, *supra* note 17; Robyn, *supra* note 12; Suzan Bayhan et al., The Future is Unlicensed: Coexistence in the Unlicensed Spectrum for 5G (2018).
21. Gary Cook, Clicking Clean: Who Is Winning the Race to Build a Green Internet? 15 (2017).
22. IEA, *supra* note 1, at 103.
23. Cook, *supra* note 21, at 8–13 (2017).
24. *See* IEA, *supra* note 1, at 16–18; Policy Connect, Is Staying Online Costing the Earth? (2018); Jonathan G. Koomey, H. Scott Matthews and Eric Williams, *Smart Everything: Will Intelligent Systems Reduce Resource Use?* 38 Ann. Rev. Envtl. Resources 311 (2013).
25. European Environment Agency, Circular by Design: Products in the Circular Economy 19 (2017).
26. US Census Bureau, E-Stats 2016: Measuring the Electronic Economy 2 (2018).
27. Ishan Chatterjee et al., McKinsey & Co., The Decade Ahead: Trends that Will Shape the Consumer Goods Industry 10 (2010).
28. Press Release, Amazon, Prime Members Again Enjoyed the Biggest Global Shopping Event in Amazon History this Prime Day (July 18, 2018).
29. Reuters, *China Faces 160,000 Tonnes of Packaging Waste after Singles' Day Buying Binge*, The Straits Times, Nov. 17, 2017.
30. *See* Cedric Gossart, *Rebound Effects and ICT: A Review of the Literature, in* ICT Innovations for Sustainability 435 (M.L. Hilty and B. Aebischer eds., 2015); Tilman Santarius, *Digitization, Efficiency and the Rebound Effect* (2017), www.degrowth.infoen/2017/02/digitizatoin-efficiency-and-the-rebound-effect/.

31. *See, e.g.*, Sui and Rejeski, *supra* note 1, 155, 157 (impact of online book purchase).
32. *See generally* Conrad B. MacKerron, Waste and Opportunity 2015: Environmental Progress and Challenges in Food, Beverage and Consumer Goods Packaging (2015); European Environment Agency, Waste Prevention in Europe – the Status in 2014 (2015).
33. Olivia Gagan, *E-Tailers Must Wrap Up a Better Package*, Raconteur, Sept. 21, 2017.
34. Matt Richtel, *E-Commerce: Convenience Built on a Mountain of Cardboard,* NY Times, Feb. 16, 2016.
35. Amazon, Frustration-free packaging, www.aboutamazon.com/sustainability/packaging/frustration-free-packaging.
36. Directive of the European Parliament and of the Council Amending Directive 94/62/EC on Packaging and Packaging Waste, May 30, 2018, Art. 1(6).
37. OECD, Extended Producer Responsibility (EPR) and the Impact of Online Sales 31 (2018).
38. PayPal, PayPal Cross-Border Consumer Research 2018: Global Summary Report 7 (2018); UPS, UPS Impulse of the Online Shopper™ Study: Global Study, Executive Summary 9 (2018).
39. *Cf.* OECD, *supra* note 37, at 6, 25–33 (risk of free-riding for international online sales in extended producer responsibility context).
40. *Cf.* Institute for European Environmental Policy, Capacity Building for Environmental Tax Reform 44–60 (2017) (discussing existing pay-as-you-throw fees).
41. *See* OECD, Environmentally Related Taxes in OECD Countries 15 (2001) (distinguishing environmental taxes and fees).
42. *See, e.g.*, Arthur Holland Michel, Amazon's Drone Patents 1 (2017); Alan Levin, *Toddler's Popsicle-by-Air Marks First in US Drone Delivery*, Bloomberg, Aug. 8, 2018, www.bloomberg.com/news/articles/2018-08-08/toddler-s-popsicle-by-air-marks-milestone-in-u-sdrone-delivery. Regulation of commercial delivery drones varies significantly by country. *See* Therese Jones, Rand Corp., International Commercial Drone Regulation and Drone Delivery Service iii (2017).
43. Martin Joerss et al., McKinsey & Co., Parcel Delivery: The Future of Last Mile 7 (2016). *See also* Jones, *supra* note 42, at iii.
44. *See* Joshuah K. Stolaroff et al., *Energy Use and Life Cycle Greenhouse Gas Emissions of Drones for Commercial Package Delivery*, 9 Nature Comm. 409 (2018); Miguel Figliozzi, *Drones for Commercial Last-Mile Deliveries: A Discussion of Logistical, Environmental and Economic Tradeoffs* (Civil and Environmental Engineering Faculty Publications and Presentations 416, 2017); Andrew J. Lohn, Rand Corp., What's the Buzz? The City-Scale Impacts of Drone Delivery (2017); Timothy R. Gulden, Rand Corp., The Energy Implications of Drones for Package Delivery: A Geographic Information System Comparison 10 (2017).
45. Lohn, *supra* note 44, at 20; Andrew Christian and Randolph Cabell, Initial Investigation into the Psychoacoustic Properties of Small Unmanned Aerial System Noise 18–20 (2018).
46. Marta Villar Ezcurra, *Noise Pollution Taxes: A Possibility to Explore, in* Innovation Addressing Climate Change Challenges: Market-based Perspectives 113, 119 (M. Hymel et al. eds., 2018).
47. *See Code General des Impots* [Internal Revenue Code] *art. 1609 quatervicies A* (Fr.); Aircraft Noise Levy Act 1995 (Austrl.); Aircraft Noise Levy Collection Amendment Bill 2001 (Austrl.).
48. *See* Regulation (EU) 2018/1139 of the European Parliament and the Council of 4 July 2018, 2018 O.J. (L 212) 1.
49. *See, e.g.*, Singer v. City of Newton, 284 F. Supp. 3d 125 (D. Mass. 2017); Regulation (EU) 2018/1139, *supra* note 48.
50. Nellie Bowles, *San Francisco Measure Targets a Tech Staple: The Free Lunch*, NY Times, Aug. 1, 2018, B1.
51. L. David Goodman, *In New York and Virginia, Amazon Is Sold on a Deal*, NY Times,

Nov. 14, 2018, A.1. Amazon subsequently withdrew its plans to locate a headquarters in New York in response to local opposition.

52. Kirk Johnson, *Lessons Seattle Can Teach Other Cities About Amazon*, NY Times, Nov. 17, 2017, A13.
53. Kevin Kelleher, *San Francisco's Home Prices Soared an Average of $205,000 in Past 6 Months*, Fortune, July 6, 2018.
54. Mark Noack, *Twin MV Tax Measures Coast to Victor*, Mountain View Voice, Nov. 7, 2018.
55. *Id.* City of Mountain View, Proposed Ordinance, www.mountainview.gov/civicax/filebank/blobdload.aspx?BlobID=27111.
56. Marlize van Romburgh, *Mountain View Mulls Taxing Large Employers Like Google Millions*, Silicon Valley Bus. J., May 9, 2018.
57. City of Mountain View, Business License Tax Measure P, Ballot Measure, https://www.mountainview.gov/depts/manager/2018_potential_general_revenue_measures.aspl; City of Mountain View, Impartial Analysis, www.mountainview.gov/civicax/filebank/blobdload.aspx?BlobID=27115; Natasha Mascarenhas, *Google Tax to Go Before Voters as Tech Giant's Hometown Puts Proposal on Ballot*, San Francisco Chronicle, June 26, 2018.
58. Khalida Sarwari, *Cupertino Shelves Proposed 'Head Tax' on Apple Employees for Now*, Mercury News, July 31, 2018.
59. *Id.*
60. http://notaxonjobs.com/.
61. David Streitfeld and Claire Ballentine, *Amazon Played Hardball on New Tax. Now Seattle is Killing the Tax*, NY Times, June 13, 2018, at B1.
62. Karen Weise, *Microsoft Pledges $500 Million to Ease Seattle Housing Crisis*, NY Times, Jan. 17, 2019, at A1.
63. *See generally* Richard F. Dye and Richard W. England, Assessing the Theory and Practice of Land Value Taxation (2010); Planning Committee, London Assembly, Tax Trial. A Land Value Tax for London? Feb. 2016; Letter from Sadiq Khan, Mayor of London, to Tom Copley, City Hall, Nov. 2, 2016.
64. *See, e.g.*, OECD, Environmentally Related Taxes in OECD Countries 15 (2001); Eurostat, Environmental Taxes: A Statistical Guide 9 (2001).
65. *See generally* Saron Feigon et al., Private Transit: Existing Services and Emerging Directions, Transit Cooperative Research Program (2018); Shared-Use Mobility Center, Shared-Use Mobility: Reference Guide (2015).
66. *See, e.g.*, Feigon et al., *supra* note 65, at 25–26; Nordic Council of Ministers, Environmental Impacts and Potential of the Sharing Economy 47–57 (2017); Shared-Use Mobility Center, *supra* note 65, at 14–15.
67. *See generally* International Transport Forum, The Shared-Use City: Managing the Curb (2018).
68. Press Release, Office of the Mayor, Mayor de Blasio, Signs for-Hire Vehicle Legislation (Aug. 14, 2018).
69. Emily Badger, *What's the Right Number of Taxis?* NY Times, Aug. 11, 2018, B1.
70. Emma G. Fitzsimmons and William Neuman, *This Time It's Uber's Turn to Wage an Uphill Battle*, NY Times, July 28, 2018, at A15.
71. Press Release, City of Beverly Hills, Beverly Hills to Prohibit the Use of Motorized Scooters for Six Months (July 24, 2018).
72. Feigon, *supra* note 65, at 32–36.
73. City of Santa Monica, Staff Report 3006 (2018).
74. Ordinance No. 2578 (June 26, 2018); City of Santa Monica Shared Mobility Device Pilot Program Administrative Regulations (Sept. 25, 2018); City of Santa Monica, David Martin, Final Administrative Decision (Aug. 30, 2018).
75. Santa Monica Administrative Regulations, *supra* note 74, §3.5; City of Santa Monica, Staff Report 3006 (2018); City of Santa Monica, Frequently Asked Questions About the Shared Mobility Pilot Program (2018).

76. Max A. Bushell et al., Costs for Pedestrian and Bicyclist Infrastructure Improvements 12 (2013).
77. U.S. Government Accountability Office, Pedestrians and Cyclists: Cities, States and DOT Are Implementing Actions to Improve Safety 23 (2015).
78. David Martin, City of Santa Monica, City Council Report (Aug. 28, 2018); City of Santa Monica, Frequently Asked Questions About the Shared Mobility Pilot Program (2018).
79. Bird, Save Our Sidewalks Pledge, March 27, 2018, www.bird.co/sos-pledge-mar272018.
80. Shared Mobility Principles for Livable Cities, Principle 7, www.sharedmobilityprinciples.org.
81. International Transport Forum, *supra* note 67, at 35, 80–81.
82. *See* Farah Diba Abrantes Braga, Giuliana Isabella and José Afonso Mazzon, *Do Digital Wallets as Payment Method Influence Consumer in Their Buying Behavior?* XXXVII Encontro de ANPAD 4 (2013).
83. *Id.* at 5.
84. Pew Charitable Trusts, Who Uses Mobile Payments? Survey Findings on Consumer Opinions, Experiences 1, 3 (2016).
85. *See* Braga et al., *supra* note 82; Drazen Prelec and Duncan Simester, *Always Leave Home Without It: A Further Investigation of the Credit-Card Effect on Willingness to Pay*, 21 Marketing Letters 21:1, 5–12 (2001); Manoj Thomas, Kalpesh Kaushik Desai and Satheeshkumar Seenivasan, *How Credit Card Payments Increase Unhealthy Food Purchases: Visceral Regulation of Vices*, 38 J. Consumer Research (2011); Priya Raghubir and Joydeep Sirvastava, *Monopoly Money: The Effect of Payment Coupling and Form on Spending Behavior*, 14 J. Experimental Psychology: Applied, no. 3, 213 (2008); Greg B. Davies, *The Realities of Spending*, 2 Argent, no. 6, 22 (2003).
86. Braga et al., *supra* note 82.
87. Nelson D. Schwartz, *Credit Cards Encourage Extra Spending as the Cash Habit Fades Away*, NY Times, March 25, 2016 (quoting Richard Feinberg, Purdue University).
88. Amy Finkelstein, *E-ZTax: Tax Salience and Tax Rates* (Nat'l Bureau of Econ. Research, Working Paper No. 12924, 2007).
89. A.C. Pigou, The Economics of Welfare 168 (1920).
90. William J. Baumol and Wallace E. Oates, T*he Use of Standards and Practices for Protection of the Environment*, 73 Swedish J. Econ. no. 1, 1971, 42–54.

2. Is the low level of tax on e-commerce contributing to an environmentally unfriendly increase in transport?

Marta Villar Ezcurra*

1. INTRODUCTION

E-commerce companies in the EU currently have an effective average tax rate of half that of their traditional counterparts, according to data from the European Commission.[1] In fact, the state of taxation of certain e-commerce activities[2] – especially those relating to tangible goods – is a source of global concern.[3] The main worry for tax administrations is the lack of taxation on e-commerce sales of tangible goods in the countries where those goods are sold and consumed. This is why policymakers and legislators have recently taken a number of steps towards a model in which e-commerce activities are taxed in a fair, efficient and growth-friendly way.

There is no doubt that the tax landscape is evolving very quickly, on the assumption that the digital economy[4] has positive environmental effects. However, the question of potential adverse environmental effects remains, such as the increase in long-distance freight transport to the detriment of local production. In particular, the question is whether the difference in tax treatment is creating imperfect competition that enables some entities to assume transport costs which are impossible for others with a higher tax burden, and thus to compete favourably with local production.

European statistics seem to confirm this analysis, because transport charges are a major obstacle to e-commerce. Although the majority (59 per cent) of EU enterprises receiving orders via websites or apps during 2016 reported no difficulty in making web sales to other EU Member States, almost four in ten (38 per cent) reported hampering factors. These factors were primarily economic: transport charges were described as the 'main impediment to cross-border web sales within the EU', particularly the high costs of delivering and returning products (27 per cent).[5]

The current tax model also raises the question of whether the minimum corporate taxation burden for e-commerce activities and other productive factors – especially for labour – are leading e-commerce companies to assume costs and structure distribution channels that are environmentally harmful.

This chapter considers whether environmentally unfriendly symptoms of transport caused by e-commerce are the natural result of, or in some way influenced by, the current international tax framework. It also considers what kinds of mitigation strategies should be implemented to strengthen the protection of the environment. The chapter is structured as follows: section 2 briefly examines the tax implications of the digital sale of tangible assets and highlights the low level of taxation of many operators in the international digital market. Section 3 focuses on the general relationship between the digital economy and good environmental practice. Section 4 addresses the importance of transport activities to e-commerce. Section 5 considers whether there is any relationship between the increase in transport and the low level of taxation of e-commerce. In Section 6, possible policy actions that might equalize the tax burden for e-commerce companies are discussed. The conclusion summarizes the main findings.

2. TAX IMPLICATIONS OF DIGITAL SALES OF TANGIBLE ASSETS

The tax implications of the digital sale of goods raise a lot of issues that have not been thoroughly studied. So far, emphasis has been placed on the fact that these sales are not taxed in the countries where the goods are sold and consumed. The problem that this represents from the perspective of tax collection in those countries has been highlighted several times. However, so far there is a lack of in-depth analysis on the impact of unbalanced taxation on models for the production and distribution of goods at a global level.

It is a statistical truth that e-commerce is driving a significant increase in transport.[6] However, not all circumstances giving rise to this increase have been sufficiently analysed. In particular, further analysis is required as to whether and to what extent the low or non-existent taxation of many e-commerce companies might allow them to assume higher transport costs.

Although, for obvious reasons, it is not easy to find data on the structure of unbundled costs of large-scale e-commerce companies, some information from international bodies sheds light on this issue.

The digital economy is increasingly becoming the mainstream economy and is being promoted at an international level as a source of societal improvements. The consequent difficulty of 'ring-fencing' the digital economy from the rest of the economy was recognized in the 2018 Organisation for Economic Co-operation and Development (OECD) Interim Report as part of the Action Plan on Base Erosion and Profit Shifting (BEPS).[7] At the same time, the digital economy presents major challenges for the international tax system.[8] These challenges arise from issues such as nexus, data and characterization in the digital sector. As the European Parliament has recognized, the digital economy exacerbates existing BEPS issues. Multinational enterprises (MNEs) use complex mechanisms to achieve 'double non-taxation' and generate so-called 'stateless income' in onshore or offshore low tax jurisdictions. Moreover, they often take advantage of the exceptions provided in Article 5 of the OECD's Model Tax Conventions to avoid 'permanent establishment' (PE) status. In addition, 'tax treaties between jurisdictions of the payer and recipient may be abused by treaty shopping to avoid the payment of withholding taxes in the high-tax jurisdiction by means of establishing shell companies in tax havens'.[9]

The increasing number of EU investigations into tech giants shows that tax planning and tax avoidance practices are rife in the digital sector, enabling the world's biggest companies to get away with paying close to zero taxes. Although the European Commission should be commended for its proactivity, the investigations are seen as a temporary solution to tax avoidance and are being constrained by EU case law, the four fundamental freedoms and the lengthy investigation process.[10]

For the purpose of this chapter, the main issue to point out is the fact that a substantial part of the digital businesses of big e-commerce companies is structured in such a way that the sellers are located in tax havens or low taxation jurisdictions, or at least enjoy special regimes for these types of activities.[11] Businesses are transforming their supply and demand chains, as well as their internal organization, to fully exploit the advantages afforded by information and communications technologies.[12]

Digital platforms have a monopoly on their networks and geographical boundaries are blurred. Therefore, the allocation of activities and income to a particular fiscal jurisdiction becomes more complex. MNE strategies and markets have transformed, and continue to transform, business models. MNEs enjoy significant benefits of reduced taxation based on tax planning structures which are considered 'aggressive'. A number of actions have been taken to combat this phenomenon of aggressive tax planning at a national, international and EU level. These measures include anti-avoidance rules that are referred to in tax conventions (both bilateral and multilateral) as well as in EU Directives and unilateral tax law. Besides, production is generally carried out in countries with low labour costs and e-commerce companies often are not taxed in end consumer countries. In the EU, although there is no specific tax data on tangible goods which are electronically traded, it is estimated that on average, domestic digitalized business models are subject to an effective tax rate of only 9 per cent. This represents less than half that applicable to traditional business models, which face an effective tax rate of 21 per cent.[13]

The truth that there is little or no taxation of e-commerce companies in all or some jurisdictions where they conduct activities raises three levels of discrimination than can influence the transport of goods: (1) the difference in treatment with respect to e-commerce companies as regards the standard level of taxation; (2) the difference in treatment with respect to traditional operators marketing equivalent or similar products in relevant state; and (3) the difference in treatment with respect to e-commerce companies established in the local state where the goods are commercialized, and which are therefore residents or PEs.

3. THE GENERAL RELATIONSHIP BETWEEN THE DIGITAL ECONOMY AND ENVIRONMENTAL GOOD PRACTICE

There is a commonly held belief that the digital economy leads to positive environmental effects. These have generally been summarized as the 'three Ds' of the new economy: dematerialization, decarbonization and demobilization.[14] For example, by moving businesses online and marketing via pixels instead of paper, e-commerce can reduce the need for wasteful products such as printed catalogues, telephone directories, newspapers and magazines.

Despite the growing literature on the three Ds, a closer look quickly reveals that their potential positive environmental impacts are only one side of the story. The Internet has already dramatically increased mass production on a global scale.[15] Other available studies on e-commerce also show that it is somewhat costlier than the traditional system.[16]

Digital technologies can make transport safer and more efficient;[17] but on the other hand, in terms of energy consumption, just-in-time delivery tends to create a situation in which trucks are moving half empty. E-commerce also tends to favour faster transportation modes, which can increase fuel consumption exponentially. When we opt for trucks instead of boats or rail, energy use increases by a factor of four to five.[18] Moving the same package by airfreight again increases energy use dramatically. The growth of e-commerce has further stimulated the expansion of the overnight delivery business. Moreover, it is very likely that the increase in transport energy consumption may offset the energy savings from consumers travelling less to local stores, unless e-commerce is seamlessly integrated with both business-to-business (B2B)[19] and business-to-consumer (B2C) operations.[20] Finally, an important issue arises when the business/tax model of the digital economy based on tangible goods shows that the long-distance transport of goods has become an element of the business model itself; this could increase transport substantially.

The need to promote environmental good practice in an integrated way was considered by the European Commission in a proposal issued in July 2016, entitled *The European strategy for low-emission mobility*,[21] which showed how different initiatives in related fields are linked and how synergies can be achieved. The main elements of this EU strategy include: (1) increasing the efficiency of the transport system by making the most of digital technologies;[22] (2) promoting smart pricing and further encouraging the shift to lower-emission transport modes; and (3) speeding up the deployment of low-emission alternative energy for transport – such as advanced biofuels, electricity, hydrogen and renewable synthetic fuels – and removing obstacles to the electrification of transport. Regarding the move towards zero-emission vehicles, while further improvements to the internal combustion engine are needed, the strategy argues that Europe needs to accelerate the transition towards low and zero-emission vehicles. EU legislation currently refers to low-emission vehicles as vehicles with tailpipe emissions below 50 grams per kilometre. These include some plug-in hybrids, full electric cars and fuel cell (ie, hydrogen-powered) vehicles; the latter two examples also constitute zero-emission vehicles.[23] The strategy further reiterates the EU's commitment to pursuing global efforts to control emissions from international aviation and maritime transport.

Finally, we must not forget that one particular concern about the role of trade in increasing greenhouse gas emissions is its link to transportation services. International trade involves countries exporting goods in which they have a comparative advantage and importing other goods from their trading partners. This process of international exchange requires the transport of goods from the country of production to the country of consumption. Thus, international trade expansion is likely to lead to increased use of transportation services.[24]

4. THE IMPORTANCE OF TRANSPORT ACTIVITIES FOR DIGITAL MARKETS

The relationship between the transport sector and the digital economy is evidenced by the fact that transport is the second largest sector in the European Union in terms of turnover in e-commerce. It represents almost one-quarter of Europe's greenhouse gas emissions and is the main cause of air pollution in cities.[25]

In 2017, about 22 per cent of all turnover of enterprises in the transportation and storage industries was linked to e-commerce. About 20 per cent of EU businesses sell online, which accounts for 18 per cent of their turnover. Among EU Member States, Ireland had the highest share of B2C sales (23 per cent), while Sweden had the highest share of B2B sales (18 per cent). The share of turnover generated from B2C sales was also highest in Ireland (9 per cent), while that from B2B sales was highest in Belgium (10 per cent).[26]

The boom in online shopping and changes in consumer behaviour have resulted in changes in demand for passengers and freight transport. The influence of the digital economy on transport has been systematically considered by some authors.[27] However, in the area of production, logistics and planning of transportation may increase distance. Research has demonstrated that consumer-to-consumer e-commerce influences both the amount of personal travel and the distances travelled by consumers.[28]

Therefore, despite the environmental argument that e-commerce reduces transportation and collateral costs because there are fewer trips to shopping malls, among other things, the fact is that e-commerce systems generally rely on a transportation system that is more energy and pollution intensive, as aircraft replace trucks and rail.[29]

One particular concern about the impact of international trade on greenhouse gas emissions is the link to transportation services.[30] Moreover, as customers are frequently given the option to return delivered products free of charge, and as companies try to get their products to consumers more quickly, non-sustainable transportation may increase.

Thus, from an environmental point of view, the key question should be how the environmental performance of each value chain can be improved[31] – for example, through better volume utilization of vehicles, avoidance of express delivery by airfreight, minimization of packaging,[32] greater use of traffic light technology and truck platooning,[33] and tax mitigation strategies which prevent e-commerce companies from maintaining their current competitive advantages.

In addition, the fiscal impact on e-commerce companies which sell tangible goods should be as neutral as possible, in order to avoid increased international transport of goods that may occur if these companies engage in tax planning that minimizes taxation in consumer countries.

The main issue is the extent to which the competitive advantage of a reduced tax burden leads to a substantial increase in the transportation of goods that otherwise would not occur.

5. IS THERE ANY RELATIONSHIP BETWEEN THE INCREASE IN TRANSPORT AND THE LOW LEVEL OF TAXATION ON INTERNATIONAL E-COMMERCE COMPANIES IN THE TANGIBLE ASSETS MARKET?

In the current tax framework, income from digital sales of imported products is not subject to corporate income tax (CIT) in consumer states. As a consequence, the purchase of local products online or through traditional commerce is discouraged, thus unnecessarily increasing the transportation of goods. The existing tax system incentivizes the delocalization of sales, through which sellers can avoid tax residence, PEs and other tax nexuses with consumer states. It is obvious that current tax treaty rules concerning the definition of a PE[34] incentivize a business model for e-commerce of tangible assets that prevents all activities in consumer states that would imply the existence of a PE and the CIT associated thereto. That is, the business model avoids the establishment of offices, factories, workshops, warehouses, shops, authorized agents and other nexuses, depending on the applicable treaty provisions or local regulations on PEs. In addition, e-commerce creates significant new regulatory policy challenges, because 'the network effects and economies of scale associated with digitalization can cause rising inequality and generate barriers to market entry'.[35]

Although there is no data in the academic literature or in the reports of institutional organizations on the relationship between transport activities and the level of taxation on e-commerce companies, the marginal costs associated with transport, coupled with the importance of avoiding PE connections, suggest a strong link between tax planning and an increase in international transport. The available data on estimated Cost, Insurance and Freight (CIF) and Free on Board (FOB) margins in international trade provide a solid basis for a comparison between the cost of international transport and the avoidance of taxes.[36]

The substantial reduction in the standard tax burden has created a powerful financing tool which allows e-commerce companies to assume higher transport costs in an anti-competitive way. For example, Amazon reportedly attributed $7.29 billion of its net sales in 2013 – or 9.8 per cent of its global total – to the UK, even though almost that entire sum comprised website transactions handled through the group's European trading hub in Luxembourg. Amazon's main UK company, which operates its warehouses and supports sales and purchase activities, had a reported turnover of £449 million for 2013 and a tax charge of £4.2 million.[37] According to the Eurostat database, the share of turnover from e-commerce spent on transportation and storage companies (with ten employees or more) in

2015 amounted to 81 per cent in Ireland, 37 per cent in the UK and 23 per cent in Croatia.[38]

This tax advantage for certain operators could therefore be pushing e-commerce companies in the wrong direction, in terms of their environmental footprint and sustainability.

6. POSSIBLE ACTIONS TO EQUALIZE THE TAX BURDEN FOR E-COMMERCE COMPANIES

The growing use of e-commerce has been described as 'the first of the termites' that is busily gnawing away at the foundations of the tax system.[39] As the current international tax system dates back to the 1920s, consensus is growing that the traditional concepts of 'source' and 'residence' should be replaced with 'origin' and 'destination'. This has become a pressing issue due to the challenges posed by e-commerce, such as the absence of a physical presence or a taxable nexus.[40] In considering how to improve current patterns, it is crucial to distinguish long-term tax reforms from interim measures.

According to international tax rules, the global allocation of taxation rights on the profits of all businesses relies on the presumption of a physical presence through the cornerstone concept of the PE and corresponding transfer pricing and profit attribution rules. These rules are challenged by the digitalization of the economy, which allows businesses to generate profits without establishing a physical presence in every relevant jurisdiction. The result is a perception that e-commerce companies do not pay their fair share of tax in all jurisdictions in which they conduct activities. This issue goes beyond the BEPS concerns, which have already been targeted by multiple anti-tax avoidance measures.[41]

On the one hand, international concerted actions are based on the recognition of low taxation. While the OECD clearly aims to tax profits in line with economic activity[42] and the EU promotes legislative measures,[43] a conceptualization of the terms 'value creation' and 'business models in the digital economy' is needed, apart from examining new business models.[44] An updated March 2018 UK Report proposes that the rules in the OECD Model Tax Convention – particularly Articles 5, 7 and 9 – as well as the OECD profit attribution guidelines that underpin those articles be modified to allow user jurisdictions to tax non-resident companies with a PE in their jurisdiction (under the modified Article 5) on profits attributable to value created by local users, and that a method be established for determining such value that is consistent with the changes to Article 9.[45]

On the other hand, some countries have reacted unilaterally. However, their actions may be characterized as defensive measures and short-term solutions. They include the UK Diverted Profits Tax, the Australian Multinational Anti-Avoidance Law and Diverted Profits Tax, and India's Equalization Tax[46] and the proposed new nexus based on a concept of 'significant economic presence'. France, too, has an online audiovisual content/advertising levy;[47] and Italy has initiatives such as the voluntary disclosure procedure and the levy on digital transactions (web tax).[48]

As a result, a significant number of MNEs have taken proactive measures to realign their tax arrangements with their real economic activity, either by reconsidering their transfer pricing positions or by relocating and on-shoring valuable assets, such as intangibles. With the exchange of country-by-country reports beginning in 2018 for the 2016 tax year, further evidence of the impact of the BEPS measures is anticipated in the coming years.[49] Furthermore, country-level implementation of the wide-ranging BEPS package is already having an impact, with evidence emerging that some MNEs have already changed their tax arrangements to better align with their business operations. The measures are already delivering increased revenues for governments – for example, over €3 billion in the EU alone as a result of the implementation of the new International Value Added Tax/Goods and Services Tax Guidelines. Also, the widespread implementation of the BEPS package, including recent EU directives, as well as some aspects of US tax reform, should neutralize the very low effective tax rates of some companies.

Nonetheless, the BEPS measures do not necessarily resolve the question of how rights to tax are shared between jurisdictions, which is part of the long-term issue.[50] The March 2018 UK Report considered whether, in the case of remote sales, the principles of the international tax system are being undermined by the ability of e-commerce companies to generate revenues from markets in which they have a limited physical presence. The UK Report challenged the idea that 'cross-border selling is unique to digital businesses, arguing that globalisation and technological improvement are increasing the ability of businesses in all sectors to centralise core economic functions and sell remotely into foreign markets'. It also challenged the idea that 'the increasing ability of a business to sell to customers in a market in which it has limited local presence somehow undermines the existing principle of the international tax system'.[51] The channels through which user participation creates value for a business:

> seem least relevant to businesses that sell acquired goods on an online platform (e-retailers) or digital software/hardware providers. For these businesses, user participation appears to be a less important source of value and less integral to the success of the business compared to more traditional functions such as the design, development and provision of a product or service.[52]

The UK Report further distinguishes between users and customers, and argues that:

> the principal role that customers serve to most businesses will continue to be paying for the goods or services that a business provides. Furthermore, while traditional multi-sided and intermediation business models do exist, the constraints to scale and remote operation mean that the value of customers/users will always be limited or substantially captured in the jurisdiction in which those customers/users are located.[53]

Finally, the courts are also taking a stance on this issue, changing the framework in a way that will certainly impact on taxation in the digital economy. For example, in *South Dakota v Wayfair*,[54] the US Supreme Court addressed the question of whether an out-of-state online seller could be held responsible for a sales tax in the consumer's state, which required an interpretation of the Commerce Clause in the US Constitution.[55] Acknowledging that 'the physical presence rule has been the target of criticism over many years from many quarters', the court concluded that the substantial nexus requirement was satisfied in this case based on both economic and virtual contact that the respondent had with the state. To the court, the volume of business conducted on an annual basis 'could not have occurred unless the seller availed itself of the substantial privilege of carrying on business in South Dakota'. This decision – the first sales tax jurisdiction case heard by the US Supreme Court in 25 years – is expected to have a significant impact not only on online sales across the country, but potentially also beyond, because the US 'nexus' is a similar concept to the PE in international taxation.[56]

As Vito Tanzi argues, 'governments might develop ways to monitor electronic commerce and electronic money or they may introduce new taxes', such as bit taxes or the Tobin tax. While the political mood, especially in the United States, seems to be against imposing new taxes on e-commerce, 'at least in the short term, progress might be made in clarifying how e-commerce transactions can be taxed within the existing tax framework'.[57]

In any case, e-commerce of tangible goods should be subject to its own specific tax measures for CIT and sales tax purposes, necessarily different from those addressing taxation of the digital economy as such. The current challenge is to fight against delocalization, non-taxable profits and unfair tax competition.

7. CONCLUSIONS

The current tax treatment of major international e-commerce companies is clearly unsatisfactory. This has been demonstrated by both international organizations and legislatures, as well as by expert committees in most of the countries that have heeded this issue.

Irrespective of whether it is necessary to address the fiscal situation of major e-commerce companies for reasons of tax collection and competition, there are also environmental reasons that suggest a thorough analysis of the issue is required. No or low taxation of such companies may be leading to increased long-distance international transport of goods, to the detriment of other market activities that are more advantageous from an environmental point of view.

It is clear that when we talk about environmental effects, we do so from a global perspective and not from the exclusive point of view of the consumer state, which in many cases could benefit itself from the immediate environmental effects of e-commerce.

Finally, despite the difficulties of obtaining precise data on the effects of the tax treatment of major e-commerce companies, there is no doubt that all measures implemented to restore fair competition will remove the incentives to incur higher transport costs. To this end, more non-legal statistical studies of location patterns and transportation patterns are needed.

All in all, successfully responding to the important tax and environmental challenges presented by the digital economy will require policy makers to draw on hitherto hidden creative reserves. Ultimately, effective action in this regard will demand complex international agreements and new international tax standards and proceedings.

NOTES

* This research is part of Project 587904: 'EU-China Comparative experiences and contributions to global governance in the fields of climate change, trade and competition', funded by the European Commission.

1. See EUROPEAN COMMISSION (2018), Press release, Brussels, 21 March 2018, 'Digital Taxation: Commission proposes new measures to ensure that all companies pay fair tax in the EU', http://europa.eu/rapid/press-release_IP-18-2041_en.htm, last accessed 4 December 2018.
2. 'Electronic commerce' can be defined as 'the sale or purchase of goods and/or services whether between businesses, households, individuals, governments and other public or State organisations, conducted over computer networks by methods specifically designed for the purpose of receiving or placing of orders'; OECD, 2011, 'Guide to measuring the information society 2011', OECD Publishing. http://dx.doi.org/10.1787/10.1787/9789264113541-en, last accessed 4 December 2018.
3. See, among others, Olbert M and Spengel, Ch (2017), 'International Taxation in the Digital Economy: Challenge Accepted?', *World Tax Journal*, February 2017, 3–46. This article critically outlines the OECD's view and includes recent literature contributions on the matter.
4. The 'digital economy' can be defined as 'the global network of economic and social activities that are enabled by platforms such as the Internet, mobile and sensor

networks'; UNITED NATIONS DEPARTMENT OF ECONOMIC AND SOCIAL AFFAIRS (2014), *Protecting the Tax Base in the Digital Economy*, 5.

5. EUROSTAT E-COMMERCE STATISTICS (2017), data extracted in December 2017 as a result of the 2017 survey on 'ICT usage and e-commerce in enterprises'; http://ec.europa.eu/eurostat/statistics-explained/index.php/E-commerce_statistics#Transport_charges_main_impediment_to_cross-border_web_sales_within_the_EU, last accessed 4 December 2018.
6. See Mokhtarian, PL (2004), 'A conceptual analysis of the transportation impacts of B2C e-commerce', *Transportation* 31 (3) (August), 2004, 28; https://escholarship.org/uc/item/74m9x4sh, last accessed 4 December 2018.
7. See OECD Interim Report 2018, 'The Challenges Arising from Digitalisation (Inclusive Framework on BEPS)', para 15. The Interim Report identifies three characteristics that are frequently observed in certain highly digitalized business models: scale without mass; heavy reliance on intangible assets; and the role of data and user participation, including network effects. It was noted, however, that countries have different views on whether and to what extent these features represent a contribution to value creation by the enterprise.
8. OECD, 'Addressing the Tax Challenges of the Digital Economy – Action 1: 2015 Final Report', 16.
9. See EUROPEAN PARLIAMENT (2006), 'Tax Challenges in the Digital Economy. Study for the TAXE 2 Committee', 16.
10. Id, 8.
11. See TELECOM ADVISORY SERVICES, LLC, 'The impact of taxation on the digital economy, Regulatory and Market Environment' (2016), ITU Regional Economic and Financial Forum of Telecommunications/ITC for Africa, Abidjan, Côte d'Ivoire, 19 January 2016.
12. See OECD (2011), 'Guide to measuring the information society 2011', OECD Publishing, n3, 14; Ayres, RU and Williams, E (2004), 'The digital economy, Where do we stand?', *Technological Forecasting and Social Change*, Vol 71, Issue 4, May 2004, 315–339; Zimmermann, H-D (2000), 'Understanding the Digital Economy: Challenges for New Business Models'; https://ssrn.com/abstract=2566095 or http://dx.doi.org/10.2139/ssrn.2566095, last accessed 4 December 2018.
13. See keynote speech by Commissioner Moscovici at the 'Masters of Digital 2018' event, Brussels, 20 February 2018.
14. See Sui, D and Rejeski, D (2002), 'Environmental Impacts of the Emerging Digital Economy; The E-for-Environment E-Commerce?', 29 *Environmental Management*, No 2, 2002, 156; https://doi.org/10.1007/s00267-001-0027-X, last accessed 4 December 2018.
15. The ease of pointing and clicking itself causes people to buy more. See Sui, D and Rejeski, D (n14), 159.
16. See Scott Matthews, H, Hendrickson, CT and Soh, DL (2001), 'Environmental and Economic Effects of E-Commerce. A case study of book publishing and retail logistics', *Transportation Research Record Journal of the Transportation Research Board* 1763 (1), 6–12.
17. They enable seamless door-to-door mobility, integrated logistics and value-added services. See EUROPEAN COMMISSION (2016), 'A European Strategy for Low-Emission Mobility', Brussels, 20 July 2016, COM (2016) 5101 final, 3.
18. Rejeski, D (1999), 'Electronic Impact', *The Environmental Forum*, July/August 1999, 34.
19. At present, more than 90 per cent of e-commerce is B2B.
20. See Sui, D and Rejeski, D (n14), 157.
21. EUROPEAN COMMISSION (n17).
22. The broad impact of ITC on road freight transportation combines an increasing trend caused by the growth in e-commerce with a decreasing trend caused by improved transportation efficiency. See Yoshimoto, R and Nemoto, T (2005), 'The impact of information and communication technology on road freight transportation,' *IATSS Research* Vol 29, no 1.
23. EUROPEAN COMMISSION (n17), 2, 7.

24. The work programme of the Committee on Trade and Environment (CTE) covers the main issues at the intersection of trade and environment. A number of issues indirectly relating to climate change – such as the environmental benefits of removing trade restrictions in the energy and forestry sectors and the effect of energy efficiency labelling on market access – have been discussed in the CTE. See in the official website of the WTO, 'The impact of trade opening on climate change', www.wto.org/english/tratop_e/envir_e/climate_impact_e.htm, last accessed 4 December 2018.
25. EUROPEAN COMMISSION, https://ec.europa.eu/clima/policies/transport_en, last accessed 4 December 2018.
26. See EUROSTAT, 'Digital economy & society in the EU. A browse through our online world in figures', 2018 ed.
27. Banister, D and Stead, D (2004), 'Impact of Information and Communications Technology on Transport Reviews', Vol 24, no 5, 611–632.
28. See Weltevreden, JWJ and Rotem-Mindali, O (2009), 'Mobility effects b2c and c2c e-commerce in the Netherlands: a quantitative assessment', *Journal of Transport Geography* 17, 83–92; Kos-Labedovicz, J and Urbanek, A (2017), 'Do Information and Communication Technologies influence transport demand? An exploratory study in the European Union', *Transportation Research Procedia* 25, 2660–2676.
29. Scott Matthews, H, Hendrickson, CT and Soh, D (2001), 'The Net Effect: Environmental Implications of E-Commerce and Logistics', Ref: 0-7803-6655-7/01/$10.00, 2001 IEEE, 192.
30. WTO (n24).
31. See, for example, the proposals made by Bottani, E and Casella, G (2018), 'Minimization of the environmental emissions of closed-loop supply chains: a case study of returnable transport assets management', *Sustainability MDPI*, 27 January 2018.
32. See Ficher, K (2003), 'E-Commerce. Sorting Out the Environmental Consequences', *Journal of Industrial Ecology*, Vol 6, No 2 (doi/epdf/10.1162/108819802763471762).
33. See 'The environmental cost of free two-day shopping', Climate Lab T1-E7, University of California.
34. The current norms are based on the PE rule for active business income and withholding tax for passive investment income. Under the current rule, a PE necessitates human activity or at least some form of physical presence in the source country; this is not always necessary for digital transactions. For a comparative perspective, see The General Report, 'Withholding tax in the era of BEPS, CIV and digital economy', IFA 2018 Seoul Congress (2018), *Cahiers de droit fiscal international*, vol 103, 248, 249.
35. United Nations Conference on Trade and Development (2018), 'Trade and Development Report 2018', Ch III, 86. One way of addressing rent-seeking strategies in a digital world would be to break up the large firms responsible for market concentration. An alternative would be to accept the tendency towards market concentration, but regulate that tendency with a view to limiting a firm's ability to exploit its dominance.
36. Miao, G and Fortanier, F (2017), 'Estimating Transport and Insurance Costs of International Trade', OECD Statistics Working Papers, 2017/04, OECD Publishing, Paris; http://dx.doi.org/10.1787/8267bb0f-en, last accessed 4 December 2018, 10. For instance, Table A6 (Annex V) shows CIF-FOB margins estimated by importing countries at between 1.6 and 8.1 per cent, 34.
37. See 'US tech giants launch fierce fightback against global tax avoidance crackdown', available at www.theguardian.com/business/2015/jan/21/us-tech-tax-avoidance-google-amazon-apple, last accessed 4 December 2018.
38. See Kos-Labedovicz, J and Urbanek, A (2017), 'Do Information and Communication Technologies influence transport demand? An exploratory study in the European Union', *Transportation Research Procedia* 25, 2671.
39. Tanzi, V (2001), 'Globalization, Technological Developments, and the work of fiscal termites', *Brookline Journal of International Law*, Vol 26, Issue 4, 1264; Murphy, R (2013), 'Over here and undertaxed: Multinationals', *Tax Avoidance and You*, Brain Shots, Vintage Digital.

40. See EUROPEAN PARLIAMENT (2006), 'Tax Challenges in the Digital Economy. Study for the TAXE 2 Committee', 67.
41. Council conclusions on 'Responding to the challenges of taxation of profits of the digital economy', COM (2017) 547 final.
42. OECD, 'Addressing the Tax Challenges of the Digital Economy – Action 1: 2015 Final Report', 16 (OECD/G20 2015). About digital economy in general, see OECD (2017), Digital Economy Outlook, 2017, OECD publishing, Paris; http://dz.doi.org/10.1787/9789264276284-en, last accessed 4 December 2018.
43. See EUROPEAN COMMISSION Communication of 18 April 1997: 'A European Initiative in the sector of Electronic Commerce', COM (1997) 157 final, Brussels and Proposal for a Council Directive on the common system of a digital services tax on revenues resulting from the provision of certain digital services, Brussels, 21 March 2018, COM (2018) 148 final 2018/0073(CNS).
44. See Olbert, M and Spengel, Ch (2017), 'International Taxation in the Digital Economy: Challenge Accepted?', *World Tax Journal*, February 2017, 72.
45. HM TREASURY, 'Corporate tax and the digital economy: position paper update', March 2018, 20; https://assets.publishing.service.gov.uk/government/uploads/system/uploads/attachment_data/file/689240/corporate_tax_and_the_digital_economy_update_web.pdf, last accessed 4 December 2018.
46. The equalization tax is confined to B2B transactions in India so far, but, if it survives it will perhaps make a dent in B2C transactions as well. See Lee and Yoon, 'General Report Subject 2: Withholding tax in the era of BEPS, CIVs and digital economy', IFA 2018 Seoul Congress (*supra* note 34), 255.
47. Article 1609 *sexdecies* B of the General Tax Code, Act No 2016-1918 of 29 December 2016 amending the Finance Act for 2016.
48. The Italian 2018 Budget Law introduced a new 'tax on digital transactions' ('web tax').
49. See OECD Interim Report 2018, 'Brief on The Challenges Arising from Digitalisation (Inclusive Framework on BEPS)', para 13.
50. Id at para 3.
51. HM TREASURY, 'Corporate tax and the digital economy: position paper update' (*supra* note 45), 5.
52. Id, 11–12.
53. Id, 11, points 2.47, 2.48 and 2.32.
54. *South Dakota v Wayfair, Inc, et al*, 585 US 2018, No 17-494. Argued 17 April 2018, decided 21 June 2018.
55. US Const, Art I, Section 8, cl 3.
56. See Jansen, D, 'South Dakota v Wayfair – Insights and Analysis', posted in The News, Noteworthy cases on 21 June 2018; www.stateandlocaltax.com/in-the-news/south-dakota-v-wayfair-insights-analysis/, last accessed 4 December 2018.
57. Tanzi, V (n39) at 1277.

3. Tax incentives for green investments: limits to state cutbacks. A reflection on legitimate expectations and fair and equitable treatment of investors

Jerónimo Maillo*

1. INTRODUCTION

Can a State which has heavily incentivized long-term green investments for several years subsequently change the applicable framework, thus reducing the benefits for investors? If so, can these cutbacks apply to existing and operational energy plants, or should they be limited to future plants? Is it sufficient to ensure the reasonable profitability of existing plants? Can the whole productive life of an existing plant be taken into account in calculating whether profitability is reasonable? Do any of these measures qualify as an illegal retroactive application of the law? Do they violate the principle of legitimate expectations or can they be considered to constitute unfair or inequitable treatment of investors? What limitations apply to the cutback of green tax incentives according to general principles of law and the Energy Charter Treaty (ECT)?

These are some of the very interesting questions put forward in more than 30 cases commenced against Spain following law reforms in 2010 and (mainly) 2013–14 which reduced the incentives introduced for renewable energies in 2007. This chapter will explore these issues in the case law of both the Constitutional Court and the Supreme Court, and will compare them with arbitration awards issued by bodies such as the Stockholm Chamber of Commerce (SCC) and the International Centre for Settlement of Investment Disputes (ICSID) of the World Bank. It will mainly focus on the limits to State cutbacks according to general principles of law and the ECT – in particular, the need for fair and equitable treatment of investors, and related aspects such as the concept of legitimate expectations and the principle of non-retroactivity. However, to the extent that this is necessary, it will also address correlated issues such as the intersection between the EU State aid regime and the principle of legitimate expectations; the need to notify to the European Commission as State aid any new payments due as the result of an arbitration award; and the possible consequences of the different treatment of national, European and foreign investors following the recent arbitration awards against Spain.

2. THE SPANISH CASES: IMPORTANCE AND FACTUAL FRAMEWORK

This section will briefly describe the factual and regulatory framework in which these cases arose – in particular, the reforms to the incentives implemented in Spain that led to the filing of compensation claims before both the Spanish courts and international arbitration bodies. This exercise will also be useful to identify the main focus of this research and to better understand its quantitative and qualitative importance.

In 2007, in the context of a growing economy and a healthy public budget, the socialist party in government adopted important incentives for renewable energy generation.[1] The aim was to attract and promote green investments and make Spain a leader in the renewable energy field – not only to promote climate change goals (as required by the EU), but also to further the strategic development of the Spanish economy. However, by 2010, the context had drastically changed. The global economic crisis had had a severe impact on the Spanish economy, the country's future economic prospects looked bleak and the growing tariff deficit was starting to be perceived as unsustainable. Therefore, reforms[2] were adopted to cut back on green incentives. In particular, feed-in tariffs for solar energy and incentives for wind generation were reduced. Furthermore, a 25-year limit and an annual cap for feed-in tariffs were imposed. These changes were perceived as relevant cuts to the incentives which nonetheless did not modify the fundamentals of the initial framework. However, the tariff deficit continued to increase, necessitating further reforms.

In 2013, with the Popular Party in power, more radical reforms were passed[3] to abrogate the feed-in tariffs, while ensuring through a new calculation method that operators could still achieve 'reasonable profitability' from their investments. While the 2010 reforms had already been challenged before national courts and arbitration bodies, the 2013–14 reforms generated most of the court and arbitration actions and are thus the main focus of this chapter. The beneficiaries of the 2007 incentives claimed that the reforms violated the principles of legal certainty, legitimate expectations and non-retroactivity of the law, and thus constituted unfair and inequitable treatment of investors according to Spanish, EU and international law.

The quantitative importance of these claims is huge, as the investors are suing Spain in more than 30 cases for a total amount of more than €7.5 billion.[4] From a qualitative perspective, the judgments and arbitration awards will have to strike a balance between the need for legal certainty, which is essential to attract investment, and the necessary scope for public authorities to reform the regulatory framework when circumstances change without having to pay significant compensation. This may affect the credibility of the State – in this case, Spain – in its efforts to incentivize the green investment which is essential to meet EU and international goals to combat climate change and protect environment; but may also extend further to other types of investment. Furthermore, whether and under what circumstances it is still possible to resort to international arbitration, as well as the final balance struck by international arbitration awards, are issues that will have an impact on investments both in Europe and at a global level. In the context of an intense debate over investment treaties, with a key issue being which mechanisms of alternative dispute resolution are available, the outcome of these cases may have great significance far beyond Spanish borders.

3. THE LEGAL ANALYSIS: A DOUBLE STANDARD OF ASSESSMENT?

3.1 Outlining the General Picture

This section will analyse relevant case law of the Spanish courts and international arbitration bodies. It will identify some similarities, but also a lot of differences that may be creating a substantive double standard of assessment – a double level of protection for investors. This substantive double standard may be reinforced by the different procedural possibilities for international arbitration depending on whether the investor is Spanish, European or from a third country.

Finally, this section will introduce a special feature of the Spanish cases: the lack of State aid notification to the European Commission in relation to the 2007 green incentives regime. In the author's opinion, the intersection between EU State aid rules and the principle of legitimate expectations is a key issue that needs to be explored and that may influence the final outcome of these cases.

3.2 The Positions of the Constitutional Court and Supreme Court

Both the Constitutional Court and the Supreme Court have consistently held that the reforms of 2010 and 2013–14 did not violate the general principles of legal security, legitimate expectations, non-retroactivity and fair and equitable treatment of investors.[5]

3.2.1 Legal certainty and legitimate expectations

According to the Constitutional Court and the Supreme Court, the principle of legal security and its corollary, that of legitimate expectations, do not imply that economic actors are entitled to expect that a specific regulation in a specific sector at a given time will remain unchanged. Regulatory stability is compatible with legislative changes when these are foreseeable and aimed at defending the general interest. In this respect, the measures at issue did modify the previous regime, but they were not unpredictable;[6] they were also made in the general interest, given the difficulties prevailing in the sector as a whole, and the need to achieve the necessary economic balance and ensure the proper management of the system. A 'prudent and diligent economic operator' could have foreseen that the regulatory changes were feasible, necessary and even probable, given: (1) the existence of consistent case law holding that although the Spanish legal system guaranteed the operators of renewable energy production facilities the right to a reasonable return on their investments, it did not guarantee that the remuneration framework would remain unaltered[7] or entitle them to a very high profit level that could be contrary to superior public interests[8]; (2) the significant progress that had already been made (beyond what had been expected) in increasing the share of renewable energy in the Spanish energy mix; and (3) above all, the increasing tariff deficit and the serious threat this presented to the viability of the electricity system. The accumulated debt of the electricity system exceeded €26 billion and the structural deficit in the system had reached €10 billion annually, so the system risked bankruptcy if this imbalance were not corrected.

Furthermore, reasonable profitability was guaranteed. Article 30.4 of Law 54/1997, as per the wording set out in Royal Decree-Law 9/2013, provided that this reasonable profitability was based, before taxes, on the average yield in the secondary market of the State's public ten-year bonds, plus an appropriate differential. This differential was set by the first additional provision of Royal Decree-Law 9/2013 at 300 basis points, without prejudice to its possible revision every two years. For existing facilities with a premium regime on the date of entry into force of Royal Decree-Law 9/2013, as the value of the corresponding public bonds was 4.398 per cent, the reasonable profitability established by the Royal Decree-Law was 7.398 per cent.

3.2.2 Non-retroactivity

According to the Constitutional Court, Article 9.3 of the Constitution does not impose an absolute prohibition on retroactivity, which would effectively 'freeze' the legal order. So-called 'authentic' and 'improper' retroactivity should be distinguished. The former, which is applicable only to rights already consolidated and fully acquired – and not to pending, future or conditional rights and expectations – is prohibited. The latter – which affects unfinished situations, still in progress – is not. There is no proscribed retroactivity where a rule regulates *pro futuro* legal situations created prior to its entry into force or whose effects have not been consummated.

In the case at issue, the new remuneration regime took effect from the date of entry into force of the new regulations. It had an impact on legal situations created before the entry into force of that rule and that continued to produce effects; but it did not imply a prohibited retroactivity, since it did not affect acquired rights of the owners of such facilities or legal situations already exhausted or consummated.

By contrast, if the 'reasonable profitability' threshold for a facility had been exceeded at the time the new regime took effect, and the return of the amount beyond that threshold had been demanded, this would constitute authentic retroactivity. However, this was expressly prevented by Section 4 of Law 24/2013, which provided that in no case could the new remuneration model result in a claim for remuneration received prior to 14 July 2013, even if it was found that on that date, the profitability threshold had been exceeded. Therefore, there was no prohibited retroactivity in the case at hand.

However, dissenting opinions were issued by Judge Hon Mr Eduardo Espín Templado and Judge Hon Mr D Eduardo Calvo Rojas (to which Judge Hon Mrs Isabelle Perelló Domenech adhered) with regard to the judgment of the Third Section of the Administrative Chamber (Appeal 650/2014). This concerned an action against Royal Decree 413/2014 and Order IET/1045/2014 – rules for the development of Royal Decree-Law 9/2013. In this case three of the seven magistrates considered that there was prohibited retroactivity, because according to these rules, the changes applied to the entire life of each facility – that is, not only *pro futuro*, but from the initial commencement of operations. Each installation was assigned a model type according to its technical characteristics and the compensation was calculated in accordance with the parameters established in Order 1045/2014 for that category from the outset of its life; this could have the effect of reducing the remuneration to zero. The new calculation model did not take into account the real amounts that had been invested or specific data on actual activities – such as operating hours, operating costs, financial costs and electricity sales revenue – but rather applied standard values based on the criteria and parameters established by the new model across the whole life of the facility. According to the dissenting magistrates, in order to respect the principle of non-retroactivity, expressions such as 'throughout its regulatory life' and 'reasonable profitability' should have been interpreted as referring to the life of the facility after the entry into force of Royal Decree 413/2014 and Order IET/1045/2014 only, and not as though the new calculation model had been in force throughout the entire life of the facility.

3.3 The Position of International Arbitration Bodies

Some investors brought claims before international arbitration bodies such as the SCC and ICSID where this possibility was available under bilateral or multinational treaties, including the ECT. These international bodies decided cases involving both the 2010 and 2013–14 reforms, with very different outcomes. The basis for these arbitration reviews was primarily the principle of fair and equitable treatment of investors;[9] for example, Article 10.1 of the ECT[10] provides that:

> Each Contracting Party shall, in accordance with the provisions of this Treaty, encourage and create stable, equitable, favourable and transparent conditions for Investors of other Contracting Parties to make Investments in its Area. Such conditions shall include a commitment to accord at all times to Investments of Investors of other Contracting Parties fair and equitable treatment.

In general, the 2010 reforms were upheld and no compensation was awarded to investors. For instance, in *Charanne v Spain* (21 January 2016), the SCC decided not to award compensation as the 2010 reforms were not retroactive, were not unfair and were within the reasonable margin for reforms that the legislature has. The SCC found that investors could not have reasonably expected that there would be no changes at all to the regulatory regime that could reduce the value of their investment. Moreover, there were good reasons for the changes – in particular, the need to address the tariff deficit. The SCC stated that Spain had a regulatory right – albeit not an unfettered right – to make changes. In its view, the measures enacted in 2010 did not 'fall outside the acceptable range of legislative and regulatory behaviour'[11] because they had not 'entirely transformed and altered the legal and business environment under which the investment was decided and made'.[12] There was a similar outcome in *Isolux* (12 July 2016), in which the SCC again concluded that there had been no violation of the principle of legitimate expectation and no unfair treatment of investors. In *Isolux*, the position was even clearer as the investment had been made in October 2012 – that is, at a stage when it must have been clear to the investors that significant changes to the regime were likely. The SCC also accepted in both cases that the cutbacks could apply to operational plants insofar as they applied only to future payments, and not to payments already made to the investors.

However, the cases involving the 2013–14 reforms had very different outcomes. The SCC awarded compensation in *Novoenergia* (15 February 2017), although a Swedish court subsequently annulled the award for lack of competence. Nevertheless, the award reveals that the SCC considered the more radical reforms of 2013–14 to constitute unfair treatment. The SCC stated that the challenged measures were radical and unexpected. They fell 'outside the acceptable range of legislative and regulatory behaviour' and 'entirely transform[ed] and alter[ed] the legal and business environment under which the investment was decided and made'.[13] Moreover, the reforms had a significant detrimental economic effect on the investors. It is not necessary for the value of an investment to be destroyed entirely in order to find that a breach has occurred;[14] therefore, the fact that Spain had guaranteed reasonable profitability was not enough.[15] Determining whether the principle of fair and equitable treatment has been violated is more complex, involving a balancing exercise which weighs the State's regulatory interests against the investors' legitimate expectations and reliance.[16]

The ICSID has already decided three cases involving the 2013–14 reforms (*Eiser*,[17] *Masdar*[18] and *Antin*[19]), awarding compensation in all three.

Overall, the arbitrators considered that the 2013–14 reforms had much more radical effects than the 2010 reforms; that they were based on totally new economic fundamentals;[20] that excessive past profitability ratios had not been shown – if this were relevant, which might not be the case;[21] that the legislative changes were unreasonable and not foreseeable; and that the specific context of the plants had not been sufficiently taken into account.[22] All of this caused a very significant decrease in investors' returns, regardless of whether their profitability was still reasonable. For instance, in *Masdar*, the tribunal noted that Masdar had invested in the knowledge that the level of incentive went beyond the mere prospect of a reasonable return.[23] It further highlighted that the level of incentive on offer influenced not only the decision to invest, but also the design and development of the specific project. Without that precise incentive (eg, with only a reasonable return), the investment may have not been made in the first place, or may have been made very differently. As the tribunal stated in *Antin,* 'the issue at hand is not whether the New Regime provides a "reasonable return", but rather how such "reasonable return" is determined'.[24]

The question remains open as to whether 'specific commitments' to individual investors are needed to create legitimate expectations of regulatory stability, or whether such expectations may be derived from general legislation and general documents, press releases, presentations and reports provided by the public authorities.[25] This debate also encompasses the questions of what constitutes a 'specific commitment' and what is sufficient to confirm its existence. If a specific commitment exists, then legitimate expectations have been created and a sudden or drastic change to the regulatory framework will constitute a breach of the principle of fair and equal treatment. In *Masdar*, for instance, the tribunal found that a specific commitment existed based on the following evidence: (1) an individual resolution addressed to each of the investors concerned stating that they had been admitted to the Register for the Special Regime Applicable to Renewable Energy Plants (*Registro Administrativo de Instalaciones de Producción en Régimen Especial*) in due time and therefore that the benefits of Royal Decree 661/2007 were applicable to them; and (2) individual letters issued by the Spanish public authorities, upon request of the investors concerned, confirming that the remuneration applicable to their installations consisted of the tariffs, premiums, and upper and lower limits and supplements as established in Royal Decree 661/2007.

In *Antin*, the tribunal bypassed this discussion, finding that there had been a breach of the principle of fair and equitable treatment and legitimate expectations, as the elimination of the essential features of the regime set forth under Royal Decree 661/2007 constituted a change that was too drastic, disproportionate, unreasonable and unexpected at the time the decision to invest was made.[26] The tribunal also asserted that the new regime left too much discretion to the government as to how to calculate a 'reasonable return' (especially considering future revisions). Moreover, the tribunal was not convinced that the tariff deficit could justify the elimination of the key features of the initial regime and its replacement with a wholly new regime based on no identifiable criteria, as it was not persuaded that the feed-in tariff had played a significant role in the accumulation of the tariff deficit.[27]

3.4 A Procedural Double Standard

As a substantive double standard exists, it is relevant to determine whether and to what extent it is possible to bring a case before international arbitration bodies, which represent the most favourable forum for investors. This latter possibility requires the existence of a bilateral or multilateral treaty in which the State has accepted this alternative dispute resolution mechanism. For instance, Article 26 of the ECT (to which both Spain and the EU are parties) allows for the possibility of settling disputes through arbitration. Article 26 was invoked by the investors in all six cases on the Spanish energy reforms decided thus far by the SCC and ICSID (*Charenne*, *Isolux*, *Novenergia*, *Eiser*, *Antin* and *Masdar*). In all of these cases, Spain contended that there was a lack of jurisdiction as the ECT cannot apply to intra-EU disputes. However, in all six cases the tribunals dismissed this defence and asserted their jurisdiction.

Nevertheless, a relevant judgment was subsequently issued by the European Court of Justice (ECJ) in the *Achmea* case.[28] The dispute concerned a similar arbitration clause – Article 8 of the Agreement on encouragement and reciprocal protection of investments between the Kingdom of the Netherlands and the Czech and Slovak Federative Republic – under which an investor from one Member State, in the event of a dispute concerning investments in the other Member State, could bring proceedings against that Member State before an arbitral tribunal. Basing its decision on the autonomy of EU law, as well as Articles 267 and 344 of the Treaty on the Functioning of the European Union (TFEU), the ECJ concluded that such clauses cannot be included in international agreements between Member States. According to the ECJ, such clauses call into question not only the principle of mutual trust between Member States, but also the preservation of the particular nature of the law as established by the EU Treaties, and ensured by the preliminary ruling procedure provided for in Article 267 TFEU. They are therefore incompatible with the principle of sincere cooperation and contrary to the principle of autonomy of EU law.[29]

Although the judgment concerned a bilateral investment treaty, a similar reasoning may also apply to Article 26 of the ECT; at least, this is what the European Commission argues.[30] If this is correct, intra-EU investment disputes would have to be resolved before national courts (and the ECJ), rather than arbitration tribunals. Therefore, in national disputes which do not fall under the scope of bilateral investment treaties or the ECT, and (following *Achmea*) in intra-EU disputes, investors' sole recourse is to the national courts and the ECJ. On the contrary, in extra-EU disputes, investors may still have both channels open: litigation and arbitration. Therefore, a procedural double standard may be added to, and may reinforce, the substantive double standard.

Logically, it remains to be seen whether ICSID and other arbitration bodies will respect this conclusion or will continue to assert their jurisdiction, even after *Achmea*. In the case of the SSC, the arbitration award in *Novenergia* was challenged on these grounds before a Swedish court, which confirmed the SCC's lack of jurisdiction, thus extending the reasoning of *Achmea* to ECT cases. It is conceivable that this may not be the outcome in the US courts, where claimants have already started to seek enforcement of the ICSID arbitration awards against Spain.[31]

3.5 EU State Aid Rules and Legitimate Expectations

There is one argument which has not yet been considered by any of the arbitration tribunals, but may be crucial to the final outcome of these cases. It relates to the limits on the principle of legitimate expectations imposed in State aid cases.

All of the green incentives offered by Spain (both under the regime from 2007–10 and following the 2013–14 reforms) constituted State aid under EU law. According to Article 108 TFEU, a State that wishes to grant any new aid should first notify the European Commission accordingly and suspend implementation until authorization has been received from the Commission. If the State fails to notify, the aid is unlawful and therefore recovery of the aid with interest may be ordered.

Furthermore, recipients of the aid cannot plead legitimate expectations, as they should know that aid which has not been duly notified is unlawful. It is relatively easy for recipients to check whether this procedure has been followed and what the outcome was. This is confirmed by longstanding case law of the ECJ which was consolidated well before 2007, when the green incentives were launched.[32]

As Spain did not notify the European Commission of the green incentives of 2007–10, these constituted unlawful State aid. The investors, as diligent recipients of the aid, should have known that they cannot claim legitimate expectations. The European Commission recently reconfirmed this in relation to the 2007–10 green incentives:

> In the very specific situation of the present case, where a Member State grants State aid to investors, without respecting the notification and stand-still obligation of Article 108(3) TFEU, legitimate expectations with regard to those State aid payments are excluded. That is because according to the case-law of the Court of Justice, a recipient of State aid cannot, in principle, have legitimate expectations in the lawfulness of aid that has not been notified to the Commission.[33]

It is true that the European Commission distinguishes in the legal reasoning between intra-EU and extra-EU situations. In relation to the former, it states:

> In an intra-EU situation, Union law is part of the applicable law, as it constitutes international law applicable between the parties to the dispute. As a result, based on the principle of interpretation in conformity, the principle of fair and equitable treatment cannot have a broader scope than the Union law notions of legal certainty and legitimate expectations in the context of a State aid scheme.[34]

However, regarding the latter, the Commission ends up arriving at the same outcome: the impossibility of recognizing legitimate expectations and therefore a breach of the principle of fair and equitable treatment. It states: 'In an extra-EU situation, the fair and equitable treatment provision of the ECT is respected since no investor could have, as a matter of fact, a legitimate expectation stemming from illegal State aid.'[35]

The Commission further insists that the impossibility of recognizing legitimate expectation in such a scenario has already been explicitly recognized by arbitration tribunals – in particular, by another ICSID tribunal.[36]

Finally, the Commission emphasizes that any compensation which an arbitration tribunal were to award an investor based on Spain's modification of the green incentives 'would constitute in and of itself' notifiable State aid and be subject to the standstill obligation.[37] The Commission is the only competent authority to approve such aid.

The Commission further highlights that Commission decisions are a part of EU law and as such are also binding on arbitration tribunals where they apply EU law; the exclusive forum for challenging the validity of such decisions is the ECJ.[38]

It seems that the investors ignored this key issue and were not sufficiently diligent. Spain will surely present this argument in subsequent arbitrations; and unless tribunals decide to ignore EU law or disregard its importance by making a more general assessment of the principle of fair and equitable treatment, it will be hard for them to conclude that the investors had legitimate expectations. This defence may prove sufficient for Spain to avoid the award of compensation. In any case, if an award is granted, Spain will have to notify it to the European Commission as State aid and respect the standstill obligation until the Commission has decided accordingly. It seems very likely that the Commission would find that such an award is not justified, as there were no legitimate expectations. The investors may then challenge the Commission's decision before the ECJ, but with little or no possibility of success. Therefore, it is understandable why the investors concerned are trying to enforce the awards in the US courts, which may prove a more favourable forum.[39]

NOTES

* This research was initiated and partially developed while the author was a Fulbright Visiting Scholar at Harvard Law School (2017–18).

1. Royal Decree 661/2007.
2. Royal Decree 1565/2010 and Royal Decree 14/2010.
3. Royal Decree 9/2013 and Law 24/2013, subsequently developed by Royal Decree 413/2014 and Order IET/1045/2014.
4. *El País*, *Economia*, '*Los fondos demandan a España en EEUU para que pague los arbitrajes de renovables que perdió*', 22 August 2018.
5. See, among others, Judgments of the Spanish Constitutional Court 270/2015 of 17

December; 19/2016 of 4 February; 29/2016 of 18 February; 30/2016 of 18 February; and 61/2016 of 17 March. See also, among others, Judgments of the Spanish Supreme Court (Administrative Section) 40/2011 of 12 April 2012; 35/2011 of 12 April 2012; 62/2011 of 19 June 2012; 60/2011 of 24 September 2012; 71/2012 of 15 September 2012; 566/2010 of 26 June 2012; 261/2013 of 26 June 2013; 118/2013 of 16 March 2015; and 1259/2016 of 1 June 2016.

6. However, see the dissenting opinions of Judge Hon Mr Eduardo Espín Templado and Judge Hon Mr D Eduardo Calvo Rojas (to which the Judge Hon Mrs Isabelle Perelló Domenech adhered) regarding the judgment of the Third Section of the Administrative Chamber (Appeal 650/2014). The magistrates considered that it was not foreseeable, even at a point in time close to the introduction of the changes in 2014, that Royal Decree 413/2014 and Order IET/1045/2014 would establish such radical changes with such retrospective and detrimental scope, and without any transitional period. For further details see section 3.2.2.
7. See, among others, Judgments of the Spanish Supreme Court (Administrative Section) 12/2005 of 25 October 2006; 11/2005 of 20 March 2007; 149/2007 and 152/2007 of 9 December 2009; 40/2011 of 12 April 2012; 48/2011 of 13 September 2012; 64/2011 of 15 October 2012; 138/2011 of 10 December 2012; 232/2012 of 29 January 2013; 193/2010 of 29 May 2013; and 118/2013 of 16 March 2015.
8. See Opinion of Judge Hon Xiul Ríos regarding Judgment of the Spanish Constitutional Court 270/2015 of 17 December.
9. Regarding the principle of fair and equitable treatment of investors, see, among others, Gaukrodger, D (2017), 'Addressing the balance of interests in investment treaties: The limitation of fair and equitable treatment provisions to the minimum standard of treatment under customary international law', OECD Working Papers on International Investment, 2017/03, OECD Publishing, Paris; Kalicki, J and Medeiros, S, 'Fair, Equitable and Ambiguous: What Is Fair and Equitable Treatment in International Investment Law?, 22 *ICSID Rev - Foreign Investment Law Journal* (2007), pp24–54; Dias Simoes, F, 'When Green Incentives Go Pale: Investment Arbitration and Renewable Energy Policymaking', 45 *Denv J Int'l L & Pol'y* 251 (2017); Potesta, M, 'Legitimate Expectations in Investment Treaty Law: Understanding the Roots and the Limits of a Controversial Concept', *ICSID Review*, Vol 28, No 1 (2013), pp88–122; Zeyl, T, 'Charting the Wrong Course: The Doctrine of Legitimate Expectations in Investment Treaty Law', 49 *Alta L Rev* 203 (2011).
10. On the ECT, see, among others, Coop, G, '20 Years of the Energy Charter Treaty', *ICSID Review*, Vol 29, No 3 (2014), pp515–524.
11. *AES Summit Generation Limited and AES-Tisza Erömü Kft v Republic of Hungary*, ICSID Case ARB/07/22, Award, 23 September 2010, para 9.3.73; *Novenergia II – Energy & Environment (sca), Sicar (Luxembourg) ("claimant") v Kingdom of Spain*, SCC Case V 2015/063, para 688.
12. *CMS Gas Transmission Company v The Argentine Republic*, ICSID Case ARB/01/8, Award 12 May 2005, para 275. *Novoenergia*, para 688.
13. *Novenergia*, para 695.
14. The claimants showed that their plants had suffered a reduction in profits of 24–32 per cent between 2013–16.
15. *Novenergia*, para 692.
16. *Novenergia*, para 694.
17. *Eiser Infrastructure Limited and Energia Solar Luxembourg S.À R.I. v Kingdom of Spain,* ICSID Case ARB/13/36, 4 May 2017.
18. *Masdar Solar & Wind Cooperatief U.A. v Kingdom of Spain*, ICSID Case ARB/14/1, 16 May 2018.
19. *Antin Infrastructure Services Luxembourg S.à.r.l. and Antin Energia Termosolar B.V. v Kingdom of Spain*, ICSID Case ARB/13/31, 15 June 2018.
20. *Eiser*, paras 389 and 391; *Antin*, para 560.
21. *Eiser*, para 402. See below the discussion on *Masdar* about whether a reasonable return is sufficient to avoid a breach of the principle of fair and equitable treatment.

22. *Eiser*, para 403; *Antin*, para 565. In *Antin*, the main concern of the tribunal was that under the new regime, the 'reasonable rate of return' was not based on any identifiable criteria and therefore left too much discretion to governmental decisions, in stark contrast to the initial regime. See in this regard paras 563–568, especially 568.
23. *Masdar*, para 496.
24. *Antin*, para 562.
25. See, for instance, the discussion on *Masdar*, paras 490 et seq.
26. *Antin*, para 560.
27. *Antin*, paras 57–572.
28. Judgment of the Court (Grand Chamber) of 6 March 2018, *Slowakische Republik v Achmea BV*, C-284/16, ECLI:EU:C:2018:158. For comments on this ruling, see, among others, Melchionda, L, 'The European Court of Justice ruling in Achmea v. Slovak Republic: more questions than answers', *Diritto del commercio internazionale* 2018 pp337–359; Simon, D, '*L'arbitrage en matière d'investissement remis en cause par la Cour de Justice?*' Europe 2018 May nº 5 pp5–9; Villar, M, '*Implicaciones del caso «Achmea» en asuntos fiscales: límites al arbitraje, jurisdicción exclusive del TJUE y convenios de doble imposición internacional*', *Quincena Fiscal 1-2, Enero* 2019, pp147–182; and the Declaration of the representatives of the governments of the Member States, of 15 January 2019 on the legal consequences of the judgment of the Court of Justice in Achema and on investment protection in the European Union.
29. *Achmea*, paras 58–60.
30. European Commission Decision of 10 November 2017, C (2017) 7384 final, State aid SA40348 (2015/NN) – Spain Support for electricity generation from renewable energy sources, cogeneration and waste, paras 160–163.
31. This is the case for the awards in *Eiser* and *Antin*. See *El País, Economía*, 22 August 2018, '*Los fondos demandan a España en EE UU para que pague los arbitrajes de renovables que perdió*'.
32. See, among others, ECJ Judgments in Case C-5/89, *Commission v Germany*, EU:C:1990:320, para 17; Case C-169/95, *Spain v Commission*, EU:C:1997:10, para 51; Case C-334/99, *Germany v Commission* EU:C:2003:55, para 41; Case T-366/00, *Scott v Commission*, T:2007:99, para 61; Case C-91/01, *Italy v Commission*, EU:C:2004:244, para 65; Case C-24/95, *Land Rheinland-Pfalz v Alcan Deutschland*, EU:C:1997:163, paras 13–14 and 25.
33. European Commission Decision of 10 November 2017, C (2017) 7384 final, State aid SA40348 (2015/NN) – Spain Support for electricity generation from renewable energy sources, cogeneration and waste, para 158.
34. Ibid, para 64.
35. Ibid.
36. *Electrabel S.A. v Republic of Hungary*, ICSID Case ARB/07/19.
37. European Commission Decision of 10 November 2017, C (2017) 7384 final, State aid SA40348 (2015/NN) – Spain Support for electricity generation from renewable energy sources, cogeneration and waste, para 165. See also European Commission Decision 2015/1470 of 30 March 2015, State aid SA38517 (2014/C) (ex 2014/NN) implemented by Romania – Arbitral award *Micula v Romania* of 11 December 2013.
38. European Commission Decision of 10 November 2017, C (2017) 7384 final, State aid SA40348 (2015/NN) – Spain Support for electricity generation from renewable energy sources, cogeneration and waste, para 166.
39. See also Tamás Kende, T, 'Arbitral Awards Classified as State Aid under European Union Law', *ELTE Law Journal*, 2015 (1), pp37–56.

PART II

Fiscal Environmental Policies for Urban Concentration

4. Smart cities: can business improvement districts reduce the environmental footprint of urban areas?

Helena Villarejo Galende, María Luisa Esteve Pardo and Clara Peiret García*

1. INTRODUCTION

The United Nations estimates that by 2050, approximately 6.4 billion people will be living in urban centres.[1] Urban growth presents enormous challenges for contemporary cities, with economic efficiency and environmental sustainability at the forefront of those challenges. Smart city initiatives aim to respond to such challenges through the use of technology and innovation, and afford the opportunity to rethink the way that citizens are provided with services.

Although, in general terms, the definitions of a 'smart city' all have the use of technology to improve the sustainability and efficiency of public services in common, the literature on the subject calls for a holistic 'smart city' concept that places less emphasis on the use of information and communication technology (ICT) and more on citizen participation and public-private partnership:

> We believe a city to be smart when investments in human and social capital and traditional (transport) and modern (ICT) communication infrastructure fuel sustainable economic growth and a high quality of life, with a wise management of natural resources, through participatory governance.[2]

Public-private partnerships between local governments and the private sector – such as business improvement districts (BIDs), where businesses invest collectively through compulsory charges to help make local improvements – can contribute to finding solutions by working closely with the community and tailoring technology to local needs. In the context of the question, 'What do twenty-first century technologies enable us to do better?', although BIDs may not provide all the answers to metropolitan sustainable development issues, they can provide platforms where those answers might be found. By acting small but aiming high, BIDs can play a progressive engaging role on the sustainable development front.[3]

BIDs have proved to be a creative and very efficient mechanism of urban governance, capable of satisfactorily combining the public and private interests at play. This means that they can also play a significant role in the field of urban freight flows and the way in which deliveries are made. BIDs can develop smart city projects that help to reduce the environmental footprint of commercial logistics and meet other corporate social responsibility goals.

This chapter explores the need to recognize the role of 'middleman' organizations such as BIDs (not yet developed in Spain) to tackle the challenges of urban growth via cutting-edge technology, and to promote public participation in designing and implementing smart and sustainable measures that will transform our cities for the twenty-first century.

To develop a global vision of BIDs and the potential they offer, this chapter is structured as follows. First, the model and its origins are defined, and the countries in which it has been implemented are outlined. Next, the mechanism through which these entities operate is described, dissecting the technicalities on how BIDs are created and funded and discussing the actions they take. Following on from this, our proposal for implementing the BID model in Spain is presented. The final section analyses how BIDs can contribute to creating smarter, more sustainable cities by working hand in hand with local governments.

2. DEFINITION AND ORIGINS

2.1 Definition

'BIDs' can be defined as 'self-assessment districts that are usually initiated and governed by property or business owners, enabled by state laws, and authorised by local governments to provide public services in designated urban and suburban areas'.[4]

The uniqueness of this model lies in the way it operates. BIDs are created through a democratic process between property owners or businesses within a delimited geographical area, which agree to endow their district with additional public services. Those extra services are funded via a compulsory assessment or levy that all property owners or businesses in the area must pay.[5] Although traditionally these services included additional cleaning, supplemental security or consumer marketing and branding of the district, the model has since evolved and in recent years sustainability-related measures have become increasingly important.[6] It can be said that, despite the evolution of their activities, BIDs have always aimed to promote and regenerate the areas in which they operate.[7]

2.2 Origins

The BID model originated in Canada in the mid-1960s, as a private sector-led initiative to regenerate downtown areas and combat the problem of free-riders that a group of Toronto business owners was facing. Those free-riders were benefiting from the actions and improvements that a voluntary business association was funding – a situation that led its members to explore the possibility of creating a privately managed autonomous entity with the power to impose a charge on all business owners in the district.[8] To do so, specific enabling legislation had to be passed. In 1969, the Province of Ontario took this step and six months later, the City of Toronto passed By-law No 170-70, which resulted in the world's first BID: Bloor West Village.[9] The model quickly spread throughout Canada and then into the USA, where there are now over 1000 BIDs, of which 75 are in New York City alone. BIDs have since appeared all over the world, from Australia to Japan to Europe, including Germany, the Netherlands, Ireland, Sweden and the UK.[10] This fact exemplifies the flexibility and adaptability of this urban policy,[11] as well as its success as a model of governance.

The first European country to adopt the model was the UK, when the Local Government Act was passed in 2003. The model was slowly phased in throughout the country (the legislation was developed in 2004 for England, 2005 for Wales, 2006 for Scotland and 2013 for Northern Ireland), and has resulted in the creation of more than 300 BIDs to date.[12] In Germany, the process of introducing the model was pioneered by the city-state of Hamburg, which passed the enabling legislation in December 2004 and saw the birth of its first two BIDs (BID Sachsentor and BID Neuer Wall) shortly after. In 2007, the Federal Code of Urban Planning (*Baugesetzbuch*-§171f BauGB) was modified. In particular, a new paragraph was added under the heading 'Private initiatives in urban development' ('*Private Initiativen zur Stadtentwicklung*'). This enabled *Länder* to pass specific laws to promote private initiatives aimed at developing and regenerating specific urban areas.[13] To date, 10 *Länder* have authorized the creation of these entities.[14] There are now 30 fully functioning BIDs in Germany and almost 100 being developed[15] – a phenomenon that has led some authors to declare the 'BIDization' of German cities.[16]

The rapid growth in the number of BIDs is a response to a series of socio-economic and political factors: the decline of city centres, together with urban sprawl caused by the development of extensive motorway networks, the proliferation of new commercial formats, the problems of organizing and financing local governments, and the tendency to turn to public-private companies and partnerships to promote urban regeneration.[17]

Upon analysing the model's origins and expansion, three main ideas can be discerned. First, the fact that multiple business associations from very different locations around the globe have decided to adopt this model unequivocally demonstrates the advantages that it presents – in particular, the obvious improvement of the areas in which they have been established. Second, the ease with which the model has been adapted to such differing legal systems highlights its flexibility in both cultural and technical terms. Third, with regard to the formal aspects of the model, this adaptability also produces a wide range of variations between the different countries that have adopted BIDs. These divergences become clearest when their functioning requirements are analysed.

3. FUNCTIONING, FUNDING AND ACTIONS UNDERTAKEN

3.1 The Creation Process

As discussed above, the distinctive way that BIDs operate constitutes their main peculiarity. Although many countries have adopted the model and some variations can be observed (even from state to state within federal countries), BIDs are usually created through a municipal decision and authorized by state law. In the USA, business and property owners in the area in question usually lead the process and propose the boundaries for the BID, the business plan and how it will be funded.[18] It is also common among states to establish a two-stage procedure to constitute a BID. First, stakeholders (property owners, shopkeepers and business owners) carry out a ballot in which they vote whether to authorize the creation of a BID in the area. Second, the local authority must pass an ordinance (a city government statute) by which the BID is formally established and its boundaries, functions, budget and manner of funding are approved. It can therefore be concluded that the process of establishing a BID is democratic, as it must be aligned with the majority's interests. Moreover, some states set relatively high approval rates and weighted voting systems that combine criteria on the number of property owners and the property value they represent to secure the general interest.

In the UK – specifically, in England and Wales – the BID 'levy' is paid by business owners, who are also those eligible to vote in a ballot that must pass a double test. First, the BID proposal must be approved by a simple majority of businesses; second, those voting in favour must represent a majority of the aggregate rateable value of the hereditaments voting.[19] Unlike in the rest of the UK, in Scotland, property owners also take part in the initial plebiscite. Moreover, Scottish legislation sets a minimum turnover – 25 per cent of those eligible to vote both by number and by rateable value – for the ballot to be binding.[20]

In Germany, it is property owners who decide: they pay and they vote. The initial BID proposal must be backed by just 15 per cent of the property owners in the proposed area, representing at least 15 per cent of the total surface area in question.[21] Once the business plan of the future BID is accepted by the local authority, the application is made public for one month. If the affected property owners who explicitly reject the proposal do not represent more than one-third of the total (again in both quantitative and qualitative terms), the BID will be approved by the local government and all the property owners within the boundaries of the BID will be charged an additional tax based on the value of their properties.[22]

3.2 Funding

In terms of the BID funding system, all existing legislation stipulates that a charge must be paid to fund the actions of the BID – a burden that will have been accepted beforehand by those eligible to vote in the initial ballot. As with the constituent system of the BID, funding methods also vary from country to country. For instance, in the USA, the formula for payment is called an 'assessment' or 'BID fee', and is legally configured as a tax aimed at specifically funding any actions developed by the BID.[23] In general terms, the amount that property owners must pay represents 8–10 per cent of the real estate tax charge and constitutes the main funding source for the BID. Depending on the value of the business premises, the size of the district and the tax revenue formula used, figures can vary from thousands to millions of dollars per year.[24]

Canada, on the other hand, offers greater flexibility. Each business improvement area (BIA) establishes the amount of money that it wants to dedicate to promoting and enhancing the area. This proposal must be approved by the local government; once it has given the green light to the budget, funds are proportionally distributed among BIA members according to the share they represent in relation to the total property tax value in the area.[25]

The main difference between the British and US model is that in England and Wales, it is business owners (or business premises tenants), rather than property owners, who are obliged to pay the corresponding

BID 'levy', which is collected annually by the local tax authorities along with their non-domestic business rates bill.[26] This extra charge does not usually exceed 1.5 per cent of the rateable value of the business and can vary substantially from one BID to another.

In Germany, a 'special tax' (*Sonderabgabe*) must be paid by property owners within the district. This is calculated using two parameters: the BID's budget and the total rateable value of the encumbered properties. It is commonly established that the rate cannot exceed 10 per cent of the initial property value, notwithstanding that the actual burdens of existing German BIDs are considerably lower.[27] The local government collects the tax and, after deducting the corresponding administrative costs, hands the remaining amount over to the BID.

Altogether, all the models studied show that the levies paid by BID members are the BID's principal source of income. The levies are generally collected by the city council along with other local taxes and subsequently transferred to the management body of the BID (usually constituted as a non-profit organization) to fund the actions and services previously laid out in its business plan.

This system of funding based on fees or levies is one of the most salient features of the BID model. It addresses two of the major issues that pre-BID schemes faced – free-riders and the lack of a constant budget – and therefore it allows both professional management and effective actions. The compulsory BID charge has been the key feature for the success of the model worldwide.[28]

3.3 The Actions Undertaken

Although the actions of the respective BIDs can vary significantly from one to another, they are usually focused on three main pillars:[29] (1) cleaning, maintenance and enhancement of public spaces (ie, cleaning and maintaining the streets, removing graffiti, collecting litter, paving walkways, improving signposting and lighting, installing benches and rubbish bins, planting trees and flowers); (2) security and safety for the area and its businesses (through employing private security staff and installing security cameras to prevent crime and to make business owners, staff and consumers feel safer); and (3) marketing and promoting the BID area through different activities and events.

However, and as was briefly pointed out earlier in this chapter, a shift in BID measures has been perceived for some time now. For instance, several BIDs have started to work on projects concerned with improving sustainability, such as supporting eco-friendly urban freight initiatives[30] or developing local community actions in the interest of the common good.[31]

Such actions take place over a delimited period, usually lasting between three and five years. At the end of this, the BID must revalidate its mandate to keep operating. In other words, a new proposal for the BID must be submitted, which is then voted on by the stakeholders.[32] Usually, renewal rates among BIDs are strikingly high and participation levels in second and subsequent ballots tend to increase[33] – a fact that showcases local agents' satisfaction with the model.

Overall, it is important to bear in mind that BIDs do not seek to replace the local authority in providing services;[34] nor can they be used to justify the local government withdrawing and causing the privatization of public spaces. Analyses have been conducted on this particular point,[35] and have concluded that no significant differences between the public services provided by the local authority in BID and non-BID areas could be discerned. Moreover, countries such as Germany have explicitly established by law that BIDs cannot administer essential public services or activities that involve the exercise of public authority.[36]

Hence, having presented the features of BIDs, it may be concluded that these entities constitute the perfect breeding ground for new urban initiatives. BIDs have proved to be a creative and very efficient mechanism of urban governance, capable of satisfactorily combining the public and private interests at play. This is due to two key features: (1) the initial democratic process guarantees the involvement of all stakeholders; and (2) the sustained source of funding allows for the provision of urban services to be effectively improved.

Introducing the BID model to Spain could serve to boost not only urban commercial areas, but also other environments where there is economic activity, such as industrial parks and tourist destinations. BIDs could well be the best response to the problems that the urban economy is currently facing in Spain and a good way of solving the pressing financing needs that have arisen as a result of the economic crisis. Many public administrations, private organizations and political parties have expressed their interest in the potential development of this model. Considering its long history and proven success, we believe that the time has come to introduce the BID model to Spain.[37]

4. THE PROPOSAL FOR ADOPTING THE BID MODEL IN SPAIN

In brief, our proposal establishes that Spanish BIDs would have the following characteristics.[38]

The initiative to establish a BID must always come from a significant group of economic operators located in a specific area of a municipality.

However, under our proposal, not only retailers' associations can take the initiative, but also any group of economic agents with a common interest in the area. Gathering the support needed to go ahead with the proposal falls, of course, to the steering group.

Once a significant proportion of the economic operators in the area support the initiative, the steering group will ask the local government for approval. Initially, a BID proposal must be presented to the council, which will then check whether the proposed actions are aligned with the general interest and do not encroach on public competences or replace the public sector. Once the local government has authorized the proposal, it will be submitted for public scrutiny. If a majority of the economic operators affected agree, or alternatively if a significant proportion do not vote against it, the local authority will approve the BID. The option of introducing weighted voting systems should also be considered.

Once the BID has been approved by the local government, its collaboration with the BID will be formalized by signing an agreement or public contract whereby the BID commits to carry out the proposed business plan and to apply the funds correctly. The agreement or contract can be terminated if breached.

BIDs are managed by private non-profit bodies or public-private partnerships. Membership of the BID is voluntary and any economic operator obliged to pay the BID charge can become a member. While membership is not mandatory, payment of the BID charge is. The organization of the BIDs can be more or less complex, and could include a general assembly, a board of directors, a chairman, a manager and an operational team. In any case, the local authority will be represented on the organs of government of the BID as a non-voting member, to ensure that the BID's activities are consistent with the public interest.

The actions and services of the BID can focus on aspects from image campaigns, event organization and other services (to promote, regenerate and enhance the attractiveness of the area)[39] to sustainability-related measures and partnerships with the local authority to develop a cohesive urban policy. However, the services that BIDs provide are in addition to those offered by local governments and must therefore run concurrently with them, and by no means replace them. Two dangers are thereby avoided: the BID will not replace the public sector in its duties and powers; and the local authority will not reduce or withdraw the services it provides in the area on the grounds that the BID is now responsible for them.

The budget of the BID is mainly covered by the BID charge. This levy is established by municipal ordinance once the enabling law has been passed and is paid by those who carry out economic activity in the area. The amount of the BID charge is to be calculated based on the budget of the BID and the rateable value of the business premises – although relief extensions may be available based on, for example, the type of activity undertaken (eg, charity, cultural or general interest activities).[40] While the local authority will collect the charge together with the local property rates (*Impuesto sobre Bienes Inmuebles*), the levy will be itemized separately on the bill and the amount collected in BID charges will later be handed over to the BID's governing body. Additional income sources for the BID can also be considered, such as voluntary contributions by specific taxpayers or companies, public aid, payment for its services and external investment.

BIDs have a limited lifespan – that is, they are approved to operate for four or five years. The usual effective term in comparative law is five years, after which the BID can be renewed if the same prerequisites as applied in the initial set-up are complied with. Limitations such as this on the effective term of BIDs maximize accountability and taxpayers' assessments of how the income from the levy has been managed.

The local government is responsible for monitoring and supervising the BID to ensure that the business plan is being effectively implemented, and that the BID charges are being used correctly (ie, in accordance with the budget). The powers assigned to the local authority should be strictly limited to monitoring and supervising the BID, as comparative experience has shown that any greater local government intervention leads to the BID becoming simply a local authority instrument whose initiative is stifled.

5. CAN BUSINESS IMPROVEMENT DISTRICTS REDUCE THE ENVIRONMENTAL FOOTPRINT OF URBAN AREAS?

Introducing the BID model to Spain could not only serve to boost urban commercial areas, but also help to deal with the new challenges posed by the current retail revolution and even address some environmental issues. In accordance with the principle of subsidiarity,[41] innovative actions taken at the local level tend to be more pragmatic.[42]

E-commerce is reshaping the retail sector. One of the most significant new trends is a reduction in 'physical' stores and an increase in digital purchase channels. This implies a 'distribution revolution', in order to provide fast, convenient and secure package delivery. Commercial logistics are becoming increasingly complicated and their environmental impact cannot be ignored.

In this context, BIDs can play a key role by developing new strategies and availing of twenty-first century technologies, thus contributing to the wellbeing of agents both inside and outside the BID. On the internal level, BIDs could organize workshops and campaigns to raise awareness among members and clients of environmental issues, and help them to embrace sustainability as a core value. They could also take a step further to help small retailers go green and organize collective purchase orders for common store supplies such as reusable shopping bags, less toxic cleaning products, recycled wooden cabinets and shelves, energy-efficient lighting and eco-friendly electronic devices. These orders could be stored in a BID-owned warehouse outside the BID area and freighted to businesses when necessary. The delivery could be carried out by a shared eco-friendly van, which would allow street traffic and greenhouse emissions in the district to be reduced. Moreover, the BID could negotiate off-peak delivery hours with the local authority to further relieve congestion.

Moreover, BIDs could reverse the damage that e-commerce causes to business-to-people trade by creating a distribution centre in a warehouse located inside the area where online orders could be delivered, assembled and collected by clients. These deliveries could be managed through a BID app, based on existing models such as Amazon or Uber, which would allow clients to track and collect their packages and pay for them through secure payment systems based on the blockchain technology that makes it possible to carry out a digital transaction without revealing any more information than is absolutely necessary. Alternatively, BID members could create a home delivery service that uses zero-emission vehicles, such as cargo cycles, as some BIDs in London have already started to do.[43]

Finally, the corporate social responsibility of BIDs could be enhanced by developing synergies in partnership with local authorities. Existing BID technologies could be offered to urban planners to help them establish urban policies both in the BID area and in the rest of the city.[44] This collaboration could be based on open data and shared repositories, always respecting data protection. For instance, as measuring pedestrian traffic is important for planning and managing cities, an effective way to do so could involve using lidar sensors, low-resolution cameras, trace detectors that count passers-by without storing images or, in any event, devices that would guarantee data anonymization – a technique highly recommended by the EU General Data Protection Regulation (GDPR). An example of how the local authority could take advantage of the information provided by the BID would be by accessing the BID's footfall registers and analysing pedestrian patterns in the area. The partnership between the BID and the local authority could also employ existing sensors and install new ones for a multitude of purposes, from measuring traffic to detecting parking slots in the area, and from studying how often litter bins are used to determining pedestrian flow or occupancy rates.

To sum up, BIDs might not solve all the sustainability problems that cities are currently facing, but they can contribute by collaborating with local authorities to provide a platform where innovative and 'smart' solutions can be developed.[45] Moreover, BIDs constitute a perfect example of open government, given that discussion with and between stakeholders and a fluid relationship between the public and private sectors are essential in deciding what actions these entities will undertake. We must remember that a BID project will succeed only if it convinces its stakeholders that it offers solutions to urban problems and contributes to the general interest and common wellbeing.

6. CONCLUSIONS

BIDs came into being almost 50 years ago to solve very specific problems relating to depressed urban downtown areas. Their success in solving these issues has led them to spread all over the globe, gaining recognition among both their members and external agents such as local authorities, as well as the public as a whole. This is attested to by the high approval rates achieved in renewal ballots, by the number of countries that have adopted the model and by the interest they are sparking in areas where they have yet to be implemented.

The flexibility and adaptability of BIDs have allowed them to evolve and adapt to changing times and circumstances. Environmental sustainability and 'smart' solutions to urban problems have been added to the list of traditional objectives pursued by these entities as they collaborate ever more closely with local governments.

BIDs can now play a key role by helping to reduce greenhouse emissions using eco-friendly shared delivery vehicles, address traffic problems by changing delivery hours and grouping common orders, and reduce the environmental footprint of businesses by raising awareness or promoting green purchasing among their members. Furthermore, BIDs have established more solid relationships with local authorities by sharing their knowledge with urban planners. In this respect, the technology that BIDs possess, such as footfall sensors and parking slot detectors, can be used not only in the BID area itself, but in the city as a whole.

However, this public-private relationship must be clearly defined in terms of both competences and the use of any data gathered. The countries that have adopted this model have very precisely defined the line between the actions taken by the public sector and those developed by the BID. It must be made very clear that under no circumstances can BIDs replace local authorities or local authorities withdraw their obligations towards their citizens. Furthermore, now more than ever it is essential to provide data protection to guarantee privacy among users, and in Europe the recently introduced GDPR legislation clearly advocates for this. Therefore, it is fundamental to implement newly developed tools such as encryption through blockchain and/or data anonymization.

Implementing the BID model in Spain would help to resolve some of the most pressing issues currently affecting urban areas. BIDs would allow existing town management organizations to count on a reliable source of funding – something that currently constitutes one of their main difficulties. The lack of a predictable budget and their dependency on public subsidies damage their potential to undertake effective measures that would benefit both their own members and society in general. In establishing a compulsory contribution, these organizations would be able to develop long-term strategies and the democratic nature of the BID would increase the level of engagement among stakeholders.

This would also prevent free-riders from benefiting from the activities of surrounding businesses. Presently in Spain, those free-riders are typically the biggest business premises and thus those that would have to pay a higher contribution to a hypothetical BID. Consequently, town centre associations would see not only the so-called 'parasites' disappearing, but also their own budgets significantly increasing. Hence, passing the enabling legislation that would allow municipalities to levy a BID charge is essential. If this initial step is not taken, the BID model cannot be implemented in Spain.

Finally, in bringing the model to Spain, cities would also benefit from the collaboration between public and private sectors, as BIDs would act as a catalyst to promote and strengthen this relationship. Public authorities should build on these partnerships to develop collaborative projects for the sake of the common good, focusing on urban sustainability and environmental enhancement, as well as on how the use of technology could provide smart solutions with which to solve current challenges. It is essential that Spanish cities continue developing community-driven and local actions in keeping with the 'act small, but aim high' strategy that BIDs embody.

NOTES

* This chapter is part of the Project 'Public-private partnership and fiscal consolidation: BIDs and ECAs' (DER2015-65148-C2-1-P), financed by the Spanish Ministry of Economy and Competitiveness (2015 call).

1. See the United Nations 2018 Revision of World Urbanization Prospects, https://population.un.org/wup, last accessed 18 January 2019.
2. Caragliu, A, Del Bo, C and Njkamp, P (2009). 'Smart cities in Europe'. Paper presented at the Conference III Central European Conference in Regional Science, 7–9 October, Košice, Slovak Republic, p50.
3. See Lorne, F and Welsh, M (2013). 'Sustainable Development and Business

Improvement Districts Theoretical Basis for Community Actions at the Local Level', *The International Journal of Sustainability Policy and Practice*, Vol 8 (4): 1–14, p8; and Zygiaris, S (2013). 'Smart City Reference Model: Assisting Planners to Conceptualize the Building of Smart City Innovation Ecosystems', *Journal of the Knowledge Economy*, Vol 4, Issue 2: 217–231.

4. Morçöl, G and Wolf, J (2010). 'Understanding Business Improvement Districts: A New Governance Framework', *Public Administration Review*, 70(6): 906–913, p906.
5. Mitchell, J (1999). *Business improvement districts and innovative service delivery*, The PricewaterhouseCoopers Endowment for the Business of Government, New York, p6.
6. See Lorne, F and Welsh, M (2013). Id 3, at 8; and Browne, M, Allen, J and Alexander, P (2016). 'Business Improvement Districts in Urban Freight Sustainability Initiatives: A Case Study Approach', *Transportation Research Procedia*, Vol 12: 450–460.
7. Villarejo Galende, H (2014). '*Colaboración público-privada para la revitalización de espacios urbanos: la introducción de los Business Improvement Districts en el ordenamiento jurídico español*', *Revista de Gestión Pública*, III (2): 235–277, p249.
8. Houstoun, LO (1997). *BID: Business Improvement Districts*, Washington, DC: Urban Land Institute.
9. Hoyt, LM (2006). 'Importing ideas: The transnational transfer of urban revitalization policy', *International Journal of Public Administration*, Vol. 29: 221–243, p229.
10. Ward, K and Cook, I (2017). 'Business Improvement Districts in the United Kingdom: Territorialising a "global" model?' in Deas, I and Hincks, S (eds), *Territorial Policy and Governance: Alternative Paths*. London: Routledge: 127–146.
11. Ward, K (2006). '"Policies in motion", urban management and state restructuring: The trans-local expansion of Business Improvement Districts', *International Journal of Urban and Regional Research*, 30 (1): 54–75; Cook, IR (2008). 'Mobilising urban policies: the policy transfer of US Business Improvement Districts to England and Wales', *Urban Studies* 45 (4): 773–795.
12. Turner, C (2017). *National Business Improvement District Survey*. British BIDs, p7. Available at https://cdn.britishbids.info/publications/National-BID-Survey-2017-a4.pdf?mtime=20180227104106, last accessed 18 January 2019.
13. Kreutz, S (2009). 'Urban Improvement Districts in Germany: New legal instruments for joint proprietor activities in area development', *Journal of Urban Regeneration and Renewal*, Vol 2, 4: 304–317 and Eick, V (2012). 'The co-production of purified space: hybrid policing in German Business Improvement Districts', *European Urban and Regional Studies*, 19 (2): 121–136.
14. DIHK (2017). *Deutscher Industrie- und Handelskammertag* – BID News 30/2017, www.dihk.de/themenfelder/wirtschaftspolitik/info/bidnews/aktuell/bidnews-30-17-engl/at_download/file?mdate=14996923408, last accessed 18 January 2019.
15. Costela Sánchez, A (2018). 'German Business Improvement Districts (BIDs) as a model for Spain', *GIGAPP Estudios Working Papers*, 80: 33–48; www.gigapp.org/ewp/index.php/GIGAPP-EWP/article/view/89/112, last accessed 18 January 2019.
16. Eick, V (2012). Id 13, at 124–125.
17. Hoyt, LM and Gopal-Agge, D (2007). 'The Business Improvement District Model: A Balanced Review of Contemporary Debates', *Geography Compass*, 1 (4): 946–958, p948.
18. Briffault, R (1999). 'A Government for Our Time? Business Improvement Districts and Urban Governance', *Columbia Law Review*, 99 (2): 365–477.
19. Cook, IR (2009). 'Private sector involvement in urban governance: The case of Business Improvement Districts and Town Centre Management partnerships in England', *Geoforum*, 40: 930–940.
20. Id 10 at 140.
21. Esteve Pardo, ML (2015). '*Financiación de actuaciones público-privadas de promoción del comercio urbano mediante tributos: la experiencia alemana*', *Quincena Fiscal*, 22: 21–47, p32.
22. Kreutz, S (2009). Id 13, at 308.
23. Id 18, at 370.

24. Id 5, at 17.
25. Id 17, at 949.
26. Cook, IR (2008). Id 11.
27. Jaguttis, M (2014). *Gesteuerte Freiheit: Das Urban Governance Instrument des Improvement Districts und Verfassungsrecht*. Tübingen: Mohr Siebeck, pp162–165 and id 21, at 40.
28. Jaguttis, M (2014). Id 27, at 155; and Esteve Pardo, ML (2017). '*Una propuesta de adaptación del modelo BID (Business Improvement District) a nuestra realidad*', *Impulso a la actividad económica en los municipios: cuestiones tributarias de interés*. Barcelona: Huygens: 13–42.
29. Hochleutner, BR (2003). 'BID fare well: The democratic accountability of Business Improvement Districts', *New York University Law Review*, Vol 78: 374–404; Ward, D (2006). Id 11 and id 5.
30. Browne, M, Allen, J and Alexander, P (2016). Id 6.
31. Lorne, F and Welsh, M (2013). Id 3.
32. Id 22 and id 10, at 141.
33. Costela Sánchez, A (2016). '*Los Business Improvement Districts (BIDs): implantación en Europa, experiencia en el Reino Unido, y futuro*'. *GIGGAP VII Congreso Internacional en Gobierno, Administración y Políticas Públicas*. Madrid. p10; www.gigapp.org/administrator/components/com_jresearch/files/publications/2016-234.pdf, last accessed 18 January 2019.
34. Id 18, at 400.
35. Meltzer, R (2010). 'Clean and Safe for All? The interaction between Business Improvement Districts and local government in the provision of public goods', *National Tax Journal*, 64 (3): 863–890.
36. Kersten, J (2007). Business Improvement Districts *in der Bundesrepublik Deutschland – Urban Governance zwischen privater Inititative und staatliche Zwang*', *Umwelt- und Planungsrecht (UPR)*, No 4: 121–129 and Jaguttis, M (2014). Id 27, at 93–96.
37. Villarejo Galende, H and Esteve Pardo, ML (2018). 'New Forms of Urban Governance: Business Improvement Districts and the Challenges of Their Introduction in Spain', Proceedings of the 6th Creative Cities Conference, Orlando (USA), University of Central Florida-Scientific Association ICONO14: 1046–1064; https://doi.org/10.7195/piccc.00054, last accessed 18 January 2019.
38. Id 37, at 1054–1056.
39. Id 15, at 42–45.
40. Id 33, at 10–11.
41. The general aim of the principle of subsidiarity is to guarantee a degree of independence for a lower authority in relation to a higher body or for a local authority in relation to central government. It therefore involves the sharing of powers between several levels of authority, a principle which forms the institutional basis for federal states. The idea of having decisions taken as closely as possible by the people is clearly at the basis of some provisions on federalism, regionalism and local autonomy. The subsidiarity principle was formally enshrined by the Maastricht Treaty in the European Union legal system. See Schilling, T (1995). 'Subsidiarity as a Rule and a Principle, or: Taking Subsidiarity Seriously; https://jeanmonnetprogram.org/archive/papers/95/9510ftns.html#f33, last accessed 18 January 2019.
42. Lorne, F and Welsh, M (2013). Id 3, at 4.
43. Id 30, at 453.
44. In this regard, it is interesting to follow the Sidewalk Toronto initiative, developed by Sidewalk Labs working in partnership with the tri-government agency Waterfront Toronto and the local community, to tackle the challenges of urban growth through cutting-edge technology. See more at www.sidewalklabs.com/, last accessed 18 January 2019.
45. Lorne, F and Welsh, M (2013). Id 3.

5. The costs and benefits of extended producer responsibility: an evaluation of the Italian waste electrical and electronic equipment (WEEE) management system

Edoardo Croci and Francesco Colelli*

1. INTRODUCTION

Extended producer responsibility (EPR) schemes can provide a flexible new fiscal approach to improving waste management, as they provide a reliable source of funding for the collection and recycling of waste (Organisation for Economic Co-operation and Development (OECD), 2016). Within the European Union, Member States have established take-back EPR systems for the four waste streams identified in EU Directives: packaging, batteries, end-of-life vehicles and waste electrical and electronic equipment (WEEE). European EPR systems for WEEE management vary considerably in terms of their design, rules for ensuring producer compliance, financial schemes, stringency of targets and local authority involvement (Monier et al, 2014). The economic and environmental performance of EPR systems is an interesting area of research, as – depending on the model and the waste streams considered – such performance appears to be rather mixed (OECD, 2013; 2016).

This chapter aims to carry out a cost-benefit analysis, both at present and up to 2030, of the EPR scheme for the management of WEEE in Italy. The chapter proposes three scenarios for the production, use and generation of WEEE and three scenarios of waste management that determine the amount that will be recycled up to 2030. These scenarios are based on different institutional, behavioural and technological factors. The industrial costs (collection, distribution, treatment and recycling) and the benefits of WEEE management in these scenarios are estimated. The benefits include both economic benefits, stemming from lower imports of raw materials generated by recycling (aluminium, iron, plastic, copper, glass and lead); and environmental benefits, which focus on reductions in greenhouse gas (GHG) emissions due to the correct preparation of equipment for recycling and the consequent disposal of gas mixtures contained in EEE, as well as the emissions saved due to the recycling of these materials.

2. THE STATUS OF THE ITALIAN WEEE MANAGEMENT SYSTEM

The Italian EPR system for the management of WEEE, regulated under EU Directive 2012/19/EC and National Decree 49/2014, was created in 2008. Within this system, a key role is played by the national producer responsibility organizations (PROs), which are responsible for the collection of WEEE from collection centres managed by the municipalities; the transport of WEEE to treatment facilities; the treatment of WEEE according to the proper environmental and safety criteria; the recycling of materials; and the disposal of residual waste. These operational activities are financed by contributions paid by EEE producers, which in turn choose to join a PRO based on the services offered and the financial contributions required (competitive system). PROs are required to operate without profit, to take the legal form of a consortium and to manage a quantity of WEEE proportional to the market share of their respective producers. A private consortium of PROs acts as a Clearing House, to ensure fair competition by monitoring PROs' activities and promoting the coordination of operational activities. In practice, this option is adopted only for 'professional WEEE', which is defined as waste generated by EEE that does not fall within the definition of 'household EEE' and that is intended for professional use. 'Household WEEE' is defined as waste from EEE used by households and from EEE with similar characteristics of household appliances used by non-household consumers (EC, 2012). As an alternative to signing up to one (or more) consortia, producers and importers can fulfil their obligations by organizing an individual system. In total, around 300 individual producers and importers have been operating in Italy since 2008 and have been active only in the professional WEEE sector (MATTM, 2018). In 2017, PROs managed over 296000 tons of household WEEE, or 4.89 kilograms (kg) per inhabitant – an increase of 4.66 per cent on the previous year. The quantity of domestic WEEE collected in 2017 corresponded to about 36 per cent of the average put on the market in the previous three years. The collection of domestic WEEE has been increasing steadily since 2013 (Eurostat, 2018). As for professional WEEE, the latest data available shows that in 2016, 76317 tons of waste were managed by collective and individual systems (CdC RAEE, 2018). The return rate of the professional supply chain therefore stands at around 50 per cent of the consumption input. The WEEE collection target set by Directive 2012/19/EC for the three-year period 2016–18 is 45 per cent of EEE put on the market (EEE production plus imports, net of exports). From 2019, the target collection rate will be set at 65 per cent of EEE put on the market, or alternatively at 85 per cent of WEEE generated. Moreover, further to Directive 2012/19/EC, EU WEEE management systems will undergo a significant market expansion in 2018. (For an evaluation of the impact of this market expansion in Europe, see EC, 2014; Croci and Colelli, 2017.) Due to a lack of data on the specific products to be included in the new expanded system, the following analysis is restricted to the WEEE currently managed by PROs and individual systems.

3. METHODOLOGY

This research estimates the volume of EEE products put on the market. In addition to EEE sales reported in the official statistics, it considers an important and often overlooked share of the EEE market: the volumes sold by producers and importers that free-ride the system. Based on historical EEE units sold and the probability distribution of the lifetime of each type of EEE product, the research quantifies the number of units of EEE that will become waste in a given future year. As future EEE sales and thus future WEEE generation are uncertain, a scenario analysis is conducted to assess the sector's main market and technological trends. Different macro and microeconomic factors, consumer practices and technological eco-innovations (eg, dematerialization and refurbishing) are included to develop three scenarios of EEE production, use and waste generation. The three different WEEE management scenarios are developed based on operational, institutional and behavioural factors. Industrial costs estimates are based on industry data and include collection, logistics, treatment and recycling costs. The economic benefits are estimated by calculating the decrease in raw material imports due to secondary material production through recycling (aluminium, iron, plastic, copper, glass and lead). The environmental benefits are estimated by taking into consideration the GHG emissions avoided from the substitution of primary raw materials and the correct treatment of WEEE components. Emissions relating to raw materials production are considered using a lifecycle approach. Emissions generated by WEEE management operations are accounted for in order to calculate the net environmental benefit. Other relevant elements of waste management, such as externalities relating to landfill or the abandonment of waste, are not quantified.

4. SCENARIO ANALYSIS OF WEEE MANAGEMENT

4.1 Quantification of EEE and WEEE

The data on the volume of EEE put on the market (PoM) was obtained from the official database of Eurostat and from data published annually by the WEEE Coordination Center (Eurostat, 2018; CdC RAEE, 2018). Relying exclusively on institutional sources, however, would underestimate the real size of the national market. Some EEE producers and importers ('free-riders') are not currently registered with the national accounting system. Although uncertain, this share is estimated at about 25 per cent of total PoM (Remedia, 2012). This share was therefore added to the official PoM in order to map the 'effective' PoM amount. The assumptions for each type of EEE are reported in the appendix. EEE in the national system is classified in five groups: R1 (cooling and freezing equipment), R2 (large household appliances), R3 (televisions and monitors), R4 (mixed WEEE) and R5 (lamps).

As a second step, the amount of waste generated was estimated. This calculation was based on three elements: the quantity of 'stock' equipment already present in households, the quantity of EEE placed on the market between 2016–30 and the definition of a profile of the useful life of the EEE, as a proxy for the actual process of use of the EEE. The first two factors were obtained from historical data derived from institutional sources (Eurostat, 2018) and from the PoM trends elaborated in the following paragraph. The life profile of EEE can be reconstructed according to the 'distributed lifespan' method, which is based on a distribution function of the probability that the product ceases to be used in each year following its purchase. The level of waste generated was obtained by multiplying this probability with the historical series of product sales (Streicher-Porte et al, 2005; Oguchi et al, 2008; Dwivedy and Mittal, 2010). The probability distribution of EEE lifetime reported by Magalini et al (2012) was adopted in the calculations. With regard to WEEE generated in the professional sector, the volumes of WEEE generated from the levels of PoM were calculated taking into consideration the fact that only approximately 38 per cent effectively becomes waste; the remaining 62 per cent enters the professional second-hand channel (Remedia, 2012). This phenomenon affects the WEEE groups slightly differently. The professional EEE flows identified in the three different scenarios were multiplied by the coefficients reported for each group following an 'average lifespan' method.

4.2 Scenario Analysis of EEE and WEEE Flows

Volumes of EEE and WEEE are influenced by several factors. In particular, two major macro-factors were identified: consumption factors and production factors. As regards consumption factors, two socio-economic variables were considered: EEE unit demand evolution and consumer management of EEE. The former was estimated based on two elements: forecasted growth of national gross domestic product (GDP) and historical sectoral sales trends. The evolution of PoM generally relates to growth in aggregate national production or to other variables linked to the national economic system (Huisman et al, 2008; Huisman, 2010). Three different scenarios of sales growth from 2017–30 were assumed. The central scenario corresponds to the average growth rate of each EEE sector, calculated as the mean of the annual change in sales volumes for the 2013–15 period. 'High' and 'low' sales scenarios were developed by assuming respectively a higher and a lower growth rate of sales than the historic average. The level of such growth rate average was set as equal to the range of GDP growth projections produced by the Italian Central Bank (2017). This data is based on the PRODCOM database, which provides the value of volumes produced, imported and exported each year from 1996–2015. Due to its heterogeneity, seven sub-groups were identified for group R4.

In addition to these trends, variables relating to consumer behaviour were included in relation to specific product categories. In fact, consumer management of EEE greatly influences consumption trends, net of general macroeconomic growth and sector growth. For example, for the commodity class 'laptops and notebooks', the average volume of EEE per household was assumed to increase progressively based on historical trends. Particular attention was also given to the impact on PoM of reuse practices and the development of second-hand markets. The impact attributed to these factors was based on a recent survey of Italian EEE consumers' behaviour (IPSOS, 2017). The assumptions on the share of products that may enter such markets is reported in the appendix. This analysis was carried out for domestic EEE only; for professional EEE, only the impact on consumption due to GDP growth was estimated, due to a lack of data.

As for the production factors, two different factors were considered: products' technological innovation and reconditioning. Products' technological innovation was assessed by analysing the evolution of the average weight of EEE. Due to a lack of data, other elements such as the evolution of product durability and of material composition could not be considered. Taking these missing aspects into consideration would constitute an important element of further research. The assumptions on technological evolution, based on historical trends in recent years for a selection of EEE types, are reported in the appendix.

In addition to the variables relating to product innovation, reconditioning activities were considered for consumer products and information and communications technology devices, such as mobile phones and personal computers; and to a lesser extent for refrigerators and washing machines (Moller et al, 2015). The average European WEEE reconditioning rate stood at 1–2 per cent in 2012 on total WEEE collected (EC, 2017). The highest rate, equal to 8 per cent, was registered in the United Kingdom (EC, 2017). As for Italian reconditioning activities, it is assumed that this market could range from 0–10 per cent of WEEE collected by 2030, given the other EU benchmarks. The general assumptions in the three scenarios are presented in Table 5.1. In accordance with the calculation of PoM in the current years as outlined in section 4.1, the scenarios assume no irregularities in EEE producers' declarations to the National Registry, so that the total quantities represent the 'effective' PoM. Based on different assumptions concerning the variables identified, three different scenarios are developed: 'sustained growth', 'conservative' and 'circular development' (Table 5.1).

In the 'sustained growth' scenario, flows of EEE consumption for domestic EEE reach 2 200000 tons in 2030 – a 100 per cent increase on 2015 – while flows of professional EEE PoM reach 600000 tons. As for

Table 5.1 Factors included in the EEE PoM scenarios

	Consumption		**Production**	
	Evolution of demand	Consumer EEE management	Technological innovation	Alternative markets
'Sustained growth'	Demand growth above the historical average	No second-hand market development	Historical technological trends	No development of reconditioning
'Conservative'	Historical demand growth	Low second-hand market development	Historical technological trends	Slow development of reconditioning
'Circular development'	Demand growth below the historical average	High second-hand market development	New virtuous technological trends (dematerialization)	Fast development of reconditioning

the generation of WEEE, domestic waste reaches 1.6 million tons in 2030, while professional waste reaches 228 000 tons. In the 'conservative' scenario, flows of EEE consumption for domestic EEE reach 1 500 000 tons in 2030 – a 41 per cent increase on 2015 – while flows of professional EEE PoM reach 550 000 tons. As for the generation of WEEE, domestic waste reaches 1.22 million tons in 2030, while professional waste reaches 223 000 tons. In the 'circular development' scenario, flows of EEE consumption for domestic EEE reach 1 070 000 tons in 2030, with no real substantial increase compared to 2015. Flows of professional EEE PoM are stable at around 500 000 tons. As for the generation of WEEE, domestic waste remains stable throughout the period, while professional waste reaches 218 000 tons in 2030. The difference between the three scenarios increases over time, as a consequence of the impact of the growth trends of the national economic system and the EEE sectors. Moreover, the circular practices included in the model (reuse, reconditioning and dematerialization) begin to take hold between 2020–25.

4.3 Scenario Analysis of WEEE Collection

In order to conduct a cost-benefit analysis of WEEE management, the volumes of WEEE collected must be assessed. Four streams of WEEE can be identified (CdC RAEE, 2018; Huisman et al, 2015; Remedia, 2012): WEEE managed by PROs; WEEE recycled inadequately by the informal sector, equal to around 31 per cent of WEEE generated; WEEE mistakenly thrown away by households (mainly in groups R4 and R5), equal to 11 per cent of WEEE generated in 2016; and WEEE treated according to 'illegal' procedures, including unauthorized abandonment, treatment and scrapping, equal to 18 per cent of WEEE generated in 2016. Although no national figures were available, we emphasize that some illegally managed WEEE and used EEE in Italy may be exported to other countries, especially developing countries; EU-wide illegally exported used EEE and WEEE amounts to roughly 13 per cent of waste generated (Huisman et al, 2015). Therefore, part of the environmental impact associated with incorrect WEEE management practices may arise in these countries, rather than at a national level.

A scenario analysis is applied based on assumptions as to the different waste destinations. Three scenarios are developed for the period 2017–30:

- 'Operational efficiency': WEEE collected by municipal centres and managed by PROs grows at the average historical rate.
- 'Regulatory enforcement': this scenario couples the operational efficiency of PROs with the progressive erosion of informal operations

by 2030. For this reason, WEEE incorrectly treated through this channel is considered easier to reduce through stronger regulatory enforcement than WEEE illegally shipped abroad or managed by other operators, as the former operations are easier to track.

- 'Correct consumer practices': this scenario couples the operational efficiency of PROs with the progressive end of incorrect household waste management practices. Households become better informed of WEEE regulation and act accordingly. This is effected through the dissemination of information campaigns and enhanced opportunities to bring WEEE to municipal collection centres, due to the increased number of such collection centres (CdC RAEE, 2017).

The volumes of WEEE collected in 2030 reach 587 million tons under the 'operational efficiency' scenario, 871 million tons under the 'regulatory enforcement' scenario and 752 million tons under the 'correct consumer practices' scenario. Adding all factors would imply a collection of 1936 million tons in 2030. The rate of collection henceforth differs under each scenario. The yearly value is calculated by taking into consideration the volumes collected (in the numerator) as well as the PoM[1] (in the denominator):

Volume collected / PoM (average of the three previous years)

The value of the return rate in 2030 varies depending on how the two variables evolve in the three WEEE collection scenarios and the three EEE PoM scenarios. Under the 'sustained growth' scenario, the operational efficiency of PROs would lead to a 31 per cent collection rate; regulatory enforcement would lead to a 57 per cent collection rate; and correct consumer practices would lead to a 42 per cent collection rate. Under the 'conservative' scenario, the operational efficiency of PROs would lead to a 36 per cent collection rate; regulatory enforcement would lead to a 66 per cent collection rate; and correct consumer practices would lead to a 49 per cent collection rate. Under the 'circular development' scenario, the operational efficiency of PROs would lead to a 39 per cent collection rate; regulatory enforcement would lead to a 71 per cent collection rate; and correct consumer practices would lead to a 53 per cent collection rate. The value differs from the official rate of collection because in this estimation, the 'effective' share of PoM is used as the denominator. Due to the lack of information on the factors affecting the operation of individual PROs, the collection rate of professional WEEE is assumed to be stable in all scenarios.

5. COST OF WEEE MANAGEMENT

The system's cost estimates are based on industrial data and include collection, logistics, treatment and recycling costs. Investment expenditure is considered within the yearly costs, together with operating expenditure. The costs of collection centres are covered by the municipal tax for separate collection services and amounted to €136 per ton of WEEE in 2015 (ISPRA, 2016). In order to offset the costs relating to municipal management and incentivize the achievement of quantitative thresholds that would facilitate economies of scale, PROs award financial bonuses to those collection centres that achieve specified efficiency targets. These bonuses totalled €15.9 million in 2017 – an average of €54 per ton of WEEE (CdC RAEE, 2018). The average logistics costs relating to the transport of WEEE from collection centres to treatment plants amount to €100 per ton, based on previous research (Favot, 2015) and industrial data (Remedia, 2012; Ecodom, 2016). As for treatment costs, PROs provide financial incentives to treatment plants for the treatment of some classes of WEEE and charge for other classes whose treatment generates a profit. WEEE average treatment costs equate to €233 a ton (b2wee, 2018). These are compensated in part by the sales of raw materials and in part by the financial incentives provided by the PROs. As revenues are highly sensitive to raw material prices, treatment plants usually receive a fee or pay a charge to the PROs which is indexed to such prices. We assume that the net cost of treatment and recycling is represented only by the net contribution that the PROs pay to the facilities. The estimated total amount of revenues of PROs amounts to €12–13 million, based on the quantities managed in 2017; while the cost of the incentives amounts to €17–18 million (CdC RAEE, 2018). The resulting net cost of WEEE treatment and recycling operations for the EPR system is €5.4 million. The structural costs of PROs include communication costs and the costs of financing the activities of the coordination centres. The former are assumed to amount to about €2–3 million and the latter to €10 million (Remedia, 2017; Ecodom, 2017). As for professional WEEE, only logistics and treatment costs are considered, due to the nature of the operational activities; the data required to apply the values of domestic WEEE estimates to professional WEEE management operations is not available. In total, the logistics and treatment costs of professional WEEE are estimated to amount to €100–120 per ton. All of these costs are assumed to be paid by the individual system managed by the EEE producer. Summing up the various elements, the estimated costs of domestic WEEE management in 2017 amount to €98.7 million. Of that, 40 per cent is covered by municipalities through the tax for separate collection services; the remaining 60 per cent is covered by the financial contributions that domestic EEE producers pay to the collective PROs. When professional EEE management is also taken into consideration, the total costs increase by roughly €10 million, to a total of €110 million. By summing up the contributions of collective and individual systems for domestic and professional WEEE, the financial contribution of EPR reaches 65 per cent of the total system costs.

5.1 The Evolution of WEEE System Costs

This section quantifies the costs of the EPR system under the different WEEE management scenarios developed in section 4.3. In addition to the industrial cost estimates reported above, the possible role of economies of scale in driving down future EPR system costs – in particular, logistics costs – is considered. Economies of scale in WEEE logistics are highlighted by the recent operational activity of PROs: the three-year period 2015–17 saw a percentage increase in both the quantities collected and the number of trips carried out by PROs, with the first rate of growth greater than the second, at 13.5 per cent and 10 per cent respectively (CdC RAEE, 2018). Assuming that the operational performance of PROs continues to improve at the same rate, the total system costs would reach different levels depending on the WEEE management scenario. As for primary collection, treatment and recycling, a lack of data constrained the possibility to quantify possible economies of scale. Therefore, the current average costs were used for the cost projection up to 2030. An assessment of economies of scale for these activities in the waste management chain is left to future research. In the 'business as usual scenario', EPR system costs are lower than in the other two, because the volumes of WEEE managed are lower. The estimates do not consider the costs of WEEE managed by the informal sector and by the illegal sector, as well as the costs of WEEE inadequately managed by households. Total yearly costs in 2030 range from €200 million in the 'operational efficiency' scenario to €270 million in the 'correct consumer practices' scenario and €287 million in the 'regulatory enforcement' scenario.

6. BENEFITS OF WEEE MANAGEMENT

6.1 Economic Benefits of WEEE Management

The production of secondary raw materials through the national recycling industry avoids the need to import those raw materials, generating an important economic saving – particularly for a country such as Italy, which is dependent on imports of these resources. The positive impact is calculated based on both the volumes of individual materials recovered and the respective market prices. The materials considered in this analysis are aluminium, iron, plastic, copper, glass and lead. The primary raw materials prices adopted are reported in the appendix. It is important to point out that the prices of these raw materials influence the relative advantage of official EPR collection and recycling as against illegal and informal activities, as when the prices of raw materials are lower, the incentives to deviate WEEE flows away from the official system are also lower. The savings in 2030 amount to €190 million in the 'operational efficiency' scenario, €311 million in the 'regulatory enforcement' scenario and €265 million in the 'correct consumer practices' scenario.

6.2 Environmental Benefits

The environmental impacts of WEEE management considered are the GHG emissions saved: (1) through the correct preparation for recycling of EEE and the consequent disposal of the gas mixtures contained therein (measured in terms of tons of carbon dioxide (CO_2) equivalent); and (2) through the recycling of materials derived from managed technological waste (measured in terms of equivalent tons of CO_2). In the first case, the impacts derive from the avoided emission of chlorofluorocarbons (CFCs) contained within refrigerators, air conditioners and other equipment in group R1 with Global Warming Potential (GWP); for example, 1 kilogram of CFCs has the same GWP as over 12 tons of CO_2 (IPCC, 1996). In the second case, the benefits derive from the use of a secondary raw material, rather than a primary raw material that must be extracted, processed and transported.

GHG emissions reductions are considered net of the emissions relating to the operation of the system – in particular, preparation for recycling, recycling, combustion of materials for energy production and logistics and disposal activities (Remedia, 2017; Ecodom, 2017). In total, the management of WEEE in 2015 resulted in a reduction of more than 1.1 million tons of CO_2 equivalent. Avoided emissions in 2030 amount to 2.28 million tons of CO_2 equivalent in the 'operational efficiency' scenario, 2.98 million tons of CO_2 equivalent in the 'regulatory enforcement' scenario and 259 000 tons of CO_2 equivalent in the 'correct consumer practices' scenario. To obtain a monetary quantification of the avoided externalities, the social cost of carbon values given by the Environmental Protection Agency – equal to €35 per ton in 2020 and €40 per ton in 2030 – was adopted (EPA, 2017). In 2030 the management of WEEE could result in yearly economic savings of €91 million in the 'operational efficiency' scenario, €120 million in the 'regulatory enforcement' scenario and €103 million in the 'correct consumer practices' scenario.

7. CONCLUSIONS

This chapter has quantified the net industrial costs of WEEE management, as well as the environmental and economic benefits. The Italian EPR model for WEEE management has helped to shift the financial burden from municipalities and taxpayers to producers: currently 60 per cent of WEEE management costs are covered through the charges paid by producers to PROs. Different macro and microeconomic factors, consumer practices and technological eco-innovations (eg, dematerialization and refurbishing) were considered in order to estimate three scenarios of EEE production, use and waste generation. The 'circular development' scenario in 2030 is characterized by a volume of WEEE which is more than 30 per cent lower than that in the 'sustained growth' scenario. Sustainable consumption and production practices can play an important role in reducing the amount of waste generated. The benefits were calculated by estimating the value of primary raw materials saved thanks to the recovery of WEEE and the GHG emissions saved thanks to reductions in the production of primary raw materials and the treatment of CFCs. The results show that in 2017, the net benefits amounted to over €35 million. The scenario analysis of WEEE collection practices shows that in 2030, the operational efficiency of PROs could lead to increased system yearly net benefits of up to €80 million. Successful regulatory enforcement, ending the illegal or informal treatment of WEEE by unauthorized treatment facilities, is the scenario that would yield the highest yearly net benefits, totalling over €140 million. The scenario whereby households bring all small WEEE to municipal collection centres instead of dumping them or keeping them idle at home would yield yearly net benefits of almost €100 million.

NOTES

* Luigi Bocconi University. Centre for Geography, Resources, Environment, Energy and Networks (GREEN).

1. The collection rate estimated should not be directly compared to the present rate, as in the case of this chapter's estimations, the PoM is higher than the institutional PoM due to the effect of free-riders, as explained in section 4.1.

REFERENCES

Italian Central Bank (2017). *Bollettino economico* 2017.
B2WEEE (2018); www.b2bweee.com/; last accessed 1 November 2018.
CECED (2016). Report Home Appliance Europe 2015–2016.
Centro di Coordinamento RAEE (2017). *Rapporto Annuale* 2016.
Centro di Coordinamento RAEE (2017). *Rapporto Impianti di Trattamento.*
Centro di Coordinamento RAEE (2018). *Rapporto Annuale* 2017.
Croci, E and Colelli, FP (2017). '*Sfide e prospettive del sistema nazionale di gestione dei RAEE alla luce dell'entrata in vigore dell'ambito di applicazione aperto.*' IEFE – Università L Bocconi Research Report N 27, October 2017.
Huisman, J, Botezatu, I, Herreras, L, Liddane, M, Hintsa, J, Luda di Cortemiglia, V, Leroy, P, Vermeersch, E, Mohanty, S, van den Brink, S, Ghenciu, B, Dimitrova, D, Nash, E, Shryane, T, Wieting, M, Kehoe, J, Baldé, CP, Magalini, F, Zanasi, A, Ruini, F, Männistö, T, and Bonzio, A, *Countering WEEE Illegal Trade (CWIT) Summary Report, Market Assessment, Legal Analysis, Crime Analysis and Recommendations Roadmap*, 30 August 2015, Lyon, France.
Dwivedy, M and Mittal, RK (2010). 'Estimation of future outflows of e-waste in India'. *Waste Management* 30(3): 483–491.
Ecodom (2017). *Rapporto di Sostenibilità* 2016.
Environmental Information Agency (2014). VHK's Ecodesign Impact Accounting.
European Commission (2014). Frequently Asked Questions on Directive 2012/19/EU on Waste Electrical and Electronic Equipment.
European Commission (2017). Report from The Commission to The European Parliament and the Council on the Commission pursuant to Directive 2012/19/EU.
European Commission (2017). WEEE compliance promotion exercise, Final Report.
European Commission (2018). Directive (EU) 2018/849–852.
Eurostat (2018). WEEE generation dataset.
Favot, M (2015). 'Why manufacturers of electrical and electronic equipment (EEE) create producer responsibility organizations (PROs) to comply with the WEEE directive? The case of ERP Italia Srl with focus on costs.' *Environmental Engineering and Management Journal.*
Huisman, J (2010). 'WEEE recast: from 4kg to 65%: the compliance consequences.' UNU Expert opinion on the EU WEEE Directive. Bonn, Germany, United Nations University.
Huisman, J, Magalini, F, Kuehr, R, Maurer, C, Ogilvie, S, Poll, J, Delgado, C, Artim, E, Szlezak, J and Stevels, A (2008). *Review of Directive 2002/96 on Waste Electrical and Electronic Equipment (WEEE)*. Bonn, Germany, United Nations University.
IPCC (1996). Contribution of Working Group I to the Second Assessment Report of the Intergovernmental Panel on Climate Change. UNEP – WMO Final Report.
IPSOS (2017). *Gli italiani e i RAEE: indagine IPSOS-Ecodom.*
Magalini et al (2012). 'Household WEE generated in Italy', Ecodom – IPSOS Report.
MATTM (2018). Registro AEE; www.registroaee.it/RicercaProduttoriFI, last accessed 1 November 2018.
Michel, A, Attali, S, and Bush, E (2015). 'Energy efficiency of White Goods in

Europe: monitoring the market with sales data'; analysis and report by Topten International Services.

Moller, M and Baron, Y (2015). Background report for the development of an EMAS Sectoral Reference Document.

OECD (2001). *Extended Producer Responsibility: A Guidance Manual for Governments*, OECD Publishing, Paris; http://dx.doi.org/10.1787/9789264189867-en.

OECD (2013). *What Have We Learned About Extended Producer Responsibility in the Last Decade? A Survey of the Recent Economic EPR Literature*, ENV/EPOC/WPRPW(2013)7/FINAL; http://spot.colorado.edu/ ~daka9342/OECD_EPR_KO.pdf.

OECD (2016). *Extended Producer Responsibility: Updated Guidance for Efficient Waste Management*, OECD Publishing, Paris; http://dx.doi.org/10.1787/9789264256385-en.

Oguchi, M, Murakami, S, Tasaki, T, Daigo, I and Hashimoto, S (2010). 'Lifespan of Commodities, Part II', *Journal of Industrial Ecology* 14(4): 613–626.

Remedia (2012). *Il Sistema Nazionale di gestione dei RAEE Studio dei flussi e proposte per il raggiungimento dei target europei.*

Remedia (2017). *Rapporto di Sostenibilità 2016.*

Streicher-Porte, M, Widmer, R, Jain, A, Bader, HP, Scheidegger, R and Kytzia, S (2005). 'Key drivers of the e-waste recycling system: Assessing and modelling e-waste processing in the informal sector in Delhi', *Environmental Impact Assessment Review* 25(5): 472–491.

Van der Voet, E, Kleijn, R, Huele, R, Ishikawa, M and Verkuijlen, E (2002). 'Predicting future emissions based on characteristics of stocks', *Ecological Economics* 41(2): 223–234.

APPENDIX

Table 5A.1 *Scenario analysis input values*

Share of undeclared PoM over total effective PoM (Remedia, 2012)

R1	R2	R3	R4	R5
16%	22%	58%	50%	44%

Share of reusable products over total household EEE (IPSOS, 2017)

Microwave	5%	Telephone with/without cord	6%
Oven	1%	Digital camera	15%
Dryer	6%	Wireless headphones/ headphones	14%
Personal computer	3%	Audio-video equipment	20%
Mobile phone chargers	7%	Video camera	34%
Mobile phone	5%	Mp3 player	20%

Yearly average of EEE weight change assumptions (EIA, 2014; Michel et al, 2015)

EEE	Business as usual	Minimum	Maximum
Refrigerator	1%	0%	2%
Washing machine	1%	0%	2%
Dishwasher	0%	−1%	1%
Dryer	0%	−1%	1%
CRT monitor	−4%	−2%	−8%
LCD monitor	7%	6%	8%
Personal computer (including central unit, mouse and keyboard)	−5%	−2%	−8%
Complete laptop (including mouse, screen and keyboard)	−5%	−2%	−8%
Notebook	−5%	−2%	−8%
Other small appliances	0%	−1%	1%

Primary raw material prices in 2017 (€/ton) (Remedia, 2017)

Aluminium	1500	Copper	4400
Iron	200	Glass	40
Plastic	300	Lead	1700

Tons of CO_2 equivalent saved per ton of materials recovered (Remedia, 2017)

Aluminium	9.96	Copper	3.24
Iron	1.47	Glass	0.7
Plastic	0.7	Lead	1.89

Tons of CO_2 equivalent saved per ton of WEEE containing CFCs (Remedia, 2017)

R1 WEEE	15.59

6. Fiscal policy for decarbonization of energy in Europe, with a focus on urban transport: case study and proposal for Spain

David Robinson, Pedro Linares Llamas, Xiral López-Otero and Renato Rodrigues*

1. INTRODUCTION

In this chapter, we argue that fiscal policy in Europe is not aligned with decarbonization. We propose reforms to improve this alignment. We also report on a case study to model the impact of implementing a version of the proposed fiscal reforms in Spain. This case study illustrates that such fiscal reforms would be valuable, especially in reducing carbon dioxide (CO_2) emissions, and reveals the need for a transition plan to send clear investment signals and address the political economy frictions of introducing new low carbon technologies.

Section 2 introduces two fiscal policy trends in the EU in evidence during the period 2008–15: (1) rising taxes and levies on electricity and (2) relatively unchanged rates of taxation on transport fuels. Over that period, electricity decarbonized quickly, but transport did not. Partly as a consequence of these different fiscal trends, electricity may have become less competitive in comparison to transport fuels, slowing down the process of decarbonizing transport through electrification. This section proposes fiscal policy reforms to encourage investors and consumers to move towards lower carbon solutions, including electric vehicles.

Section 3 presents a case study that assesses the potential impact of these fiscal policy reforms in Spain. It includes a brief introduction to Spanish fiscal policy and emissions, and to the models used in the study. It summarizes the short-term impact of the proposed reforms on: demand, prices and output for different energies; CO_2 and other emissions; gross domestic product (GDP); and the distributional impact on final consumers.

Section 4 proposes fiscal policy reforms for Spain, with a focus on the road transport sector. Some of these reforms could negatively affect that sector and the economy in the short term, but would have long-term beneficial effects. The proposal therefore includes a transition plan to minimize the short-term impact of the reforms, while offering long-term signals to encourage investment in low carbon transport technologies and to smooth political economy frictions. Section 5 draws conclusions.

2. TWO ENERGY-ENVIRONMENTAL FISCAL TRENDS IN EUROPE

Two fiscal policy trends in evidence in the European energy sector – especially in the period between 2008–15 – are not aligned with the goal of decarbonization:

- Rising taxes and levies on electricity finance renewable power, whose ‘extra costs’ cannot be recovered in the market. These renewables contribute to lower CO_2 emissions and carbon intensity in the EU energy sector.
- Taxation on transport fuels has remained relatively flat during a period in which the trend of CO_2 emissions from transport has also remained static.

2.1 Rising Taxes and Levies on Electricity[1, 2]

Between 2008–15, electricity prices in the EU – especially residential prices – increased. On average, residential prices in euro cents per kilowatt hour (€ cents/kWh) rose by 3.2 per cent per annum. Over this period, prices increased from 16.7 to 20.8 € cents/kWh – approximately 25 per cent in nominal terms and 12 per cent in real terms. Meanwhile, CO_2 emissions from electricity fell due to lower demand, lower fossil fuel generation and a sharp increase in renewable power.[3] Eurelectric reported that the carbon intensity of electricity generation fell by 35 per cent between 1990–2014.[4] As electricity decarbonized, final electricity prices rose to finance this decarbonization.

To explain rising final prices, we refer to the European Commission’s disaggregation of prices into three cost components: energy, networks and taxes/levies (referred to here as the ‘government wedge’, the ‘policy wedge’ or the ‘wedge’).[5] Energy costs in the power sector include the wholesale market price plus a small retail supply cost. Network costs include the fixed and variable costs of transmission and distribution networks. The wedge includes everything else, especially value added tax (VAT) and taxes or levies that fund policies, including, especially, support for renewable power, cogeneration (CHP) and certain consumer groups.

Between 2008–15, the energy component in final electricity prices in Europe fluctuated and fell, in nominal terms from 7.6 to 7.5 € cents/kWh and in real terms to 6.7 € cents/kWh (a 12 per cent reduction over this period). As a share of rising final electricity prices, the energy component fell from 46 per cent to 36 per cent. This decline reflects, *inter alia*, excess generation capacity and the penetration of zero marginal cost renewables.

Meanwhile, network costs rose in nominal terms from 4.3 to 5.4 € cents/kWh and in real terms from 4.3 to 4.9 € cents/kWh. Network costs remained the same as a share of the final price, at 26 per cent.

By contrast, taxes and levies rose from 28 per cent to 38 per cent of final residential electricity prices. That corresponds to an increase from 4.6 to 7.9 € cents/kWh, up 72 per cent in nominal terms and 54 per cent in real terms.

In Figure 6.1, we can see the increasing importance of tariff support for renewables and CHP in the EU. Governments supplemented the income that these technologies could earn in electricity markets. This can be considered as a subsidy to cover the 'extra costs' of an immature low carbon technology or as compensation for their contribution to reducing emissions in a market that did not reward them adequately. Over the period, the renewables/CHP support costs rose on average from 14 per cent to 33 per cent of the increasingly large wedge.

This trend towards rising taxes and levies on electricity was especially

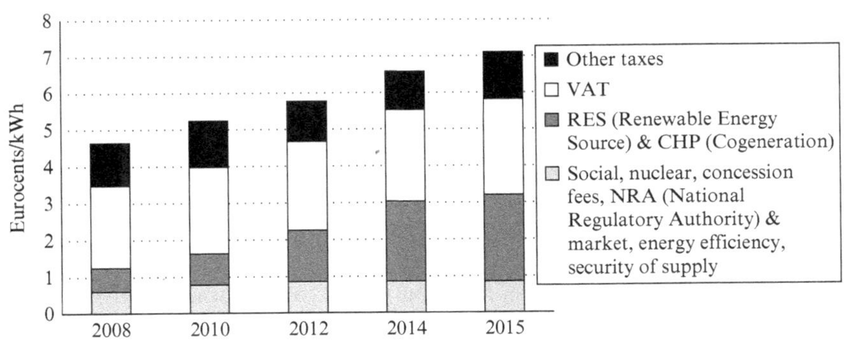

Source: Energy prices and costs in Europe (COM (2016) 769 Final, SWD (2016) 420 Final).

Figure 6.1 Composition of EU weighted average taxes and levies on electricity for households (DC), in nominal terms, 2008–15

pronounced in Spain, where residential prices rose by 48 per cent between 2008–15, from 15.6 to 23.1 € cents/kWh. During that period, taxes and levies increased substantially, to 11.6 € cents/kWh, accounting for most of the increase in final prices. In 2015, Spain's wedge was about 50 per cent of the final residential electricity price. That helps to explain why Spain's residential electricity prices are among the highest in Europe. The main sources of the wedge in Spain are similar to those in Europe – namely VAT and renewables/CHP support.

2.2 Flat Taxation Trend in Real Terms for Transport Fuels

While taxes and levies on electricity have risen quickly to fund various public policies, notably decarbonization, the trend in transport fuel taxation has been different. Figure 6.2 illustrates that the average rates of fuel taxes have been relatively flat in Europe since 2000, with taxes on diesel lower than those on gasoline. This taxation corresponds to a period when greenhouse gas emissions from the transport sector were either rising (2000–08) or fluctuating around a pretty flat trend in response to demand (falling from 2008–13 and rising from 2013–16).[6]

Real end user prices (including taxes) of transport fuel fluctuated after 2000, mainly reflecting crude oil prices. Despite a slight rise in real end-user prices over the past two decades, transport demand has continued to increase. Since August 2012, end prices have fluctuated around a downward trend, supporting increased transport demand.[7]

Taxes on transport fuels are significant as a share of the final price in Europe. However, the European Environmental Agency has argued that current taxation of road fuels has not been used as an environmental policy measure, and that if it were, this could reduce the attendant environmental damage:

> The extent to which fuel taxes have been used to internalise environmental externalities has not significantly changed during the period in question. Taxes on transport fuels have not been widely used in Europe as an environmental policy measure that can directly influence transport demand levels. Such a tax would reduce the environmental harm caused by the sector.[8]

Our concern relates to the signals being sent to consumers and investors by the fiscal trends for transport fuels and electricity. Whereas electricity has been decarbonizing rapidly, the transport sector has not. There is little evidence to suggest that taxation of transport fuels reflects the growing concerns about climate change and local pollution, whereas the fiscal burden on electricity has grown precisely due to the sector's decarbonization. Consequently, fiscal policy may be making electricity less competitive

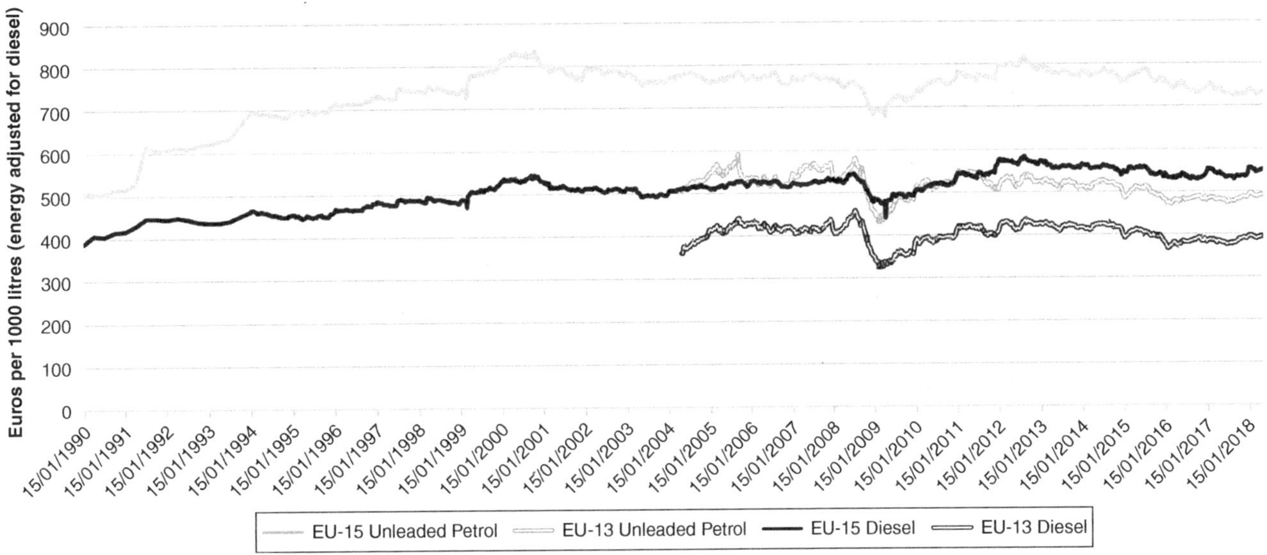

Source: European Environment Agency, 'Transport Fuel Prices and Taxes', www.eea.europa.eu/data-and-maps/indicators/fuel-prices-and-taxes/assessment-7, last accessed 17 April 2019.

Figure 6.2 Consumption-weighted average rates of real transport fuel taxes in the EU, 1990–2018

against transport fuels, slowing the process of decarbonizing transport through electrification.

An extreme version of the trends described for Europe is evident in Spain. The fiscal burden on electricity in Spain has risen more than the average for Europe, largely due to the Spanish sector's decarbonization prior to 2012. Meanwhile, CO_2 emissions from transport in Spain are rising, while tax rates on transport fuels are among the lowest in Europe: about 80 per cent of the EU average for gasoline and 77 per cent for diesel. For many years the Organisation for Economic Co-operation and Development, the International Monetary Fund and special national expert commissions have recommended that Spain introduce energy-environmental taxation throughout the economy, particularly for transport fuels. The case for increasing taxation of transport fuels in Spain is well known.[9]

2.3 Conclusion on Fiscal Trends and Recommendations for Reform

First, the European electricity sector is being rapidly decarbonized through increased penetration of renewables, with the costs borne by electricity consumers through rising levies and taxes. This increase in electricity prices is a problem for the most vulnerable customers, unless they are well protected. Second, demand and emissions from transport have risen in Europe since 1990; energy-environmental fiscal policy has not yet been adopted in many European countries with the aim of decarbonizing transport. Third, the competitive position of electricity in the transport sector may be deteriorating as a result of fiscal policies that make decarbonized electricity more expensive relative to fossil fuels.

We therefore propose four energy-environment fiscal policy recommendations for Spain.[10] First, the polluter pays principle should apply, at least for those emissions that most affect climate change and local pollution: CO_2, nitrogen oxide (NOx) and sulphur dioxide (SO_2). These taxes should apply to emissions in all sectors.

Second, evidence increasingly points to the benefits of introducing fiscal policy changes in the broader context of a green tax reform, where taxes on 'bads' can replace taxes on 'goods' such as employment, sometimes producing a 'double dividend'. We follow the general practice of proposing fiscal policy changes that are neutral in the sense that they do not increase the overall tax burden. However, we note here that when government increases taxes to cover expenditures, it makes more sense to tax 'bads' than 'goods', and to tax in accordance with the Ramsey principle (where demand elasticity is lowest).

Third, policy costs that are delivering public goods – notably, renewables to combat climate change – should be recovered through the general government budget. This allows the government to decide how best to spread the cost burden of decarbonization and removes one of the barriers to decarbonization via electrification. It makes little sense to make decarbonized electricity less competitive in transport and other energy end markets when one of the aims is to decarbonize those end markets. In the words of Professor David Newbery:

> It thus follows that the revenue needed to finance renewables and other public goods should come from general taxation raised in the least distorting ways consistent with distributional objectives – either through income taxes or a uniform rate of VAT, and not by selectively charging single products like electricity. (Newbery, 2015)[11]

Finally, plans to increase taxation of transport should send efficient long-term signals, but the actual increases will also cause political economy frictions if introduced too quickly. Indeed, governments have been reluctant to introduce or raise taxes on certain fuels due to the relevance of the transport sector to the economy, and to the impact on those most negatively affected by higher transport taxes. Any reform should include a transition plan that aims to influence investment decisions (generation, vehicles, buildings) and maintain the support of society during the transition.

3. SPANISH CASE STUDY

We have carried out a case study designed to assess the implications of fiscal policy reforms in Spain following the guidelines summarized in the previous section. The rationale for the reforms applies especially well to Spain, due to emissions and pricing trends applicable to electricity and transport fuels. CO_2 emissions fluctuate from one year to the next, reflecting changes in underlying costs, economic conditions and other factors. Nevertheless, over the period 2008–16, the trend is clear: emissions from the Spanish electricity sector fell far more (41 per cent) than emissions from the transport sector (14 per cent). Emissions from the electricity sector will continue to fall as renewable energy penetration continues and coal is phased out. The challenge now is to reduce emissions from the rest of the economy – especially from transport, which accounts for about 33 per cent of Spanish energy-related CO_2 emissions (and 28 per cent of total GHG emissions) and is the largest emitting sector in Spain.[12]

3.1 Scenarios and Assumptions

We modelled the very short-term impacts of three scenarios, along with some sensitivities related to relevant parameters: (1) polluters pay CO_2, NOx and SO_2 taxes throughout the economy; (2) policy costs (the government wedge) to support renewables/CHP and electricity consumers on the islands are passed from the electricity tariff to the public budget; and (3) a combination of these two scenarios. For each scenario, we assessed the impact on demand, prices and output for different energies; CO_2 and other emissions; GDP; and the distributional impact on final consumers.

Under Scenarios 1 and 3, we modelled the impact of introducing a lower or higher tax (€10 or €30 per tonne) on CO_2 emissions in all sectors of the economy and a lower or higher tax (€1000 or €2000 per tonne) on SO_2 and NOx emissions.[13] Given that some sectors are already subject to the European Emissions Trading Scheme (ETS) and to its carbon allowance price, we assume that under the €10 scenario, ETS sectors would not be affected.

Under Scenarios 2 and 3, we modelled the impact of passing the renewable/CHP support costs from the electricity tariff to the public budget, assuming that these costs would be recovered either from a new tax on the energy sector (on the basis of energy sales or on the basis of the price elasticity of the different products, Ramsey-style), or more widely from all productive sectors of the economy.

We assume that the rest of charges and taxes currently affecting the energy sector are unchanged. However, since some taxes (VAT or the electricity tax) are *ad valorem*, taking renewable/CHP costs away from the electricity tariff would also reduce the revenue from these taxes. We also assume that the new taxes introduced will be recycled in the economy in the context of a green tax reform, either through a reduction in labour taxes or through a lump-sum transfer.

To estimate the impact on consumption of the change in prices, we used the short-term elasticities calculated for Spain by Labandeira et al (2016).[14] We used short-term rather than long-term elasticities to be consistent with the modelling methodology. Long-term elasticities incorporate investment decisions (changing appliances or changing fuel). Although long-term elasticities would be realistic within the time horizon considered, the simulation models applied are static – that is, they do not consider the possibility of new investments. Therefore, we considered it to be more robust to make investment assumptions exogenous and hence used short-term elasticities.

Finally, for the distributive analysis, we used the Spanish Household Budget Survey for 2015. The share of electricity expenses decreases with income level, whereas the share of gasoline and diesel expenses increases up to the sixth or seventh decile and then decreases. The share of natural gas is quite stable across income deciles.

3.2 Modelling

We combine two types of modelling, in order to account better for all possible impacts of the proposed fiscal tax reforms in Spain. The first model is a microeconomic one, which estimates changes in demands of the different energy vectors from changes in prices through an exogenously assumed price elasticity (explained earlier). This model therefore represents the direct impact of the price changes induced by taxes, and also the impact on CO_2 emissions (which are assumed to be proportional to demand).

We also use this model to assess distributive changes in households and simulate the changes induced in the different household deciles by the introduction of the different tax schedules.

However, this microeconomic model is rather limited, in that it does not account for the price adjustments induced by changes in demand or for the indirect effects on the rest of the economy. Nor can the model estimate the changes in the electricity sector resulting from how the different technologies and fuels move along the merit order curve.

These indirect and induced effects have been assessed, as in previous exercises in the literature,[15] with a general equilibrium model (GEM),[16] which also features particular details for the electricity generation sector (the latter allowing us to represent changes in fuels and technologies in this sector). This GEM model represents the adjustment in the economy to the new simulated taxes. For example, faced with an increase in electricity prices due to a new environmental tax, the demand of the sectors that consume electricity will be lower, which in turn will result in lower electricity prices. This effect cannot be captured by the microeconomic model. However, our GEM model is also limited in the following ways:

- It uses a not-fully updated social accounting matrix of the Spanish economy, which means that some of the results may not correspond to what would happen in the current economy.[17]
- GEM models in general are not well suited to represent major changes in the economy. Although the taxes simulated here are not that large, the simulation of the removal of government wedges in the electricity price tests the limit of the model.
- Finally, the GEM model does not represent in detail all of the final energy markets in which electricity competes with fossil fuels – in particular, transport, heating and industry.

In spite of the limitations of both approaches, we think that their combined use provides a reasonable approximation to the expected impacts.

3.3 Results

The results vary depending on the specific assumptions – for instance, the level of the environmental taxes, how much coal is in the mix at the outset, what is done with the additional environmental tax revenues and how the renewable policy costs are shared. However, we arrive at some conclusions that are robust under almost all scenarios and sensitivities.

The various tax schedules produce different effects on electricity prices. New CO_2 taxes (or increases over current ETS prices) increase electricity prices by around 1 per cent and reduce demand by less than 0.5 per cent. Taxes on NOx or SO_2 result in even lower electricity price increases and similar reductions in demand. However, when we take the government wedges out of the electricity tariff, prices are reduced by between 20–30 per cent, resulting in electricity demand increases of between 4–10 per cent.

The changes in electricity demand, together with the changes in demand for other fuels, affect CO_2 emissions that depend on the competition between gas and coal in electricity generation. When this competition is unchanged, emissions reductions are small (between 1–3 per cent). But when gas becomes cheaper as a result of the tax reform and therefore replaces coal in the merit order, emissions reductions can reach 7 per cent. It is interesting to note that removing government wedges from the electricity price might increase emissions (since it results in an increase in gas use, not compensated by reductions in other sectors). When we combine the different instruments, in Scenario 3, emissions reductions lie between 3–5 per cent. It should be noted that in our simulations, we assume that some coal-based electricity remains. If coal disappears before the reform, then total emissions will be lower, but so will be the reductions induced by the tax reform.

Tax revenues could be significant – up to €9500 million, enough to compensate the cost of renewables/CHP and extra-peninsular support that is passed from the electricity tariff to the government budget.

The effects on GDP, which can only be estimated with the GEM model, are generally modest and negative. As explained below, this impact is due mainly to the increase in transportation costs caused by higher petrol and diesel prices, and the fact that the Spanish freight transportation system is highly dependent on trucks. Reductions in GDP are more significant the larger the impact on transport costs, due to the relevance of transport in the Spanish economy. These larger changes in transport costs correspond to NOx taxes or to sharing the electricity wedge with all fuels. On the other hand, when transport demand increases (and hence GDP improves), CO_2

emissions also rise, so there seems to be a clear trade-off between these two elements. Here it is important to remember that our model does not represent long-term effects: when the economy is given enough time to adjust, the impacts on GDP will be softer.

Finally, our analysis of the distributive effect of the tax reform shows very clearly that any reduction in electricity prices results in an overall increase in available income for households, with this increase being progressive: it is larger for lower-income households, whereas higher-income households see reductions in income. This effect is observed across all the simulations.

Table 6A.1 in the Appendix provides more detail about the results for selected scenarios.

4. PROPOSAL FOR SPAIN, WITH A FOCUS ON TRANSPORT

Our modelling focused on short-term impacts. Although the results of Scenario 3 were broadly positive in terms of emissions reductions and distributive impact, there were also some concerns, especially relating to transport. Increased taxes on transport increase the cost of most goods in the economy (which are transported by road); and this, like any other price shock (eg, an increase in oil prices) translates into lower demand and a reduction in the share of value added (which is what we measure in general equilibrium models).

Over the longer term, the benefits of the reform should become more apparent, provided that companies and individual consumers make investment decisions that favour efficiency and decarbonization – for instance, through purchasing electric vehicles or adopting other forms of sustainable transport (eg, walking, autonomous shared vehicles), rather than holding onto old internal combustion engine (ICE) vehicles or buying new ones.

We conclude that Spain should adopt a fiscal reform that includes two key components, along with a transition plan. First, we recommend a new economy-wide tax/levy on CO_2, NOx and SO_2. Our proposal is that the CO_2 tax for transport, heating and other sectors not covered by the EU ETS be consistent with the price in the EU ETS. Although we did not model the impact, we also think that Spain should adopt a rising floor for CO_2 prices and do so in conjunction with other like-minded EU countries. Even with the recent reform of the EU ETS, which has seen prices rise from €5 to €25 in a few months, the significant volatility of that price (it fell 20 per cent from the maximum in a few days) could undermine investment decisions in favour of decarbonization (eg, renewables, electric vehicles) and slow the closure of coal-fired stations. A CO_2 price floor (as adopted in Great Britain) would provide clearer long-term signals favouring investment in low carbon products.

The second proposal is to pass gradually the policy costs associated with renewables and other public goods to the government budget, thus allowing the government to decide how best to redistribute those costs. This reform would also help to make decarbonized electricity more competitive with fossil fuels in transport, heating and industrial markets.

The third proposal is to design a transition plan to provide long-term signals and smooth the legitimate political economy frictions, especially in the transport sector. These frictions include the higher cost of fuel for people driving gasoline and diesel vehicles, especially professional service providers and people below the poverty line. The transition should also aim to reduce the potential short-term macroeconomic cost, however small, resulting from an increase in the cost of transport. That transition should aim to incentivize investment decisions that are consistent with the objective of encouraging both decarbonization and cleaner air.

We propose the following transition for freight transport. First, we recommend a predictable yearly rise in the tax on diesel (Gasoil A) over a ten-year period. Second, we favour a congestion charge for access to city centres. In the absence of a congestion charge, which we much prefer, we would recommend a well-defined timetable for restricting access to give people time to adjust their expectations when making investment decisions. Third, we recommend compensation for early retirement of the most polluting vehicles. For private transport, we propose a similar set of reforms, but with policies designed to promote public transportation and alternatives to limit the economic harm of restricting private transport (or increasing its cost) and enhance the environmental benefit.

All tax exemptions and rebates should only be for the most vulnerable. The aim is to avoid free-riding – in particular, subsidizing people who would in any case be ready to invest in a low carbon vehicle.

One issue to emphasize is that as ICE vehicles lose market share, the tax revenue from fossil fuel excise duties and CO_2 emissions will decline. A strategy will be needed to replace these tax revenues. One proposal gaining support is to tax all vehicles on the basis of their emissions, their effect on noise, the distance they travel and their contribution to congestion.[18]

5. CONCLUSION

Decarbonized electricity is key to the deep decarbonization of the rest of the economy. As the penetration of renewable power increases, it is critical to ensure that this intermittent power can be efficiently integrated. Although the costs of renewables have fallen substantially, other costs (eg, storage and flexible decarbonized generation) to enable further penetration may require financial support until renewables can recover their costs through well-designed markets. We argue that the historic 'extra' costs to support renewables (which we have modelled) and at least some of the 'extra' new costs (which we have not modelled) should be treated as public goods and be recovered through the public budget. This will enable further electrification (and decarbonization) of the economy.

We also argue that the polluter should pay for environmental externalities, wherever they occur in the economy. Excise taxes on diesel and gasoline are substantially lower than the European average, especially for diesel. We support their gradual increase in order to signal the government's intent to encourage investments in lower carbon alternatives. We also support equivalent taxation on fossil fuels in the power sector. Ultimately, we seek to promote competition between decarbonized electricity and other decarbonized sources of energy, such as hydrogen, throughout the economy.

Finally, we recommend that fiscal reforms provide long-term signals for low carbon investment and operations, as well as transition arrangements to smooth the inevitable political economy frictions and to protect the most vulnerable from the consequences of the reform.

NOTES

* This chapter is based mainly on a research project carried out for Endesa. The contents are the authors' sole responsibility. They do not necessarily represent the views of the institutions with which the authors are affiliated, their members or Endesa.

1. Data in this section on European electricity prices and their cost components come from 'Energy prices and costs in Europe', European Commission (COM (2016) 769 Final), 30 November 2016, in addition to the staff document that accompanies that report: https://ec.europa.eu/energy/sites/ener/files/documents/swd2.pdf, last accessed 17 April 2019.
2. For more information on electricity fiscal policy trends, see Robinson, David (2016). 'A comparison of US and EU electricity prices: the relevance of the government wedge', *Oxford Energy Forum* 104; and Robinson, David (2015). *Análisis comparativo de los precios eléctricos en la Unión Europea y los Estados Unidos: una perspectiva española*, Eurocofin.
3. European Environment Agency, 'Small cut in EU's total greenhouse gas emissions in 2016 but transport emissions keep increasing', 31 May 2018; www.eea.europa.eu/highlights/small-cut-in-eus-total, last accessed 17 April 2019.
4. 'Electrification of society – A Bright Future for Europe', www.eurelectric.org/media/1136/electrification_report_-_a_bright_future_for_europe-2017-030-0291-01-e.pdf, last accessed 17 April 2019.
5. 'Energy prices and costs in Europe', European Commission (COM (2016) 769 Final), 30 November 2016.
6. European Environment Agency, 'Small cut in EU's total greenhouse gas emissions

in 2016 but transport emissions keep increasing', 31 May 2018; www.eea.europa.eu/highlights/small-cut-in-eus-total, last accessed 17 April 2019.

7. European Environment Agency, 'Transport fuel prices and taxes', www.eea.europa.eu/data-and-maps/indicators/fuel-prices-and-taxes/assessment-7, last accessed 17 April 2019.
8. European Environment Agency, 'Transport fuel prices and taxes', www.eea.europa.eu/data-and-maps/indicators/fuel-prices-and-taxes/assessment-6, last accessed 17 April 2019.
9. The 2018 report by the Spanish Committee of Experts on the Energy Transition (*Comisión de Expertos de Transición Energético: Analisis y propuestas para la descarbonización*) provides a history of the reports favouring the introduction of energy environmental taxation reforms. It also makes its own recommendations, which are broadly in line with those proposed in this chapter; www6.mityc.es/aplicaciones/transicionenergetica/informe_cexpertos_20180402_veditado.pdf, last accessed 17 April 2019.
10. These correspond to most of the proposals in Robinson, David (2017). 'Fiscal Policy for Decarbonization of Energy in Europe', Oxford Institute for Energy Studies; www.oxfordenergy.org/wpcms/wp-content/uploads/2017/09/Fiscal-policy-for-decarbonization-of-energy-in-Europe-EL-25.pdf, last accessed 17 April 2019.
11. Newbery, David (2015). 'Reforming UK energy policy to live within its means', Cambridge Working Papers in Economics. See also Robinson, David (2017). 'Fiscal Policy for Decarbonization of Energy in Europe', Oxford; www.oxfordenergy.org/wpcms/wp-content/uploads/2017/09/Fiscal-policy-for-decarbonization-of-energy-in-Europe-EL-25.pdf, last accessed 17 April 2019.
12. *Inventario Nacional de Emisiones, Ministerio para la Transición Ecológica*, Government of Spain.
13. Although the external costs of these pollutants are generally estimated to be much larger – between €8000 and €13 000 per ton – taxes on them have generally been set much lower. For example, in Denmark the tax is €3400 per ton of NOx and €1500 per ton of SO_2. NOx emissions vary with technology, so the taxes on them should be contingent on this.
14. The assumed elasticities are: −0.203 for electricity; −0.242 for natural gas, −0.201 for diesel and −0.253 for gasoline. See Labandeira, X, Labeaga, JM, López-Otero, X (2016). 'Un metaanálisis sobre la elasticidad precio de la demanda de energía en España y la Unión Europea', *Papeles de Energía*, 2, 65–93.
15. See, for example, Bovenberg, AL and Goulder, L (1996). 'Optimal Environmental Taxation in the Presence of Other Taxes: General Equilibrium Analyses', *American Economic Review* 86(4).
16. Rodrigues, R, et al, 2014. 'Electricity load level detail in computational general equilibrium – Part I – Data and calibration', *Energy Economics*, 46: 258–266, 2014.
17. Although the electricity sector has been calibrated for the current one.
18. See Labandeira, X, 'Crisis and Reform of Road Transport Taxation', 19th Global Conference on Environmental Taxation, CEU, Madrid, 28 September 2018.

APPENDIX

Table 6A.1 Summary of modelling results

Scenario	Electricity price		Electricity demand		Fiscal revenues (M€)		CO_2 emissions		GDP	Distributive impact
	Micro	Macro	Micro	Macro	Micro	Macro	Micro	Macro		
Tax on CO_2 €10/t	–	−0.12%	–	–	1274	2302	−0.83%	−0.05%	−0.12%	−0.105% (avg) −0.047% (1 Dec) −0.112% (10 Dec)
Tax on CO_2 €30/t	1.39%	1.84%	−0.28%	−0.48%	4425	6892	−2.55%	−7.19%	−0.33%	−0.343% (avg) −0.192% (1 Dec) −0.348% (10 Dec)
Tax on NOx and SO_2 €1000/t	0.22%	0.28%	−0.05%	−0.17%	484	1625	−0.19%	−0.15%	−0.11%	−0.043% (avg) −0.024% (1 Dec) −0.044% (10 Dec)
Tax on NOx and SO_2 €2000/t	0.72%	0.90%	−0.15%	−0.72%	1105	2806	−0.35%	−6.92%	−0.19%	−0.092% (avg) −0.059% (1 Dec) −0.092% (10 Dec)
Renewable and extra-peninsular costs support to public budget	−30.73%	−19.18%	6.24%	10.69%	−8361	−7208	0.55%	4.19%	0–2.23%	0.781% (avg) 1.291% (1 Dec) 0.386% (10 Dec)
Renewable and extra-peninsular costs support to energy tax	−20.34%	−21.39%	4.13%	10.56%	0	0	−3.04%	2.71%	−0.34%	0.030% (avg) 0.615% (1 Dec) −0.251% (10 Dec)
Renewable and extra-peninsular costs support to energy sector (Ramsey)	−18.56%	−15.66%	3.77%	7.05%	0	0	−2.58%	1.75%	0%	0.052% (avg) 0.551% (1 Dec) −0.177% (10 Dec)

Table 6A.1 (continued)

Scenario	Electricity price		Electricity demand		Fiscal revenues (M€)		CO_2 emissions		GDP	Distributive impact
	Micro	Macro	Micro	Macro	Micro	Macro	Micro	Macro		
High tax on CO_2, NOx and SO_2, policy wedges to budget	−25.19%	−19.14%	5.11%	9.79%	−1805	2480	−2.46%	−4.73%	−0.50%	0.250% (avg) 0.877% (1 Dec) −0.100% (10 Dec)
High tax on CO_2, NOx and SO_2, policy wedges to energy tax	−22.32%	−19.71%	4.53%	9.66%	0	2432	−3.24%	−5.12%	−0.91% −1.21%	0.005% (avg) 0.674% (1 Dec) −0.316% (10 Dec)
High tax on CO_2, NOx and SO_2, policy wedges to energy sector (Ramsey)	−21.69%	−12.84%	4.40%	6.41%	0	2496	−3.17%	−4.43%	−0.57% −1.43%	0.012% (avg) 0.650% (1 Dec) −0.289% (10 Dec)
Low tax on CO_2, NOx and SO_2, policy wedges to budget	−30.51%	−20.38%	6.19%	− 9.73%	−6599	−3275	−0.48%	2.46%	−0.23%	0.632% (avg) 1.219% (1 Dec) 0.229% (10 Dec)
Low tax on CO_2, NOx and SO_2, policy wedges to energy tax	−25.81%	−20.55%	5.24%	9.47%	0	−3200	−3.65%	2.99%	−0.53% −0.11%	0.039% (avg) 0.795% (1 Dec) −0.326% (10 Dec)
Low tax on CO_2, NOx and SO_2, policy wedges to energy sector (Ramsey)	−24.10%	−15.08	4.89%	6.30%	0	−3286	−3.25%	1.28%	−0.32%	0.061% (avg) 0.732% (1 Dec) −0.253% (10 Dec)

Note: Impacts are shown as percentage change over the initial situation. In the case of the distributive impact, we show the average percentage change in household income, as well as for the first and last deciles.

Source: Own elaboration.

7. A proposed green tax reform for Cyprus and its co-benefits for urban sustainability

Theodoros Zachariadis

1. INTRODUCTION

European countries generate most of their revenues through labour and income taxation. In 2016, direct taxes (comprising income taxes, corporate taxes, capital taxes and social security contributions) accounted for 65 per cent of total tax revenues in the European Union (EU) – and for 54 per cent of the corresponding revenues of the government of Cyprus (European Commission and Eurostat, 2018). At the same time, activities causing environmental degradation and depletion of scarce natural resources (eg, consumption of electricity, fuels and water, as well as production of waste) account for a small fraction of government finances: in 2016 they accounted for 6.3 per cent and 8.8 per cent of total tax revenues in the EU and Cyprus respectively. As a fraction of gross domestic product (GDP), these revenues have receded in the last two decades (more so in Cyprus than in the EU as a whole).[1] Thus, the current structure of European tax systems causes high labour costs; this endangers economic growth and employment, and rewards (or does not discourage) overexploitation of natural resources. At the same time, it encourages tax evasion and undeclared labour.

Low taxation of polluting and resource-depleting activities constitutes a hidden environmentally harmful subsidy, because these activities are often taxed below their socially optimal levels – that is, the costs of pollution or resource depletion are not covered by the existing taxes. According to international organizations, such subsidies amount to many billions of euros each year around the world, causing a significant loss of tax revenues and discouraging international attempts to mitigate climate change and improve the efficient use of natural resources (International Monetary Fund (IMF), 2015; Organisation for Economic Co-operation and Development (OECD), 2013). Environmental fiscal reform can correct this disparity by shifting the focus of government taxes and levies from labour and income to environmentally harmful activities.

As shown in the review of Withana et al (2013), several European countries have already introduced environmentally oriented fiscal reforms. Apart from saving energy and improving the environment, environmental taxes can produce better economic results than conventional taxes. Several studies have found that, depending on whether and how the additional public revenues generated from environmental taxation are recycled in the economy, an environmental fiscal reform may also be beneficial for economic growth. Even energy taxation, although leading to rising energy bills, tends to produce a benefit for consumers overall when compared with other forms of taxation (European Commission, 2013; Vivid Economics, 2012). If the environmental tax increases are accompanied by reductions in labour taxation, the overall effect can be beneficial in both macroeconomic and environmental terms.

Such reform reduces distortions in economic activity and changes relative economic prices, thereby encouraging innovation and investment in green economy sectors, which can create a competitive advantage for national economies. Countries may also use the revenues of green taxes to pay back public debt (Rausch, 2013) or to broaden the tax base if there is a large informal labour market (Markandya et al, 2013). According to Edenhofer et al (2015), some of the revenues should be used for infrastructure investments that enhance productivity. Higher levels of public infrastructure have been shown to be related to economic growth, reduced inequality and improvements in human wellbeing (Jakob and Edenhofer, 2014). Major international organizations such as the OECD, the IMF and the World Bank have underlined that green tax reforms are the most efficient way to ensure both fiscal sustainability and environmental protection (OECD, 2013; Parry et al, 2014).

This chapter sets out a proposal for a green tax reform in the Republic of Cyprus – the first to be submitted in the country up to now – to be implemented over a period of six years. It consists of three major elements – carbon, water and waste taxation – in the form of a carbon emissions tax, a water charge and a landfill tax respectively. This chapter provides an assessment of the annual tax revenues generated and, where possible, an estimate of the corresponding environmental improvements in the form of energy savings, emissions reductions and water savings, as well as the effects on firm competitiveness and social equity. As the intention of this proposal is to implement a revenue-neutral fiscal reform, the additional revenues raised through this reform can be used to reduce labour or other taxation, in order to increase employment and economic output; this latter point, however, is beyond the scope of this chapter.

2. CURRENT STATUS OF ENVIRONMENTAL TAXES AND ENVIRONMENTALLY HARMFUL SUBSIDIES IN CYPRUS

2.1 Structure of Tax Revenues

In 2016 the total tax revenues of the government of Cyprus amounted to €6.1 billion or 34 per cent of national GDP – well below the EU average of 39 per cent. Indirect taxes accounted for 46 per cent of these revenues, while the shares of direct taxes and social security contributions were 29 per cent and 25 per cent respectively (European Commission and Eurostat, 2018). Environmental taxes, as defined by Eurostat, amounted to 2.9 per cent of national GDP – somewhat higher than the EU average of 2.4 per cent – and accounted for 8.8 per cent of total tax revenues; this fraction was lower than in the early 2000s, when environmental taxes accounted for 12.3 per cent of total revenues. Three-quarters of all environmental tax revenues came from fuel taxation. Conversely, there is essentially no taxation on pollution or the consumption of natural resources; hence, revenues from such taxes are almost zero and Cyprus ranks among the last countries in the EU for this category of tax.

2.2 Environmentally Harmful Subsidies

The term 'environmentally harmful subsidies' denotes broadly economic measures that – directly or indirectly – distort competition between technologies and lead to lower relative prices (and hence preferential treatment) of activities that cause environmental degradation or overconsumption of resources.

In line with this general definition, and with the findings of relevant studies (eg, *Umweltbundesamt*, 2017), the following environmentally harmful subsidies in Cyprus have been identified:

- According to the Excise Taxes Law 91(I)/2004, liquid fuels used for power generation are exempt from excise taxes. This exemption constitutes a subsidy of fossil fuel-based power generation in comparison to renewable power generation. On the basis of data from 2017, the revenues forgone by the government due to the lack of excise taxes on fuels used by the Electricity Authority of Cyprus (and the corresponding value added tax) amount to around €15 million per year.
- Agricultural gas oil is also legally exempt from excise taxes, which discourages energy conservation and the use of renewable energy in

this sector. Revenues forgone amount to a few thousand euros per year.

- Automotive diesel oil enjoys a lower excise tax rate than automotive petrol. As diesel-powered vehicles generally cause greater health problems due to the higher emissions of particulate matter and nitrogen oxides, the preferential tax treatment of diesel oil constitutes an indirect subsidy. Depending on how this subsidy is defined, forgone revenues amount to a few million euros per year.
- Although Cyprus suffers from higher water stress than any other EU country (Eurostat, 2015), water prices include only a tiny charge of €0.01 per cubic metre to account for the costs of water scarcity and the costs of environmental pollution due to this scarcity. This essentially zero taxation level constitutes an indirect subsidy, encouraging the over-exploitation of valuable water resources and the increased use of energy-intensive desalination. The size of the subsidy is especially pronounced in the case of irrigation water.
- No tax or charge is applied to the production of municipal waste in proportion to the amount of waste generated. This leads to high amounts of waste being disposed of in landfill and discourages waste reduction and recycling initiatives. It should be noted that Cyprus ranks second in the EU for the amount of municipal waste generated per capita (Eurostat, 2017).

It is important to keep in mind that these subsidies have historically been granted by the government in order to achieve other general policy goals such as social equity and rural development. Although they lead to environmentally harmful behaviour, it is not recommended that they all be abolished immediately. It is important, however, to be aware that these subsidies exist and have both environmental and fiscal costs to society, and to keep them in mind when designing tax policy reforms.

3. PROPOSED INTRODUCTION OF ENVIRONMENTAL TAXES

3.1 Carbon Tax

The main policy proposal is to introduce a carbon tax for the use of fuels in all sectors that are not subject to the EU Emissions Trading System (ETS). All fuels are petroleum based, since coal and natural gas are not used in the Cyprus energy system. The carbon tax would be introduced gradually over the six-year period 2020–25, at annual increments of €20 (at 2015 prices)

Table 7.1 Increase in the excise tax of oil products used in Cyprus due to the gradual introduction of the proposed carbon tax

(Eurocents'2015 / litre)	2020	2021	2022	2023	2024	2025
Petrol	4.60	9.20	13.80	18.40	23.00	27.60
Automotive diesel	5.43	10.86	16.29	21.71	27.14	32.57
Heating diesel	5.43	10.86	16.29	21.71	27.14	32.57
Liquefied petroleum gas	3.04	6.08	9.12	12.17	15.21	18.25
Fuel oil	6.04	12.09	18.13	24.17	30.21	36.26

Table 7.2 Projected net increase of government revenues up to 2040 after implementation of the proposed carbon tax

(Million Euros'2015)	2020	2021	2022	2023	2024	2025	2030	2035	2040
According to energy model	70.6	139.5	202.3	259.2	311.5	360.4	320.0	317.1	315.6
Assuming inelastic fuel demand	72.5	145.8	214.8	280.6	346.0	412.0	406.9	405.4	404.2

per tonne of carbon dioxide (CO_2). This means that the carbon tax could reach €120 (at 2015 prices) per tonne of CO_2 by 2025 and would remain at this level at real prices thereafter (ie, it would be adjusted for inflation each year after 2025).

This carbon tax would affect all economic sectors except those of electricity, cement production and brick and tile production, as these sectors are subject to the EU ETS. As a result, implementation of the tax would not affect electricity prices, but would affect the prices of oil products depending on their carbon content, as shown in Table 7.1.

In order to assess the changes in fuel consumption, public revenues and carbon emissions, we employed recent projections of an energy forecast model that we developed and that is being used by national energy authorities (Zachariadis et al, 2017). Table 7.2 displays the projected net change in public revenues for two cases: one using the price elasticities of our model, thereby assuming that higher retail fuel prices will reduce fuel demand and thereby reduce some of the anticipated tax revenues; and a second case with the assumption of an entirely inelastic fuel demand. The latter case is unrealistic, but it offers an overview of the possible range of effects depending on the response of consumers and firms to this tax. It is evident from Table 7.2 that additional tax revenues (from both the carbon tax and the additional value added tax calculated on the carbon tax) are projected to gradually increase and stabilize at around €320–400 million (at 2015 prices).

As regards the effect on energy consumption, Figure 7.1 shows the demand forecast for a baseline case without a carbon tax and for the linearly increasing carbon tax as proposed in this study. It is apparent that the proposed tax will mainly affect the road transport sector, as it will lead to an increase in fuel prices. Conversely, energy consumption in residential and commercial buildings is expected to be affected only marginally, because the proposed tax will not affect electricity prices and the residential and tertiary sectors of Cyprus are highly electrified.

Figure 7.2 presents the projected evolution of non-ETS CO_2 emissions in Cyprus with and without the application of the carbon tax, and the additional tax revenues raised. Despite the considerable reduction in carbon emissions, it is worth noting that the implementation of such a tax is not enough to decarbonize the Cyprus economy sufficiently for the country to comply with its commitment to reduce greenhouse gas emissions of non-ETS sectors by 24 per cent by 2030 compared to 2005 levels.

Starting in 2026, the carbon tax is expected to lead to energy savings in the order of 100–130 000 tonnes of oil equivalent per year or 6–8 per cent of total energy demand. Apart from environmental benefits, this change will reduce the energy dependency of Cyprus and can lead to savings of €70–95 million (at 2015 prices) per year, thanks to lower fuel imports. This would help to substantially reduce the current accounts deficit of the Republic of Cyprus.

The increase in fuel taxes shown in Table 7.1 will lead to higher fuel prices and hence increased expenditures by households and firms. After 2025, when the full amount of carbon tax will be in force, fuel prices will be 27–42 per cent higher than in 2014–15. Percentagewise, prices will increase less for automotive petrol, as the price of this is already relatively high; and will increase most for heating oil, which has comparatively low prices and a relatively high carbon content.

Environmental taxes – like all other types of taxes – are subject to considerations of political costs. It is therefore necessary to explore the effect of the proposed carbon tax on the cost of living of households. Table 7.3 displays the maximum anticipated additional expenditures of households due to higher retail prices of automotive and heating fuels by net income decile. The average additional burden is expected to lie at €519 per household per year, or 1.1 per cent of the average net income. This will range between €151–€890 for the poorest and richest households respectively; with the exception of the top income groups, the additional burden corresponds to an almost constant fraction (1.2–1.5 per cent) of the income of other income groups. This means that – in contrast to the

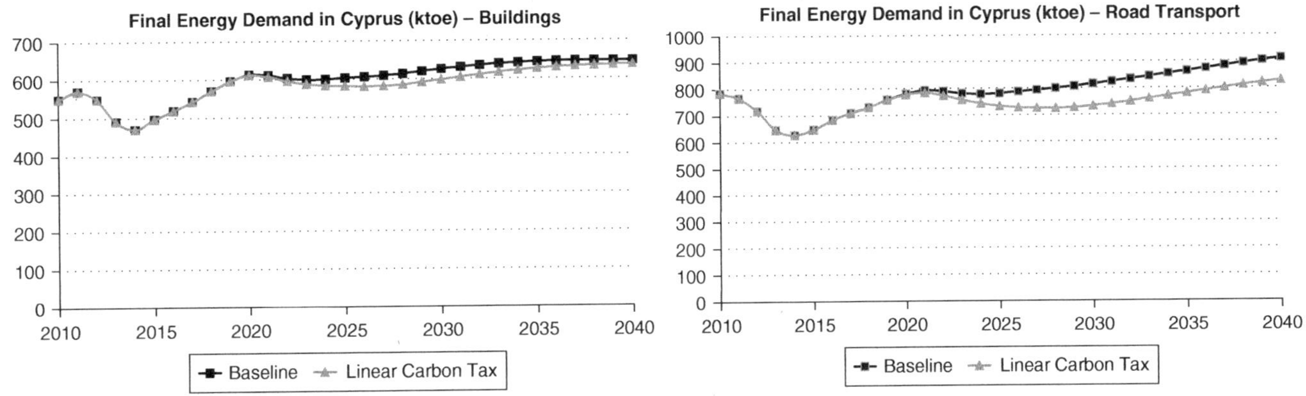

Figure 7.1 *Projected evolution of final energy demand in buildings and transport in Cyprus with and without implementation of the proposed carbon tax*

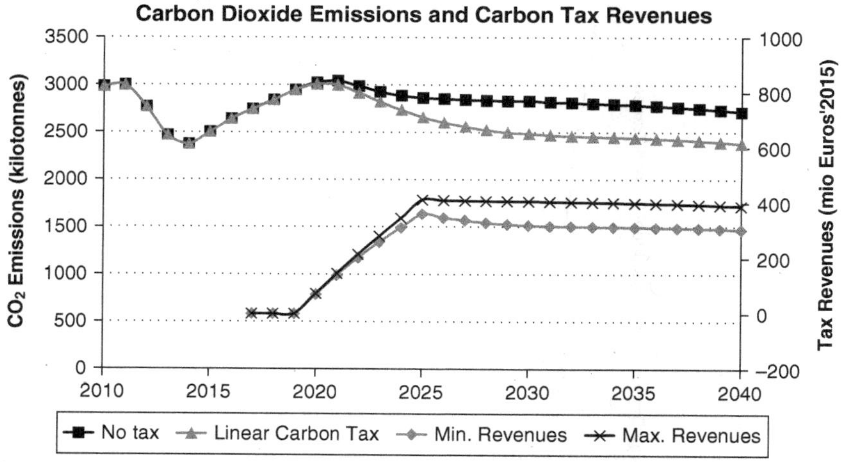

Figure 7.2 *Projected evolution of non-ETS CO_2 emissions in Cyprus with and without implementation of the proposed carbon tax (left axis); and range of projected revenues from carbon taxation (right axis), which can be used to reduce the tax burden on labour*

Table 7.3 *Additional expenditures of households by income group in 2025 due to the introduction of the proposed carbon tax*

(Euros'2015)	Extra expenditure for heating fuels	Extra expenditure for transport fuels	Total extra expenditure	Fraction of net income
Lowest 10%	52.35	98.50	150.85	1.3%
10%–20%	75.04	176.10	251.15	1.4%
20%–30%	75.64	274.49	350.13	1.5%
30%–40%	82.09	317.17	399.26	1.3%
40%–50%	113.03	374.02	487.05	1.3%
50%–60%	118.09	425.67	543.76	1.2%
60%–70%	158.90	467.30	626.20	1.2%
70%–80%	181.49	561.54	743.03	1.2%
80%–90%	172.81	546.65	719.46	1.0%
Top 10%	283.24	607.16	890.40	0.8%
All households	131.46	387.12	518.58	1.1%

Source: Family Expenditure Surveys of Cyprus for 2009 (processed by Dr Alexandros Polycarpou, Economics Research Centre of the University of Cyprus).

perception that such a tax is regressive and affects low-income households more – the effects of the carbon tax will be uniform across most Cypriot households.

As regards the effect of the carbon tax on the production costs and competitiveness of Cypriot enterprises, it is possible to draw some conclusions from an earlier study that explored the effects of higher fuel and electricity prices by sector of the economy (Ketteni et al, 2013). This study showed that although energy is complementary to capital and labour in most sectors, higher energy prices have very low adverse effects on investments and employment in Cypriot firms. Sectors with a comparatively higher share of fuel costs are (1) mining and quarrying and (2) transport and communications, but even there the effects of the carbon tax seem to be manageable. As a part of the green tax reform, the government can foresee temporary tax credits or other rebates that can alleviate the adverse effects of selected economic sectors. On the other hand, implementation of the carbon tax should be seen by firms as an opportunity for energy efficiency investments that can increase productivity and hence offer economic advantages in the medium term.

3.2 Water Scarcity Charge

It is proposed that an additional water charge be implemented for both domestic and irrigation water supply, in the order of €0.10 (at 2015 prices) per cubic metre (cm), phased in gradually over two years – €0.05/cm in 2020 and an additional €0.05/cm in 2021. From 2022 onwards, this charge would be kept at least constant in real terms (ie, it would be adjusted for inflation each year).

The amount of €0.10/cm comes from studies carried out for the Water Development Department of Cyprus so that the country can achieve recovery of the full costs of water supply, in line with the requirements of the EU Water Framework Directive 2000/60/EC (WDD, 2010). More specifically, this amount corresponds to the estimated water scarcity cost (resource cost) and the environmental cost from overexploitation of water resources. National Regulation 128/2014, adopted by the government of Cyprus in February 2014, provides for the implementation of such charges and the first such decision was made in 2017. Zachariadis (2010) provided a different assessment on the basis of economic welfare analysis, leading to substantially higher scarcity costs than those of governmental studies. However, as water pricing is always a socially and politically sensitive issue, it was preferred to keep the modest cost estimates of the government; but one should keep in mind that these most likely will not lead to full recovery of the social costs of water use.

Based on official statistics about the quantities of water billed to residential, industrial and agricultural consumers, this water charge is estimated to bring in additional revenues in the order of €10 million (at 2015 prices) per year – €6 million from water charges for domestic and industrial water and €4 million from charges for irrigation water. All households, firms and farmers are expected to pay this charge. Revenues will be collected through water bills. According to the national Regulation mentioned above, revenues from charges for the resource and environmental cost of water will go to the general government budget; no specific earmarking of any revenues is foreseen.

The water-saving potential of such a charge can be assessed on the basis of two existing studies: an econometric analysis of residential water demand in the three major urban areas of Nicosia, Limassol and Larnaca (Polycarpou and Zachariadis, 2013); and a simulation of long-term effects of water scarcity (Zachariadis, 2010). According to these studies, long-term price elasticity of residential water demand lies around −0.25 to −0.3. This could lead to potential water savings – if the proposed water pricing were implemented – in the order of 1.5–2 million cubic metres per year of residential and industrial water. Another 1–2 million cubic metres per year could be saved through the enforcement of proper irrigation water pricing in agriculture in line with the full cost recovery principle. Such water savings would help to enrich groundwater aquifers, especially those in coastal areas that are increasingly suffering from salinization. Moreover, these savings could help to reduce the dependence on water from desalination plants, which may cause damage to marine ecosystems in their proximity; these plants also require large amounts of electricity to produce freshwater and, since most electricity in Cyprus is produced in thermal power plants burning fuel oil and gas oil, desalination is the cause of substantial carbon and air pollutant emissions as well.

Water pricing is politically sensitive in view of the fact that water is an absolutely necessary good. It is therefore important to assess the social equity effects of such a policy. As far as residential water consumers are concerned, Zachariadis (2010) conducted a preliminary (ex-ante) analysis of distributional impacts from the adoption of water pricing. According to the Family Expenditure Surveys carried out by the Statistical Service of Cyprus for the years 2003 and 2009, domestic water expenditures represent less than 0.5 per cent of total household expenditures on average; this fraction increases somewhat – but is still less than 1 per cent – for the poorest 20 per cent of households.

This means that water expenditures of Cypriot households are regressive, but represent a very low fraction of household income. If the proposed water charge is imposed (ie, €0.10/cm), the average household may have to pay €19–28 more per year for water; this may range between

€12–17 for low-income households (or 0.1 per cent of their income) and €27–40 for high-income households (or 0.05 per cent of their income). Thus, the concerns of consumer associations and some policymakers over social equity are somewhat exaggerated and should not necessarily deter authorities from adopting these water charges.

3.3 Landfill Tax

Municipalities and firms are charged with different amounts per tonne of waste that they dispose of, depending on the landfill in which they deliver their waste. In the modern Koshi landfill site, for example, where the waste of the Larnaca and Famagusta areas is disposed of, charges have reached €80 per tonne; whereas in the old landfill sites of Kotsiatis and Vati, serving the areas of Nicosia and Limassol respectively, landfill charges have been less than €10 per tonne. Apart from the unequal and hence unfair treatment of citizens of the country, depending on where they live, the low landfill rates constitute an environmentally harmful subsidy, leading to inefficient waste management because they do not encourage reducing, reusing or recycling waste streams. This is in sharp contrast with the legal commitments of the Republic of Cyprus in view of the EU's Circular Economy Package, which requires that very small fractions of total waste should be disposed of in landfills by 2030 (European Commission, 2014).

It is therefore recommended that a uniform landfill tax be gradually introduced in all areas of Cyprus, which could reach €60 per tonne of waste by 2022 (at 2015 prices) – starting with €15 per tonne in 2019 and increasing by €15 per tonne each year up to 2022. A part of this tax is meant to recover the financial costs of waste treatment; the rest would correspond to a green tax encouraging alternative waste management options in line with the relevant EU policies. Evidently, this tax is in line with good practices in many EU countries. The expected revenues should amount to about €15–20 million (at 2015 prices) when the full tax is implemented. These revenues, however, may be expected to decrease after some years, because the amount of waste reaching landfill will be reduced as a result of the tax. Obviously, in order to reap the anticipated environmental benefits in waste treatment, proper surveillance should be enforced in order to avoid illegal waste dumping.

The implementation of a landfill tax need not have adverse distributional consequences. If local authorities collect waste charges from their citizens with 'pay as you throw' systems, which impose a waste charge that depends on the weight of waste generated in a household, then they can collect the required revenues to pay the landfill taxes in a socially fair and environmentally effective way.

4. IMPLICATIONS FOR URBAN SUSTAINABILITY

The savings in automotive fuel consumption mentioned above as a result of the carbon tax can lead to considerable reductions in emissions of air pollutants in urban areas. Based on emission factors of passenger cars provided by the European Environment Agency (EEA) Emissions Inventory Guidebook (EEA, 2013), as well as information collected from national air pollution authorities, the decrease in transport fuel consumption shown in Figure 7.1 can lead to savings in automotive emissions of nitrogen oxides in the order of 520–580 tonnes from 2030 onwards; and to savings in sulphur dioxide emissions of about 4 tonnes per year. Taken together, and using widely accepted assumptions about the cost of pollutant emissions in urban areas (eg, see Zachariadis and Hadjikyriakou, 2016), the reduction in just these two pollutants could reduce environmental damage costs in Cypriot urban areas by about €7 million per year (at 2015 prices).[2]

These calculations do not include an assessment of avoided environmental damages from other pollutants (eg, particulate matter), and also do not include benefits from avoidance of other transport-related costs such as congestion, noise and traffic accidents. Zachariadis (2008) assessed the external costs from the use of vehicles in urban roads of Cyprus to exceed €1 per kilometre during peak traffic hours. Of those costs, 90 per cent are associated with congestion, but accidents and noise also have a sizeable economic impact. In the absence of a detailed transport model, which could simulate the effect of a carbon tax through the cost of transport use to traffic loads in a Cypriot city, it is not possible to offer a reasonably plausible assessment of the effect of the carbon tax on these externalities – but one can state with confidence that several millions of euros could be saved per year due to improved urban traffic conditions thanks to the implementation of the carbon tax.

5. CONCLUSIONS

Cyprus faces serious energy and environmental challenges, which may be exacerbated in the future because of climate change. Compared with other European countries, it has low energy productivity, high amounts of municipal waste per capita and the worst water scarcity problem. National commitments for implementing EU legislation in relation to greenhouse gas emission reduction and improved waste management will become increasingly difficult to meet in the near future.

In view of these challenges, a fiscally neutral green tax reform can significantly contribute towards the transition to a path of economically and environmentally sustainable development. This chapter has outlined a proposal for one part of the tax reform – the implementation of environmental taxes at a level that is comparable to the economic costs that these environmental issues pose to society. More specifically, we propose the gradual implementation of a carbon tax to those sectors that are not subject to the EU ETS, a water scarcity charge, and a landfill tax for municipal and industrial waste that is disposed of in landfill. We have demonstrated, to the extent possible, the environmental benefits and the increase in public revenues that these taxes will bring about in the medium and long run. We have also assessed the effect of these taxes on firm competitiveness and social equity, underlining that potential adverse impacts of these measures will be manageable and should not be used as an excuse for not proceeding with a green tax reform.

This chapter has not dealt with the second part of the reform – namely, the reduction in labour or other taxes that could be facilitated by increased government revenues from green taxation. This is an equally important part of the reform, as the government could spend the higher public revenues by providing targeted aid to vulnerable households in order to alleviate adverse distributional impacts and reducing labour costs, thus boosting employment in the economy. Political acceptance of the reform will crucially depend on how the additional environmental tax revenues are deployed within the economy of Cyprus.

The international experience has shown that the adoption of a gradual green tax reform can have substantial positive effects on both the environmental and economic performance of a country. Our assessment shows that urban areas may benefit from considerable improvements in air quality and reductions in pollution costs if the proposed carbon tax is implemented. Further effects – such as reductions in road congestion, accidents and noise – which have not been quantified in our study highlight the substantial side benefits of green taxation. It is therefore recommended that the national economic authorities of Cyprus proceed with this reform in order to enable the transition to a more productive, more resource-efficient and less polluting economy.

NOTES

1. See also summary statistics on environmental taxes on Eurostat's webpage: http://ec.europa.eu/eurostat/statistics-explained/index.php/Environmental_tax_statistics, last accessed 22 April 2019.
2. Assumptions: nitrogen oxide emission factors of average in-use cars: 0.16 and 0.65 grams per kilometre for petrol-powered and diesel-powered cars respectively; sulphur content of both petrol and diesel fuel equal to 50 parts per million; fuel consumption of average

in-use cars: 7.7 and 5.9 litres per 100 kilometres for petrol-powered and diesel-powered cars respectively; marginal damage cost of emissions: €20,000 per tonne of nitrogen oxide and €30,000 per tonne of sulphur dioxide; 50 per cent of total vehicle kilometres are travelled in urban areas.

REFERENCES

Edenhofer O, Jakob M, Creutzig F et al (2015). 'Closing the emission price gap'. *Global Environmental Change* 31, 132–43.

EEA (2013). EMEP/EEA *Emission Inventory Guidebook 2013*, Technical Report No 12/2013, European Environment Agency, Copenhagen.

European Commission (2013). Tax Reforms in EU Member States 2013: Tax Policy Challenges for Economic Growth and Fiscal Sustainability. Report No 5/2013 of 'European Economy' series, Directorates-General for Economic and Financial Affairs and for Taxation and Customs Union; doi: 10.2765/40142.

European Commission (2014). Communication from the Commission to the European Parliament, the Council, the European Economic and Social Committee and the Committee of the Regions: Towards a circular economy: A zero waste programme for Europe, COM(2014)398 of 2 July 2014.

European Commission and Eurostat (2018). 'Taxation trends in the European Union – 2018 Edition', Luxembourg; doi:10.2778/025314.

Eurostat (2017). 'Energy, Transport and Environment Indicators – 2017 Edition', Luxembourg; doi:10.2785/964100.

Eurostat (2015). Online information on the Water Exploitation Index, available at https://ec.europa.eu/eurostat/web/products-datasets/-/t2020_rd220, last accessed 22 April 2019.

IMF (International Monetary Fund) (2015). 'How Large Are Global Energy Subsidies?' Working Paper WP/15/105. Washington, DC.

Jakob M and Edenhofer O (2014). 'Green growth, degrowth, and the commons'. *Oxford Review of Economic Policy* 30, 447–68.

OECD (2013). *Climate and Carbon. Aligning Prices and Policies*. Paris, France.

International Renewable Energy Agency (2015). *Renewable Energy Roadmap for the Republic of Cyprus*, January. Available at www.irena.org/publications.

Ketteni E, Mamuneas T and Zachariadis T (2013). 'The Effect of EU Energy and Climate Policies on the Production Sectors of the Economy of Cyprus – Final Results'. Economic Policy Paper 01-13, Economics Research Centre, University of Cyprus, February 2013. Available at http://ucy.ac.cy/erc/documents/DOP_1-13.pdf, last accessed 22 April 2019.

Markandya A, González-Eguino M and Escapa M (2013). 'From shadow to green: Linking environmental fiscal reforms and the informal economy'. *Energy Economics* 40, S108–S118.

Parry IWH, Heine D, Lis E and Li S (2014). *Getting Energy Prices Right: from Principle to Practice*. International Monetary Fund, Washington, DC. ISBN: 978-1-48438-857-0.

Polycarpou A and Zachariadis T (2013). 'An Econometric Analysis of Residential Water Demand in Cyprus'. *Water Resources Management* 27, 309–17.

Rausch S (2013). 'Fiscal consolidation and climate policy: an overlapping generations perspective'. *Energy Economics* 40, S134–S148.

Umweltbundesamt (German Federal Environment Agency) (2017). 'Environmentally Harmful Subsidies In Germany – Updated Edition 2016', Dessau-Roßlau, Germany. Available at www.umweltbundesamt.de/en/publikationen/umweltschaedliche-subventionen-in-deutschland-2016.

Vivid Economics (2012). 'Carbon taxation and fiscal consolidation: the potential of carbon pricing to reduce Europe's fiscal deficits'. Report prepared for the European Climate Foundation and Green Budget Europe, May 2012.

WDD (Water Development Department) (2010). 'Costs and Pricing of Water Services in Cyprus', April 2010 (in Greek). Available at www.moa.gov.cy/moa/wdd/Wdd.nsf/all/82D260F5DEAC3827C2257A29002AED9F/$file/Enimerotiki_Timologisi.pdf?openelement.

Withana S, ten Brink P, Kretschmer B, Mazza L, Hjerp P and Sauter R (2013). 'Evaluation of environmental tax reforms: International experiences'. A report by the Institute for European Environmental Policy (IEEP) for the State Secretariat for Economic Affairs (SECO) and the Federal Finance Administration (FFA) of Switzerland. Final Report, Brussels, 2013.

Zachariadis T (2008). 'Road to Nowhere: An Assessment of Social Costs from the Use of Cars in Cypriot Cities'. *Cyprus Economic Policy Review* 2, 51–80.

Zachariadis T (2010). 'Residential water scarcity in Cyprus: Impact of climate change and policy options'. *Water* 2, 788–814.

Zachariadis T and Hadjikyriakou C (2016). *Social Costs and Benefits of Renewable Electricity Generation in Cyprus*. SpringerBriefs in Energy. Springer International Publishing, doi: 10.1007/978-3-319-31535-5.

Zachariadis T, Michopoulos A, Vougiouklakis Y, Struss B, Piripitsi K and Ellinopoulos C (2017). 'In-Depth Assessment of the Energy Efficiency Potential in Cyprus'. *Cyprus Economic Policy Review*, Vol 11, No 2, pp86–112.

8. The agricultural conundrum: encouraging climate-friendly agriculture through economic instruments in North America

Emma Akrawi*

1. INTRODUCTION

As populations swell and people migrate from rural areas to sprawling cities, issues around agricultural production demand increasing attention. Who will feed these growing populations, on what land and with which methods of production? Such an analysis necessitates an understanding of emissions. The food chain emits up to half of all anthropogenic emissions – from agricultural production and associated land use change and deforestation to processing, transport, retail and waste.[1] Yet many climate policies excuse agriculture from emissions standards, failing to account for its significant contribution to global greenhouse gas emissions.

This chapter considers the role of agriculture in carbon pricing. It begins by painting a backdrop of agriculture's treatment in North American environmental law, depicting the exceptional position that agriculture has enjoyed and unpacking the perceived tension between agricultural livelihoods and emissions reductions. It then transitions to a case study of California's climate policy, featuring its carbon pricing mechanism, cap-and-trade. The chapter evaluates California's treatment of agriculture and its potential to encourage climate-friendly agriculture through a cap-and-trade offset protocol for carbon farming – a suite of practices that mitigate emissions by sequestering atmospheric carbon in the soil. Ultimately, the chapter acknowledges the barriers to tucking agriculture under the carbon pricing wing: agricultural exceptionalism in environmental law, the complexity of agricultural emissions and the trouble that offsets pose. As such, the best path forward for California, and a lesson to jurisdictions in the U.S. and abroad, may be to dedicate more carbon pricing revenue to farmland conservation and soil carbon sequestration.

2. AGRICULTURAL EXCEPTIONALISM AND CARBON PRICING

A brief tour through agriculture's relationship to United States (U.S.) environmental law informs the challenge of including agriculture under a carbon pricing mechanism. Agriculture has historically enjoyed preferential treatment under the law. "Agricultural exceptionalism" in the U.S. harks back to the Constitution, which guarantees each state two Senators and in doing so safeguards the rural voice.[2] Agriculture's standing persisted due to the American agrarian ideal: that farming was not an industry, but a way of life.[3] Policies arose in defense of the "family farm" ideal. Most Americans still envision family farms as small, diversified operations where farmers steward the land.[4] Modern farming tells a different story. The U.S. Department of Agriculture (USDA) touts that 97 percent of U.S. farms are "family farms," covering over half of the nation's cropland and producing 60 percent of U.S. agricultural output.[5] The USDA defines a "family farm" as a farm where the "majority of the business is owned by the operator and individuals related to the operator"[6] – a definition unrelated to the size of the farm or family members serving as farmworkers. Larger farms are more likely to have greater operating profit margins than small farms,[7] and as such would be better suited to bear increased costs.

Agricultural exceptionalism permeates environmental laws in the United States.[8] Federal environmental statutes – including the Clean Water Act, the Safe Drinking Water Act, the Clean Air Act, and the Comprehensive Environmental Response, Compensation, and Liability Act – relieve agriculture of some or all regulatory burdens.[9] For instance, the Clean Water Act exempts from its regulated point sources of pollution agricultural irrigation return flows, which can carry sediment, pesticides, and fertilizers.[10] Even where statutes do apply to agriculture, as with large concentrated animal feeding operations, regulatory agencies have been reluctant to take action, as with the U.S. Environmental Protection Agency's failure to measure factory farm pollution.[11] At the state level, all 50 states have passed right-to-farm laws that shield farms from nuisance lawsuits.[12] For example, a right-to-farm law might bar a neighbor from suing a livestock operation for its unreasonable odor.

The political power of agriculture is felt in California's regulations. In recent years, California managed to pass a law regarding short-lived climate pollutants including methane, but the dairy industry restricted the agency's role in regulating livestock methane. Under the law, the California Air Resources Board (ARB) cannot regulate livestock emissions until 2024, and any regulations must be technically and economically feasible for the industry based on a number of enumerated factors.[13] Dairy is the highest-earning agricultural commodity in California.[14] California agriculture's political will is unsurprising, given that it rakes in around $40 billion in one year,[15] which is six times the revenue from all cap-and-trade auctions combined.[16]

On the national stage, excepting agriculture carries costs. With the modern shift from diversified farming to large crop monocultures come decreased labor costs, but also social and environmental externalities that the public must bear.[17] Air and water quality, pollinator and habitat loss, soil deterioration, and healthcare exemplify costs that industrial agriculture has shifted to the public.[18] For instance, as nutrient pollution has increased, municipalities have had to spend more on water treatment.[19] As such, industrial agriculture product prices do not reflect the true cost of food. In addition, most subsidies fund commodity crops including corn and soy. And very little of that corn feeds people. Forty percent of U.S. corn is processed for ethanol biofuel and 36 percent for livestock feed; and most of the remainder is exported or reduced to high fructose corn syrup.[20] Carbon pricing mechanisms seek to change behavior through their economic signals. But given agricultural subsidies, a small increase in costs on emissions-intensive farmers might not be enough to make practices such as carbon farming – which often comes with a time lag – cheaper to implement than subsidized crops.

Even in the context of carbon pricing in the U.S., the political power of agriculture is palpable. When the U.S. House of Representatives was considering an emissions trading bill in 2009, the agricultural lobby attained language codifying a list of agricultural offsets of questionable scientific certainty, as well as a ban on excluding any future offsets.[21] Recent state carbon tax proposals in Washington and Vermont exempted dyed farm fuel. [22] Farmers contend that taxing farm fuel emissions is unfair because agricultural lands sequester large amounts of carbon. In addition, farmers insist that they are unable to pass the costs of carbon pricing onto consumers due to the need to keep food prices competitively low.

Agricultural exceptionalism reaches internationally as well. In British Columbia, for instance, the initial carbon tax covered agricultural fuel. However, five years after the tax was enacted, the government decided to exempt agricultural fuels,[23] offering scant basis for its decision apart from a desire to maintain "the affordability and competitiveness of locally produced agricultural products."[24] One study of the effect of the British Columbia carbon tax on agriculture found that "despite the sector being singled out as 'at risk' by the provincial government," there was "little evidence that the carbon tax was associated with any statistically significant effects on agricultural trade or competitiveness between 2008–2011."[25] Also, when compared with other highly traded industries, agriculture's fuel use was found average.[26] The authors emphasized how sector exemptions undermine the tax: exemptions are "an extremely costly way to preserve employment in the exempted sector, and are inferior to other support mechanisms that governments can use."[27] Thus, while politically appealing, the agricultural exemption was economically inefficient and undermined the tax's goal.

Along with the scientific complexity of measuring agricultural emissions, agricultural exceptionalism prevents carbon pricing from embodying agriculture's negative climate impact.

3. AN OVERVIEW OF AGRICULTURE'S ROLE IN CALIFORNIA CAP-AND-TRADE

California's overarching climate change policy addresses agriculture,[28] but its carbon pricing mechanism, cap-and-trade, fails to cover most agricultural emissions. In 2013, California began enforcing cap-and-trade compliance obligations. The declining cap purports to cover around 85 percent of the state's fossil fuel emissions by covering large (at least 25 000 metric tons of carbon dioxide (CO_2) equivalent per year) industrial sources, electricity generators and importers, and fuel distributors.[29] ARB distributes tradable allowances, and entities must submit the number of allowances equal to their emissions or employ a limited percentage of offsets.[30]

Cap-and-trade fails to cover most food and agriculture emissions, with the exceptions of fuel emissions from large food processors and agricultural diesel.[31] Cap-and-trade's recent inclusion of transportation fuels indirectly brought agricultural diesel under the cap by covering fuel suppliers.[32] For covered entities under the cap, emissions stem from fossil fuel combustion, but with agriculture, fuel use is a small part of the picture. Agriculture comprises 8 percent of California's total greenhouse gas (GHG) emissions.[33] Within these agricultural emissions, farm fuel contributes just 13 percent; while methane and nitrous oxide from livestock production account for the majority, at 66 percent; and nitrous oxide and carbon dioxide from soil management practices make up 20 percent.[34] Thus, the vast majority of agricultural emissions involve a complex combination of biological, physical, and chemical processes that renders them a challenge to quantify. For instance, nitrous oxide emissions occur as a result of fertilizer application. But the amount of emissions depends on a host of variables: the type of fertilizer, soil type, climate, irrigation, crop management practices, and even the soil depth at which the fertilizer is applied.[35]

Given these complexities with agricultural emissions, it is no wonder cap-and-trade efforts focus on large, easily quantifiable, fuel-based emitters.

Even if it is unfeasible to bring most agricultural emissions under the cap, there may be potential to reward agriculture's positive climate impacts through a cap-and-trade offset for carbon-sequestering farming practices. The next two sections consider carbon offsets, first delving into a discussion of offsets generally before analyzing the potential for developing a cap-and-trade offset for carbon farming.

4. THE TROUBLE WITH OFFSETS

The purposes of offsets in an emissions trading scheme such as California's cap-and-trade are twofold. First, offsets make the carbon pricing tool more appealing for the covered entities. Second, offsets incentivize the target sectors, which can be sectors that are not covered by the cap.[36] In theory, offsets allow for the most cost-effective reduction of a given amount of emissions because the target entity can reduce emissions more cheaply than the covered entity.[37] This theoretical cost saving is especially true for land use practices, which offer some of the most affordable implementation opportunities.[38] This section analyzes some of the troubles that offsets pose.

California first allowed covered entities to offset up to 8 percent of their emissions, but has recently restricted offsets further. Between 2021–25 a covered entity may offset up to 4 percent of its compliance obligation, and between 2026–30 it may offset up to 6 percent.[39] In both cases, the new policy requires that "no more than one-half [of the offsets] may be sourced from projects that do not provide direct environmental benefits" in California.[40] Environmental justice advocates had criticized offsets because out-of-state offsets extinguish the co-benefits from local emissions reductions by covered entities.[41] The recent tightening of offsets will likely mean a diminished incentive for ARB to develop new offset protocols going forward.[42]

Legally, California requires offsets to achieve reductions that are "real, permanent, quantifiable, verifiable, and enforceable by the state board."[43] Offsets must also be additional, meaning that they would not have otherwise occurred.[44] Lastly, projects must reduce an "equivalent" amount of emissions and do so over the "same time period" as the direct emissions reduction would have.[45] This last point is not often discussed, but could come into play with a carbon sequestration offset because gains with soil carbon sequestration often require a decade or more to realize. Offsets that fail to meet the above requirements undermine the carbon pricing instrument because they allow emissions to exceed the cap.

Additionality is one of the biggest challenges with offsets. One study of Kyoto's Clean Development Mechanism offsets found that 85 percent failed to ensure additionality.[46] Departing from the Clean Development Mechanism's project-specific, case-by-case analysis of offsets, California offsets are standards-based protocols, meaning that regulations dictate protocol requirements.[47] In 2012, Citizens Climate Lobby and Our Children's Earth Foundation brought litigation challenging ARB's standards-based approach to offsets, including its livestock manure protocol. Plaintiffs argued that the standards-based protocol violated "additionality" because it permitted projects that would have happened without the offset.[48] The court upheld ARB's standards-based approach to offsets as "additional." In regard to the livestock manure protocol, the court decided that low installation figures meant that methane digesters were not a business-as-usual practice and thus could be considered additional.[49] As Professor Ramo notes, ARB "simply assumed that if a farmer were to use this technology then it would only be due to its offset protocol and therefore be additional."[50] In fact, around the same time, the USDA had pushed the profitability of digesters and the dairy industry had pledged to reduce emissions, rendering the answer to the additionality question a "murky"[51] one.

Currently, California has six offset protocols, two of which are agricultural: livestock manure and rice cultivation,[52] both of which can be implemented in U.S. states outside California. The livestock manure offset incentivizes large livestock farms to install methane digesters, which capture methane from manure that would otherwise enter the atmosphere. The rice protocol also targets methane emissions, encouraging farmers to adopt one of three alternatives: "dry seeding, early drainage, or alternate wetting and drying."[53] These two offsets address activities that contribute a minimal percentage of California's total emissions. Livestock manure emits about 1 percent of California's emissions (about 15 percent for U.S. emissions), and rice production accounts for far less than 1 percent of California's emissions.[54] Agricultural soil management contributes comparable emissions to livestock manure,[55] and carbon farming can play a role in mitigating soil management emissions, as well as in sequestering atmospheric carbon.

5. AN OFFSET FOR CARBON FARMING?

Farmers need an incentive to adopt carbon-sequestering practices. Does it make sense for that financial incentive to come in the form of a carbon offset? The answer is a mixed bag. On one hand, a carbon farming offset would complement existing California offsets and could provide an incentive for farmers. On the other hand, a carbon sequestration offset faces quantifiability and permanence hurdles, as well as the critiques of offsets more generally.

"Carbon farming" refers to "a suite of crops and practices that sequester carbon while simultaneously meeting human needs."[56] Carbon farming practices are those "that are known to improve the rate at which CO_2 is removed from the atmosphere and converted to plant material and/or soil organic carbon."[57] Carbon farming practices include reduced tillage, perennial crops, cover cropping, manure and compost application, agroforestry (integrating trees with crops and/or livestock), and more.[58] In addition to its mitigation potential, carbon farming offers many co-benefits: improving water quality from reduced sediment and chemical runoff, enhancing soil capacity to withstand drought, reducing soil erosion, reducing fossil fuel use, boosting productivity, and improving biodiversity.[59] In its 2014 Agriculture Working Paper, California noted the "enormous opportunities to increase biological carbon sequestration in both vegetation and soils," drawing down atmospheric emissions.[60] The working group added, "Sequestration of carbon in soils provides almost 90 percent of the global potential for agricultural mitigation."[61]

Financial incentives are necessary for farmers to adopt carbon sequestering practices. Some farmers might be able to absorb the costs of a carbon tax or regulatory mandate to adopt carbon farming practices. However, many cannot, and increased costs can price out farmers and drive development on agricultural lands. In *The Carbon Farming Solution*, Eric Toensmeier writes, "the more incentives are available for farmers, the more carbon they can draw down."[62] This section evaluates the potential for developing a California cap-and-trade offset protocol for carbon farming. It looks at quantifiability, additionality, time, permanence, and costs.

5.1 Quantifiability

Perhaps the biggest challenge to a carbon farming offset is the ability to accurately quantify carbon sequestration. Not only is there a huge variety of farming practices that sequester carbon, but within each practice there are variables such as climate, soil type, plant variety, livestock components, soil amendment application, and precipitation.[63] In contrast, the emissions mitigated by a methane digester are easily calculable.[64]

At present, there are methods of satellite imaging to estimate aboveground biomass to extrapolate the carbon stored in trees.[65] In contrast, there is currently no affordable way to accurately measure soil carbon.[66] However, such tools are being developed and could be ready in around five years.[67] An affordable soil carbon measuring tool would enable widespread verification of soil carbon sequestered on farms. Even without such a device, potential to quantify soil carbon remains. The COMET-Planner tool, developed through a joint effort by the U.S. Natural Resources Conservation Service and Colorado State University,[68] estimates soil carbon sequestration rates for 34 different practices.[69] California has partnered with COMET-Planner's developers on a California-specific version of the tool to implement in its Healthy Soils Program,[70] which uses cap-and-trade revenue to support farms building soil carbon.[71]

Another consideration with carbon farming quantifiability is whether there might be a tradeoff with other greenhouse gas emissions. For example, conservation tillage reduces fossil fuel use and conserves soil carbon and water quality, but in the United States it is usually accompanied by increased herbicide use, which contributes to higher nitrous oxide emissions.[72]

5.2 Additionality

The same additionality issues inherent with any carbon offset are compounded by carbon farming. Because of the wide variety of techniques that can sequester carbon in the soil, some practices would likely seem more "additional" than others based on how prevalent they currently are. For example, conservation tillage is used on less than 2 percent of California cropland currently, but in some parts of the United States the practice is more common due to USDA incentives in the 1960s and 1970s.[73]

5.3 Time

Offsets must achieve equivalent emissions "over the same time period" as the reduction by the covered entity would have taken.[74] In other words, if a covered entity could have taken a certain number of years to reduce its emissions, the offset replacing those reductions must occur within the same number of years. This requirement could pose a problem for carbon farming. A number of carbon farming practices take time to establish and for soil carbon to accumulate. In addition, interactions with other biological processes may take time to even out. For instance, studies have found that nitrous oxide emissions increase in the initial years after the introduction of conservation tillage, but longer-term studies of a period of ten years or more found a reduction in nitrous oxide emissions.[75]

5.4 Permanence

Permanence is a concern with all offsets, but governments have been especially wary of offsets in the land use realm for fear of impermanence.[76]

Carbon sequestered through soil and biomass can return to the atmosphere through human action or natural disaster.[77] Even if a farmer has been practicing no-till for a number of years, tilling the soil at some point would release carbon benefits to the atmosphere. Likewise, natural disasters including fires, floods, and pest infestations contribute to loss of sequestered carbon.[78] California recently endured its largest wildfire on record – a colossal loss of carbon.[79] Two questions arise from the permanence of land use offsets. First, what can be done about unintended carbon loss from natural disasters? Second, is it possible to make carbon farming practices permanent?

The EU Emissions Trading Scheme has not permitted land use offsets due to permanence concerns, but California offers offset protocols for U.S. forestry. For purposes of California's forestry protocol, 100 years is considered permanent.[80] One way in which California's forestry offset considers permanence is by creating an insurance mechanism of a "Forest Buffer Account" to account for carbon lost through forest "reversal."[81] As the protocol states, "If a Forest Project experiences an unintentional reversal of credited GHG reductions," then "ARB offset credits from the Forest Buffer Account will be retired in an amount equal to the total amount of carbon that was reversed."[82]

Because California provides forestry offsets, it seems logical that it could offer carbon farming offsets without violating permanence. However, one key point distinguishes forestry from many carbon farming practices: time. Unlike with the relatively long-term scale of timber growth, many carbon farming practices are not inherently permanent for a 100-year period. Some agroforestry may be able to overcome this hurdle with incorporation of longer-term tree crops. However, other carbon-sequestering practices, such as reduced tillage, do not inherently ensure a long timeline. A farmer can decide to till the soil at any time, reversing the positive impacts of the sequestration.

Tools such as conservation easements may help ensure that carbon farming offsets are permanent. A conservation easement is a legal agreement between a landowner and easement holder to permanently restrict certain use and development rights in order to protect the land. Under the U.S. tax code, landowners can qualify for a tax deduction by dedicating a perpetual conservation easement on lands including farmland.[83] The code imposes no requirements for conservation farming practices in order to qualify, but land trusts or governments accepting the easements can exert their own standards and encourage carbon farming practices. California's 2030 Natural and Working Lands Concept Paper suggests mandating climate-friendly practices through conservation easements in order to increase permanence.[84] As an analogy, the forestry offset protocol requires landowners of "avoided conversion projects" to record a perpetual conservation easement.[85]

Management plans in conjunction with an easement may offer some remedy. A conservation easement can require that management comply with the management plan, which can impose affirmative obligations that evolve over time with best management practices. For example, in California's Lassen Foothills, The Nature Conservancy employed detailed restrictions on development and an affirmative obligation on ranchers to leave a certain level of residual dry matter on the ground at the end of the season.[86] Residual dry matter provided a quantifiable metric for overgrazing that could be monitored over time.[87] In the context of carbon farming, conservation easements hold potential.

5.5 Cost

Having assessed whether carbon farming can meet the legal requirements of offsets, it is equally important to consider whether a carbon farming offset would be a financial draw to farmers. Many carbon farming practices involve upfront investments.[88] As the Economic and Technology Advancement Advisory Committee Report cautioned:

> Establishing and monitoring the amount of carbon stored could be difficult if it requires more work than the value of the credit. In addition, transaction costs may be too high for an individual farmer to play directly in the carbon market.[89]

This economic hurdle could be particularly challenging for carbon farming. Transaction costs could be the reason that the urban forest offset program has yet to take off.[90]

Alberta offers a number of agricultural offset protocols through its Carbon Competitiveness Incentive Regulation, which requires facilities that emit over 100 000 tons of GHGs a year to report and reduce emissions.[91] The agricultural offsets include a protocol for conservation tillage, as well as protocols for livestock, waste, and renewable energy.[92] The conservation tillage protocol has proven popular among Alberta's farmers, with one estimate touting that 75 percent or more of land now uses no-till.[93] Thus far, these carbon payments for reduced tillage have persisted despite conservation tillage gaining independent popularity for preventing soil erosion.[94] But the offset is nearing a 40 percent adoption rate, at which point it would be considered common practice and could be dropped as an offset.[95]

To overcome the transaction cost hurdle, payments are made through private aggregators, which verify and package farmer credits together to sell to the large covered entities.[96] Some aggregators pay farmers a flat fee for credits and others offer a price based on the marketplace.[97] Either way, the amount of the credit the farmer receives is discounted to cover the aggregator's costs, including the aggregator's work to verify the credit.[98] Typically, a farmer takes home around 60 percent of the credit, while the aggregator collects the remaining 40 percent.[99] Alberta dictates a value of tonnes per acre of carbon sequestered for each of two types of land: Parkland (0.11 tonnes/acre) and Dry Prairie (0.06 tonnes/acre).[100] In order to determine the carbon price a farmer would receive, one can multiply the given carbon sequestration rate in tonnes per acre by the carbon price that the offset credits sell for in the market (currently between $20 and $25 per tonne of CO_2 equivalent).[101] Applying an upper-end price of $25 per tonne, this calculation rewards the farmer approximately $1.65 per acre for Parkland and $0.90 per acre for Dry Prairie.[102] Given these low prices, the conservation tillage offset protocol only attracts large farms with thousands of acres.[103]

Similarly, California could calculate an offset for a carbon farming practice by multiplying the COMET-Planner sequestration figure in tonnes of carbon sequestered by the price of a cap-and-trade allowance. In the August 2018 cap-and-trade auction, the clearing price was $15.05.[104]

In addition to transaction and upfront costs for the farmer, it would be necessary to consider the administrative costs in developing a carbon farming protocol. The ARB process for developing offset protocols is intensive and can take years.[105]

6. CONCLUSION

California provides a useful case study for agriculture's role within carbon pricing instruments. California's cap-and-trade program does not cover food or agricultural emissions apart from fuel use at large food processing plants and farm diesel. It is difficult for carbon pricing mechanisms to cover agricultural emissions for two main reasons. First, agriculture's political power, as evidenced by its exceptional treatment in North American environmental law, coupled with challenging economics for farmers, makes financially burdening agriculture politically infeasible. Second, the scientific complexity of agricultural emissions, most of which occur through biological interactions rather than through fuel combustion, makes them impossible to capture under current carbon pricing models.

Given the challenges of encouraging climate-friendly agriculture through a cap, this chapter turns to the question: Can carbon pricing mechanisms successfully reward carbon-sequestering agriculture through offsets? Carbon farming mitigates atmospheric greenhouse gas emissions by sequestering carbon in soils. Farmers need incentives to adopt these practices. And generally, the more carbon that an agricultural practice sequesters, the costlier it is to implement.[106] The Alberta case study demonstrates that soil carbon sequestration offsets are possible. However, it also highlights how small per-acre offset payments are only enticing to large farms. In addition, general concerns with offsets endure, including additionality and permanence considerations.

Limited potential exists for California to draft a carbon farming offset protocol. It might be feasible for California to apply COMET-Planner sequestration figures and model an offset protocol on Alberta's conservation tillage protocol for a variety of carbon farming practices. California currently offers two offset protocols within agriculture. However, the shortcomings of offsets in general, the state's recent tightening of offset amounts, and the unique challenges with developing a carbon farming protocol lead toward the conclusion that California's approach to reducing agricultural emissions should not rely on cap-and-trade offsets.

Agriculture is challenging to incorporate under carbon pricing mechanisms. But the story need not end there. Carbon pricing revenue presents an opportunity to direct attention to agriculture. In its 2018–19 expenditure plan, California dedicates auction revenue to five agricultural initiatives: agricultural diesel engine replacements ($112 million), dairy farm methane reductions ($99 million), food processor incentives ($64 million), Healthy Soils Program ($5 million), and on-farm renewable energy ($4 million).[107] In addition, the Sustainable Agricultural Lands Conservation Program continually receives cap-and-trade revenue ($34 million in 2017–18).[108] While bringing agriculture under the cap tends to benefit larger farms which can pay, targeting agriculture's climate impact with grants allows for solutions that cater to smaller farms. For example, grant funding for dairy methane reductions acknowledges that the livestock methane offset protocol is only feasible for large farms that can afford a $2–$9 million digester installation.[109] In contrast with targeting agriculture's positive impact through offsets, agriculture grants guarantee local impact. Funding for replacing farm equipment, for instance, improves air quality in California.[110]

Going forward, California can continue to expand revenue support for its farmland conservation and soil carbon sequestration efforts. The Healthy Soils Program allocates funding to soil carbon sequestering practices and demonstration farms.[111] The Sustainable Agricultural Lands Conservation program funds farmland conservation easements in areas of California confronting intense development pressure from urban sprawl. In one study, an acre of urban land in Yolo County, California, emitted 70 times more greenhouse gases than an acre of cropland, making farmland conservation and infill development within existing urban areas essential for climate goals.[112] As urban dwellers continue to multiply, the need to recognize the carbon sequestration potential of farmland is more important than ever. Other jurisdictions may wish to adopt California's approach of dedicating carbon pricing revenue toward climate-friendly agriculture.

NOTES

* J.D.'19, Vermont Law School. The author would like to thank Professor Janet E. Milne for her essential mentorship and support.

1. Eric Toensmeier, The Carbon Farming Solution: A Global Toolkit of Perennial Crops and Regenerative Agriculture Practices for Climate Change Mitigation and Food Security 12 (2016).
2. Susan Schneider, *A Reconsideration of Agricultural Law: A Call for the Law of Food, Farming, and Sustainability*, 34 Wm. & Mary Envtl. L. & Pol'y Rev. 935, 938 (2010).
3. *Id.* at 940.
4. *Id.* at 943, 945.
5. USDA, Structure and Finances of U.S. Farms: Family Farm Report (2014).
6. USDA Economic Research Service, www.ers.usda.gov/topics/farm-economy/farm-household-well-being/glossary/#familyfarm (last accessed August 11, 2018).
7. *Id.* at 7.
8. Nicole E. Negowetti, *Exposing the Invisible Costs of Commercial Agriculture: Shaping Policies with True Costs Accounting to Create a Sustainable Food Future*, 51 Val. U. L. Rev. 447, 458 (2017) ("Agriculture is the only major industrial sector that is routinely exempted from baseline environmental standards").
9. *Id.* at 459–64.
10. *Id.* at 459 (discussing Section 402 of the Clean Water Act).
11. *See* Georgina Gustin, *EPA's Failure to Regulate Factory Farm Pollution Draws New Scrutiny*, Inside Climate News (November 28, 2016), https://insideclimatenews.org/news/22112016/epa-regulate-factory-farm-emissions-pollution (last accessed April 22, 2019).
12. Peter J. Wall, *Land Use and Agricultural Exceptionalism*, 16 San Joaquin Agric. L. Rev. 219, 226 (2007).
13. Cal. Health & Safety Code § 39730.7 (effective January 1, 2018).
14. Governor Edmund G. Brown, et al., First Update to the Climate Change Scoping Plan: Building on the Framework 9 of Appendix C: Agriculture Working Paper (2014).
15. *Id.* at 11.
16. Governor Edmund G. Brown, California State Budget 2018–19 (stating that since cap-and-trade's inception in 2013, California has appropriated $6.9 billion in auction proceeds).
17. Negowetti, *supra* note 8, at 449.
18. *See generally id.*
19. *Id.* at 467.
20. Jonathan Foley, *It's Time to Rethink America's Corn System*, Scientific American (March 5, 2013), www.scientificamerican.com/article/time-to-rethink-corn (last accessed April 22, 2019).
21. Donald T. Hornstein, *The Environmental Role of Agriculture in an Era of Carbon Caps*, 20 Health Matrix 145, 172 (2010) (discussing agricultural influence over the American Clean Energy and Security Act). *See also* Lauren Bernadett, Comment, *Agricultural Soil Carbon Sequestration Offset Programs: Strengths, Difficulties, and Suggestions for*

Their Potential Use in AB 32's Cap and Trade Program, 31 UCLA J. Envtl. L. & Pol'y 198, 216–17 (2013) (discussing the corn industry).
22. S.B. 6203, 65th Leg., (Wash. 2018); S.B. 284 (Vt. 2018).
23. British Columbia Ministry of Finance, June Budget Update 2013/14-2015/16 65 (2013).
24. *Id.*
25. Nicholas Rivers and Brandon Schaufele, The Effect of British Columbia's Carbon Tax on Agricultural Trade 4 (2014).
26. *Id.* at 15.
27. *Id.* at 14.
28. California Global Warming Solutions Act of 2006, Cal. Health & Safety Code § 38566 (effective January 1, 2017).
29. Cal. Code Regs. tit. 17 § 95812. *See also* Brown, et al., *supra* note 14, at 93.
30. *See* Brown et al., *supra* note 15, at 93.
31. *See* Cal. Code Regs. tit. 17 § 95812.
32. Telephone Conversation with Syd Partridge, Manager of Mandatory Reporting Requirements, Cal. Air Res. Bd. (August 15, 2018).
33. Ryan Byrnes et al., *Review of Research to Inform California's Climate Scoping Plan: Agriculture and Working Lands*, 71 Cal. Agric. 160, 160 (2017).
34. *Id.* at 1.
35. Duke Nicholas Inst. for Envtl. Policy Sol., Greenhouse Gas Mitigation Opportunities in California Agriculture 11–21 (2014).
36. Bernadett, *supra* note 21, at 210–11.
37. Alan Ramo, *The California Offset Game: Who Wins and Who Loses?*, 20 Hastings W.-N.W. J. Envtl. L. & Pol'y 109, 119 (2014).
38. *Id. See also* Toensmeier, *supra* note 1, at 314 ("sequestering carbon in soil is the most cost-effective mitigation strategy").
39. § 38562(E)(i).
40. *Id.* It will be interesting to see how "direct environmental benefits" will be defined and whether litigation will ensure over the definition.
41. Ramo, *supra* note 37, at 129.
42. Telephone Interview with Tim O'Connor, Environmental Defense Fund (August 8, 2018).
43. Cal. Code Regs. tit. 17, § 38562(d)(1) (effective July 25, 2017).
44. § 38562(d)(2).
45. § 38562(d)(3).
46. Dr. Martin Cames, et al., How Additional is the Clean Development Mechanism? 11 (2016).
47. Ramo, *supra* note 37, at 125.
48. *Citizens Climate Lobby v. Cal. Air Res. Bd.*, 2013 WL 861396 (Cal. Super. Ct. 2013).
49. *Id.* at 16.
50. Ramo, *supra* note 37, at 134.
51. *Id.* at 135 ("[I]s a new digester a result of the federal initiative, the dairy industry's commitment, the particular circumstances of a farm where converting methane may be profitable, or the impact of the offset protocol? And if the answer is murky, would not that be true of the validity of the offset?").
52. *Compliance Offset Program*, Cal. Air. Res. Bd., www.arb.ca.gov/cc/capandtrade/offsets/offsets.htm (last accessed April 22, 2019).
53. *Rice Cultivation Projects Compliance Offsets Protocol*, Environmental Defense Fund, www.edf.org/sites/default/files/one-pager_final.pdf (last accessed November 16, 2018).
54. *Manure Management*, Cal. Air Res. Bd., www.arb.ca.gov/ag/manuremgmt/manuremgmt.htm (last accessed August 12, 2018) (stating that two years in a row, livestock manure accounted for around 1 percent of California's emissions). Duke Nicholas Inst., *supra* note 35, at 6 (stating that rice cultivation only contributed to 1.8 percent of California's *agricultural* emissions).
55. *Id.*

56. Toensmeier, *supra* note 1, at 1.
57. *Carbon Farming*, Carbon Cycle Institute, www.carboncycle.org/carbon-farming/ (last accessed August 15, 2018).
58. *See* Toensmeier, *supra* note 1, at 30 (depicting a table of carbon farming techniques, their mitigation potential, and implementation readiness).
59. *See* Bernadett, *supra* note 21, at 216–17. *See also* ETAAC Final Report 6–12 (2008).
60. Brown, et al., *supra* note 14, at 2 of Appendix C: Agriculture Working Paper (2014).
61. *Id.* at 5 of Appendix C: Agriculture Working Paper.
62. Toensmeier, *supra* note 1, at 36.
63. *See* Bernadett, *supra* note 21, at 222.
64. *Id.*
65. Telephone Interview with Eric Toensmeier, author of The Carbon Farming Solution (August 8, 2018).
66. Toensmeier, *supra* note 1, at 325.
67. Telephone Interview with Eric Toensmeier, *supra* note 65.
68. *Commonly Used NCRS Tools-COMET Farm,* www.nrcs.usda.gov/wps/portal/nrcs/detail/national/programs/?cid=*stelprdb1261363* (last accessed November 16, 2018).
69. *COMET-Planner*, www.comet-planner.com/ (last accessed August 12, 2018).
70. *See* http://bfuels.nrel.colostate.edu/health/Home (last accessed November 16, 2018). *See also* Cal. Air Res. Bd., California 2030 Natural and Working Lands Climate Change Implementation Plan: Concept Paper 8 (May 2018).
71. *California Healthy Soils Initiative,* CDFA, www.cdfa.ca.gov/healthysoils/ (last accessed August 12, 2018).
72. Bernadett, *supra* note 21, at 225.
73. ETAAC Final Report 6-12 (2008). *See also id.* at 223.
74. Cal. Code Regs. Tit. 17 § § 38562(d)(3).
75. Duke Nicholas Inst., *supra* note 35, at 23–24.
76. Telephone Interview with Kelley Hamrick, Program Manager of Ecosystem Marketplace, Forest Trends (July 25, 2018).
77. Brian C. Murray and Lydia P. Olander, Mitigation Beyond the Cap: Addressing Impermanence Risk and Liability in Agriculture, Land Use Change, and Forest Carbon Projects 2 (2008).
78. *Id.* at 3.
79. Cal Fire, *Top 20 Largest California Wildfires,* www.fire.ca.gov/communications/downloads/fact_sheets/Top20_Acres.pdf (last accessed November 18, 2018).
80. Cal. Air Res. Bd., Compliance Offset Protocol U.S. Forest Projects 60 (2014).
81. *Id.*
82. *Id.*
83. *See* 26 U.S.C. § 170(h).
84. Cal. Air Res. Bd., *supra* note 70, at 12.
85. *Id.* at 16.
86. Adena R. Rissman, *Conservation Easements: New Perspectives in an Evolving World: Evaluating Conservation Effectiveness and Adaptation in Dynamic Landscapes,* 74 Law & Contemp. Prob. 145, 159–60 (2011).
87. *Id.* at 161.
88. *See* ETAAC Final Report 6–12 (2008).
89. *Id.* at 6–13.
90. *See* Hamrick, *supra* note 76.
91. *Carbon Competitiveness Incentive Regulation*, www.alberta.ca/carbon-competitiveness-incentive-regulation.aspx (last accessed August 12, 2018).
92. *Agricultural Carbon Offsets – An Introduction*, www1.agric.gov.ab.ca/$Department/deptdocs.nsf/all/cl16248 (last accessed August 12, 2018).
93. *Alberta's Farmers Cash in on 'Tillage Credits,'* The Globe and Mail, www.theglobeandmail.com/report-on-business/albertas-farmers-cash-in-on-tillage-credits/article555123/ (last accessed August 12, 2018).

94. *See id.*
95. *Carbon Credit Program Ain't What it Used to Be,* Alberta Farmer Express, www.albertafarmexpress.ca/2017/09/11/carbon-credit-program-aint-what-it-used-to-be/ (last accessed August 12, 2018).
96. *Id.*
97. *Carbon Offsets for Agricultural Practices – Frequently Asked Questions*, www1.agric.gov.ab.ca/$Department/deptdocs.nsf/all/cl14135 (last accessed November 16, 2018).
98. *Id.*
99. Email with Doug Cornell, Product Owner at Farmers Edge, an approved aggregator (November 13, 2018).
100. *January 2018 Offsets Update,* www1.agric.gov.ab.ca/$Department/deptdocs.nsf/all/cl11618/$FILE/All-Protocols-Update-Sheet-180129.pdf (last accessed November 16, 2018).
101. Email with Doug Cornell, Product Owner at Farmers Edge, an approved aggregator (November 13, 2018).
102. Author's calculations: $25 x 0.11 tonnes/acre = $2.75/acre x 0.6 =$1.65/acre Parkland. $25 x 0.06 tonnes/acre= $1.50/acre x 0.6= $0.90/acre Dry Prairie.
103. Email with Doug Cornell, Product Owner at Farmers Edge, an approved aggregator (November 13, 2018).
104. International Carbon Action Partnership, USA – California Cap-and-Trade Program, available at https://icapcarbonaction.com/en/?option=com_etsmap&task=export&format=pdf&layout=list&systems[]=45 (last accessed November 16, 2018).
105. Telephone Interview with Tim O'Connor, *supra* note 43 (noting that the recent rice protocol addition took around three years for ARB to develop).
106. Toensmeier, *supra* note 65; *See also* Negowetti, *supra* note 8, at 467 ("[F]arming systems that deliver significant health, social, and environmental benefits, such as building soil fertility and locking atmospheric carbon into the soil, usually pay higher costs to deliver these benefits.").
107. Mac Taylor, The 2018–19 Budget: California Spending Plan 55 (2018), available at https://lao.ca.gov/reports/2018/3870/spending-plan-2018.pdf (last accessed April 22, 2019).
108. California Climate & Agriculture Network, Sustainable Agricultural Lands Conservation Program, available at http://calclimateag.org/wp-content/uploads/2018/03/CSA-Fact-Sheet-2018-SALC-Final.pdf (2018) (last accessed April 22, 2019).
109. California Climate & Agriculture Network, *Livestock Methane,* http://calclimateag.org/solutions/livestockmethane (last accessed August 14, 2018).
110. *FARMER Program to help farmers upgrade equipment, reduce pollution,* ww2.arb.ca.gov/news/farmer-program-help-farmers-upgrade-equipment-reduce-pollution (last accessed November 18, 2018).
111. California Dept. of Food and Agriculture, *Healthy Soils Program,* www.cdfa.ca.gov/oefi/healthysoils/ (last accessed November 18, 2018).
112. California Climate & Agriculture Network, *Sustainable Agriculture Lands Conservation Program,* http://calclimateag.org/salcp/ (last accessed November 18, 2018).

PART III

Challenging Issues for Transport Taxes

9. External costs and environmental taxation: the role of transport sectors within the Italian economy

Andrea Molocchi*

1. INTRODUCTION

This chapter aims to verify the coherence of the Italian environmental tax framework with the polluters pays principle, as measured through the external environmental costs of different sectors, with a particular focus on transport; and to make recommendations for environmental tax reform within the context of the broader Italian fiscal system.

The chapter is organized in five sections. Section 2 describes the policy context, the aims of the chapter and the main definitions adopted. In section 3, an introductory analysis of environmental taxes (Eurostat definition) in Italy is conducted, with a particular focus on transport and vehicle taxes. Section 4 presents an estimation of the external costs generated by different sectors of activity based on official data and methods, such as Istat's account of air emissions by NACE[1] sector (National Accounting Matrix including Environmental Accounts (NAMEA)) and the newly released government guidelines for evaluating the external costs of public infrastructure.[2] The external costs of different NACE sectors are then compared with the levels of environmental taxes paid by those same sectors. This facilitates a consistency analysis with the polluter pays principle, focusing in particular on the three transport NACE sectors (land transport, which includes road and rail transport services; maritime transport; and aviation) and on the power sector, the environmental taxation of which is potentially linked to the issue of current taxation of electrified transport.

Section 5 discusses the boundaries and assumptions of this approach, and clarifies the need for further research. Section 6 proposes a cross-sectoral environmental taxation reform in Italy, with a particular focus on transport.

2. THE NATIONAL FISCAL POLICY CONTEXT

According to the latest available data from Eurostat (for 2016), fiscal pressure in Italy is at 42.9 per cent of gross domestic product (GDP) – that is, 7 per cent above the average EU level (40.0 per cent).[3] By taking into account the impact of the shadow economy on GDP, the Court of Public Accounts has highlighted that the real fiscal pressure on legal activities in Italy is much higher (53 per cent in 2015). Despite this context of high taxation, environmental taxes – which, according to Istat, accounted for only 8.2 per cent of fiscal revenues in 2016 – can play a larger role. An environmental fiscal reform could help the government to achieve three longstanding objectives: (1) easing taxes on labour, (2) reducing tax evasion, and (3) funding innovation-based industrial policies targeted at the realization of increasingly ambitious climate change mitigation goals. As will be shown in detail in the following sections, to achieve these objectives, the current environmental tax regime should be comprehensively reformed in accordance with the polluter pays principle, both by increasing the rates of existing environmental taxes and by identifying and removing 'hidden' tax exemptions and allowances for the most polluting activities.

In early 2014, a Government Delegation Act on taxation (Law 23/2014, 'Provisions for a fairer, transparent and growth-oriented tax system') attempted to enact, *inter alia*, a specific reform of environmental taxation, with the primary aims of reducing the tax burden on labour and boosting growth through investment in green technologies. In the one and a half years available for approval of the necessary Legislative Decrees, the Government enacted many Decrees, but it did not advance any regulation on environmental taxation. This was mainly because the Delegation Act issued by Parliament linked the national environmental taxation reform to approval of the European Commission proposal to reform Directive 2003/96/EC on energy taxation – a step which never took place. When Jean-Claude Juncker became president of the European Commission, he shelved the fuel tax harmonization reform in the EU.

In 2015 important international initiatives to enhance sustainable development – such as the United Nations (UN) Agenda 2030 and the Paris Agreement – were introduced. At a national level, an important Environmental Act (Law 221/2015) was also approved; this contains provisions to increase public action relating to sustainable development and the green economy, to promote a circular economy and to assess the environmental compatibility of current subsidy schemes through an annual Report to Parliament called the 'Catalogue of Environmentally Harmful and Environmentally Friendly Subsidies'. The first Catalogue was issued by the Ministry of Environment, Land and Sea in February 2017;[4] it examined about 130 existing subsidy schemes (both direct incentives and fiscal allowances) across all sectors of the economy and all main forms of taxation, with an overall financial cost to the State budget of about €41 billion a year, highlighting more than 50 environmentally harmful subsidy schemes with an overall value of €16.1 billion. The Catalogue has paved the way for a possible environmental fiscal reform, consistent with fair implementation of the polluter pays principle in the national taxation system, to progressively reduce scores of environmentally harmful subsidies that undermine the achievement of the environmental and financial targets of the Paris Agreement and the UN Agenda 2030.

2.1 Definitions and Boundaries of Analysis

Some preliminary clarifications and definitions are needed. The 'polluter pays principle' is a principle recognized in EU Treaties that is also used as a reference in environmental taxation.[5] In this chapter, an integral, yet simplified approach to the polluter pays principle is proposed, based on the calculation of 'standardized' environmental external costs and subsequent comparison with environmental taxes paid by sectors of activity. External costs are those damages generated by an economic or social activity that fall on third parties and on the environment, and that are not already covered by the same activity (eg, through insurance premiums, environmental taxes or compensation fees). Environmental external costs are those attributed to environmental impact factors due to a specific activity. They are usually calculated through the impact pathways approach – a model that links impact factors to the relevant environmental media and the latter to the final damage receptors. This model, widely developed in research projects such as ExternE,[6] estimates the final risks to ecosystems, human health and material assets due to specific impact factors relating to economic activities, and then aggregates the different risk types by means of the same unit of measurement (monetary base), representing willingness to pay to avoid a specific risk. Unlike the concept of damage, external costs by definition relate to the decision making inherent in an activity which bears its own 'internal' costs and generates the environmental impact factors (eg, gaseous emissions, liquid discharges, littering of waste, noise emissions) that result in the final damages.

In this chapter a pre-tax definition of environmental external costs is assumed (damages due to the activity), in order to allow for a comparison of external costs with environmental taxes.

3. ENVIRONMENTAL TAXES IN ITALY

This section describes the environmental tax regime in Italy, to facilitate an understanding of the data on the total amount of taxes paid by different sectors, which will be presented in the next section. Istat – the National Statistical Institute – monitors environmental tax revenues in Italy by applying the definition provided by Eurostat: environmental taxes are 'compulsory payments to the government, where the benefits provided to the taxpayer are not directly linked to the payment' and where 'the tax base is a physical unit (or a *proxy* of it) of something that has a proven, specific negative impact on the environment'.[7] Under this EU-agreed definition, the purpose stated by the tax legislature is not necessarily relevant, while the tax base is of primary importance. Moreover, environmental taxes include a wide range of pricing mechanisms, such as excise duties on energy products, emissions trading, system charges in energy bills, vehicle taxes, charges with specific purposes and other taxes without any stated purpose, but with a tax base that impacts on the environment.

Istat classifies environmental taxes in the following categories: energy taxes, transport taxes, pollution taxes and resource taxes. In Italy, pollution and resource taxes – both of which have environmental aims and relate to a base that has a negative environmental impact – account only for about 1 per cent of environmental tax revenues. Energy taxes account for the majority of environmental tax revenues, at 81 per cent, followed by transport taxes, at about 18 per cent.[8] Energy taxes include excise duties on fossil fuels, which totalled about €30 billion in 2016 (51 per cent); excise duty and system charges for electricity consumption (the latter are used to finance renewable energy plants and have been increasing over the past decade), which totalled about €17 billion (29 per cent); and revenues from the Emissions Trading System (ETS) (auctions of emission permits), which totalled about €411 million (0.7 per cent). Vehicle taxes amounted to about €10.5 billion in 2016, while vehicle registration fees amounted to €1.8 billion (3.1 per cent); a greater contribution was made by circulation taxes (€6.6 billion in 2016, or 11.3 per cent of environmental tax revenue), which are specifically regulated by regions under a detailed scheme that considers both engine power and emissions standards (Euro classes).

While, under certain conditions, taxes on fuels and vehicles can be considered as instruments to implement the polluter pays principle, excise duty and system charges for electricity consumption cannot be considered optimal methods of implementing this principle, as the final consumer cannot do anything to influence the way that electricity is produced:[9] he or she can only reduce consumption, even if a share of this is produced from renewable sources. The high environmental taxes imposed on electricity consumption – which totalled €17 billion in 2016, corresponding to an average tax rate of about 5.7 eurocents per kilowatt hour consumed, or one-third of the average final average price of electricity in Italy[10] – represent a major obstacle to the diffusion of electric vehicles and to achieving the expected emissions reductions in the transport sector.[11] This is an area where an environmental fiscal reform could intervene, rebalancing taxes on electricity consumption through increasing other environmental taxes, inspired by a cost-effective implementation of the polluter pays principle (coverage of marginal external costs).

The phase-out of environmentally harmful subsidies benefiting the transport sector is an additional area for policy intervention. The Catalogue of Environmentally Harmful and Environmentally Friendly Subsidies, produced by the Italian Ministry of Environment, Land and Sea,[12] provides a detailed picture of subsidies in the Italian transport sector. Maritime and air transport are totally exempt from fuel excise duties, with a respective tax revenue loss of €457 million and €1551 million in 2016. Road transport freight services benefit from a 34.7 per cent tax discount on diesel fuel excise duty, with an overall tax revenue loss of about €1296 million.[13]

4. THE POLLUTER PAYS COMPARISON: ENVIRONMENTAL TAXES PAID BY SECTORS AS COMPARED WITH EXTERNAL COSTS GENERATED

In this section, the external costs estimated for NACE sectors and households are compared with the environmental taxes paid by those same sectors, to verify the consistency of the polluter pays principle.

External costs are estimated for greenhouse gases, major air pollutants, heavy metals and noise in relation to available environmental accounts, which follow the same principles and sector classification as the National Economic Accounts (so-called 'satellite accounts' of the System of Economic-Environmental Accounting). These external costs can thus be compared with economic accounts produced by Istat, such as those on environmental taxes paid by different economic sectors.

4.1 External Costs Methodology

For the purpose of estimating environmental external costs, this chapter applies the relevant section of the Italian Guidelines for the Evaluation of Investments in Public Infrastructure (MIT, 2017, see note 2), approved by the Italian Government Committee for Economic Planning and released in June 2017. This section of the Guidelines is based on international and European studies that have used the impact pathways approach to estimate the external costs associated with different environmental impact factors (eg, air emissions) due to economic and social activities – particularly those studies and handbooks aimed at providing standardized and recommended damage values to be used in cost-benefit analysis (eg, Ricardo – AEA (2014);[14] Exiopol (2010);[15] and NEEDS (2008)).[16]

The starting point is to model environmental impact factors relating to the activities under analysis. This data set is provided for different sectors of economic activity (production perspective) and for three types of household activities (consumption perspective) in the NAMEA – an account produced by Istat in cooperation with the Italian National Agency for Environmental Protection that calculates the annual quantities of different types of air emissions across all sectors of economic activity (NACE rev 2, disaggregation level of 64 branches), and for households (transport, heating, other) following the residence principle. This allows emissions data to be fully integrated with basic economic data in the National Accounts (eg, value added, production, jobs).

For each sector, the NAMEA aggregates data on emissions from characteristic production processes, from secondary activities and from ancillary activities, such as in-house heating and transport. The NAMEA covers the following emission types:

- seven greenhouse gases (carbon dioxide (CO_2), nitrous oxide, methane, hydrofluorocarbons, perfluorocarbon, sulphur hexafluoride and nitrogen trifluoride);
- seven main air pollutants (sulphur oxides, nitrogen oxides (NO_x), non-methane volatile organic compounds, carbon monoxide, ammonia, fine particles and coarse particles); and
- nine heavy metals (cadmium, arsenic, nickel, lead, mercury, chromium, copper, selenium and zinc).

As regards impact pathways of air emissions and monetary evaluation, this chapter refers to the recommended approaches and values in the climate change and air pollution sections of the Guidelines.[17] These sections of the Guidelines rely on a wider, EU-harmonized approach, as set out in the European Commission Handbook on external costs of transport.[18] The exercise conducted in this chapter may thus serve as a national test for the possible subsequent extension of the suggested approach to all EU Member States.

4.2 External Costs Results

The latest available data for estimating the external costs relating to emissions in different sectors of activity in Italy is from 2015. The estimate also includes the external costs of noise from different transport modes (road, rail, aviation), by allocating noise results for Italy calculated by CE Delft (2011).[19] The total estimated external costs due to air emissions and noise produced across the 64 sectors of economic activity and households slightly exceed €79 billion at 2015 prices.[20] As regards the distribution of these costs between impact factors, CO_2 emissions account for 45 per cent, followed by fine particles at 20 per cent, NO_x at 11 per cent, ammonia at 7 per cent, methane (the second biggest contributor to human-induced climate change) at 6 per cent, sulphur oxides at 3 per cent and transport noise at 2 per cent.

The estimated external costs are mainly due to economic sectors (€52.5 billion, corresponding to 66.4 per cent of the total), while household activities account for €26.5 billion (33.6 per cent). In a further breakdown between the main economic sectors (agriculture, industry and services) and the three household consumption types (transport, heating and other activities), industry ranks first (€28.9 billion of external costs, accounting for 67 per cent of CO_2 emissions); household heating ranks second (€17.3 billion);[21] services rank third (€12.9 billion); agriculture ranks fourth (€10.7 billion);[22] and household transport ranks fifth (€9 billion).[23]

4.3 The Comparison with Environmental Taxes

The polluter pays comparison is made possible by an additional account on environmental taxes elaborated by Istat,[24] which separates the environmental tax revenues paid by residents (both economic activities and households) from those paid by non-residents, and then details the environmental taxes paid by each sector with the same level of disaggregation as in the NAMEA account of emissions (64 NACE sectors).[25] The reference year for the comparison is 2015, since external costs have been estimated based on environmental impact factors from that year. The comparison can be made at different levels of disaggregation.

Figure 9.1 shows the results at a macro level (first level of disaggregation). Strong inconsistencies are evident in agriculture and industry, while the service sector pays close to the optimal level. Household is the only sector that seems to pay more than its external costs. The aggregated net gap that stems from these sectoral differences amounts to about €25 billion at the national level.

Very strong inconsistencies are confirmed at the highest disaggregation level of 64 sectors (see Figure 9.2). At least four sectors pay very little in

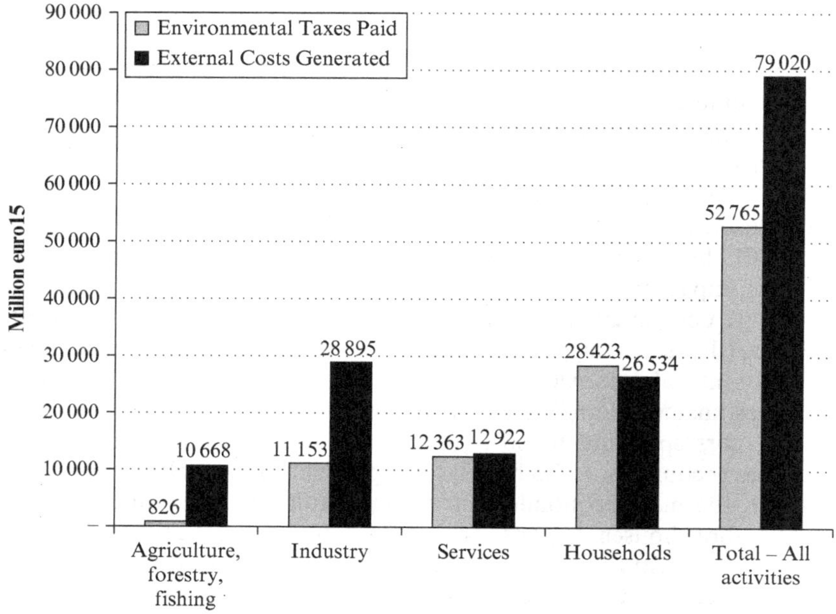

Source: Istat for environmental tax revenues; author for external costs estimate (MIT 2017, see note 2, for unitary external costs reference values).

Figure 9.1 Comparison between environmental taxes paid and external costs generated by economic sectors and households (first level of disaggregation), Italy, € million, 2015

comparison to the external costs they generate: maritime transport (0.7 per cent);[26] air transport (5.4 per cent); agriculture and farming (7.5 per cent); and power and gas (9.9 per cent). Land transport covers 64 per cent of its external costs.[27] Many manufacturing branches do not cover their external costs, particularly coke and refining (12 per cent); glass, ceramic, cement and other mineral products (23 per cent); metallurgy (30 per cent); paper (31 per cent); pharmaceutics (40 per cent); chemical products (48 per cent); and food, beverages and tobacco (67 per cent).[28]

5. DISCUSSION

Before drawing conclusions in the following section, we must address the assumptions and limitations of this analysis. First, not all main

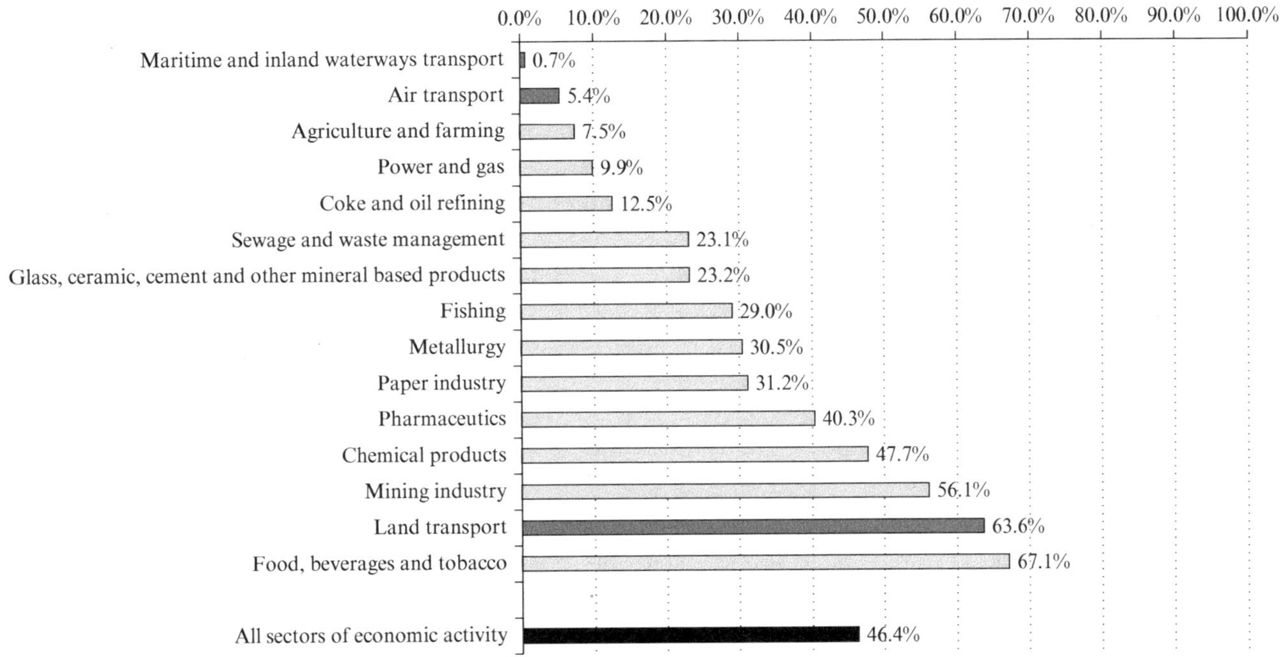

Note: The 64 available branches have been ordered by increasing value of the indicator. Due to space constraints, only the first 15 branches not covering external costs are shown. Transport sectors are highlighted in dark grey. The national economy average (black bar) is provided as a benchmark.

Source: Istat for environmental tax revenues; author for external costs estimate (MIT 2017, see note 2, for unitary external costs reference values).

Figure 9.2 Environmental tax revenues as percentage of external costs, by economic sector (maximum disaggregation level), Italy, 2015

environmental external costs of economic activities have been quantified. The impact pathway methodology should be further developed to assess external cost categories relating to probably significant impact factors, such as land consumption due to increased urbanization (new transport infrastructure, parking areas and expansion of residential or commercial areas). Second, some major non-environmental external cost categories relating to transport activities – such as road accident costs and traffic congestion – were excluded from the calculation due to lack of data or difficulties in integrating available local data into the adopted macro scale model. This has resulted in an underestimation of external costs relating mainly to the NACE sectors 'land transport services' and 'household transport'. Moreover, the inventory of environmental taxes monitored by Istat should be expanded to include local or specific environmental tax revenues (eg, pesticides tax, city centre access or congestion charges, regional taxes on extraction of raw materials), as pointed out by the last European Environment Agency Report on environmental taxes.[29] However, the main assumption underpinning the comparison relates to the old national practice of earmarking revenues from transport fuel excise duties for specific non-environmental purposes (to finance emergency costs of natural disasters such as earthquakes, international peace-keeping missions and public finance emergencies). When assessing implementation of the polluter pays principle through environmental taxation, in order to allow for a fair comparison, these costs should be subtracted from state environmental tax revenues, as in such cases taxation follows a specific cost coverage principle that is additional to the polluter pays principle. At present, the lack of official data on revenues relating to the earmarking of environmental taxes for non-environmental purposes prevents such a calculation from being made. The choice in this chapter to consider 100 per cent of environmental tax revenues as the amount that polluters pay as compensation for their environmental damages should be considered a cautious assumption.

6. CONCLUSIONS: TOWARDS AN ENVIRONMENTAL TAXATION REFORM

Environmental taxes in Italy should be revised within the broader framework of a comprehensive tax reform aimed at reducing taxes on labour while fulfilling public budget constraints. According to the European Commission report on taxation trends in the EU, Italy has the highest implicit tax rate on labour[30] of all EU Member States, at 42.6 per cent – seven percentage points higher than the EU average. An environmental tax reform would afford a great opportunity for Italy to reduce the taxes on labour.

The model adopted in this chapter facilitates an assessment of the potential revenues that could be raised through an environmental tax reform aimed at covering the external costs of economic activities and providing general guidelines for achieving economy-wide consistency with the polluter pays principle. The recommended reform would aim to:

- abolish current direct subsidies or tax expenditures (exemptions or allowances) benefiting sectors that do not cover their environmental external costs through tax (ie, the polluter should not be paid); and
- gradually increasing the ordinary rates of environmental taxes to a level that covers the sector's external costs (ie, the polluter should pay).

Focusing on the NACE transport sectors (ie, aviation, maritime transport, land transport), the adopted model has shown that all three do not cover their external costs. In aviation and maritime transport, the main options for an environmental tax reform consistent with the polluter pays principle are: (1) abolishing the exemption on fuel excise duties by gradually increasing fuel excise rates, starting with domestic flights and national cabotage; (2) implementing a globally extended ETS (agreed in 2016 by the International Civil Aviation Organization for aviation, with an initial pilot phase starting from 2021, but not yet agreed for maritime transport); and (3) increasing vehicle taxes (eg, aircraft landing tax, ship anchorage tax) by applying differentiated rates based on the environmental and energy performance of aircraft and vessels. More specific recommendations for Italy should emerge from a feasibility analysis taking into account international and EU legislation.[31]

With regard to land transport, the environmental external costs estimate provided in section 4 shows that there is room to proceed in the coming years with the gradual abolition of the reduced rate of excise duty applied to diesel fuel for road freight and passenger services, as commenced in the Financial Stability Law 2015 (Euro 0 and older vehicles) and confirmed in the Financial Stability Law 2016 (Euro 1 and Euro 2 vehicles). The increasing availability of competitive alternative fuels for freight transport such as compressed natural gas and liquefied natural gas – the distribution infrastructure for which is promoted by Legislative Decree 256/2016, transposing Directive 2014/94/EU – has made the abolition of this environmentally harmful subsidy a real opportunity.

With regard to non-transport sectors of economic activity, significant potential would appear to be afforded by a tax reform inspired by the polluter pays principle in the NACE gas and power sector. This is because the environmental taxes paid in this sector are less than €1 billion,[32] while the sector's external costs bill is ten times higher, at €10 billion. Such intervention is complicated by the fact that in Italy, the two environmental taxes paid through electricity consumption (excise duty on electricity and system charges for renewable sources) amounted to €17 billion in 2016 (€15.2 billion in 2015). These two 'user-oriented' environmental taxes together amount to 31 per cent of the final average electricity price, increasing to 36.5 per cent when value added tax (VAT) revenue on these taxes is included.[33] As noted in section 3, these taxes are not consistent with optimal implementation of the polluter pays principle and are hindering the diffusion of energy-efficient innovations such as electric vehicles (eg, battery cars; electric buses and trams; electric trains for urban, suburban and high-speed inter-urban use)[34] and electric heat pumps.[35] To tackle this issue, it is suggested that an exemption from both electricity excise duty and system charges be introduced in favour of so-called 'dedicated uses of electricity' that require an additional monitoring system for specific consumption types (eg, electric car recharging). The financial cost of this environmentally favourable subsidy could be recovered through the revenues from the proposed fiscal reform aimed at covering each sector's external costs – that is, through the €9 billion in tax revenues that may potentially be obtained in the power sector from (1) the expected increase in ETS prices driven by EU policy by 2030 and (2) increases in both the excise duty rates for fossil fuel generation and the tax rates for sulphur dioxide and nitrogen oxide power plant emissions.[36] According to this proposal, vehicle charging would benefit from a tax reduction of about one-third of the final electricity price. The fiscal barrier that is currently hindering electric mobility in Italy could thus be overcome within the broader framework of an environmental tax reform.

To sum up, even if there are good reasons to look beyond environmental external costs in determining environmental taxation levels and structures, it is clear that the polluter pays principle can play an important role in reducing the tax pressure on labour and increasing alternative revenues from the taxation of polluting activities. The proposed reform aims to promote robust green growth, with a reduction in labour cost and a consistent environmental tax framework boosting green innovation with a view towards achieving ambitious environmental goals.

The polluter pays principle is a powerful instrument for tackling environmental issues through taxation, beginning with existing taxes on energy and transport and then gradually expanding this approach to encompass the taxation of specific pollutants and natural resources. Measuring external costs can provide valuable information for reforming existing environmental taxes, phasing out environmentally harmful subsidies and introducing calibrated environmentally friendly subsidies to support the adoption of high-efficiency innovations.

NOTES

* The views expressed in this chapter are of those of the author and should not be attributed to the Ministry of Environment, Land and Sea, Sogesid or any other organization with which he cooperates.

1. NACE (*Nomenclature générale des Activités économiques dans les Communautés Européennes*) is the classification of economic activities established for use within the EU. The last revision (rev 2) is defined in Regulation 1893/2006 of the European Parliament and the Council of 20 December 2006.
2. MIT (2017): *Guidelines for the Evaluation of Investments in Public Infrastructures*, Italian Ministry for Infrastructure and Transport, June 2017; www.mit.gov.it/node/5272, last accessed 10 December 2018.
3. http://appsso.eurostat.ec.europa.eu/nui/submitViewTableAction.do, last accessed 25 October 2018.
4. MOELS (2017): *Ministero dell'Ambiente, della Tutela del Territorio e del Mare, Direzione generale per lo sviluppo sostenibile (SVI) – Unità di Assistenza Tecnica Sogesid S.p.A., Catalogo dei sussidi ambientalmente favorevoli e ambientalmente dannosi*, December 2016; www.minambiente.it/pagina/catalogo-dei-sussidi-ambientalmente-dannosi-e-dei-sussidi-ambientalmente-favorevoli, last accessed 10 December 2018.
5. An overview of EU policy areas in which the polluter pays principle is implemented is provided in Molocchi A, *Chi inquina, paga? Tasse ambientali e sussidi dannosi per l'ambiente. Ipotesi di riforma alla luce dei costi esterni delle attività economiche in Italia. Ufficio di Valutazione d'Impatto del Senato della Repubblica, documento di valutazione* n. 6, December 2017, www.senato.it/4746?dossier=2295, last accessed 28 October 2018.
6. ExternE (1995): European Commission DGXII, *Externalities of Energy, vol 1–6*, EUR 16520–16525, Brussels. ExternE (1999): European Commission DGXII, *Externalities of Energy, vol 7–10*, EUR 19083–18836–18887–18528, Brussels, 1999. ExternE (2005): Bickel P, Friedrich R, *Externalities of Energy, Methodology update*, 2005; www.externe.info/externe_d7/?q=node/30, last accessed 18 November 2018.
7. Eurostat (2013), *Environmental taxes – A statistical guide*, European Union, Luxembourg, Publication Office of the European Union; http://ec.europa.eu/eurostat/documents/3859598/5936129/KS-GQ-13-005-EN.PDF, last accessed 10 December 2018.
8. Istat, *Revenues of environmental taxation,* edition November 2017, http://dati.istat.it/Index.aspx?QueryId=10998.3, last accessed 25 October 2018.
9. The excise duty and system charges levied on electricity consumption mean that the users pays, rather than the polluter. The polluter pays principle assumes that the best way to tax is where and when pollution is generated, in order to stimulate prevention through individual behaviour change or, at corporate level, through changes in management systems (eg, investment in environmental mitigation, organizational changes, supply chain changes).
10. €18.3 per kilowatt hour. See RSE, *Anatomia dei costi in Bolletta*, updated edition 2016, *Alkes edizioni*, Milano, Table 4.22.
11. The net energy and emissions savings generated by electric cars are linked to country-specific conditions, which are satisfied in the case of Italy but may not necessarily be satisfied in other countries. By considering factors such as the Italian energy mix, power plant energy efficiency, transmission losses and car battery recharging losses, Molocchi (2012) estimated a 38 per cent primary energy saving gained from energy consumption of electric cars per kilometre as compared to the declared average fuel consumption per

kilometre of new conventional cars sold in Italy. Even higher savings are estimated for CO_2 emissions, due to the prevailing contribution of natural gas and the increasing contribution of renewable energy sources to the national energy mix (respectively at 45 per cent and 35 per cent of gross production in 2016). See Molocchi A (2012), *Introductory presentation to the AREL Workshop "L'auto elettrica"* – 9 May 2012, in Seminari AREL, *Osservatorio Energia e Ambiente*, 2/2012; www.arel.it/ricerche/osservatorio-energia-e-ambiente/lauto-elettrica-9-maggio-2012, last accessed 27 October 2018.
12. MOELS (2017); see note 4.
13. A diesel excise duty discount was introduced for freight and passenger transport services under DPR 277/2000, as modified by art 6, paragraph 2 of Legislative Decree 26/2007 and art 61, paragraph 4 of Decree Law 1 of 24 January 2012. The Stability Law for 2015 (art 1, paragraph 233 of Law 190/2014) excluded from the subsidy those diesel vehicles with Euro 0 emission standard or lower. The Stability Law for 2016 (art 1, paragraph 645 of Law 208/2015) further restricted the scope of application of this discount by excluding Euro 2 or lower emission standard diesel vehicles from 1 January 2016. The current reduced rate is €403.16 per 1000 litres (ordinary rate €617.40 per 1000 litres).
14. Ricardo – AEA (2014), *Update of the Handbook on External Costs of Transport*, Report for the European Commission – DG MOVE, 8 January 2014; https://ec.europa.eu/transport/sites/transport/files/themes/sustainable/studies/doc/2014-handbook-external-costs-transport.pdf, last accessed 27 October 2018.
15. Exiopol (2010): Müller W, Preiss P, Klotz V and Friedrich R, *External Cost Values for EE SUT Framework, Final report providing external cost values to be applied in an EE SUT framework*, Exiopol DIII.1.b-2, IER University Stuttgart, March 2010; www.feem-project.net/exiopol/index.php, last accessed 27 October 2018.
16. NEEDS (2008): Preiss P, Friedrich R and Klotz V, *Report on the procedure and data to generate averaged/aggregated data*, Deliverable n1.1 – RS 3a, NEEDS project, 6th FRP; www.needs-project.org/2009/Deliverables/RS3a%20D1.1.zip, last accessed 27 October 2018.
17. The methodological framework adopted for this chapter is methodologically consistent, but differs in the reference marginal damage values for emissions adopted by the author in previous exercises aimed at estimating external costs of air emissions in Italy for sectors of economic activity (Molocchi 2014b, 2017). There are three reasons for this: (1) the Italian Guidelines recommend a higher range of CO_2 values, with a central value of €90 2010/t (originally taken from Kuik, O, Brander, L and Tol, RS, 2009, 'Marginal abatement costs of greenhouse gas emissions: A meta-analysis', *Energy Policy*, vol 37, no 4, pp1395–1403); (2) in the Italian Guidelines, only two stack height classes are considered for damages associated with major air pollutants (sulphur dioxide, NO_x, ammonia, non-methane volatile organic compounds and particulate matter), instead of the three classes proposed in Exiopol (2010) and adopted in the author's previous works; and (3) in the Italian Guidelines, damage values for particulate matter are differentiated for three classes of exposed population (urban, suburban, rural), instead of the two classes proposed by Exiopol (2010). Molocchi A (2017), *Polluters make others pay. A Sector based Assessment of external costs for a tax reform in Italy*. Paper presented at GCET 17, 22–23 September 2016, Groningen. *Nuova Energia, bimestrale dello sviluppo sostenibile*, n 1 (part I) and n 2 (part II), 2017; www.nuova-energia.com/index.php?option=com_content&task=view&id=5274&Itemid=146, last accessed 28 October 2018; Molocchi A, Aspromonte D (2014b), *Così può cambiare la fiscalità ambientale. Verso un sistema più equo, trasparente e orientato allo sviluppo sostenibile. Nuova Energia, bimestrale dello sviluppo sostenibile*, n 2, 2014; www.nuova-energia.com/index.php?option=com_content&task=view&id=4084&Itemid=141, last accessed 28 October 2018.
18. Ricardo – AEA (2014), see note 14.
19. CE Delft, Infras and Fraunhofer ISI (2011), *External Costs of Transport in Europe. Update study for 2008*. Delft CE Delft November 2011; www.CE_Delft_4215_External_Costs_of_Transport_in_Europe_def-1.pdf, last accessed 20 October 2018.
20. This amount corresponds to about 4.8 per cent of the same year's GDP at market prices.

21. As to the external costs of household heating, 66 per cent are due to fine particle emissions. Fine particle emissions from this source increased from 78 096 tonnes in 2011 to 108 140 tonnes in 2015 (a 38 per cent increase), due to the diffusion of biomass heating appliances (pellets and wood). This side effect of climate and energy policies is clearly highlighted by the external costs valuation approach.
22. The high external costs estimated for agriculture are mainly due to the effects of non-combustion emissions from animal farms and fertilizers. In particular, 52 per cent of all agriculture external costs are due to ammonia emissions generated by the use of nitrogen fertilizers and by the diffused practice of open-air storage of livestock manure (agriculture released about 378 000 tons of methane in 2015 – 98 per cent of the national total).
23. As to household transport external costs, 56 per cent are due to CO_2 emissions, 19 per cent to NO_x emissions and 11 per cent to fine particle emissions. The latter are steadily declining (a 26 reduction between 2011–15) as a result of car fleet renovation and are now relatively low (9019 tonnes in 2015) as compared to household heating.
24. Istat (2017), *Environmental tax revenue*, Istat Datawarehouse, November 2017 edition; http://dati.istat.it/Index.aspx?DataSetCode=DCCN_IMPAMB1, last accessed 28 October 2018.
25. Unfortunately, Istat's account of environmental taxes paid by different sectors does not include a differentiated account of taxes paid by households for the three NAMEA household categories (ie, transport, heating and other household activities). This limits the polluter pays comparison to the whole household category, without further disaggregation.
26. For maritime transport and fishing, marginal damage unitary values for air pollutant emissions in sea areas have been applied, as recommended in Ricardo – AEA (2014), see note 14. These values have been calculated for emissions in the Mediterranean Sea area by NEEDS (2008), see note 16.
27. Even assuming the abolition of the current subsidy (the diesel excise duty discount), the sector's revenue would remain lower than its external costs.
28. Since the environmental taxes paid by nine of the 19 manufacturing branches are more than their external costs (indicator >100 per cent), this means that these branches are subsidizing the other ten manufacturing branches for their non-covered external costs (only the first seven manufacturing branches are depicted in Figure 9.2).
29. EEA – European Environmental Agency (2016), *Environmental Taxation and EU environmental policies*, EEA Report 17/2016; www.eea.europa.eu/publications/environmental-taxation-and-eu-environmental-policies/download, last accessed 25 October 2018.
30. European Commission, Directorate General of Taxation, Taxation Trends Report 2018. The implicit tax rate on labour is given by the sum of personal income tax, employee social security contributions and the employer's social security contributions and other payroll taxes; https://ec.europa.eu/taxation_customs/business/economic-analysis-taxation/taxation-trends-eu-union_en, last accessed 28 July 2018.
31. Specific recommendations – such as the amount of a certain excise rate increase or the features of a pollutant differentiated port tax – are beyond the scope of this chapter and require further research and specific modelling.
32. Molocchi, Recchini and Tudini (2018) estimated that 30 per cent (about €300 million) of the sector's environmental tax payments relate to the ETS and current excise duties on fuels used for electricity generation; the remaining 70 per cent are due to other forms of environmental taxes, such as the excise duty on electricity consumption by offices and excise duties paid for transport (eg, company cars, in-house freight transport). See Molocchi A, Recchini E and Tudini A, *Polluter Pays Principle implementation in the Italian electricity sector. A comparison of environmental taxes with the air emissions external costs of thermal power plants*. Presentation for the Sixth IAERE Annual Conference, 15–16 February 2018, University of Turin; www.iaere.org/conferences/2018/02presentations.html, last accessed 20 October 2018.
33. VAT is also calculated on excise duties and system charges. RSE (2014) estimates an

average implicit rate of 17.6 per cent for VAT paid on electricity bills by all consumer types (this implicit rate falls between the 22 per cent ordinary rate and the preferential 10 per cent rate applicable to domestic users and to agriculture and certain manufacturing sectors). RSE, *Anatomia dei costi in Bolletta, Alkes edizioni*, 2014.

34. Molocchi A (2010), 'Electric cars or high-efficiency transport networks?', *Economics and Policy of Energy and the Environment* LIII(1):2010, DOI: 10.3280/EFE2010-001002; www.francoangeli.it/riviste/sommario.asp?anno=2010&idRivista=10, last accessed 15 December 2018.
35. Molocchi A, Aspromonte D (2014a), '*Pompe di calore elettriche a vantaggio dell'ambiente*', *Nuova Energia, bimestrale dello sviluppo sostenibile*, n 1, 2014; www.nuova-energia.com/index.php?option=com_content&task=view&id=3943&Itemid=141, last accessed 28 October 2018.
36. ETS, fuel excise duties and emission taxes are paid by fossil fuel-based plants (and not by renewable plants): producers would eventually transfer the increase to the price of energy sold on the electricity wholesale market, increasing the sale price and profits for renewables. The government could at least partially neutralize the expected increase in the final electricity price through a corresponding reduction in the electricity excise duty and system charges. Details of this proposal are described in Molocchi, Recchini, Tudini (2018), note 34.

10. An environmental take on Australia's traffic congestion 'crisis': using road pricing to achieve sustainable transport

Vanessa Johnston

1. INTRODUCTION

Road transport plays a vital role in Australia, where the economy relies on moving people and goods both within sprawling cities and across a vast continent, and where cultural and social identity is characterized by ownership and use of private vehicles. Unsurprisingly, road transport makes a substantial contribution to Australia's annual greenhouse gas emissions, which not only continues to grow, but is resistant to change. In particular, the transport task is becoming more difficult in major cities due to road congestion, overcrowding and a lack of alternatives for domestic, commercial and freight transport.

It is becoming clear that transport behaviour in Australia is unsustainable, evidenced most acutely by the current traffic congestion 'crisis' in major Australian cities. While a range of factors contributes to 'unacceptable' levels of congestion,[1] recent data on travel in Australia indicates that congestion is unacceptable based on two crucial factors: increased duration and variability of travel time.[2] Moreover, the estimated cost of traffic congestion is high, reaching A$10.2 billion in Melbourne and A$12 billion in Greater Sydney annually by 2030.[3] Accordingly, while the value of reducing congestion varies by both location and time of day,[4] reducing congestion will benefit not only transport users, but Australia's entire economy.[5]

From traditional engineering and economic perspectives, congestion is respectively caused by inadequate road infrastructure[6] and by the lack of clear pricing signals about road infrastructure use.[7] A complex range of policies and laws governs the way that users access and pay for transport services (including infrastructure) in Australia. While policies and laws relating to road transport activities are the most relevant to traffic congestion, congestion is a challenge for all land-based transport modes, including public transport (train, tram, bus) and active transport (cycling, walking). In the states most acutely affected by congestion – Victoria and New South Wales – laws already impose charges designed to address congestion in specific areas, as well as fixed and time-of-day tolls on specific roads, to manage congestion at peak times.[8] Recent government and industry reviews on traffic congestion recommend that congestion be managed in the short term by expanding existing congestion levies within inner-city parking charges.[9] In the long term, reviews recommend the development of an 'integrated system-wide road pricing scheme' to ensure that users pay appropriately to access and use roads,[10] although little detail is given about the form that such scheme might take. While additional infrastructure and specific congestion charges may reduce specific instances of congestion, these initiatives do not address the underlying causes, which is necessary to manage congestion in the long term. Long-term solutions should address the importance and reliance that Australians place on private vehicle transport, including the regulatory framework that sustains such position.

Consequently, creating a sustainable, low-carbon transport system in Australia that alleviates the current congestion crisis requires a paradigm shift: a new perspective that can intervene in the self-reinforcing relationship between existing transport regulations and private vehicle/transport demand. Considering congestion from an environmental perspective provides fundamental support to re-examine existing transport laws and regulations, and to support the development of a road pricing scheme that addresses traffic congestion as a matter of sustainability.

This chapter examines the connection between congestion and sustainable development in Australia. If congestion can be framed as a matter of sustainability, then environmental taxation literature can arguably be applied to guide reforms of existing laws and regulations to improve the sustainability of Australia's road transport system and manage congestion in the long term.

2. WHY IS CONGESTION A MATTER OF SUSTAINABILITY?

In addition to being an infrastructure or economic problem, traffic congestion is a problem of sustainability – or more accurately, lack thereof. From an environmental perspective, congestion is encouraged by social, cultural and political conditions that create and sustain demand and preference for private vehicle transport. According to a historical analysis of state and territory transport policies by Curtis and Low, Australia's current approach to road transport is based on engineering and economic 'storylines' to 'predict and provide' for the future with the most efficient allocation of resources. These storylines have created 'path dependence'[11] towards motor vehicles and against public and active transport modes.[12] Explained in these terms, it is unsurprising that the current legal framework in Australia's transport sector fails to account for the social and environmental costs of road transport, facilitating the existing patterns of unsustainable transport. Conversely, these same unsustainable transport patterns and reliance on motor vehicles encourage resistance towards regulatory measures that address underlying vehicle demand.[13] Creating a low-carbon transport system in Australia requires these issues to be addressed. Without limitation, the resulting traffic congestion has adverse practical implications for the liveability of Australian cities and for greenhouse gas emissions which contribute to climate change. Liveability of cities and climate change are important indicators of sustainable development.

The concept of sustainability and sustainable development was first articulated in the 1983 Brundtland Report, in relation to regulating international environmental and economic issues, as development 'that meets the needs of the present without compromising the ability of future generations to meet their own needs'.[14] While it has been discussed in various contexts since then, sustainability is the foundation for the current global framework for international cooperation: the United Nations' 2030 Agenda for Sustainable Development, an action plan for people, the planet and prosperity intended to strengthen universal peace and eradicate poverty.[15] The lofty objectives of this Agenda will be achieved through State Parties meeting 17 Sustainable Development Goals (SDGs) relating to different aspects of sustainable development.[16] As a State Party to the Agenda, Australia is obliged to participate in achieving SDGs at an international level.[17] While there is no specific goal for 'sustainable transport', transport is a vital component of SDG 11 on creating sustainable cities and SDG 13 on mitigating climate change. However, according to the latest SDG Global Index Report on international progress towards achieving the SDGs, Australia is ranked 35th out of 156 states in relation to these goals, with 'insufficient' performance on transport matters under SDG 11 and 'highly insufficient' performance across all aspects of SDG 13.[18] Consequently, national efforts to address congestion by improving the sustainability of Australia's transport system not only benefit Australia at a domestic level, but also enable Australia to fulfil its international commitments to contribute to global sustainable development.

Pursuant to SDG 11, State Parties should 'provide access to safe, affordable, accessible and sustainable transport systems for all' in striving to create sustainable cities and communities.[19] While private road transport will remain a necessary part of Australia's transport system in some capacity, SDG 11 demands that State Party governments and local authorities collaborate to find solutions to future mobility needs that minimize environmental impact while making transportation safer and more affordable for all.[20] According to Curtis and Low, sustainable transport in reference to cities must be interpreted broadly and can be achieved when mobility is integrated with the wider human purposes of the city itself.[21]

State Parties are also encouraged to take urgent action to combat climate change under SDG 13,[22] which includes action to reduce greenhouse gas emissions from road transport activities.[23] More specifically, since the adoption of the Paris Agreement on climate change in 2015, State Parties will be required to mitigate emissions from road transport activities in order to satisfy 'nationally determined contributions' to mitigate greenhouse gas emissions by 2030.[24] Under the Paris Agreement, Australia has committed to reduce national greenhouse gas emissions by 26–28 per cent below 2005 levels by 2030.[25]

The Paris Process on Mobility and Climate (PPMC) is designed to support States in transitioning towards low-carbon transport as part of achieving their 'nationally determined contributions' under the Paris Agreement.[26] The PPMC's Global Macro Roadmap encourages the reduction of greenhouse gas emissions at a national level, while providing greater access and mobility in and around large cities, according to three key pillars of 'shifting', 'avoiding' and 'improving' transport.[27] According to Australia's latest National Greenhouse Gas Inventory, the transport sector accounts for 18.1 per cent (97.5 megatonnes (Mt)) of annual greenhouse gas emissions, with 84.8 per cent (82.6Mt) of those emissions arising from road transport activities.[28] Alarmingly, there has been continuous growth in emissions from road transport activities in Australia since 1990, which the government recognizes as being 'principally driven by the importance placed on motor vehicles as modes of transportation of passengers and freight'.[29] Accordingly, it is especially important that Australia implements measures in line with all three PPMC pillars in order to encourage sustainable low-carbon transport in the context of international climate change objectives.[30]

In light of SDGs 11 and 13, congestion is essentially a symptom of Australia's transport system being 'unfair, unsustainable, and inefficient'[31] – in relation not only to engineering and economic measures of performance, but also to developmental and environmental ones. In this case 'sustainability' relates not only to demand for private transport itself, but also to the types of transport demanded – predominantly emissions-intensive road transport modes compared to public or active transport alternatives. Consequently, congestion is linked to sustainable development in relation to sustainable cities and climate change by the concept of 'sustainable transport'. This concept provides a new framework in which to examine regulatory-based solutions to address congestion in Australia in the long term.

2.1 What is 'Sustainable Transport'?

While there is no quintessential definition of 'sustainable transport', we all have a general sense of what sustainable transport involves: transporting people and goods by modes of transport that have low environmental impact. In both policy and academic literature, the term 'sustainable transport' is often used interchangeably with specific transport modes such as public transport, cycling and walking. Nevertheless, sustainable transport can also be used to describe a transport system more generally as one which includes certain features or attains certain standards relating to sustainable development. How these features or standards appear in Australia depends on the nature of Australia's transport system and the characteristics of its transport users.

The PPMC pillars provide a clear and overarching framework for how sustainable transport can be achieved by States in the eyes of the international community. More specifically, these encourage 'avoiding' unnecessary travel; 'shifting' the movement of goods and people to the most efficient modes; and 'improving' the environmental performance of fuels and powertrains, inter-modality and transport management.[32] In addition, academic research indicates that transport becomes sustainable when it is both 'accessible' and 'reproducible' according to relevant performance indicators. While performance indicators referred to by scholars can be drawn directly from the PPMC pillars, vehicle greenhouse gas emissions ratios, emissions intensity and transport fuel mix may also be useful.

Transport activities designed to achieve sustainable performance indicators must be 'accessible' and 'reproducible'. 'Accessibility' means not only access in a literal sense, but also access in terms of providing users with satisfactory mobility to and from desired destinations.[33] In relation to 'reproducibility', studies indicate that transport will be sustainable when activities can be repeated not only over time, but also in ways that preserve structures and functions of natural systems at a desired level.[34] In Australia, these elements can be satisfied with various degrees of difficulty. For example, the element of accessibility is particularly demanding, as land-use planning, urban sprawl, remoteness of major cities and low (relative) population density increase the inaccessibility of many transport options due to distance, time, cost or route complexity.[35] While there are fewer challenges involved in reproducing transport activities, a sustainable transport system developed in Australia will have to accommodate a range of emerging innovations that is likely to change Australia's transport task. Innovations including intelligent transport systems, Global Positioning System (GPS) tracking, autonomous vehicles, electric vehicles, alternative fuels and ride sharing[36] have different impacts on road transport in particular. While some of these innovations may benefit sustainable transport by providing real-time date to support pricing measures (eg, GPS tracking), or as alternatives to private vehicle travel (ride sharing, car sharing), others create new challenges by avoiding traditional congestion measures (ride sharing, car sharing) and proposed road pricing reform intended to improve transport sustainability in Australia.[37] Consequently, while the term 'sustainable transport' may appear to be a simple way to express the desired nature of Australia's transport system in the future carbon-constrained economy, the concept of sustainable transport consists of complex and interrelated elements.

2.2 Elements of Sustainable Transport in Existing Policy and Regulation

In Australia, government transport policies and regulations that apply to transport activities can encourage low-carbon transport in general or contribute to an element of sustainable transport, as discussed above. In Australia, there are numerous regulations that appear to support sustainable transport in both of these ways, despite the fact that Australia's transport sector is largely unsustainable.

Victoria takes a progressive regulatory approach to pursuing sustainable transport,[38] with its *Transport Integration Act 2010* (Vic) (TIA) being the only state-level transport law to include an express objective to achieve 'sustainability' across an entire transport system at sector level.[39] However, while 'sustainability' may be interpreted literally in the TIA (not being otherwise defined), this term alone is not what supports sustainable transport in Victoria, but the combined objective of the TIA to achieve a better 'integrated and sustainable transport system in Victoria'.[40] The combination of these elements enables the TIA to facilitate 'sustainable transport', elements of which are evident in explanatory materials that justify the enactment of the TIA:

> A transport system needs to support environmental responsibility by seeking to protect the local and global environment, by mitigating negative impacts, by promoting forms of transport. . . which have the least impact on the natural environment, and by improving the environmental performance of all forms of transport. When transport and land use are integrated, they contribute to better environmental outcomes by minimising the amount of travel needed

and increasing access to sustainable transport options, including walking and cycling.[41]

The above refers to elements of sustainable transport that are easily matched with pillars of the PPMC and to academic definitions including minimizing travel, improving environmental performance, promoting low emissions and mass transport. Moreover, the sustainable transport sought by the TIA is also intended to be consistent with a 'vision statement' which recognizes the contribution that such system makes to an 'inclusive, prosperous and environmentally responsible State'.[42] Each part of the vision statement is defined in more detail in separate sections of the TIA, which include items that further support the concept of sustainable transport (as defined above) – namely priorities to minimize barriers to access[43] and promote forms of transport that reduce the contribution of transport-related greenhouse gas emissions.[44]

Apart from sector-wide regulations such as the TIA, elements of sustainable transport and the pricing instruments that can support it are identified in narrower laws enacted in many states and territories. For example, while the element of 'access' is supported in most road and passenger transport regulations across Australia,[45] the 'shift' pillar of the PPMC in particular is supported by South Australia's *Passenger Transport Act 1999* (SA).[46] Reference to sustainable transport is also made in planning scheme documents. For example, an express purpose of the Victorian planning provisions on car parking is to support 'sustainable transport alternatives to the motor car'.[47] By contrast, in New South Wales, where congestion is also acute, few regulations contain express reference to sustainable transport, either in its entirety or in relation to its elements (as defined above). While the *Passenger Transport Act 2014* (NSW) contains express objectives to 'improve access to public transport',[48] the objectives of other transport regulations relate only to governance, service delivery and safety.[49] In this case, objectives to alleviate congestion and encourage sustainable transport are contained in government policy documents[50] and travel demand management recommendations made by Infrastructure New South Wales.[51]

Consequently, elements of sustainable transport already exist (or can be implied) in policy documents and individual laws that apply to transport activities. Therefore, in terms of legal regulation, the problem of congestion, as a symptom of unsustainable transport, is not caused by the lack of a regulatory framework and policy objectives intended to promote sustainable transport. Instead, the problem of congestion (as a symptom of unsustainable transport) occurs from the failure to use or apply the law in accordance with this objective, to actually achieve this outcome. Policy and regulatory objectives to promote sustainable transport as a whole, or in part, should be used to identify, review and reform laws that entrench the demand for and reliance on motor vehicles that underpin congestion itself, including those which impose economic instruments that affect the cost of transport activities.

3. LEGAL OPPORTUNITIES TO PROMOTE SUSTAINABLE TRANSPORT

A variety of regulatory measures can be used to create and support a sustainable transport system in Australia, including 'road pricing instruments' that have been referred to in various government and industry reviews as tools capable of alleviating congestion. To date, however, recommendations to develop road pricing instruments have been vague, with minimal detail provided about the form and structure that these instruments should take as part of an 'integrated system-wide pricing scheme'.[52] That notwithstanding, guidance about how pricing measures can be imposed by law to promote sustainable transport in Australia can be drawn from economic theories and legal and transport policy commentary on social and environmental externalities.

Whether a road pricing scheme is created by enacting laws to impose a price on road use directly and/or by reforming laws that already apply to various transport activities for this purpose, environmental taxation theories and principles should be applied to ensure that the resulting laws also contribute to sustainable transport. 'Pricing' occurs via 'economic instruments' that affect 'costs and benefits of alternative actions. . . with the effect of influencing decision-making behaviour'[53] to account for the cost of social and environmental 'externalities' of specific activities. Economic instruments are imposed by laws or policy measures to increase the cost of relevant activities in line with the cost of those externalities.[54] In Australia's transport sector, relevant externalities include capital infrastructure costs, traffic accidents, congestion and greenhouse gas emissions.[55] According to Pigou, a tax can be used to internalize such externalities in the cost of relevant activities. Traditionally, taxes raise revenue for general government spending. Accordingly, in order for a tax to be used to promote sustainable transport, certain aspects of the imposing laws must be altered to accommodate this new objective. A comprehensive body of literature already exists that analyses how 'environmental taxes'[56] can achieve a 'double dividend' of dual environmental and revenue objectives. In short, an environmental tax has characteristics both in common with, and different from, traditional taxes – being simple, certain, efficient and visible,[57] but intentionally unfair or favourable towards activities that promote or contribute to the relevant environmental objective.

Laws that already affect the cost of transport activities in Australia can be reviewed in accordance with Pigou's theory and environmental tax principles to better promote sustainable transport. In Australia, road transport activities are 'heavily taxed'[58] in the sense that there are numerous laws that impose costs on users to purchase, own and use vehicles, and also road infrastructure. However, these laws affect transport costs not only via taxes (or associated tax expenditure provisions), but also via other forms of economic instruments, including levies/charges and direct financial assistance measures:

1. Taxes and duties provide revenue for general government spending.[59] For example, goods and service tax,[60] stamp duty,[61] customs duty[62] and luxury car tax[63] affect the cost of vehicles at the time of purchase. Excise and customs duties apply to liquid and gaseous transport fuels.[64] Employers pay fringe benefits tax[65] on the value of motor vehicles benefits (including vehicles and car parking) provided to employees.
2. Tax expenditure provisions provide favourable treatment to some taxpayers within the tax system. For example, select stamp duty laws include provisions that reduce the amount of tax or duty paid on the purchase price of a vehicle according to its environmental performance.[66] In relation to luxury car tax, 'fuel-efficient' vehicles enjoy a higher tax-free threshold[67] than applies to other luxury vehicles. Entities that purchase fuel for heavy vehicles travelling on public roads may be entitled to a 'credit' for part of the excise or customs duties paid on transport fuel.[68]
3. Levies, fees and charges are paid in return for a service[69] – for example, parking fees (increased by annual congestion levies in some states),[70] road tolls, vehicle licence and registration fees (all vehicles),[71] and 'road user charges' (heavy vehicles).[72] Charges also apply to public transport and commercial passenger transport services (taxi, hire car and ride-share services) which offer alternatives to private vehicle transport.
4. Direct financial assistance mechanisms pay entities directly to engage in certain desired activities.[73] For example, the 'Urban Congestion Initiative' was recently created to fund projects that target congestion in urban areas.[74] Under the 'Emissions Reduction Fund,'[75] entities may receive funding for projects that reduce or save greenhouse gas emissions from eligible transport projects.[76]

Pigou's theory and environmental taxation principles are directly applicable to laws that impose a tax or tax expenditure provision (categories 1 and 2 above) on transport activities. However, there is sufficient similarity (tax compared to charge) or equivalence (tax expenditure provision compared to direct financial assistance measures)[77] between these instruments so that Pigou's theory and environmental tax principles can guide the general reform of laws that affect transport costs in Australia.

Based on a growing body of literature,[78] there are numerous ways that existing transport laws could be reformed to contribute to promote sustainable low-carbon transport[79] based on how they influence *use* or *choice* of vehicles and fuels, and the relative attractiveness of public or active transport alternatives. At a sector level, it is important that individual laws work together to achieve sustainable transport and encourage users to 'avoid' unnecessary transport and/or least sustainable modes or options based on price, while encouraging users to 'shift' towards public (or active) transport alternatives. Revenue generated by individual taxes and charges, or by components of relevant laws designed to internalize social and environmental externalities, can be earmarked to 'improve' specific aspects of transport activities or fund projects involving desired alternative behaviours.[80] Arguably, encouraging sustainable transport will require a combination of laws that affect different transport activities. In the context of developing an integrated system-wide pricing scheme, road use pricing can be based on time, distance, location or mass.[81] These same laws can also include design features to address specific environmental externalities such as greenhouse gas emissions, linked to data disclosed under Australian design rules (new vehicles) and published in the 'Green Vehicle Guide'.[82] The design of foreign road pricing measures – including congestion levy zones in England and Singapore, Sweden's congestion tax and tolls for priority lane travel in America[83] – should be considered in the process of reform, including whether such measures could be adapted to Australian circumstances as part of a new system-wide scheme.

4. CONCLUSION

While there is general support in Australia for the development of an integrated system-wide pricing scheme which includes laws that directly price road use, while abolishing outdated or indirect road pricing measures including fuel excise duty, vehicle registration charges and stamp duty,[84] recommendations to date lack specific detail about the form and content of such a scheme. In this context, the process of identifying and classifying existing regulations that affect the cost of road transport activities is a necessary preliminary step to understand how various laws interact, generate revenue and encourage transport patterns that contribute to or undermine priorities to alleviate congestion and promote sustainable transport in the long term.

Moreover, shifting the existing paradigm through which congestion and road pricing are currently viewed – from traditional engineering and economic perspectives to an environmental perspective – will help to generate new solutions and opportunities for regulatory reform. Sustainable transport, which connects sustainable development objectives and domestic transport policy, provides new measures of performance to assess the existing laws that impose costs on transport activities to reinforce preference and demand for motor vehicles and create barriers to sustainable low-carbon transport. Importantly, this process provides an opportunity to equalize environmental, infrastructure and economic priorities in Australia's transport sector, to encourage activities that avoid, shift and improve current transport behaviours that will underpin Australia's sustainable transport system.

NOTES

1. Austroads, 'Congestion and Reliability Review' (Research Report AP-R534-16, December 2016) 41.
2. Infrastructure Partnerships Australia, *Australian Travel Metric 2017 Edition* (Report, 2017). See also Victorian Integrated Survey of Travel and Activity: Trip travel time; https://public.tableau.com/profile/vista#!/vizhome/VISTA-Trips-timeseriesAccess/Trips-methodoftravel, last accessed 16 August 2018.
3. Infrastructure Victoria, *The Road Ahead* (Report, November 2016) 24–25; Infrastructure New South Wales, *State Infrastructure Strategy 2018–2038* (Report, 2018) 138; Bureau of Infrastructure, Transport and Regional Economics, 'Traffic and congestion cost trends for Australian capital cities' (Information Sheet 74, 2016) 1.
4. Marion Terrill, 'Stuck in traffic? Road congestion in Sydney and Melbourne' (Report, Grattan Institute, 2017) 16. Bureau of Infrastructure, Transport and Regional Economics, 'Traffic and congestion cost trends for Australian capital cities' (Information Sheet 74, 2016) 27 [Table 4b] estimates the 'avoidable' social costs of congestion in Melbourne and Sydney in 2030 at A$7.57 billion and A$9.45 billion respectively.
5. Terrill, above n4, 14; Sarah Coleman, *Australia State of the Environment: Built Environment* (Report to the Australian Government Minister for the Environment and Energy, Australian Government Department of the Environment and Energy, 2017) 13.
6. Engineers Australia, *National Infrastructure Investment Update* (Report, 2016) 18–19.
7. Stephen Potter, 'Using Environmental Taxation for Transport Demand Management' in Lin-Heng Lye et al (eds), *Critical Issues in Environmental Taxation* (Oxford University Press, 2009) vol 7, 39, 41; see further Infrastructure Victoria, above n3, 18; Ken Henry, *Australia's Future Tax System* (2009) 375–376.
8. *Congestion Levy Act 2005* (Vic); *Parking Space Levy Act 2009* (NSW). See also *Perth Parking Management Act 1999* (WA).
9. Infrastructure Victoria, 'Five Year Focus: Immediate Actions to Tackle Congestion' (Report, April 2018).

10. Infrastructure New South Wales, above n3, 132 [Recommendation 46].
11. For example, Paul David, 'Path Dependence: A Foundational Concept for Historical Social Science' (2007) 1 *Cliometrica* 91.
12. Carey Curtis and Nicholas Low, *Institutional Barriers to Sustainable Transport* (Routledge, 2017) 103–133.
13. By analogy, see Anna Mortimore and Hope Ashibor, 'Australian Government's Ongoing Challenge to Achieve Fuel Efficiency Standards by 2025 can Impact on 2015 Paris Agreement' (2018) 35 *Environmental and Planning Law Journal* 280, 295.
14. World Commission on Environment and Development, *Our Common Future* (1983) ch 2.
15. *Transforming our world: the 2030 Agenda for sustainable development* GA Res 70/1 GAOR 70th plen, Un Doc A/ES/70/1 (21 October 2015) preamble.
16. Ibid.
17. Australian Government, '2030 Agenda for Sustainable Development and the Sustainable Development Goals' *Department of Energy and Environment* www.environment.gov.au/about-us/international/2030-agenda, last accessed 21 August 2018; *Sustainable Development Goals* https://sdgs.org.au/, last accessed 21 August 2018.
18. Bertelsmann Stiftung and Sustainable Development Solutions Network, 'SDG Global Index and Dashboards Report 2018: Global Responsibilities – Implementing the Goals' (Report, July 2018) 95, 3.
19. Above n15, 21–22, [11.2].
20. SDG Compass, 'SDG 11' https://sdgcompass.org/sdgs/sdg-11/, last accessed 27 August 2018.
21. Curtis and Low, above n12, 13.
22. Above n15, preamble 23 [13.2].
23. For example, United Nations Climate Summit (New York, 23 September 2014). Refer to United Nations, 'Joint Action Statement – Transport', www.un.org/climatechange/summit/wp-content/uploads/sites/2/2014/07/TRANSPORT-joint-Action-Statement.pdf, last accessed 4 September 2018.
24. Conference of the Parties, United Nations Framework Convention on Climate Change, *Adoption of the Paris Agreement,* Decision CP.21,21st sess, Agenda Item 4(b), UN Doc FCCC/CP/2015.L9 (12 December 2015); Commonwealth of Australia, 'Australia's Intended Nationally Determined Contribution to a New Climate Change Agreement', www4.unfccc.int/sites/submissions/INDC/Published%20Documents/Australia/1/Australias%20Intended%20Nationally%20Determined%20Contribution%20to%20a%20new%20Climate%20Change%20Agreement%20-%20August%202015.pdf, last accessed 23 April 2019.
25. Commonwealth of Australia, above n24.
26. Paris Process on Mobility and Climate, 'A global macro roadmap outlining an actionable vision towards decarbonised, resilient transport' (Report, November 2017); Partnership on sustainable low carbon transport, www.slocat.net, last accessed 23 April 2019.
27. Ibid.
28. Commonwealth of Australia, *Australian National Greenhouse Accounts: National Inventory Report 2016: The Australian Government Submission to the United Nations Framework Convention on Climate Change April 2018* (2018) vol 1, 43.
29. Supported by engineering and economic storylines evidence in transport policy – see Curtis and Low, above n12, 103–133. Commonwealth of Australia, above n28, vol 1, 44 [Fig 3.3] shows trends since 1990 – emissions were 58.7 per cent higher in 2016 than in 1990, and on average have increased by around 2.3 per cent annually. The transport sector will contribute 131Mt to emissions annually by 2050 if unmitigated. John Stanley, David Hensher and Chris Loader, 'Road Transport and Climate Change: Stepping off the Greenhouse Gas' (2011) 45 *Transport Research Part A* 1020, 1021. The number of vehicles registered in Australia continues to increase; see Australian Bureau of Statistics, 'Motor vehicle census, Australia, 31 January 2018' (No 9309.0, 27 July 2018).
30. Australian Government, '2017 Review of Climate Change Policies' (Department of the Environment and Energy, Report, 2017) 33–35.

31. Infrastructure Australia, *Australia Infrastructure Plan* (Report, February, 2016) 84.
32. Paris Process on Mobility and Climate, above n26.
33. Henrik Gudmundsson and Mattias Hoejer, 'Sustainable development principles and their implications for transport' (1996) 19 *Ecological Economics* 269.
34. Henrik Gudmundsson, 'Making concepts matter: sustainable mobility and indicator systems in transport policy' (2003) 55 *International Social Science Journal* 199, 205; see also H Opschoor and L Reijnders, 'Towards sustainable development indicators' in H Kuik and O Verbruggen (eds) *In search of indicators for sustainable development* (Dordrecht Klewer, 1991) 7.
35. Carey Curtis, Nicholas Low, and Bill Russell, 'Transport planning in Australia', in Curtis and Low, above n12, 41–55.
36. Infrastructure Victoria, 'Advice on Automated and Zero Emissions Vehicle Infrastructure: Future Scenarios' (Report, April 2018).
37. David Hensher, 'Tackling Road Congestion: What might it look like in the future under a collaborative and connected mobility model?' (2018) 66 *Transport Policy* A1.
38. Explanatory Memorandum to the Transport Integration Bill 2009 (Vic) 2.
39. Department of Infrastructure and Transport, *State of Australian Cities 2011* (Report, 2011) 214.
40. TIA s 1.
41. Explanatory Memorandum, above n38, 7. See meaning of 'integration' further explained at 3–4.
42. TIA s 6.
43. TIA s 8.
44. TIA s 10 (as amended by the *Climate Change Act 2010* (Vic)).
45. *Transport Integration Act 2010* (Vic) s 8, *Passenger Transport Act 2014* (NSW) s 3, *Transport Coordination Act 1996* (WA) s 3.
46. *Passenger Transport Act 1999 (SA)* s 3.
47. Victorian Planning Provisions cl 52.06, enacted under the *Planning and Environment Act 1987* (Vic) s 4A.
48. *Passenger Transport Act 2014* (NSW) s 3.
49. *Transport Administration Act 1988* (NSW) s 2A; *Road Transport Act 2013* (NSW).
50. New South Wales Government, *Future Transport Strategy 2056* (Report, 2018) 28.
51. Infrastructure New South Wales, above n3, 118.
52. Refer above n9, n10.
53. OECD, *Economic Instruments for Environment Protection* (OCDE-OECD, 1989) 12 OECD, *Economic Instruments for Environment Protection* (OCDE-OECD, 1989) 12. Further discussion of definitions associated with economic instruments is outside the scope of this chapter.
54. Arthur Pigou, *Economics of Welfare* (Macmillan, first published 1932, 1962 ed) 203; Ronald Coase, 'The Federal Communications Commission' (1959) 2 *Journal of Law and Economics* 1, 14; J H Dales, 'Pollution Rights' in *Pollution, Property & Price: An Essay in Policy-Making and Economics* (University of Toronto Press, 1968) 77, 99; Robert Stavins, 'Transaction Costs and Tradeable Permits' (1995) 29 *Journal of Environmental Economics and Management* 133. Note the work of Coase and Dales is more directly related to permits and tradeable property rights, which are not relevant in Australia's transport sector; see further Pedro Herrera Molina, 'Design Options and Their Rationales' in Janet Milne and Michael Andersen (eds), *Handbook of Research on Environmental Taxes* (Edward Elgar, 2012) 85, 85–86; Tim Roughgarden and Stephen Schneider, 'Climate Change Policy: Quantifying Uncertainties for Damages and Optimal Carbon Taxes' (1999) 27 *Energy Policy* 415, 426.
55. Austroads, 'Project evaluation part 4: Project evaluation data' (Publication AGEP04-12, 2012).
56. OECD, *The Political Economy of Environmentally Related Taxes* (2006) 16.
57. Adam Smith, 'Of the Sources of the General or Public Revenue of the Society' in *The Wealth of Nations* (L M Dent, first published 1910, 1960 ed) vol 5, ch 2; more recent

interpretations and applications of these objectives can be found in Simon James and Christopher Nobes, *The Economics of Taxation* (Fiscal Publications, 2010); Henry, above n7.

58. Henry, above n7.
59. *Matthews v Chicory Marketing Board (Victoria)* (1938) 60 CLR 263, 276; *Roy Morgan Research Pty Ltd v Federal Commissioner of Taxation* (2011) 244 CLR 97, 113; *Luton v Lessels* (2002) 210 CLR 333, 372 (Kirby J); *Australian Tape Manufacturers Association Ltd v Commonwealth* (1993) 176 CLR 480, 504.
60. *A New Tax System (Goods and Services Tax) Act 1999* (Cth) s 9–5.
61. *Duties Act 1999* (ACT); *Duties Act 1997* (NSW); *Stamp Duty Act* (NT); *Duties Act 2001* (QLD); *Stamp Duties Act 1923* (SA); *Duties Act 2001* (Tas); *Duties Act 2000* (Vic); *Duties Act 2008* (WA).
62. *Excise Act 1901* (Cth), *Excise Tariff Act 1921* (Cth) sch, *Customs Act 1901* (Cth), *Customs Tariff Act 1995* (Cth) sch 3.
63. *A New Tax System (Luxury Car Tax) Act 1999* (Cth) s 5–5.
64. *Excise Act 1901* (Cth), *Excise Tariff Act 1921* (Cth), *Customs Act 1901* (Cth), *Customs Tariff Act 1995* (Cth).
65. *Fringe Benefits Tax Act 1986* (Cth) s 6, *Fringe Benefits Tax Assessment Act 1986* (Cth) ss 7, 9–10.
66. *Duties Act 1999* (ACT) s 208; ACT Revenue Office, *Vehicle Registration Duty*, Revenue Circular DA005.7, 18 September 2017; ACT Government, 'Building an Integrated Transport Network: Reducing Emissions' (July 2016) *Green Vehicle Guide*, www.greenvehicleguide.gov.au, last accessed 20 August 2018.
67. Commissioner of Taxation, *Luxury Car Tax: What is the Luxury Car Tax Threshold and the Fuel-Efficient Car Limit for the 2018–18 Financial Year?* LCTD 2018/1, 23 May 2018, [2], [3]. See also *A New Tax System (Luxury Car Tax) Act 1999* (Cth) ss 25–1(4).
68. *Fuel Tax Act 2006* (Cth) ss 41–5, 41–20.
69. *Matthews v Chicory Marketing Board (Victoria)* (1938) 60 CLR 263, 276; this feature distinguishes a charge from a tax.
70. *Congestion Levy Act 2005* (Vic); *Parking Space Levy Act 2009* (NSW); *Perth Parking Management Act 1999* (WA).
71. BITRE, 'Public Road-Related Expenditure and Revenue in Australia' (Information Sheet 40, 23 February 2011), table 6.
72. Fuel Tax (Road User Charge) Determination 2017 (Cth); National Transport Commission *Heavy vehicle charges*, www.ntc.gov.au/heavy-vehicles/heavy-vehicle-charges, last accessed 16 August 2018.
73. Surrey and McDaniel, *Tax Expenditures* (Harvard University Press, 1985) 3.
74. Australian Government, 'Urban Congestion Initiative' (Fact Sheet, 7 June 2018), http://investment.infrastructure.gov.au/files/budget/Urban_Congestion_Initiative_Factsheet_June_2018.pdf, last accessed 15 August 2018.
75. *Carbon Credits (Carbon Farming Initiative Act 2011)* (Cth).
76. Clean Energy Regulator 'Auction June 2018: Contract Portfolio', www.cleanenergyregulator.gov.au/ERF/Auctions-results/june-2018, last accessed 16 August 2018; Clean Energy Regulator, 'Emissions Reduction Fund Register'. See further Prafula Pearce and Vanessa Johnston, 'A New Fast Lane or Just a Roadblock? Mitigating Road Transport GHG Emissions under Australia's Emissions Reduction Fund' (2016) 33 *Environmental and Planning Law Journal* 181.
77. Vanessa Johnston, *An Australian Road Transport Carbon Price* (Australian Tax Research Foundation, 2017) 47–48.
78. Potter, above n7, 41. Henry, above n7, 363, 388–389. Also Prafula Pearce, *Using Tax and Regulatory Measures to Reform Choice and Usage of Motor Vehicles* (Australian Taxation Research Foundation, 2013); Diane Kraal and Dianne Harvey, 'Fringe Benefits Tax for Cars: Some Further Considerations for Policy Change and Reform' (2009) 24 *Australian Tax Forum* 589.
79. Including traffic demand management in the context of trip number, length, time and

location of trips, mode of transport and vehicle occupancy; see further Stephen Potter in Warren (ed) *Managing Transport Energy* (Oxford University Press, 2007) 9–33.

80. Claudia Dias Soares, 'Earmarking Revenues from Environmentally Related Taxes' in Janet Milne and Michael Andersen (eds), *Handbook of Research on Environmental Taxation* (Edward Elgar, 2012) 102. For example, revenue generated from congestion levies paid under the *Parking Spaces Levy Act 2009* (NSW) s 10 is paid into a 'Public Transport Fund' to pay for infrastructure projects that contribute to greater use of public transport; www.transport.nsw.gov.au/programs/parking-space-levy, last accessed 6 August 2018.
81. Henry, above n7, 377 [recommendation 62] as proposed for heavy vehicles. Also Frontier Economics, *Heavy Vehicle Infrastructure Funding and Investment Reforms: Final Report* (December 2013).
82. Henry, above n7, 377–391; Harry Clarke and David Prentice, 'A Conceptual Framework for the Reform of Taxes Related to Roads and Transport' (Report, June 2009); Australian Government, Vehicle Standard (Australian Design Rules 81/02 – Fuel Consumption Labelling for Light Vehicles) 2008; *Green Vehicle Guide*, www.greenvehicleguide.gov.au/, last accessed 5 September 2018.
83. For example, Infrastructure Victoria, above n3, 61–70 [Appendix B1–B4].
84. Infrastructure New South Wales, above n3, 131; Infrastructure Victoria, above n3, 7, 53. Henry, above n7, 398–400.

11. Taxing vehicle use to overcome the problems of conventional transport taxes

Alberto Gago, Xavier Labandeira and Xiral López-Otero*

1. INTRODUCTION

Road transport is currently witnessing the biggest changes to the sector since the early twentieth century. Vehicle manufacturing and vehicle use have been transformed by a multitude of factors, including efforts to reduce emissions and transition towards a low-carbon economy; increased urbanization; a new regulatory attitude towards mobility; technological advancements; and changes in patterns of acquisition, possession and use of private vehicles. Alongside these far-reaching technological, social and regulatory developments, others are taking place – and will continue to do so – across all aspects relating to the sector, including fiscal aspects.

Mobility has always been of interest to the tax system – mainly because the purchase, possession and use of vehicles all indicate an ability to pay; because fuel consumption is inelastic and on a vast scale; and because tax revenue is high and stable. For decades, tax systems have used a triad of fiscal instruments – registration tax, recurring road tax and fuel tax – which have worked relatively well. However, the changes mentioned above are increasingly affecting these instruments and even challenging their existence altogether.

In academic circles, the emphasis has been on the revenue brought in by these taxes and their disconnection from the many externalities – such as global and local pollution, congestion and accidents – caused by road transport (see Delucchi, 2000; Sansom et al, 2001; Quinet, 2004; Santos, 2005; Maibach et al, 2008; van Essen, 2011; Gago et al, 2014; Korzhenevych et al, 2014; Parry et al, 2014; and Santos, 2017). Their distributive impact has also been questioned (Aasness and Larsen, 2002; European Environmental Agency, 2011); although the literature shows that taxes on transport are usually less regressive than those on other energy products (Labandeira et al, 2007; Ekins and Speck, 2011; Kosonen, 2012), and may even tend towards progressiveness under certain circumstances (Labeaga et al, 2018; Rausch et al, 2010; Sterner, 2012; Flues and Thomas, 2015).

In regulatory circles, some of these academic arguments have been used to support or draft proposals, although progress has been limited. However, in industrial and commercial areas, the changes have been much more acute. Road transport is being transformed by new technologies and products, new entrants, different patterns of use and consumption, a constrained market, new regulations on mobility and a revolution both throughout the value chain and in the behaviour of all agents (see Capgemini, 2015; Bloomberg, 2016; Kruegen and Johnson, 2016; McKinsey, 2016; BBVA Research, 2017; KPMG, 2017; and ANFAC, 2018).

These changes are affecting the accepted status that taxes on vehicles and road transport have enjoyed for many decades. Taxes on vehicle purchases are now being questioned, as are general and specific taxes on consumption. Revenues from these taxes have fallen because of the technological transition towards abandoning combustion engines or making them more efficient; and their efficiency-enhancing properties are being questioned because they are unable to internalize the main externalities in the form of local pollution or congestion. These inefficient taxes, with falling revenues, are proving unable to maintain their role in the tax system and/or to cover the costs of infrastructure, and risk breakdown of domestic markets. Comprehensive reform is therefore needed to address these failings and align these taxes with the above-mentioned transformations in the sector, and with evolving fiscal and regulatory goals.

In this context, this chapter aims to describe the current situation and present a proposal for the reform of vehicle taxation to address the challenges it faces. We believe that future transport taxation will focus on the substantial externalities; be characterized by complex fiscal structures with multiple aims; have a revenue collection capacity equivalent to or above that of today's taxes on vehicles and fuels; and function based on advanced telematic technologies that can determine in real time complex tax bases relating to the use of different types of vehicles in terms of location and time.

2. CURRENT SITUATION OF TRANSPORT TAXATION

To date, the rationale behind the imposition of road transport taxes has largely been fiscal (Gago et al, 2014). According to the latest available data, road transport taxes account for about 5 per cent of tax revenue in both the European Union (EC, 2018) and the United States (USDT, 2017; OECD, 2018) (1.8 per cent and 1.3 per cent of gross domestic product (GDP), respectively). The low price elasticity of the main source of revenue, automobile fuels (see Brons, 2008; Labandeira et al, 2017), means that taxes on them have limited effects on consumption, and therefore on the volume and stability of revenue. In fact, these figures exemplify the so-called 'optimal taxation' of goods and services because, by producing only slight alterations in consumer behaviour, they generate public revenue at low efficiency costs (Ramsey, 1927).

The revenue from these taxes is generally used without any specific assignment, although in some countries it has been used (partially or totally) to fund transport infrastructure. In the United States, the federal tax on fuels finances approximately 90 per cent of the Highway Trust Fund, which is mainly spent on the construction of highways and other transport projects (Lowry, 2015); while taxes on fuels are also the main source of revenue for states for funding their road networks and other transport infrastructure (Brouwer et al, 2016).

The second reason for imposing road transport taxes is to control externalities. As in other markets, decisions in this sector are usually adopted within an inefficient framework dominated by the presence of negative external effects of various kinds. This is because there is little consideration of the associated social costs – that is, those resulting from traffic congestion and accidents, and those generated by emissions of global (mainly greenhouse gases) and local pollutants, and noise (Parry et al, 2014).[1] Considering the relevance of such externalities and the size of the associated costs, which may be as much as 5 per cent of GDP in the European Union (van Essen et al, 2011), in recent decades some countries have tried to deal with them by changing tax rates on transport or introducing new taxes. However, the cost of these externalities is not reflected in today's prices of vehicles or fuels and gives rise to inefficient results in the absence of public intervention (Santos et al, 2010).

Within this general framework, three main categories of tax on transport are applied in many countries (Hylén et al, 2013): taxes on vehicles (purchase and recurring taxes); taxes on fuels; and taxes for access to infrastructure and cities. In particular, taxation on transport has primarily focused on the second of these, which accounts for about 75 per cent of tax revenue in this area (EC, 2018). Since there is a direct relation between the consumption of fuels and emissions of the main greenhouse gas – carbon dioxide (CO_2) – fuel tax is an efficient tool for dealing with the problem of climate change. However, since most of the most important externalities associated with road transport (eg, congestion, accidents, local pollution and noise) are not directly related to fuel consumption, but vary depending on vehicle type and place and time of use, such taxes cannot deal with them well.

3. REFORMING TAXATION ON TRANSPORT

3.1 Incremental Changes in the Current System

An initial option to address the crisis in transport taxation would simply be to avoid its use and increase other taxes to replace the revenue it brings in, using planning or conventional regulations to deal with the externalities associated with transport. In fact, most of the measures being proposed today by cities and governments to deal with transport externalities are regulations or prohibitions of different types. However, although such measures might seem more effective or fairer than pricing instruments, in practice they are substantially less efficient in mitigating transport externalities (Kleit, 2004; Austin and Dinan, 2005; Anderson et al, 2011; Jacobsen, 2013; Anderson and Sallee, 2016; Levinson, 2018),[2] and may also be more regressive (Levinson, 2018).

The second option would be to adjust existing taxes. The economic literature has focused on the analysis of two alternatives for achieving more optimal transport taxation (Parry et al, 2014): the application of broader and higher fuel taxes, and the definition of a package of new corrective taxes that would cover the various externalities with greater accuracy.

Fuel taxes have the advantage of administrative simplicity and feasibility, because they are perfectly consolidated in most tax systems and are easy to understand for taxpayers. However, they also have various shortcomings: they cannot cover most transport externalities appropriately; the rates must be very high to better internalize externalities – especially in the case of diesel (Santos, 2017) – which would generate substantial socio-economic impacts; and their revenue collecting capacity is decreasing as a result of the above-mentioned energy-efficiency improvements in the sector and a greater relative reaction to tax hikes.[3] In addition, increasing fuel tax rates to mitigate the loss in revenue would have serious distributive impacts, increasing the fiscal burden for drivers of less efficient vehicles – especially those using heavy vehicles for working and those who cannot afford new, more efficient vehicles (Jones and Bock, 2017).

Therefore, an increase in revenue and a reduction in externalities might be more efficiently realized through a specific package of new taxes. Such a package could include taxes on emissions of local pollutants, on congestion (with zone and time discrimination), and on kilometres travelled as a charge for global pollutants and to cover infrastructure and the cost of accidents. In practice, however, it would be difficult to incorporate such 'idealized' taxes within the existing tax system. In addition to public antipathy towards most new taxes, it would be difficult to coordinate and manage such a variety of instruments and there might well be distributive objections.

3.2 A Comprehensive Automated Tax on Vehicles

The above problems suggest that a far-reaching, comprehensive reform of transport taxation is needed. One initiative with significant potential is a tax on vehicle use (McLure, 2009). Such an instrument would address many of the current problems associated with transport taxation, such as reduced generation of public revenue, congestion, emissions and infrastructure deterioration (Lindsey, 2010). On the one hand, this alternative has the potential to generate more stable revenue than fuel taxes, because drivers cannot reduce their tax burden by driving more efficient vehicles (Langer et al, 2017). On the other, by using tax rates that vary by location and time, the problems of congestion and local pollution could be tackled more effectively; and a tax on real distance travelled could deal with the other externalities.[4]

In this context, our specific proposal for reforming transport taxation is to create a new tax, which we call the Comprehensive Automated Tax on Vehicles (CATV). This proposal is based on three correlated elements: on the one hand, the externalities, 95 per cent of which can be characterized as congestion, local and global pollution, accidents and noise; and on the other, both vehicle types and the fuels they use, and location and time of vehicle use, which all relate to many of the externalities.

The basic characteristics of the new CATV are summarized in Table 11.1A. The tax rate depends on the type of vehicle (grouped by technological category and age), and has three components: a toll for access to certain zones and/or for the use of infrastructure; hourly/location tax rates; and a levy on the number of kilometres travelled. For each category of vehicle, different tax rates apply depending on the zone of travel and the time of travel (possibly with a differentiation between different time brackets). A tax on distance travelled (called the 'off-peak rate' in Table 11.1) would cover the costs associated with global pollution,[5] accidents and infrastructure. For example, within a specific time bracket, a Class 1 vehicle entering Urban Area 1 might be subject to an entry rate, an hourly payment for congestion/local pollution and a tax per kilometre travelled to cover the remaining external costs. Table 11.1B relates the characteristics of each of these fiscal components (type of payment) to the externalities (or infrastructure costs) to be covered.

Table 11.1 *Characteristics of the CATV*

A. Illustration of CATV rates

	Zone 1 (urban)	Zone 2	Zone . . . (non-urban)
Vehicle type 1	Entry toll 1 Hourly rate 1a (. . .) Off-peak rate	Hourly rate 2a (. . .) Off-peak rate	Off-peak rate
	Off-peak rate	Off-peak rate	
Vehicle type . . .	Rates hourly/entrance/ off-peak	Rates hourly/entrance/ off-peak	Off-peak rate
	Off-peak rate	Off-peak rate	

B. Coverage of externalities per component of the CATV

Vehicle type 1	Payment	Externalities				
		Congestion	Local pollution/ noise	Global pollution	Accidents	Infrastructure
Entry rate	Euros	X	–	–	–	X
Hourly rate 1a	Euros/ hour	X	X	–	–	–
Off-peak rate	Euros/ km	–	–	X	X	X

4. TRANSITION TO THE CATV

As explained in the previous section, the CATV would better address the externalities associated with road transport and has significant potential to bring in revenue, which could be easily divided among the different administrations, depending on the types of externalities corrected (eg, congestion and local pollution for municipal districts; infrastructure for regional and central administrations). However, certain issues and difficulties must be addressed to guarantee the feasibility of the tax.

First, it is important to determine the different categories of vehicle and the applicable tax rates. Vehicles must be grouped according to the characteristics that relate most directly to the externalities they generate (eg, energy efficiency, emissions of pollutants, age). It is essential only that users know the exact fiscal implications of using their current vehicles, and thus it is necessary that the system also includes a registration tax, so that drivers can make more informed decisions on future vehicle purchases.[6] Tax rates should relate to the values of the various externalities, so it will be necessary to use the existing academic evidence (eg, Maibach et al, 2008; Korzhenevych et al, 2014), and attempt to apply its results to different realities through more or less sophisticated techniques.

It is essential that the fiscal structure be as simple as possible, so that users know at all times what taxes they will be subject to and can adapt their decisions and behaviour to minimize the associated negative externalities. This is a sub-optimal system, in which there must be compromises between gains in efficiency and feasible management (both in grouping vehicles by class and in structuring and quantifying the various rates).

Second, its technical functioning should be based on mature, well-known, easily accessed, advanced technology for automated calculation of the tax. All vehicles should incorporate a permanent, compulsory geolocation solution, whose technical basis and function could resemble those of the emergency call system that is compulsory for all new vehicles in the European Union as from 2018 (EP, 2015). The solution applied in Switzerland (FCA, 2017) could be used as a reference, since it involves a mechanism that cannot be tampered with and is fitted in vehicles to record characteristics of weight and emissions, and register kilometres travelled and roads used. This data is then sent periodically to the tax administration, which automatically determines the tax base, the applicable rates and the amounts due.

The greatest barrier to the introduction of a tax on vehicle use is social acceptance.[7] Several aspects must be considered in this regard, starting with the effects of the tax in terms of winners and losers: potential losses for businesses within protected areas; the costs of installing the technological support system; and the possible negative impact in terms of distribution. It seems clear that acceptance of the CATV will be greater if it can be shown that it has a significant impact on transport-related externalities and if part of the revenue generated is assigned to fund environmental initiatives or public transport infrastructure (Beuermann and Santarius, 2006; Gärling and Schuitema, 2007; Sælen and Kallbekken, 2011). Regarding its distributive impact, the literature shows that the regressive impact of taxes on vehicle use is similar to that of fuel tax (Zhang et al, 2009; McMullen et al, 2010; Larsen et al, 2012). Possible compensation for the losers would also help to increase acceptance – for example, by using revenue to reduce other taxes or for investment in infrastructure and services that would improve the distributive impact (Levinson, 2010).[8]

In addition, it is necessary to anticipate and counter possible interference with citizens' privacy, as the system involves the permanent monitoring of all moving vehicles. This would imply access to private information that not only is potentially sensitive, but also gives rise to issues such as how such information is used, processed, stored and destroyed. Research in this field is increasingly addressing these issues of privacy and data protection, in an attempt to make the accumulation of external information compatible with a certain degree of personal control, reservation and even anonymity.

Finally, it is necessary to consider the jurisdictional assignation of the CATV. First, tax bases and rates must be adapted to the scope of the externalities, in order to avoid overflow effects and loss of efficiency. Second, replacing existing taxes with the CATV might affect revenue collection at different levels of government. In this context, the proposed reform should assign regulatory capacities, tax levels and collection among the jurisdictions affected. Given that the externalities have both local and global impacts, the CATV should assign competencies and brackets to all levels of government, allowing them to participate by means of different quotas. The CATV could be constrained to keeping at least pre-reform revenue which – depending on the jurisdictional distribution of taxes – might alter the allocation of rates and bases. In sum, it will be necessary to combine these objectives in order to achieve optimal jurisdictional assignation of the CATV. Finally, there is the issue of how to treat foreign vehicles that cannot be properly tracked. In this case a simple charge levied on distance travelled within the country could be implemented, similar to the aforementioned Swiss charges on heavy vehicles.

Immediate introduction of the CATV would be very complex and costly, so this should be done gradually in order to reduce negative impacts and optimize adaptation. We therefore propose that the CATV be introduced in two phases. During the first transition phase, vehicle manufacturers would be obliged to install geolocation devices in all new vehicles, with a period established for the gradual adoption of such mechanisms in all vehicles. During this phase, conventional transport taxes would be increased to promote renovation of the fleet. Experimental pilots introducing the CATV would also be conducted, from which practical lessons could be learned towards final implementation. After analysing the results of the pilot project, at the end of this transition period – by which time the fleet would largely be equipped with geolocation devices – the CATV would be fully introduced, replacing most existing taxes levied on road transport.

5. CONCLUSIONS

The challenges facing taxation on vehicles – a traditional source of sizeable and stable revenues in many parts of the world – indicate that a radical transformation is needed if the system is to continue to meet its two main objectives: collecting revenues and correcting externalities. On the one hand, technological progress and changing consumer habits are leading to a drop in the tax revenues associated with traditional transport taxes, which will only increase in the coming years. On the other hand, concerns about the effects of the externalities associated with transport are increasing, and the effects themselves are worsening. We have observed in this study, however, that conventional transport taxation cannot cover these externalities as required.

This chapter proposes a reform of vehicle taxation that would allow existing challenges to be met, guaranteeing the feasibility of vehicle taxation in the twenty-first century. This reform would replace the traditional transport taxes with a new tax, the CATV, which can internalize the externalities associated with vehicle use by means of tax rates that vary in accordance with the type of vehicle, its zonal and hourly use, and distance travelled. Application of the tax would be based on existing geolocation technologies, which would make it possible to calculate the tax through automated processes and would guarantee the confidentiality of the information supplied.

The immediate introduction of this new system would be complex and costly, and would present problems of jurisdictional assignation and social acceptance. The transition should therefore take place gradually. The first phase would focus on the installation of geolocation devices in new vehicles and the implementation of pilot projects, as well as a considerable increase in conventional transport taxation to promote renovation of the vehicle fleet. After this initial phase, it would then be possible to introduce the CATV with greater guarantees, replacing existing taxes and optimizing the internalization of external costs, while maintaining revenue capacities.

NOTES

* Support from Naturgy Chair at the University of Vigo is gratefully acknowledged. The authors are thankful for comments and suggestions from an anonymous reviewer, José M Labeaga, Pedro Linares, Juan-Pablo Montero, Marta Villar and attendants at the Global Conference on Environmental Taxation 2019. The usual disclaimers apply.

1. These are the most important externalities, but not the only ones, caused by road traffic. For further information, see Delucchi (2000), Quinet (2004), Santos (2005), Maibach et al (2008), van Essen et al (2011) and Korzhenevych et al (2014).
2. Reducing the use of fuel through taxes is more efficient than through standards or a combination of both because, for any reduction, raising the standard (and lowering the tax) leads to greater fuel efficiency, but less distance travelled, so there will be a smaller reduction in congestion, accidents and local pollution (Anderson et al, 2011). Moreover, standards encourage the owners of used vehicles to postpone the decision to replace them

with a new, more efficient vehicle by increasing the price of new vehicles, thus reducing the efficiency of the fleet (Jacobsen and van Benthem, 2015).
3. There is growing academic evidence that consumers of fuels for transport react more to tax changes than to price changes because the former last longer and are more salient (Davis and Kilian, 2011; Li et al, 2014; Rivers and Schaufele, 2015; Lawley and Thivierge, 2016; Antweiler and Gulati, 2016; Andersson, 2017). In this context, the drop in fuel consumption might be greater than expected, resulting in an even greater loss of revenue.
4. Moreover, a programme taxing vehicle use might help to improve safety, by issuing warnings on schools, roadworks, hazardous conditions or traffic accidents; they might also provide new, added-value services for drivers such as pay-as-you-drive insurance (USDT, 2012), automatic payment for parking and tolls, or travel services depending on the location (real-time roadside assistance, identification of nearby points of interest). In addition, the system generates a large amount of anonymous data on travel that could be used to improve transport planning and operation (Sorensen et al, 2012).
5. Although all vehicles would face an off-peak rate, payments would depend on the type of car. For instance, electric vehicles would not pay for global pollution as long as the electricity sector was under a carbon pricing scheme. The same reasoning applies to the remaining externalities.
6. A registration tax would allow the principle of payment capacity to be maintained as a relevant criterion in fiscal design and would guide purchasers towards vehicles that incur lower negative externalities, thus avoiding contradictions with the functioning of the CATV.
7. This was the case with the kilometre tax in Holland (van Wee, 2010; Meurs, 2017) and the congestion taxes in New York, Edinburgh, Manchester and Birmingham (Hammadou and Papaix, 2014).
8. Recall that tackling income inequality through taxation and welfare systems is more effective and efficient than implicitly subsidizing goods – that is, setting their prices below social costs (Eliasson, 2016).

REFERENCES

Aasness, Jørgen and Erling Røed Larsen (2002), 'Distributional and environmental effects of taxes on transportation', *Discussion paper nº 321, Statistics Norway Research Department.*

Anderson, Soren T and James M Sallee (2016), 'Designing policies to make cars greener', *Annual Review of Resource Economics*, 8 (1), 157–180.

Anderson, Soren T, Ian WH Parry, James M Sallee and Carolyn Fischer (2011), 'Automobile fuel economy standards: impacts, efficiency, and alternatives', *Review of Environmental Economics and Policy*, 5 (1), 89–108.

Andersson, Julius (2017) 'Cars, carbon taxes and CO_2 emissions', Centre for Climate Change Economics and Policy Working Paper 238, available at www.lse.ac.uk/GranthamInstitute/wp-content/uploads/2017/03/Working-paper-212-Andersson_update_March2017.pdf, last accessed 22 November 2018.

Antweiler, Werner and Sumeet Gulati (2016), 'Frugal cars or frugal drivers? How carbon and fuel taxes infuence the choice and use of cars', available at https://ssrn.com/abstract=2778868, last accessed 22 November 2018.

Asociación Española de Fabricantes de Automóviles y Camiones (ANFAC) (2018), 'Annual Report 2017', available at www.anfac.com/memory/assets/memoriaanfac2017.pdf, last accessed 22 November 2018.

Austin, David and Terry Dinan (2005), 'Clearing the air: The costs and consequences of higher CAFE standards and increased gasoline taxes', *Journal of Environmental Economics and Management*, 50 (3), 562–582.

BBVA Research (2017), 'The road ahead for electric vehicles', available at www.bbvaresearch.com/wp-content/uploads/2017/02/170213_US_ElectricVehicles.pdf, last accessed 22 November 2018.

Beuermann, Christiane and Tilman Santarius (2006), 'Ecological tax reform in Germany: handling two hot potatoes at the same time', *Energy Policy*, 34 (8), 917–929.

Bloomberg (2016), 'An integrated perspective on the future of mobility', available at www.mckinsey.com/~/media/mckinsey/business%20functions/sustainability%20and%20resource%20productivity/our%20insights/an%20integrated%20perspective%20on%20the%20future%20of%20mobility/an-integrated-perspective-on-the-future-of-mobility.ashx, last accessed 22 November 2018.

Brons, Martijn, Peter Nijkamp, Eric Pels and Piet Rietveld (2008), 'A meta-analysis of the price elasticity of gasoline demand. A SUR approach', *Energy Economics*, 30 (5), 2105–2122.

Brouwer, Travis L, Karen S Doyle, Linda T Hull, David Kuhn, Humberto A Tasaico, Lorie Tudor, Gill Rogers and Daniel Yeh (2016), *Transportation Governance and Finance. A 50-State Review of State Legislatures and Departments of Transportation*, Washington, DC, USA: American Association of State Highway and Transportation Officials.

Capgemini (2015), 'Transport market monitor', Edition 25, available at www.capgemini.com/consulting/wp-content/uploads/sites/30/2017/07/151022_tmm25_en.pdf, last accessed 22 November 2018.

Davis, Lucas W and Lutz Kilian (2011), 'Estimating the effect of a gasoline tax on carbon emissions', *Journal of Applied Econometrics*, 26 (7), 1187–1214.

Delucchi, Mark A (2000), 'Environmental externalities of motor vehicle use', *Journal of Transport Economics and Policy*, 34 (2), 135–168.

Ekins, Paul and Stefan Speck (eds) (2011), *Environmental Tax Reform: A Policy for Green Growth*, Oxford, UK: Oxford University Press.

Eliasson, Jonas (2016), 'Is congestion pricing fair? Consumer and citizen perspectives', *Transport Policy*, 52 (November), 1–15.

European Commission (EC) (2018), *Taxation Trends in the European Union. 2018 Edition*, Luxembourg: Publications Office of the European Union.

European Environmental Agency (EEA) (2011), *Environmental Tax Reform in Europe: Implications for Income Distribution*, EEA Technical Report 16/2011, Luxembourg: Publications Office of the European Union.

European Parliament (EP) (2015), 'Regulation (EU) 2015/758 of the European Parliament and of the Council of 29 April 2015 concerning type-approval requirements for the deployment of the eCall in-vehicle system based on the 112 service and amending Directive 2007/46/EC', Official Journal of European Union, available at https://eur-lex.europa.eu/legal-content/EN/TXT/PDF/?uri=CELEX:32015R0758&from=EN, last accessed 22 November 2018.

Federal Customs Administration (FCA) (2017), 'Performance-related heavy vehicle charge. Overview', available at www.ezv.admin.ch/ezv/en/home/information-companies/transport--travel-documents--road-taxes/heavy-vehicle-charges--performance-related-and-lump-sum-/hvc---general---rates.html, last accessed 22 November 2018.

Flues, Florens and Alastair Thomas (2015), 'The distributional effects of energy taxes', *OECD Taxation Working Papers, 23*, Paris, France: OECD Publishing.

Gago, Alberto, Xavier Labandeira and Xiral López-Otero (2014), 'A Panorama on energy taxes and green tax reforms', *Hacienda Pública Española. Review of Public Economics*, 208, 145–190.

Gärling, Tommy and Geertje Schuitema (2007), 'Travel demand management targeting reduced private car use: effectiveness, public acceptability and political feasibility', *Journal of Social Issues*, 63 (1), 139–153.

Hammadou, Hakim and Claire Papaix (2014), 'Which policy tools to move towards low carbon mobility?', in Alexanda Hyard (ed), *Non-Technological Innovations for Sustainable Transport. Four Transport Case Studies*, London, UK: Springer, pp5–26.

Hylén, Bertil, Jari Kauppila and Edouard Chong (2013), 'Road haulage charges and taxes. Summary analysis and data tables 1998–2012', Discussion Paper 2013–8, International Transport Forum, OECD.

Jacobsen, Mark R (2013), 'Evaluating US fuel economy standards in a model with producer and household heterogeneity', *American Economic Journal: Economic Policy*, 5 (2), 148–187.

Jacobsen, Mark R and Arthur van Benthem (2015), 'Vehicle scrappage and gasoline policy', *American Economic Review*, 105 (3), 1312–1338.

Jones, Kathryn and Maureen Bock (2017), 'Oregon's road usage charge. The OReGO program', Final Report, Oregon Department of Transportation, available at www.oregon.gov/ODOT/Programs/RUF/IP-Road%20Usage%20Evaluation%20Book%20WEB_4-26.pdf, last accessed 22 November 2018.

Kleit, Andrew N (2004), 'Impacts of long-range increases in the fuel economy (CAFE) standard', *Economic Inquiry*, 42 (2), 279–294.

Korzhenevych, Artem, Nicola Dehnen, Johannes Bröcker, Michael Holtkamp, Henning Meier, Gena Gibson, Adarsh Varma and Victoria Cox (2014), *Update of the Handbook on External Costs of Transport*. London, UK: Ricardo-AEA.

Kosonen, Katri (2012), 'Regressivity of environmental taxation: myth or reality?' in Janet E Milne and Mikael Skou Andersen (eds), *Handbook of Research on Environmental Taxation*, Cheltenham, UK and Northampton, MA, USA: Edward Elgar Publishing, pp161–174.

KPMG (2017), 'Global Automotive Executive Survey 2017', available at https://assets.kpmg.com/content/dam/kpmg/xx/pdf/2017/01/global-automotive-executive-survey-2017.pdf, last accessed 22 November 2018.

Krueger, Cameron and Tiffany Johnson (2016), 'Financing the future of mobility', available at https://dupress.deloitte.com/dup-us-en/focus/future-of-mobility/transportation-ecosystem-future-of-auto-finance.html, last accessed 22 November 2018.

Labandeira, Xavier, José M Labeaga and Xiral López-Otero (2017), 'A meta-analysis on the price elasticity of energy demand', *Energy Policy*, 102 (March), 549–568.

Labandeira, Xavier, Miguel Rodríguez and José M Labeaga (2007), 'Microsimulation in the analysis of environmental tax reforms: an application for Spain', in Spadaro, Amedeo (ed) *Microsimulation as a Tool for the Evaluation of Public Policies: Methods and Applications*. Fundación BBVA, Madrid.

Labeaga, José M, Xavier Labandeira and Xiral López-Otero (2018), 'Energy tax reform and poverty alleviation in Mexico', *WP 18-01, Departamento de Economía Aplicada Universidade de Vigo*.

Langer, Ashley, Vikram Maheshri and Clifford Winston (2017), 'From gallons to miles: a disaggregate analysis of automobile travel and externality taxes', *Journal of Public Economics*, 152 (August), 34–46.

Larsen, Lisa, Mark Burris, David Pearson and Patricia Ellis (2012), 'Equity evaluation of fees for vehicle miles traveled in Texas' *Transportation Research Record: Journal of the Transportation Research Board*, 2297, 11–20.

Lawley, Chad and Vincent Thivierge (2016), 'Refining the evidence: British Columbia's carbon tax and household gasoline consumption', available at https://ssrn.com/abstract=2874417, last accessed 22 November 2018.

Levinson, Arik (2018), 'Energy efficiency standards are more regressive than energy taxes: theory and evidence', Georgetown University and NBER, available at http://faculty.georgetown.edu/aml6/pdfs&zips/RegressiveMandates.pdf, last accessed 22 November 2018.

Levinson, David (2010), 'Equity effects of road pricing: a review', *Transport Reviews*, 30 (1), 33–57.

Li, Shanjun, Joshua Linn and Erich Muehlegger (2014), 'Gasoline taxes and consumer behavior', *American Economic Journal: Economic Policy*, 6 (4), 302–342.

Lindsey, Robin (2010), 'Reforming road user charges: a research challenge for regional science', *Journal of Regional Science*, 50 (1), 471–492.

Lowry, Sean (2015) 'The federal excise tax on motor fuels and the highway trust fund: current law and legislative history', Congressional Research Service, RL30304, available at http://nationalaglawcenter.org/wp-content/uploads/assets/crs/RL30304.pdf, last accessed 22 November 2018.

Maibach, Markus, Christoph Schreyer, Daniel Sutter, Huib van Essen, Bart Boon, Richard Smokers, Arno Schroten, Claus Doll, Barbara Pawlowska and Monika Bak (2008), *Handbook on Estimation of External Costs in the Transport Sector, Version 1.1*, Delft, Netherlands: CE Delft.

McKinsey (2016), 'The future of automotive retail – a scenario based approach', available at https://denkvooruitdenkdigitaal.nl/files/000/000/092/618255%20-%20McKinseyCompany%20The%20future%20of%20Automotive%20Retail%20september%202016.pdf, last accessed 22 November 2018.

McLure, Charles E (2009), 'Taxing commercial motor fuel in the European Union: the case for an apportionment-based, destination-principle system', *International Tax and Public Finance*, 16 (3), 395–414.

McMullen, B Starr, Lei Zhang and Kyle Nakahara (2010), 'Distributional impacts of changing from a gasoline tax to a vehicle-mile tax for light vehicles: a case study of Oregon', *Transport Policy*, 17 (6), 359–366.

Meurs, Henk (2017), 'Pricing kilometres in The Netherlands', available at www.toi.no/getfile.php/1345986/mmarkiv/Forskningsprogram/Samfunnsøkonomiske%20analyser/Pricing%20kilometres%20in%20The%20Netherlands%20-%20Henk%20Meurs.pdf, last accessed 22 November 2018.

OECD (2018), 'Revenue Statistics – OECD countries: comparative tables', available at https://stats.oecd.org/index.aspx?DataSetCode=REV#, last accessed 22 November 2018.

Parry, Ian WH, Dirk Heine, Eliza Lis and Shanjun Li (2014), *Getting Energy Prices Right: from Principle to Practice*, Washington, DC, USA: International Monetary Fund.

Quinet, Emile (2004), 'A meta-analysis of Western European external costs estimates', *Transportation Research Part D*, 9 (6), 465–476.

Ramsey, Frank P (1927), 'A contribution to the theory of taxation', *Economic Journal*, 37 (145), 47–61.

Rausch, Sebastian, Gilbert E Metcalf, John M Reilly and Sergey Paltsev (2010), 'Distributional implications of alternative U.S. greenhouse gas control measures', *The B.E. Journal of Economic Analysis & Policy*, 10 (2), Article 1.

Rivers, Nicholas and Brandon Schaufele (2015), 'Salience of carbon taxes in the gasoline market', *Journal of Environmental Economics and Management*, 74 (November), 23–36.

Sælen, Håkon and Steffen Kallbekker (2011), 'A choice experiment on fuel taxation and earmarking in Norway'. *Ecological Economics*, 70 (11), 2181–2190.

Sansom, Tom, Chris Nash, Peter Mackie, Jeremy Shires and Paul Watkiss (2001), *Surface Transport Costs & Charges. Great Britain 1998*, Leeds, UK: Institute for Transport Studies.

Santos, Georgina (2005), 'Urban congestion charging: a comparison between London and Singapore', *Transport Reviews*, 25 (5), 511–534.

Santos, Georgina (2017), 'Road fuel taxes in Europe: do they internalize road transport externalities?', *Transport Policy*, 53 (January), 120–134.

Santos, Georgina, Hannah Behrendt, Laura Maconi, Tara Shirvani and Alexander Teytelboym (2010), 'Part I: Externalities and economic policies in road transport', *Research in Transportation Economics*, 28 (1), 2–45.

Sorensen, Paul, Liisa Ecola and Martin Wachs (2012), *Mileage-Based User Fees for Transportation Funding*, Santa Monica, USA: RAND Corporation.

Sterner, Thomas (2012), 'Distributional effects of taxing transport fuel', *Energy Policy*, 41 (February), 75–83.

US Department of Transportation (USDT) (2017), 'Government Transportation Financial Statistics 2014' Bureau of Transportation Statistics, available at www.bts.gov/archive/publications/government_transportation_financial_statistics/2014/table_3a, last accessed 22 November 2018.

US Department of Transportation (USDT) (2012), 'Report on the value pricing pilot program through April 2012', available at https://ops.fhwa.dot.gov/congestionpricing/value_pricing/pubs_reports/rpttocongress/vppp12rpt.pdf, last accessed 22 November 2018.

Van Essen, Huib, Arno Schroten, Mathijs Otten, Daniel Sutter, Christoph Schreyer, Remo Zandonella, Markus Maibach and Claus Doll (2011), *External Costs of Transport in Europe: Update study for 2008*, Delft, Netherlands: CE Delft, Infras y Faaunhofer ISI.

Van Wee, Bert (2010), 'The new Dutch per-kilometre driving Tax', CESifo DICE Report 2/2010, available at www.econstor.eu/bitstream/10419/167003/1/ifo-dice-report-v08-y2010-i2-p64-68.pdf, last accessed 22 November 2018.

Zhang, Lei, B Starr McMullen, Divya Valluri and Kyle Nakahara (2009), 'Vehicle mileage fee on income and spatial equity. Short- and long-run impacts', *Transportation Research Record: Journal of the Transportation Research Board*, 2115, 110–118.

12. Sharing cars: a legal and economic analysis of the taxation of B2C car-sharing models

Fanny Vanrykel, Bruno De Borger and Marc Bourgeois

1. INTRODUCTION

Recently, shared mobility has become a hot topic in urban mobility discussions. Shared transportation models, such as Ofo in Paris and Car2go in Madrid, affect people's travel behaviour, generating social, environmental and land use impacts. Notably, they can reduce car ownership and increase the use of alternative transportation modes while reducing fuel consumption, greenhouse gas emissions and the number of kilometres driven by cars, and raising environmental awareness.

In this chapter, we start from the observation that current taxes have been conceived in the context of individual car ownership, whereas new car-sharing models are based on providing access to cars for personal use. Using an interdisciplinary approach, we discuss the challenges that car sharing implies for existing car-related tax instruments from a legal and economic viewpoint, using Belgium as an example. We argue that car sharing necessitates careful reconsideration of existing ownership taxes and the planned future introduction (eg, road pricing) of new tax instruments and user charges.

2. CAR SHARING: A LITERATURE REVIEW

New consumption models have proliferated in recent years, enabling access to a wide range of services. Consumers' attitudes are shifting from buying and owning goods to paying for temporary access to them; they prefer to consume a particular quantity at a particular time and place (Wilhelms et al, 2017). While ownership remains a reality, access-based services – defined as 'transactions that can be market mediated but where no transfer of ownership takes place' (Bardhi and Eckhardt, 2012) – occupy an increasingly large share of market transactions. In such models, access is obtained by sharing/pooling goods, resources and services, facilitated by advanced technologies and peer-to-peer communities (Botsman and Rogers, 2010; Gansky, 2010). Car sharing is one of these alternative modes of consumption; it causes (disruptive) changes to the transport sector.

Car sharing is a form of shared mobility, alongside other modes such as ride sharing, bike sharing and ride sourcing. It consists of 'short-term vehicle access among a group of members who share a vehicle fleet that is maintained, managed, and insured by a third-party organization. It is typically provided through self-service vehicle access on a 24-hour basis for short-term trips' (Shaheen, Chan and Micheaux, 2015). In such a scheme, 'individuals gain the benefits of private-vehicle use without the costs and responsibilities of ownership' (Shaheen and Cohen, 2007). Car-sharing users access vehicles by joining an organization that maintains a fleet of cars deployed in lots located in different places (eg, within neighbourhoods; at public transit stations, employment centres and universities). Generally, the car-sharing operator provides gasoline, parking and maintenance, while participants pay a fee each time they use a vehicle (Shaheen and Cohen, 2007). Although the earliest experiences of car-sharing can be traced back to 1948 in Europe, growth has been particularly remarkable during the past few years, thanks to advances in information and communication technologies, and to the scaling up of platforms (Franck and Mayeres, 2016; Hildebrandt et al, 2015), especially in Belgium, Germany and the Netherlands.

Car-sharing services can be provided by automakers (eg, Car2Go and Drivenow) and car rental companies, but also by non-profit companies, under the form of peer-to-peer (P2P), business-to-consumer (B2C) or business-to-business (B2B) relations (Le Vine et al, 2014). Car-sharing models also differ regarding the type of vehicle used (eg, petrol/diesel, electric, compressed natural gas), whether the operating company has established partnerships with public authorities or private companies, and the pricing structure of their services. User prices can be set in different ways, such as a fixed fee (per day/month/year), a unit price per kilometre, a unit price per minute or a two-part tariff that combines a subscription fee with a unit charge.

The potential impact of car sharing has already been analysed in the literature. Several studies have reported evidence that car sharing generates transportation, land use, environmental and social benefits. For instance, Kopp et al (2015) indicate that car-sharing members are more multimodal than non-members. Other publications show that car sharing reduces the number of vehicle-kilometres travelled and, as a consequence, congestion (Martin, Shaheen and Lidicker, 2010; Lane, 2005). Since cars employed in car-sharing programmes are used more intensively, there is also a quicker turnover of the fleet, which implies that older models are replaced faster by (presumably) cleaner new models (Franck and Mayeres, 2016). Furthermore, one car used for car sharing replaces several vehicles (between three and 13 for round-trip car sharing) among car-sharing members, which diminishes the volume of cars and, hence, the public space (eg, roads, parking) they use (Franck and Mayeres, 2016). In addition, vehicle size can be adapted to the purpose of the trip and number of passengers. Finally, a number of authors have emphasized the benefits of car sharing for the market penetration of electric cars (Firnkorn and Müller, 2015; Wappelhorst et al, 2014; Le Vine et al, 2014).

3. THE CHALLENGES OF CAR-SHARING MODELS FOR MOTOR VEHICLE TAXES

Motor vehicle taxes were conceived as instruments allowing for taxation of the ability to pay relating to car ownership. As B2C car-sharing models are characterized by allowing access and use of such vehicles without transfer of ownership, they affect the structure of such ownership taxes. In this part of the chapter, we discuss the challenges that car-sharing models present to policy makers when redesigning car-related taxes and road charges. In particular, B2C car sharing affects both the taxable object, implying a risk of tax revenue erosion (see section 3.1), and the taxable person (owner versus user; see section 3.2). Moreover, it may engender tax competition (see section 3.3). Finally, car sharing also has implications for the implementation of future user charges (eg, road pricing, cordon pricing in cities, kilometre charges). It affects the design of new pricing systems, if these were to be introduced (see section 3.4).

3.1 Taxable Event: Risk of Tax Revenue Erosion

Motor vehicle taxes have some common features in European Member States' tax systems. In the EU, every single Member State levies a registration tax on vehicles. In addition, most European countries levy a tax on car ownership – for instance, an annual circulation tax (ACEA, 2018a).[1] These taxes are generally associated with the idea of car ownership, because they are due in the event of car purchase, car registration or car possession, regardless of the extent to which and the intensity with which the car is used.

In Belgium, there are two types of motor vehicle taxes: registration tax and annual circulation tax. Registration tax is a fixed acquisition tax, due once when the car is registered. On the contrary, annual circulation tax is a tax on ownership. It is due for periods of 12 consecutive months, with the first period starting on the first day of the month in which the vehicle is or shall be registered (Article 22 of the so-called Code of Taxes Act with equivalent effect to income taxes (ATC)). The taxable object with respect to car registration tax is defined as the use of a public road by a motor vehicle,[2] which is presumed when the (new or second-hand) car is registered with the vehicle registration department (Art 99, § 1st ATC). The same presumption applies to annual circulation tax, whose taxable object is characterized as the registration of cars.[3]

As noted, car sharing is assumed to reduce the number of cars on the road, as one car used for car sharing is predicted to replace several vehicles. To the extent that car sharing leads to the registration of fewer cars, one can expect revenues derived from motor vehicle taxes to decline (Adler, Peer and Sinozic, 2018).

There are several options to compensate for this revenue loss, the extent of which cannot easily be determined at this moment – it is likely to be limited at first, but it may become sizeable if car sharing becomes more popular. However, all have their problems. First, the effect of the reduction in the number of cars on circulation and registration tax revenues could be compensated by a higher tax rate. This seems undesirable from an economic perspective, because these taxes are very weak instruments to tackle transport congestion and environmental externalities. Second, the loss in fixed acquisition (registration tax) and circulation taxes can be compensated by higher charges on car use. This would be economically much more efficient, as user taxes are much better at internalizing congestion and other externalities than fixed taxes. A problem in the Belgian context is that the most important current user tax (the fuel tax) is under federal jurisdiction. Therefore, if one wants to compensate for the loss in fixed tax revenue for the regions with higher user charges, a deal must be negotiated between the regions and the federal level. Alternatively, compensation must be effected through a future user tax (road pricing), over which the regions arguably have jurisdiction. Third, to compensate for tax revenue losses, one might also consider differentiating the registration tax between personal ownership and car-sharing firms. However, there is no obvious economic basis for applying higher ownership taxes to car-sharing firms (see De Borger, Russo and Verhoef, 2018), and this could raise legal issues of (prohibited) discrimination.

3.2 The Taxable Person: Owner versus User

Vehicle taxes have been progressively utilized as an environmental policy tool, providing appropriate incentives to use more environmentally friendly cars. This is clear from a number of EU documents. In particular, the report *Fiscal Measures to Reduce CO_2 Emissions from New Passenger Cars* assessed the extent to which vehicle-related taxes (mainly acquisition taxes and ownership taxes) can represent effective means to reduce carbon dioxide (CO_2) emissions from new cars (TIS, 2002; COWI, 2002). This was the basis for a Communication entitled 'Taxation of passenger cars in the European Union – options for action at national and community levels',[4] which was followed by a directive proposal.[5] The proposal's purpose was twofold: to improve the functioning of the internal market and to implement the Community's strategy to reduce CO_2 emissions from passenger cars by restructuring motor vehicle taxes. Although the proposal was not adopted, 22 Member States currently base their registration tax or/and their annual circulation tax on environmental criteria, either totally or partially (CO_2, Euronorm etc).[6]

In Belgium, the tax base and rate of the motor vehicle taxes vary considerably across the regions, but the Flemish Region and to some extent the Walloon Region have used these taxes as environmental policy tools. In the Walloon Region, the registration tax depends on two criteria: (1) the cylinder capacity of the car (expressed in fiscal horsepower or in kilowatts), combined with the age of the vehicle (the amount decreases with the age of the vehicle); and (2) the eco-malus, which depends on the CO_2 emissions of the car. Such a scheme pursues a twofold objective: a social or redistributive objective, based on the first component (cylinder capacity and age); and an environmental objective, pursued by the second component (CO_2 emissions).[7] The Flemish Region bases its registration tax solely on environmental criteria: the CO_2 emissions of the vehicle, the type of fuel used and the Euronorm.[8] By contrast, in the Brussels-Capital Region, the registration tax depends on the cylinder capacity and the age of the vehicle; the tax diminishes as the age of the vehicle increases. Hence, it merely pursues social or redistributive objectives. The same tax base is used for the annual circulation tax in the Walloon Region and in the Brussels-Capital Region, whereas the Flemish annual circulation tax depends on environmental parameters.[9]

What challenges does car sharing present for the current tax system? The scaling up of car-sharing models may influence the way that taxes are designed, assuming that they strive to achieve environmental or transport policy goals. Indeed, in the case of B2C car-sharing, the taxable person – that is, the individual or legal entity which is mentioned in the vehicle registration document – will be the car-sharing (or eventually the leasing) company. Therefore, these taxes are not owed by the car users; rather – depending on both the market structure of the car-sharing industry and the pricing strategies of the car-sharing companies – the taxes will be reflected in higher user charges, either via increases in the subscription fee or via higher unit charges per kilometre or per minute, or both.

This observation has potentially important consequences. This follows from the fact that firms and individuals are affected by taxes through different channels. To be more precise, note that currently fixed acquisition and annual circulation taxes are borne by individual households, so what matters is the price elasticity of the demand for cars with respect to fixed acquisition and circulation taxes. Given that in Belgium (unlike in, for example, Denmark), these taxes currently constitute a relatively small share of the consumer cost of a car, this elasticity is quite small and the implications for car buyers and car manufacturers are relatively limited. With the introduction of car sharing, however, what matters is the price sensitivity of the car-sharing firms with respect to these taxes. This, in turn, strongly depends on the degree to which the firms can transmit the charges into higher subscription fees and per-unit charges to the customers. This in turn depends on the market structure of the car-sharing industry and the price elasticities of demand of car sharers. If the car-sharing industry becomes relatively competitive over time and demand is highly price sensitive, the car-sharing companies will bear most of the burden of the taxes, not their clients; however, if clients are not price sensitive, they will face higher charges and be worse off. At this moment, as far as we know, there is no economic model that allows for an empirical prediction of the behavioural consequences of the introduction of car sharing.

The introduction of car sharing does not affect the fact that, to the extent that in the future acquisition and circulation taxes remain relevant (they may be phased out if kilometre charges or full electronic road pricing take effect), they must reflect the environmental performance of the vehicle.

3.3 Risk of Tax Competition

Because the place of residence of the vehicle owner in B2C car-sharing models may differ from that of the vehicle user, vehicle taxes are not necessarily levied where the vehicle is used. For instance, the car-sharing company could be established in Brussels or in Paris, while car-sharing services are provided in Antwerp. Furthermore, users do not necessarily have their place of residence where the vehicle is used. This could lead to problems of double taxation, eventually breaching European freedom of establishment,[10] and at the risk of tax competition between regions or between Member States. Such considerations, although not taken in the specific context of car sharing, have justified the aforementioned proposal of the Directive on passenger car-related taxes.[11]

In Belgium, the place where the taxable person is established determines which regional regulation should be applied. It also indicates which Region benefits from the tax proceeds and which tax authorities are entitled to administer the levy (Art 5, §1, 10 & 11° of the Special Financing Law). For instance, if the owner of the car is resident in the Flemish Region, he will have to pay the Flemish registration tax to the benefit of the Flemish tax authorities. To prevent tax competition between the Regions, Article 4, § 3 of the Special Financing Law requires the conclusion of a cooperation agreement between the Regions to modify vehicle taxes in the event that the taxable person is a leasing company. However, surprisingly, this procedural obligation does not apply where the taxable person is a car renting company, although it was noted that the risk also exists in the case of renting and leasing companies. Therefore, no specific rule in Belgium currently addresses the risk of tax competition caused by B2C car-sharing models.

3.4 Road Pricing

Although the most important tax on car use is the fuel tax on gasoline and diesel, one expects that the role of fuel taxes will reduce in the future with the expected increase in market penetration of electric vehicles and with the expected shift from fuel taxes to different forms of road pricing (eg, kilometre charges, electronic road pricing, cordon charges in cities). European institutions have encouraged the use of road pricing instruments, based on the 'user pays' and 'polluter pays' principles, promoting financially and environmentally sustainable and socially equitable road transport (De Borger and Proost, 2017). In this context, transport taxes have a double function: on the one hand, they raise revenues; on the other hand, they correct market failures associated with the external costs generated by road transport (eg, pollution, CO_2 emissions, congestion, accident risks). The common economic premise is that transport taxes should aim to internalize externalities.

Many Member States have implemented a system of passenger car-use charges, in the form of either time-based charges (vignettes) – which are often levied on the full primary network – or distance-based charges (tolls), typically levied on only a limited number of road sections. By contrast, there is currently no distance-based system levied on the whole road network, although the European Commission recommends that Member States move towards distance-based road charging systems based on actual kilometres driven.

The EU initially emphasized the conditions under which Member States can impose taxes, tolls and user charges to heavy goods vehicles (HGVs).[12] In 2017, the European Commission endeavoured to extend HGV charges to passenger car use, which had hitherto been left unaddressed. In particular, the Directive proposal intends 'to make progress in the application of the "polluter pays" and "user pays" principles, thereby promoting financially and environmentally sustainable and socially equitable road transport'.[13] With the extension of its scope, the directive should ensure a more consistent tax policy across the road transport sector and further reflect external costs in road charges.[14]

This initiative echoes a number of other documents in which the Commission encourages the use of instruments allowing for the internalization of externalities associated with transport, under the form of road charges. For instance, the White Paper of March 2011 considers the use of road charges 'as an alternative way to generate revenue and influence traffic and travel behaviour'.[15] Similarly, in the communication *A European Strategy for Low-Emission Mobility*, the Commission addressed the issue of 'fair and efficient pricing in transport', indicating that '[a]cross the EU, charging should move towards distance-based road charging systems based on actual kilometres driven, to reflect better the polluter-pays and user-pays principles'.[16]

At the national level, some Member States have considered, or are considering, the adoption of a kilometre tax (also on passenger car use), applicable across their whole territory. For instance, the Netherlands discussed the introduction of such measures as early as in 1988 (Van Wee, 2010). These discussions led to draft legislation in 2009, in which a kilometre tax was based on three parameters: a flat rate per kilometre, a CO_2 component and a modulation varying in time and place.[17] However, the collapse of the government in 2010 impeded its adoption. Similarly, Finland has envisaged the replacement of taxes on vehicle ownership with a tax based on kilometres travelled and CO_2 emissions (Finnish Ministry of Communication and Transport, 2014).

In Belgium, the introduction of a 'smart kilometre tax' for passenger cars was discussed in the Flemish Region over the past decade, complementing the kilometre charge on HGVs already in place. In July 2018, the Flemish government restated its willingness to introduce such a levy, which would replace the annual circulation tax. In the Brussels-Capital Region, a recent report of the Task Force on Greening Vehicle Taxes recommends the adoption of a smart kilometre tax, to address mobility problems faced by the Region.[18] However, these discussions have not yet led to any concrete proposals.

So how would the introduction of road pricing in the future affect the desirable taxation of car-sharing companies? The issue is highly complex and little research is available. In what follows, we point out a few important preliminary findings.[19]

In the absence of road pricing, the main user tax is the fuel tax which, in the case of car sharing, we assume will be paid by the car-sharing company. Suppose further that the company charges its users a per kilometre charge (and not, for example, a fee per minute). The kilometre tax on car sharing should then be such that the unit price per kilometre for car-sharing users equals the company's marginal cost per kilometre, plus a fraction of the marginal external cost per kilometre. This fraction captures the reduction in kilometres driven by car-sharing users, owing to a small increase in the charge that is not replaced by kilometres driven by people using their own car. One can easily show that this fraction is zero when demand is perfectly elastic and one when demand is perfectly inelastic. If demand is totally inelastic, then the higher toll does not reduce overall congestion. The fraction mentioned above equals one, and the toll on car-sharing should equal the company's marginal cost per kilometre plus the full marginal external cost per kilometre. Now, suppose instead that a higher toll per kilometre on car-sharing use leads to a substantial reduction in overall car use. Then, the fraction mentioned before is less than one and the toll on car sharers can be lower than in the first case.

If road pricing is introduced so that car kilometres are taxed on the road, these charges will be paid by car-sharing users, not by the car-sharing company. For people using their own cars, the charge should reflect the marginal external cost per kilometre. In the case of car-sharing kilometres, the sum of the road charge and the kilometre price paid to the car-sharing company should be equal to the marginal external cost plus the resource cost of the car-sharing company.

The above discussion summarizes the desirable characteristics of the tax treatment of car sharing (what economists call 'second-best optimal taxes'). In practice, however, one should take into account the behaviour of the car-sharing firm. This will strongly depend on the market structure of the car-sharing market (eg, are there few companies or many offering such services? Do they compete in prices or rather in quality or other product dimensions?) and on the size of the car-sharing industry relative to the total number of cars on the road. If, initially, very few car-sharing firms operate on the market, it is quite likely that the monopoly power they have induces them to charge unit prices well above production cost. If the sector becomes large relative to the total market, but a limited number of firms dominate the market, the few operating firms will internalize the congestion effects imposed on their own customers and prices may decline. If the sector becomes highly competitive, with a large number of firms offering relatively similar services, prices will come even closer to marginal cost. The outcomes on real-world markets remain to be studied in detail.

4. CONCLUSION

With the emergence of access-based offers, consumption patterns have changed. In particular, there has been a shift from buying and owning goods to paying for temporary access and use. Platforms facilitating such services have emerged in a number of sectors and transportation is no exception. In this chapter, we focused on B2C car-sharing models. Despite their potential benefits on sustainable mobility, we showed that such models create challenges for motor vehicle taxes in several respects, especially if car sharing were to expand substantially. First, B2C car-sharing models could imply tax revenue erosion by reducing the number of cars registered. This loss in fixed acquisition and circulation taxes can be compensated by higher charges on car use. This may well be efficient from an economic point of view, as user charges are better at internalizing transport externalities than fixed charges. Second, the shift from car ownership to sharing means that the vehicle taxes mentioned are payable not by the car users, but by the car-sharing firms. Policy makers should carefully consider that firms and individuals may respond differently to these taxes. Moreover, taxes on consumers and firms may have very different welfare effects; depending both on the market structure of the car-sharing industry and the pricing strategies of the car-sharing companies, the taxes will be reflected in higher subscription fees, higher user charges or both. Further studies are required to empirically predict the behavioural consequences of the introduction of car sharing. Third, B2C car sharing creates a risk of tax competition and of double taxation, which could be addressed by the EU by harmonizing vehicle taxes. Finally, B2C car-sharing models affect the way that road charges should be designed if road pricing were to be introduced in the future.

NOTES

1. With the exception of Estonia, Lithuania and Poland.
2. Bill of Special Law of 25 May 2001, on the re-financing of the Communities and extension of regional tax competences, Chamber of Representatives 2000–01, 1183/7, p159.
3. Ibid.
4. Communication of the European Commission on the Taxation of passenger cars in the European Union – options for action at national and Community levels, COM/2002/0431 final.

5. Proposal for a Council Directive of 5 July 2005 on Passenger car related taxes, COM/2005/0261.
6. Austria, Belgium, Croatia, Cyprus, Czech Republic, Denmark, Finland, France, Germany, Greece, Hungary, Ireland, Latvia, Luxembourg, Malta, Netherlands, Portugal, Slovenia, Spain, Sweden, United Kingdom (ACEA, 2018b).
7. Arts 97–98 ATC.
8. Art 2.3.4.1.2 of the Flemish Tax Code.
9. That is, on the cylinder capacity of the car; but the amount increases or decreases based on the CO_2 emissions, the type of fuel used and the Euronorm.
10. See, for instance, ECJ 14 January 2016, *Commission v Hellenic Republic*, C-66/15.
11. COM/2005/261, op cit.
12. Directive 1999/62/EC of the European Parliament and of the Council of 17 June 1999 on the charging of heavy goods vehicles for the use of certain infrastructures.
13. Proposal of 31 May 2017 for a Directive of the Parliament and of the Council, amending Directive 1999/62/EC on the charging of heavy goods vehicles for the use of certain infrastructures, COM(2017) 275 final.
14. Proposal of 31 May 2017, op cit, p3.
15. White Paper of 28 March 2011, Roadmap to a Single European Transport Area – Towards a competitive and resource efficient transport system, COM/2011/0144 final, p15.
16. Communication from the Commission of 20 July 2016, A European Strategy for Low-Emission Mobility, COM/2016/0501 final, p4.
17. These were based on the report of the committee '*Anders Betalen voor Mobiliteit*'; Advice of 24 June 2005, available at www.rli.nl/sites/default/files/andersbetalenvoormobilitiet6-2005briefadvies.pdf, last accessed 6 August 2018.
18. Parliament of the Region of Brussels-Capital, Discussion on the Task Force on Greening Vehicle Taxes report, Session 2017–18, 703/1.
19. The following discussion is very loosely based on De Borger, Russo and Verhoef (2018).

REFERENCES

ACEA, 2018a. ACEA Tax Guide, available at www.acea.be/uploads/news_documents/ACEA_Tax_Guide_2018.pdf, last accessed 6 August 2018.

ACEA, 2018b. CO2 Based Motor Vehicle Taxes in the EU, available at www.acea.be/publications/article/overview-of-co2-based-motor-vehicle-taxes-in-the-eu, last accessed 6 August 2018.

Adler, MW, Peer, S, Sinozic, T, 2018. 'Autonomous, Connected, Electric Shared vehicles (ACES) and public finance: an explorative analysis'. Presented at WIFO Regional Economics Workshop, Vienna, September.

Bardhi, F, Eckhardt, G, 2012. 'Access-based consumption: the case of carsharing', *J Consum Res:* 39(4), pp881–898.

Botsman, R, Rogers, R, 2010. *What's Mine Is Yours: The Rise of Collaborative Consumption*, New York: HarperCollins.

COWI, 2002. *Fiscal measures to reduce CO2 emissions from new passenger cars*, Report for the European Commission, available at https://ec.europa.eu/taxation_customs/sites/taxation/files/resources/documents/co2_cars_study_25-02-2002.pdf, last accessed 6 August 2018.

De Borger, B, Proost, S, 2017. 'Tax and regulatory policies for European transport: getting there, but in the slow lane', in Parry I, Pittel K and Vollebergh H, *Energy Tax and Regulatory Policy in Europe*, Cambridge: MIT Press, pp259–295.

De Borger, B, Russo, A, Verhoef, E, 2018. 'Should car sharing be subsidized?' Presented at the ITEA Conference, Hong Kong, June.

Finnish Ministry of Communication and Transport, 2014. 'Fair and Intelligent Transport, Final Report', available at https://julkaisut.valtioneuvosto.fi/bitstream/handle/10024/77912/Fair_and_Intelligent_Transport_%28Publications_5-2014%29.pdf?sequence=1&isAllowed=y, last accessed 6 August 2018.

Firnkorn, J, Müller, M, 2015. 'Free-floating electric carsharing-fleets in smart cities: The dawning of a post-private car era in urban environments'. *Environmental Science & Policy*: 45, pp30–40.

Franck, L, Mayeres, I, 2016. 'Future trends in mobility: the rise of the sharing economy and automated transport – Annex A', report of July 2016, available at www.mind-sets.eu/wordpress/wp-content/uploads/2015/11/D3.3-Future_Trends_in_Mobility_The_rise_of_the_sharing_economy_and_automated_transport_Annex_A.pdf, last accessed 6 August 2018.

Gansky, L, 2010. *The Mesh: Why the Future of Business Is Sharing*, New York: Penguin.

Hildebrandt, B, Hanelt, A, Piccinini, E, Kolbe, L, Nierobisch, T, 2015. 'The value of IS in business model innovation for sustainable mobility services – The case of car-sharing'. *Wirtschaftsinformatik* proceedings: 68, available at http://aisel.aisnet.org/wi2015/68, last accessed 6 August 2018.

Kopp, J, Gerike, R, Axhausen, K, 2015. 'Do sharing people behave differently? An empirical evaluation of the distinctive mobility patterns of free-floating car-sharing members'. *Transportation*: 42, p449.

Lane, C, 2005. 'Philly Car Share: First-Year Social and Mobility Impacts of Carsharing in Philadelphia, Pennsylvania'. *Transportation Research Record: Journal of the Transportation Research Board*: 1927, pp158–166.

Le Vine, S, Zolfaghari, A, Polak, J, 2014. *Carsharing: Evolution, Challenges and Opportunities*, 22th ACEA Scientific Advisory Group Report, www.acea.be/uploads/publications/SAG_Report_-_Car_Sharing.pdf, last accessed 6 August 2018.

Martin, E, Shaheen, S, Lidicker, J, 2010. 'Impact of Carsharing on Household Vehicle Holdings: Results from North American Shared-Use Vehicle Survey'. *Transportation Research Record: Journal of the Transportation Research Board*: 2143(1).

Shaheen, S, Chan, N, Micheaux, H, 2015. 'One-way carsharing's evolution and operator perspectives from the Americas'. *Transportation:* 42 (3), pp519–536.

Shaheen, S, Cohen, A, 2007. 'Growth in Worldwide Carsharing: An International Comparison'. *Transportation Research Record: Journal of the Transportation Research Board*, 1992, Transportation Research Board of the National Academies, Washington DC, pp81–89.

TIS, 'Study on véhicule taxation in the member states of the European Union' – Study conducted for the European Commission – Directorate General of Taxation and Customs Union, January 2002, https://ec.europa.eu/taxation_customs/sites/taxation/files/resources/documents/vehicle_tax_study_15-02-2002.pdf, last accessed 20 February 2018.

Van Wee, B, 2010. 'The new Dutch per kilometer driving tax', CESifo DICE Report 2, pp64–68.

Wappelhorst, S, Sauer, M, Hinkeldein, D, Bocherding, A, Gla, T, 2014. 'Potential of electric carsharing in urban and rural areas', *Transportation Research Procedia*: 4, pp374–386.

Wilhelms, MP, Henkel, S, Merfeld, K, 2017. 'You Are What You Share: Understanding Participation Motives in Peer-to-Peer Carsharing', in Meyer and Shaheen (eds), *Disrupting Mobility: Impact of Sharing Economy and Innovative Transportation on Cities*, Cham: Springer International Publishing.

13. Renewable energy, smart grids and hybrid vehicles: a Brazilian case study

Elena Aydos, Rafaela Cristina Oliari and Carlos Araújo Leonetti*

1. INTRODUCTION

The environmental impacts of urban concentration and climate change will necessitate profound changes in human behaviour, including a shift in consumption, production and distribution patterns. The development of new technologies can provide partial answers to the question of how these changes will take place. In this sense, innovation can play a prominent role in climate change mitigation and adaptation, as well as supporting cities in meeting the challenges of urban concentration in the twenty-first century.

In 2013, the Brazilian government launched a public programme called Inova Energia to incentivize innovative projects in the renewable energy, electricity network and transport sectors. This chapter presents a doctrinal analysis of the Inova Energia programme in light of the World Trade Organization (WTO) Agreement on Subsidies and Countervailing Measures (SCM Agreement). Furthermore, it explores current discussions on innovation subsidies in order to assess the programme from the perspective of the principle of transparency.

Section 2 of this chapter describes the Inova Energia programme; section 3 sets out a legal analysis of the programme under the provisions of the SCM Agreement; and section 4 considers the issue of transparency and the source of revenue for the Inova Energia programme.

2. THE INOVA ENERGIA PROGRAMME

The Inova Energia programme was launched in 2013 as a coordinated action between three federal agencies: the Brazilian Electricity Regulatory Agency (ANEEL), the Brazilian Development Bank (BNDES) and the

Funding Authority for Studies and Projects (FINEP). ANEEL is the electric sector regulatory agency. BNDES is a public company that currently represents the primary resource for federal government financing of long-term projects and investments in all sectors of the Brazilian economy. FINEP is a public company, linked to the Ministry of Science and Technology, which participates in the innovation chain with the aim of providing strategic and impactful input that will help to promote sustainable development in Brazil.

The Inova Energia programme invited Brazilian companies to submit business plans for innovation projects relating to (1) smart grids and ultra-high-tension transmission, (2) electric generation from alternative sources, or (3) hybrid vehicles.

The guidelines for the Inova Energia Programme defined an 'innovation project' as:

> the execution of research, development, engineering and/or technological absorption activities; production and commercialization of innovative products, process and/or services; and other necessary actions to take those innovative results to the market, in a competitive way, aiming at the development of Brazilian companies and technologies, in one of the thematic lines mentioned above.[1]

The programme was estimated to be worth US$1.3 billion,[2] which was transferred to successful companies between 2013–17. Each innovation project received financing for up to 90 per cent of its total cost. The programme identified five different categories of support, which varied according to the type of support and the relevant funding agency. For the purposes of this chapter, these categories fell into two main groups: (1) refundable payments (loans) funded by FINEP and BNDES; and (2) non-refundable payments funded by FINEP, BNDES and ANEEL.

Proposals could be presented either individually or jointly, with one company in the group acting as leader. In addition to minimum revenue thresholds for participating companies, projects had to receive funding of at least US$400 000, have a maximum execution period of 60 months and be developed exclusively within the Brazilian territory.

Given the circumstances surrounding the sources of funding, as explained in section 4 below, it can be argued that the Brazilian government has adopted a protectionist approach to innovation, promoting domestic projects while disadvantaging international projects. In this context, it is important to assess whether the financial support provided by the Brazilian government constituted a subsidy under the terms of the SCM Agreement.

3. DID THE FINANCIAL SUPPORT CONSTITUTE A SUBSIDY?

The SCM Agreement aims to establish multilateral disciplines 'on the premise that some forms of government intervention distort international trade, [or] have the potential to distort [international trade]'.[3] Therefore, the objectives of the SCM Agreement are twofold. First, it guides and informs WTO Members pursuant to their rights and obligations relating to subsidies and countervailing measures. Second, it provides a corrective mechanism for WTO Members affected by subsidies or countervailing measures.[4]

Under the SCM Agreement, subsidies encompass a range of transactions through which a government transfers something of economic value to the advantage of a recipient,[5] ranging from the direct transfer of funds by a government or public body to any form of income or price support.[6] This differs from the broader, economics-based definitions[7] in the sense that not all government measures that confer a benefit on recipients are considered to be a subsidy.[8, 9]

The legal analysis of whether the funding provided under the Inova Energia programme constituted a subsidy involves four cumulative inquiries. The first inquiry is whether there was a financial contribution, income or price support by a government. The second inquiry is whether a 'benefit [was] thereby conferred' (Article 1.1(b)). The third inquiry concerns the 'specificity' – that is, whether the financial support was limited to specific enterprises or industries. The SCM Agreement also provides for two types of prohibited subsidies: local content and export. These are deemed to be specific and are prohibited per se. Even where a subsidy is not prohibited, a fourth inquiry determines whether a specific subsidy is actionable – that is, whether it causes injury to other Members.

3.1 First Inquiry: Financial Contribution

Under the Inova Energia programme, three Brazilian public agencies directly transferred funds to companies through loans and non-refundable payments, within the exact terms set out in Article 1.1(a)(1)(i) of the SCM Agreement.

Table 13.1 sets out the distribution of funds within each of the three areas covered by the programme.

As on average, loans accounted for 64 per cent of the total funds distributed under the Inova Energia programme, we may assume that these amounted to US$830 million, while non-refundable payments totalled approximately US$470 million.

Table 13.1 Distribution of funds under the Inova Energia programme

	Loans	Non-refundable payments
Smart grids	63%	37%
Alternative energy sources	60%	40%
Hybrid vehicles	64%	46%

Given the above, it is possible to state that the first criterion under the SCM Agreement was satisfied: the Inova Energia programme involved a financial contribution made by public bodies, through both loans and non-refundable payments, within the Brazilian territory.

3.2 Second Inquiry: Benefit Analysis

While the question of whether a financial contribution has been made is analysed from the donor's perspective, the question of whether a benefit has been conferred is analysed from the recipient's perspective.[10] Articles 1.1(a)(i) and 1.1(b) of the SCM Agreement provide that a subsidy shall be deemed to exist where there is a financial contribution by any public body and a 'benefit is thereby conferred'. These are cumulative requirements.

The SCM Agreement does not define the term 'benefit'. This term is usually interpreted in conjunction with the guidelines provided in Article 14 of the SCM Agreement. As under the Inova Energia programme, the Brazilian government granted two types of financial contribution, two different benefit assessments were required.

Approximately 36 per cent of companies received non-refundable financial contributions – that is, the funds flowed directly from the public agencies to the companies. In *Brazil – Aircraft* (Article 21.5 – Canada II),[11] the Panel acknowledged that 'in general, a non-refundable payment will confer a benefit'. Despite the peculiarities of this case, there is no doubt that the Panel considered that a non-refundable payment constitutes a benefit conferred on the recipient. Thus, it may be argued that the non-refundable payments granted by the Brazilian government under the Inova Energia programme constituted a benefit conferred on the relevant companies.

As the factual circumstances behind the loan agreements are diverse, the analysis here is more arduous. Article 14(b) of the SCM Agreement provides that:

> A loan by a government shall not be considered as conferring a benefit, unless there is a difference between the amount that the firm receiving the loan pays on the government loan and the amount the firm would pay on a comparable

> commercial loan which the firm could actually obtain on the market. In this case the benefit shall be the difference between these two amounts.

In *US – Anti-Dumping and Countervailing Duties (China)*, the Appellate Body decided[12] that:

> the benchmark loan under Article 14(b) must be a "loan which the firm could actually obtain on the market". The use of the conditional tense "could", suggests that a benchmark loan under Article 14(b) need not in every case be a loan that exists or that can, in fact, be obtained on the market.

In *EC and certain member States – Large Civil Aircraft*, the Appellate Body decided[13] that:

> There is no benefit – and therefore no subsidy – if the amounts paid by the recipient on the government loan is equal to or higher than what it would have paid on a comparable commercial loan. The amount the recipient would have paid on a commercial loan is a function of the size of the loan, the interest rate, the duration, and other relevant terms of the transaction.

Under the Inova Energia programme, the loans were granted by two federal agencies – BNDES and FINEP – whose standard lines of credit were part of their portfolio and could be accessed by any other companies that fulfilled the same criteria as those participating in the programme.

In the late 1990s, the Brazilian government initiated a significant review of its technological financing policies.[14] Several long-term loans for the financing of technology were introduced, mostly managed by FINEP and BNDES.[15] By contrast, private banks do not finance innovation in Brazil; instead, short-term private loans are used as working capital loans – that is, to finance the everyday operations of a company.[16] As pointed out by Filho and Costa,[17] in Brazil, long-term bank credit for the development of infrastructure has always been provided almost exclusively by BNDES.

Given the above, the authors were unable to identify comparable commercial loans available to assist in assessing whether a 'benefit' was conferred in this case. Despite the favourable general conditions, the loans provided by FINEP and BNDES are completely different from other available commercial loans.[18]

Private financing for innovative companies is increasingly being provided in the form of venture capital, and a new market for investment and structured merger and acquisition operations are developing fast. However, once again, venture capital activites are not comparable to loans. Venture capital involves the transfer of equity and the assumption of a certain degree of risk by investors; there are no interest rates involved. Instead, sophisticated managerial rules are set out to protect the parties.[19]

While the first inquiry (financial contribution) was satisfied in this case, it is not possible to verify whether a 'benefit' existed according to the provisions of the SCM Agreement. Therefore, a subsidy cannot be deemed to exist in relation to the loans. The next section continues with the analysis exclusively in relation to the non-refundable payments, concluding that these indeed constituted a subsidy.

3.3 Third Inquiry: Specificity

Even where a subsidy is deemed to exist, it will not be subject to Parts II, III and V of the SCM Agreement[20] unless it is 'specific' to 'certain enterprises'.[21] The Appellate Body in *United States – Definitive Anti-Dumping And Countervailing Duties on Certain Products from China*[22] clarified that the term 'certain enterprises' 'refers to a single enterprise or industry or a class of enterprises or industries that are known and particularized'.

The definition and scope of the term can be narrow or broad in a given case, depending on several factors. In the case of the non-refundable payments made under the Inova Energia programme, 'certain enterprises' would refer to technology-based enterprises in the renewable energy industry.

Article 2 of the SCM Agreement provides multiple tests to determine the specificity of the subsidy. The principles are flexible, unclear and expansionist.[23] Of particular interest is Article 2.1(b), which provides that:

> Where the granting authority, or the legislation pursuant to which the granting authority operates, establishes objective criteria or conditions governing the eligibility for, and the amount of, a subsidy, specificity shall not exist, provided that the eligibility is automatic and that such criteria and conditions are strictly adhered to. The criteria or conditions must be clearly spelled out in law, regulation, or another official document, so as to be capable of verification.

An initial assessment of the Inova Energia programme reveals that the regulations established objective general eligibility criteria for participating companies, such as nationality, development of innovation activities in the areas covered by the scheme and minimum revenue thresholds.[24] In addition, successful business plans were selected by an evaluation committee, through a case-by-case evaluation of specific and general criteria, including relevance, innovation, technical and commercial feasibility, and local technological and productive content. In fact, the Inova Energia rules were complex, ranging from objective to specific.

One possible (formal) conclusion is that, in accordance with Article 2.1(b) of the SCM Agreement, the public tender established objective criteria and conditions governing eligibility, leading to the conclusion that the subsidy was not 'specific'. However, further reflection could also lead to a different conclusion. An in-depth assessment of the public tender reveals that the rules and proceedings were complex, and the public authorities had significant discretion in the selection of participating companies. Excluding the objective criteria relating to revenue, most criteria were dependent on the discretion of the evaluation committee, whose composition was not disclosed.

Details of the winning business plans, the committee's decisions and reasoning in relation to the more specific selection criteria, the grades attributed to such criteria and the amounts effectively granted to the winning companies, among other things, have never been disclosed. Thus, even though formally objective criteria and conditions were established in the Inova Energia programme, it is impossible to verify how the programme was implemented in practice.

The question is thus whether this lack of transparency, which prevents an assessment of the criteria used to grant the financial contributions, is sufficient to affirm the existence of 'specificity' under Article 2 of the SCM Agreement. Given the above, even if the subsidy is not considered specific, the lack of transparency offends one of the essential principles that underpin the design of public policy on incentives. We address this issue separately below.

3.4 The Issue of 'Local Content'

Under Article 2.3 of the SCM Agreement, any subsidy falling under the provisions of Article 3 shall be deemed to be specific. In turn, Article 3.1(b) provides that a subsidy 'that is contingent, whether solely or as one of several other conditions, upon the use of domestic over imported goods' is prohibited.

In *US – Tax Incentives*,[25] the Appellate Body noted that Article 3.1(b) of the SCM Agreement does not prohibit the subsidization of domestic production per se, but rather the granting of subsidies that are contingent on the use of domestic rather than imported goods. The Appellate Body held that the term 'goods' may be read as a synonym for 'products', and pointed out that this term may refer to any type of good and is not confined to goods that are actually traded.

The Inova Energia programme aimed to promote the development of technology and the production and trade of innovative products. Therefore, 'local technological content' can be interpreted as the technology that would be embedded in the tradable products.

The guidelines for the Inova Energia programme stated the aim of supporting 'Brazilian companies' several times, but did not expressly include local content among the eligibility criteria. However, companies were ranked based on local technological and productive content. Therefore, companies that could demonstrate local technological and productive content were more likely to be selected.

Consequently, while the programme did not impose *de jure* contingency, it is possible that *de facto* contingency may have been imposed. The latter is also prohibited, although the evidentiary standards required in this case are higher.[26]

In *EC and certain member States – Large Civil Aircraft*, the Appellate Body[27] held that 'an evaluation of de facto contingency under Article 3.1(b) should be objectively assessed with respect to the total configuration of facts constituting and surrounding the granting of the subsidy'. In this sense, an evaluation of *de facto* contingency in the Inova Energia programme would consider relevant circumstances, such as the emphasis on the nationality of eligible companies (ie, they had to be Brazilian companies), and the assessment of innovative projects based on the use of local technology.

These two provisions of the programme indicate a preference for the selection of projects that used Brazilian technology and other goods over imported technology and goods. However, this conclusion can be verified only through an assessment of the evaluation committee's reports on how projects were graded against the selection criteria. As explained in section 4 below, this information is not available.

The question is thus whether this lack of transparency (ie, the lack of evidence on how the evaluation committee applied the 'local content' criterion) prevents a positive conclusion. Arguably, based on the objective existence of a 'local content' criterion, the Inova Energia programme may fall within the prohibition in Article 3.1(b) of the SCM Agreement.

4. THE INOVA ENERGIA PROGRAMME IDIOSYNCRASY: SOURCE OF REVENUE AND TRANSPARENCY

In addition to the assessment of the legality of the subsidy, a deeper understanding of the Inova Energia programme within the broader context of Brazilian public policy involves an analysis of the sources of the financial contributions provided by FINEP and ANEEL, as well as the lack of transparency.

4.1 Source of Revenue: Financial Contributions

Article 218 of the Brazilian Constitution provides that 'the State will promote and incentivise the scientific development, technological research, and innovation'. In order to promote research and innovation and strengthen the industrial sector, several fiscal measures and incentives for technological innovation have been implemented in Brazil in recent years.[28]

This chapter focuses on two key policy instruments: Law 10.168/200 and Law 9.9991/2000. Both laws impose taxes and charges on many sectors of the economy. The revenue collected is earmarked for financing technological projects, including a significant number of the non-refundable payments provided by the Inova Energia programme.

Law 10.168/2000 created a federal tax – known as the 'Contribution for the Intervention in the Economic Domain' (CIDE), or as 'CIDE royalties' – which is levied on all imports of technology and technical services at a rate of 10 per cent. The revenue collected is transferred to the National Fund of Science and Technological Development, which is managed and allocated by FINEP.

Arguably, the CIDE royalties are a revival of an inefficient import substitution policy implemented in the 1950s, which resulted in considerable inefficiencies and left Brazil 'internally and internationally non-competitive and with little or no creativity in technological terms'.[29] Similarly, the imposition of CIDE royalties has had the practical effect of discouraging technology imports, giving an advantage to national suppliers, which are not subject to the tax. The resources are then used to finance domestic technology, which is often less efficient and not internationally competitive.[30]

Critical issues with CIDE royalties include a lack of evidence of their effectiveness[31] and inconsistent public data regarding the destination of the revenue.[32] At the very least, it can be argued that it is counter-productive to tax the transfer of internationally competitive technology and then use the revenue to subsidize a few handpicked innovation projects.

Law 9.991/2000 provides that a certain percentage of the net operating revenue of all power distribution companies is to be invested in research and development (R&D) activities. There is no direct charge or transfer of revenue to the government; the legislation rather provides that these resources are to be managed by ANEEL.

A major issue with this policy is that it does not address the real barriers to innovation in the electricity sector in Brazil. Evidence demonstrates that the sector has sufficient resources for R&D, as well as stakeholder engagement. Rather:

> The deficit in innovation, including in relation to the development of renewable energy, can be attributed to other structural and legal hurdles, including issues with competition, barriers to entry and the current mechanisms of price control. In other words, there is no motivation to innovate.[33]

When it comes to incentivizing innovation and economic growth, as per its constitutional obligations, the Brazilian government seems to have the right intentions. However, it still lacks a deeper understanding of what is required to foster and guide innovation. In the case of renewable energy, it can be argued that financing is not the key issue. More critical hurdles to innovation include the inefficient allocation of existing resources and structural inefficiencies relating to the lack of competition and price control mechanisms.

4.2 Transparency

Classical economists, such as Marshall and Pigou, have demonstrated that subsidies can be used to internalize market failures. According to Pigou:

> it is possible for the state, if it so chooses, to remove the divergence in any field by 'extraordinary encouragements' or 'extraordinary restraints' upon investments in that field. The most obvious forms which these encouragements and restraints may assume are, of course, those of bounties and taxes.[34]

However, the use of subsidies can be controversial. A report by the United Nations Environment Programme (UNEP) concluded that 'experience in the countries analysed in this report provides evidence that, in many instances, the net effects of subsidies are negative. In other words, overall social welfare would be higher without subsidies'.[35] In terms of renewable energy subsidies, Kuntze and Moerenhout[36] analysed the relationship between local content requirements (LCR) and renewable energy policy, and established that:

> To date, it seems that most jurisdictions using LCR in renewable energy policies do not choose the correct set of tools to formulate a comprehensive policy including LCR that supports the creation of a viable innovator. This relates to one of the most important concerns: the creation of an endless, costly and ineffective LCR that is not intended to be phased out.

Literature often points to public policy design as the key issue impacting its ineffectiveness.

Maskus[37] states that 'government should justify their actions by setting out clear guidelines and benchmarks for success while limiting the length of time during which subsidies will be paid'. The author concludes that 'subsidization programs should be subject to rigorous ex-post evaluation procedures, both to find out what works and to assess effects on domestic and international competition'.

In order to capture the benefits of subsidies, the abovementioned UNEP Report set out a list of basic principles that countries should apply when designing incentive programmes. Of these, transparency is indispensable, in relation to both the costs and the beneficiaries of the subsidy programme.[38]

Since publication of the call for bids, the general guidelines of the programme and the winning companies in 2013, FINEP, BNDES and ANEEL have disclosed no relevant information regarding the implementation, effectiveness and execution of the winning projects. The business plans of the winning companies have not been made public; likewise, no information is available on on the amounts awarded to each company.

While BNDES, FINEP and ANEEL provided abundant data and information prior to launch of the programme, since 2013 these agencies have disclosed no information regarding its results. Important questions on the relationship between the developed technologies and their environmental, social and economic impacts thus remain unanswered.

The Inova Energia programme – including the application process and communications with enterprises – is managed by FINEP through its website. This website is the main channel through which information on the programme can be obtained. The authors made several unsuccessful attempts to access additional information on the programme from FINEP.

The authors also collated fragmented information from other institutions – such as the Brazilian Federal Revenue Agency, the Intellectual Property Agency and Companies House – in a bid to arrive at a better understanding of the programme and its results. However, these endeavours did not bear fruit. A thorough search of the websites of 103 participants was conducted; but only four of these companies disclosed results from the Inova Energia programme.

No information is available as to whether an *ex-ante* cost-benefit analysis of the Inova Energia programme took place. While the development of renewable energy from sources other than hydroelectric is a priority, the Brazilian authorities have not publicly demonstrated the following: (1) the criteria for determining the total cost of the project ($1.3 billion); (2) the reasons for choosing the three areas of focus; (3) the exact amount allocated to each project; (4) the reasons for the selection of winning companies, including the reasoning of the evaluation committee; (5) the progress made on each project; (6) the results achieved by the winning companies through their R&D activities; and (7) the products and services that resulted from those R&D activities. Given the lack of publicly available data, it is not possible to evaluate the impact – whether positive or negative – of these subsidies in the renewable energy sector.

5. CONCLUSION

Technological advancements in renewable energy and clean vehicles, alternative energy generation and energy measurement and distribution systems will play a pivotal role in helping Brazil to meet its (intended) nationally determined contributions under the Paris Agreement. They will also be crucial in helping cities to deal with the issues that arise from urban concentration. Given Brazil's historically limited experience with innovation, incentives for the development of innovative products and services may be needed.

While at first glance the Inova Energia programme would seem to fulfil this need, a closer analysis reveals some inconsistencies and concerns. Although there were no formal minimum content requirements, the non-refundable financial contributions provided under the programme (approximately 40 per cent of the funding awarded) can be said to have imposed *de facto* local content conditions.

The scheme's lack of transparency is also very problematic. Over four months of preparatory work for this chapter, several attempts were made to seek access to the evaluation committee's decisions, participants' business plans, the achievements and outcomes of the programme and the amounts awarded. These efforts were unsuccessful.

Finally, the source of revenue to fund the programme is also an issue. One major source – CIDE royalties – effectively taxes any attempts to import technology; another provides generous funding to companies that lack a natural motivation to innovate.

Technology does not develop by itself; rather, its development is dependent on conducive legal regimes, economic motivation and appropriate political-institutional conditions. Instead of focusing on providing financial incentives for innovation, the Brazilian government should strive to create a friendly environment for technological development and to establish a transparent path to this end, where information is publicly accessible and policy is properly evaluated.

NOTES

* Dr Elena Aydos, Senior Lecturer, University of Newcastle, elena.aydos@newcastle.edu.au; Msc Rafaela Cristina Oliari, PhD student, Federal University of Santa Catarina,

rafaelaoliari@gmail.com; Dr Carlos Araújo Leonetti, Professor, Federal University of Santa Catarina, cleonetti37@gmail.com.

1. FINEP, *Inova Energia* (2013), www.finep.gov.br/apoio-e-financiamento-externa/programas-e-linhas/programas-inova/inova-energia/81-apoio-e-financiamento/programas-e-linhas/sobre-programas-e-linhas/inova-energia?layout=blog, last accessed 21 January 2019.
2. According to the exchange rate in 2013.
3. Panel Report, *Canada – Measures Affecting the Export of Civilian Aircraft*, WTO Doc WT/DS70/R (14 April 1999) [9.119] (*Canada – Civilian Aircraft*); World Trade Organization, *WTO Analytical Index: Guide to WTO Law and Practice: Agreement on Subsidies and Countervailing Measure* (3rd edn, Cambridge University Press 2011).
4. James Windon, 'The Allocation of Free Emissions Units and The WTO Subsidies Agreement' [2010] 41 *Georgetown Journal of International Law* 189.
5. Appellate Body Report, *United States – Final Countervailing Duty Determination with Respect to Certain Softwood Lumber from Canada*, WTO Doc WT/DS257/AB/R, AB-2003-6 (19 January 2004) [51] (*US – Softwood Lumber IV*).
6. Elena de Lemos Pinto Aydos, *Paying the Carbon Price: The Subsidisation of Heavy Polluters under Emissions Trading Schemes*, New Horizons in Environmental and Energy Law (Edward Elgar 2017).
7. OECD, *Glossary of Statistical Terms* (OECD 2007). The OECD adopted an economics-based definition of a 'subsidy', as 'a result of a government action that confers an advantage on consumers or producers, in order to supplement their income or lower their costs'.
8. Panel Report, *United States – Measures Treating Exports Restraints as Subsidies*, WTO Doc WT/DS194/R (29 June 2001) ('*US – Exports Restraints*') [8.65]. Appellate Body Report, *US – Softwood Lumber IV*, WTO Doc WT/DS257/AB/R [52].
9. Aydos, 2017.
10. Petros C Mavroidis, *The Regulation of International Trade* (The MIT Press 2016) 542.
11. Appellate Body Report, *Brazil – Export Financing Programme for Aircraft AB-1999-1*, WTO Doc WT/DS46/AB/R (2 August 1999).
12. Appellate Body Report, *United States – Definitive Anti-Dumping and Countervailing Duties on Certain Products From China*, WTO Doc WT/DS379/AB/R (11 March 2011).
13. Appellate Body Report, *European Communities and Certain Member States – Measures Affecting Trade in Large Civil Aircraft*, WTO Doc WT/DS316/AB/R (18 May 2011).
14. Fátima Sandra Marques Hollanda, '*Financiamento e Incentivos à Inovação Industrial no Brasil*' (*Tese de Doutoramento, Instituto de Economia da UNICAMP* 2010) 176.
15. Gabriel Alves de Pinho, '*Financiamento Público à Inovação: um exame da alocação de recursos de subvenção econômica e operações de crédito à inovação tecnológica nas empresas*' (*Dissertação de Mestrado*, Unesp 2016) 70.
16. Hollanda, 2010, 56.
17. Ernani Filho and Fernando Costa, '*Financiamento de Longo Prazo no Brasil: um mercado em transformação*' (2013) IPEA, www.ipea.gov.br/portal/index.php?option=com_content&view=article&id=21601, last accessed 21 January 2019.
18. Hollanda, 2010, 93.
19. Christian Keuschnigg, 'Public Policy and Venture Capital Backed Innovation' (2003) Working Paper, 59th Congress of the International Institute of Public Finance, https://papers.ssrn.com/sol3/papers.cfm?abstract_id=464600, last accessed 21 January 2019.
20. Parts II, III and V of the SCM Agreement relate to prohibited subsidies, actionable subsidies and countervailing measures, respectively.
21. Marrakesh Agreement Establishing the World Trade Organization, opened for signature 15 April 1994, 1867 UNTS 3 (entered into force 1 January 1995) Annex 1A ('Agreement on Subsidies and Countervailing Measures') ('SCM Agreement') Article 2.
22. Appellate Body Report, *United States – Definitive Anti-Dumping And Countervailing Duties on Certain Products from China*, WTO Doc WT/DS379/AB/R (11 March 2011).
23. Luca Rubini, 'Ain't Wastin' Time no More: Subsidies for Renewable Energy, The SCM

Agreement, Policy Space, and Law Reform', *Journal of International Economic Law* (2012), https://doi.org/10.1093/jiel/jgs020, last accessed 21 January 2019.
24. FINEP, *Inova Energia* (2013), www.finep.gov.br/apoio-e-financiamento-externa/programas-e-linhas/programas-inova/inova-energia/81-apoio-e-financiamento/programas-e-linhas/sobre-programas-e-linhas/inova-energia?layout=blog, last accessed 21 January 2019.
25. Appellate Body Report, *United States – Conditional Tax Incentives For Large Civil Aircraft*, WTO Doc WT/DS487/AB/R (4 September 2017).
26. Petros Mavroids, Patrick Messerlin and Jasper Wauters, *The Law and Economics of Contingent Protection in the WTO* (Edward Elgar 2008) 413.
27. Appellate Body Report, *European Communities and Certain Member States – Measures Affecting Trade in Large Civil Aircraft*, WTO Doc WT/DS316/AB/R (18 May 2011).
28. Paulo Caliendo, '*Política Fiscal e Desenvolvimento Tecnológico-Empresarial: uma análise crítica sobre inovação e tributação*' [2015] (12) *Revista de Direito Brasileira* 164.
29. Karin Klempp Franco, '*A regulação da contratação internacional de transferência de tecnologia: perspectiva do direito de propriedade industrial, das normas cambiais e tributárias e do direito concorrencial*' (*Tese, Faculdade de Direito da Universidade de São Paulo* 2010) 63.
30. Ibid, 167.
31. Caliendo, 2015, 168.
32. Claudia Marchetti da Silva, '*Uma Avaliação da Instituição da Contribuição de Intervenção de Domínio Econômico como Fomento à Inovação Tecnológica*' (*Dissertação de Mestrado, Universidade Metodista de Piracicaba* 2017) 88.
33. Sergio Salles-Filho, '*Por um novo marco regulatório para o P&D ANEEL*' [2017] *Revista P&D ANEEL* 11.
34. Arthur Cecil Pigou, *The Economics of Welfare* (4th edn, Macmillan and Co., Limited 1932).
35. Anja Von Moltke, Colin Mckee and Trevor Morgan (eds), *Energy Subsidies. Lessons Learned in Assessing their Impact and Designing Policy Reforms* (UNEP, Routledge 2017) 15.
36. Jan-Christoph Kuntze and Tom Moerenhout, 'Local Content Requirements and the Renewable Energy Industry – A Good Match?', International Centre for Trade and Sustainable Development (2013), www.ictsd.org/themes/climate-and-energy/research/local-content-requirements-and-the-renewable-energy-industry-a, last accessed 21 January 2019.
37. Keith Maskus, 'Research and Development Subsidies: A Need for WTO Disciplines?' International Centre for Trade and Sustainable Development (2015), http://e15initiative.org/publications/research-and-development-subsidies-a-need-for-wto-disciplines/, last accessed 21 January 2019.
38. UNEP, 2017, 17.

PART IV

The Evaluation of Cross-Cutting Policies

14. *Ex-post* cost-benefit analysis of environmentally related tax policies: building on programme evaluation studies

Jonas Teusch and Nils Axel Braathen*

1. INTRODUCTION

How can policy analysts use empirical programme evaluation studies to perform *ex-post* assessments of environmentally related tax policies? A number of peer-reviewed academic studies identify the causal effects of environmentally related tax policies on health and environmental outcomes, especially with respect to transport policies. However, quantified effects typically represent a small subset of the potential impacts of the evaluated policies. In addition, rarely do researchers complement their econometric work with an assessment of the social costs and benefits of the policies.

Cost-benefit analysis (CBA) could enrich *ex-post* appraisals of environmentally related tax policies due to its focus on total economic surplus. Specifically, CBA allows the identification of potential trade-offs among policy objectives (Organisation for Economic Co-operation and Development (OECD), 2018a). For example, CBA will not only reveal whether the environmental consequences of a policy are as expected, but can additionally provide information on both intended and unintended co-benefits and costs – for example, with respect to local air pollution and energy poverty. *Ex-post* CBA can therefore inform a revision or discontinuation of the evaluated policy or suggest the need to improve or introduce complementary policies.

These points are developed and illustrated by reference to the French feebate programme for motor vehicles introduced in 2008 (D'Haultfœuille, et al, 2014; D'Haultfœuille, et al, 2016; Durrmeyer, 2018). The French vehicle feebate provides tax incentives for the purchase of relatively carbon dioxide (CO_2) efficient vehicles.[1]

Building on existing studies of the French feebate (D'Haultfœuille, et al, 2014; Durrmeyer, 2018), this chapter discusses and attempts to quantify the full social costs and benefits of the identified effects on the 2008 vehicle cohort, taking into account impacts on vehicle usage over the vehicle lifetime. In addition to the policy's impact on CO_2 emissions, the analysis considers the social cost of other externalities such as local air pollution and the social cost of the resulting revenue shortfall, as well as changes in producer and consumer surplus.

The chapter provides a concrete example as to how policy analysts can fruitfully tap into academic studies that credibly identify causal effects of environmentally related tax policies in the field of transport policies, but do not necessarily provide the information needed to properly inform the policy-making process.

2. BACKGROUND AND METHODOLOGY

2.1 Related Literature

Typically, programme evaluation studies focus on assessing whether the stated objective of the policy was achieved. However, evaluating whether a policy is successful on its own terms is not sufficient to conduct a CBA that seeks to uncover both intended and unintended impacts of a policy and quantify their social costs and benefits. Studies of vehicle feebates and rebates, as well as related research on differentiated vehicle purchase and circulation taxes, are cases in point.[2]

Most common is the narrow focus on the impact of the policy on CO_2 emissions and the related issue of fuel efficiency. This applies to assessments of the French vehicle feebate system (D'Haultfœuille, et al, 2014; D'Haultfœuille, et al, 2016); Swiss annual vehicle registration feebates (Alberini, et al, 2018); CO_2-based tax incentives in the Netherlands (Kok, 2015), and in France, Germany and Sweden (Klier and Linn, 2015); and fuel efficiency-related changes to the Danish registration tax on private vehicles (Mabit, 2014).

Granted, a number of related studies do engage in welfare analysis and therefore go further in the direction of CBA. However, these studies remain incomplete from the perspective of CBA, as they do not account for non-climate externalities, do not provide a comprehensive treatment of fiscal effects and generally do not estimate producer surplus effects.

All of these points apply to research on a feebate programme in the Canadian province of Ontario (Rivers and Schaufele, 2017), and to a study on Swiss annual circulation taxes that are linked to vehicle CO_2

emissions (Alberini and Bareit, 2017). A recent study of Japan's feebate policy estimates producer surplus effects (Konishi and Zhao, 2017), but does not directly provide the other information that would be needed for a CBA. Against this background, it is useful to illustrate how analysts can nevertheless usefully draw upon these studies when conducting *ex-post* appraisals.[3]

2.2 Methodology

The starting point of this chapter is D'Haultfœuille, Givord and Boutin (2014), which estimates the effects of the French vehicle feebate on CO_2 emissions. Specifically, the original article compares the vehicle fleet and its usage under the feebate to the counterfactual of no policy change over the period March–May 2008, following the introduction of the feebate in January 2008.

The original study is extended here in two main ways. First, the present analysis includes discounted future climate benefits and costs that can be expected to result from the estimated changes to the vehicle stock. Second, the original analysis is extended by modelling non-climate externalities, indirect fiscal effects and consumer and producer surplus.

External cost estimates as well as estimates of the social costs of public funds and surplus effects are taken from other studies. Given the uncertainty associated with many of these estimates, whenever possible, range estimates are established and added to the graphs.

3. REVISITING THE FRENCH VEHICLE FEEBATE SYSTEM

3.1 External Costs

3.1.1 Climate costs

The analysis of the climate effects in tonnes of CO_2 is based on the short-run effects estimated by D'Haultfœuille, Givord and Boutin (2014). The original estimates are adjusted to reflect the lifetime emissions that are the result of the feebate-induced changes to the 2008 vehicle cohort (see Annex).

Whereas the feebate programme stayed in place after 2008, changes to future cohorts are not taken into account in the present analysis, as policy changes imply that it would be inappropriate to extrapolate information on feebate-induced purchase decisions into the future. In addition, manufacturers can be expected to react to the existence of a feebate policy and adjust their vehicle portfolio accordingly, offering cleaner vehicles.

However, the feebate-induced changes to the 2008 vehicle cohort will continue to impact on the usage of this cohort's vehicles over their lifetime. Following Rivers and Schaufele (2017), it is assumed that these effects are constant over the vehicle lifetime.[4] Specifically, it is assumed that the newly purchased vehicles have a lifetime of 15 years.

Figure 14.1 reports the estimated fleet composition, rebound, fleet size and manufacturing effects of the feebate scheme. The negative fleet composition effect is due to the fact that feebate-induced cars emit less CO_2 per kilometre than the cars that would have been on the road in the absence of the feebate policy. The positive rebound effect is the result of decreased fuel cost per kilometre driven, which incentivizes consumers to drive more, causing additional CO_2 emissions. The fleet size effect is positive because the feebate increased the total sales of cars by 13 per cent compared to the no-feebate counterfactual, meaning there are now additional cars on the road emitting CO_2. The manufacturing effect is positive because the production of additional vehicles is associated with CO_2 emissions, which is only partly offset by the fact that feebate-induced vehicles are smaller than those that would have been produced otherwise.

The resulting net effect of the feebate is a reduction in CO_2 emissions of

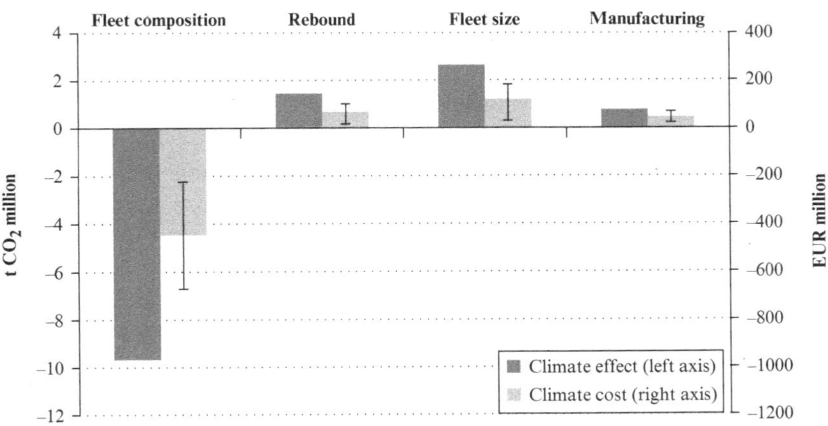

Note: Climate costs assume a social cost of carbon of 60 EUR/t of CO_2. The lower (higher) end of the range estimate refers to a carbon cost of EUR 30 (90) per tonne of CO_2. Post-2008 climate costs are discounted using a 4 per cent discount rate (Smith and Braathen, 2015).

Source: Own analysis (see Annex) based on D'Haultfœuille et al (2014).

Figure 14.1 Climate effects of feebate-induced changes to the 2008 vehicle cohort

4.8 million tonnes, which suggests that the feebate did indeed achieve its goal of reducing carbon emissions. These results are fundamentally different from the short-run effects estimated by the original paper, which found that the feebate increased quarterly emissions by 169 000 tonnes.

The explanation for these differences lies in the appraisal periods. Whereas the original analysis did not consider climate effects that materialized after the programme evaluation period (March–May 2008), this chapter not only considers the whole of 2008 (see Annex), but additionally accounts for future climate effects that result from the 2008 feebate policy. The reason for this persistence is that the changes to the 2008 vehicle cohort continue to affect vehicle usage patterns. The short appraisal period of the original study implies that in their case the emission increases of the manufacturing effect dominate.

Emitting CO_2 into the atmosphere causes damage to society. Figure 14.1 therefore also reports damage estimates of the CO_2 effects. The marginal damage caused by emitting 1 tonne of CO_2 caused by the feebate is assumed to be €60. This is within the range of the results from the Stern-Stiglitz Commission, which recommends carbon prices of at least $40–80 per tonne of CO_2 by 2020 (High-Level Commission on Carbon Prices, 2017). €30 is used as a low-end estimate (OECD, 2018b). €90 is considered a high-end estimate for the climate effects, given that the assumption on vehicle lifetime implies that effects only persist until 2022.

3.1.2 Non-climate external costs

CO_2 emissions are not the only external effect of the French feebate. The change in fleet composition could potentially decrease local air pollution per kilometre driven if new cars had better emission control technology than the cars they replaced; or could increase local air pollution per kilometre if diesel vehicles replaced petrol cars.[5] The fact that rebound and fleet size effects were positive implies that external costs associated with road use – specifically congestion, but also accidents, noise and wear and tear – will increase.

Figure 14.2 reports the non-climate externalities of additional road use triggered by the 2008 feebate programme. Non-climate external effect are most pertinent for congestion (ie, the cost of increasing other vehicles' journey time), accidents (the part of the costs exerted on other road users that is not covered by insurances) and local air pollution (mainly negative health impacts).

There are two reasons why external costs are higher for diesel than for petrol. The first is that an estimated three-quarters of the additional mileage is due to road use by diesel vehicles. With respect to air pollution, this

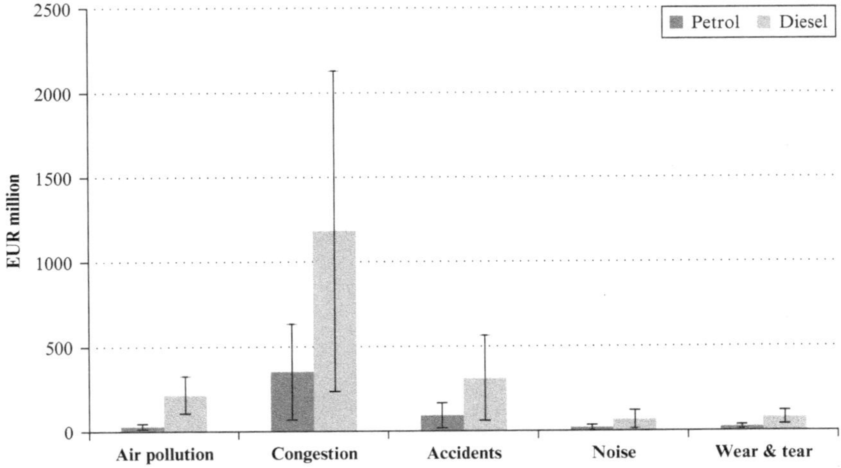

Note: Marginal external cost estimates are France-specific and taken from Santos (2017), with the exception of the estimate for wear and tear, which is from Van Dender's (2018) meta-analysis of external cost estimates in the European Union. The latter's range of estimates is also used to graph the range. Post-2008 external costs are discounted using a 4 per cent discount rate. See also Annex.

Figure 14.2 Non-climate externalities of feebate-induced changes to the 2008 vehicle cohort, in € million

effect is reinforced by the fact that according to Santos' (2017) estimate, diesel vehicles pollute twice as much per kilometre driven as petrol vehicles.

However, the magnitude of these external cost estimates is generally quite uncertain. This is reinforced by the fact that parts of these damages are from future road use. For instance, if diesel vehicles were banned from entering city centres, local air pollution damages from diesel use would decrease dramatically (and so would consumer surplus of those who own such vehicles). Similarly, technological improvements to road management systems could mean that congestion and accident costs decrease. On a futuristic note, in a world of self-driving vehicles that allow for teleworking and entertainment while being on the road, time spent in a car may no longer be time wasted; congestion cost estimates would have to be adjusted accordingly.

3.1.3 Fiscal costs

Feebate policies also affect government revenue. While the feebate was meant to pay out as much in rebates as it collected in fees, it failed to do so in practice. Specifically, it is reported to have weakened public finances by €285 million in 2008 alone (D'Haultfœuille, et al, 2014) (see Figure 14.3).[6]

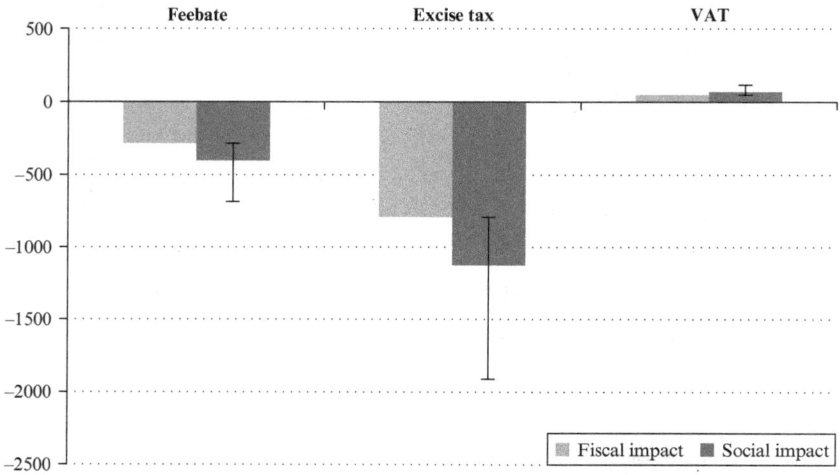

Note: The social impact baseline assumes that the marginal cost of public funds (MCF) is 1.42, whereas the lower (higher) cap of the range bar refers to a marginal cost of public funds of €1 (2.41) per tonne of CO_2. Post-2008 fiscal impacts are discounted using a 4 per cent discount rate. See also Annex.

Figure 14.3 Fiscal impacts of feebate-induced changes to the 2008 vehicle cohort, in € million

Not considered in the programme evaluation studies is that excise tax revenue has also been affected. On the one hand, fuel tax revenue per kilometre declines as the composition effect implies that cars are more fuel efficient because of the feebate. On the other hand, excise revenue increases because of rebound and fleet size effects. The composition effect dominates rebound and fleet size effect, as shown in Figure 14.3. The net excise tax effect is almost three times as large as the direct fiscal cost of the feebate.

The feebate policy additionally affects value added tax (VAT) revenue through two channels. VAT revenue increases due to higher car sales, but decreases because of lower fuel consumption per kilometre (which is only partly offset by additional road use). Figure 14.3 demonstrates that the former effect dominates somewhat, but the net effect is rather small compared to feebate and excise tax effects.[7]

Whether one focuses on direct fiscal effects or additionally considers excise and VAT issues also makes a difference when calculating the fiscal cost per tonne of CO_2 avoided – a common metric in programme evaluation studies. In the former case, it amounts to €59 per tonne of CO_2; in the latter, the fiscal cost increases to €214 per tonne of CO_2.

On the face of it, the fiscal costs from the feebate merely represent a transfer from taxpayers, which must fund the resulting revenue shortfall to those consumers that obtain a subsidy. However, the fiscal cost resulting from the French vehicle feebate may be accentuated by the fact that raising tax revenue to make up for the revenue shortfall could cause a distortion in the resource allocation in the economy – a cost typically referred to as the marginal costs of public funds (MCF) (Dahlby, 2008). Consequently, Figure 14.3 also reports the social cost of the identified fiscal effects. The baseline estimate refers to an MCF of 1.42, which is what Barrios et al (2013) have estimated for green taxes in France and is therefore appropriate if the revenue shortfall is recovered through a rise in fuel tax rates.

There is controversy as to how one ought to value MCF in the context of CBA. Several studies recommend not considering MCF at all (MCF=1) for a variety of reasons, ranging from the argument that the marginal cost of tax distortions is equal to the marginal benefit of redistribution (Jacobs and de Mooij, 2015) to pragmatic considerations (European Commission – Directorate-General for Regional and Urban Policy, 2014). The lower caps of the range bars are drawn in accordance with this view. The upper caps that bound the range, on the other hand, assume a very high MCF of 2.41, which corresponds to Barrios et al's (2013) estimate for French labour taxes.

3.1.4 Consumer and producer surplus

The French vehicle feebate affects consumer and producer surplus (profits). Given that the feebate subsidizes clean vehicles while making polluting vehicles more expensive, the programme increases consumer demand for clean vehicles while depressing demand for polluting vehicles.[8] Consumers with an underlying preference for clean vehicles thus potentially benefit, whereas consumers favouring polluting vehicles could see their surplus decrease.

In a differentiated product market, such as the market for new vehicles, producers enjoy some market power. Suppliers will therefore react to the feebate by adjusting market prices. In particular, vehicle suppliers can be expected to enjoy higher (lower) margins on clean (polluting) vehicles. Which effect dominates is an empirical question.

As D'Haultfœuille, Givord and Boutin (2014) do not estimate impacts on consumer and producer surplus, this chapter relies on a recent working paper that was prepared using a similar model on comparable data (Durrmeyer, 2018). In the model, the feebate policy affects consumer surplus in three main ways. First, consumers who buy clean vehicles benefit from a subsidy, whereas consumers of polluting vehicles must pay a tax. Second, the feebate may distort consumer choices as the rebate could

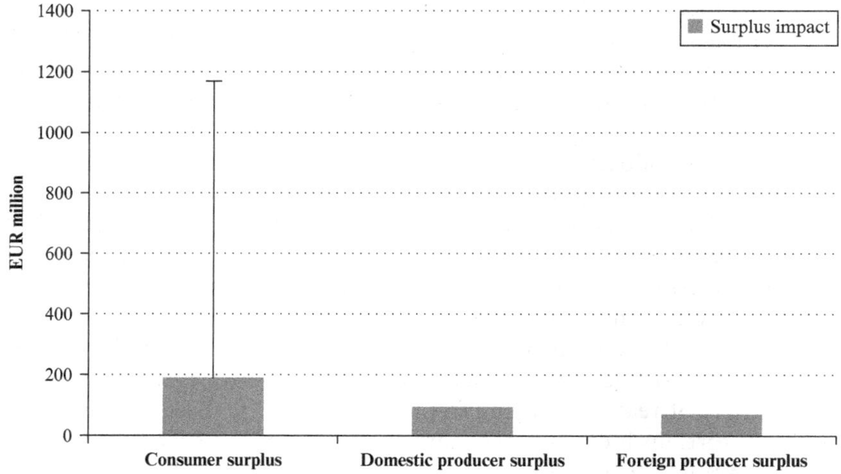

Note: Surplus effects are based on Durrmeyer (2018), see Annex. The upper cap of the consumer surplus assumes that 25 per cent of discounted future fuel cost savings represent a consumer surplus gain (Allcott and Wozny, 2014). No range bars indicate a lack of information regarding the appropriate range.

Figure 14.4 Consumer and producer surplus effects of 2008 vehicle feebate, in € million

induce consumers favouring polluting vehicles to instead buy cleaner ones and, for example, suffer from forgone performance. Third, consumers can be affected by supplier price changes.

Figure 14.4 shows that the net effect of the feebate on both consumer and producer surplus appears to be positive – before considering who funds the fiscal deficit caused by the feebate.

Modified consumer choices do not necessarily represent an allocative distortion from a social welfare perspective. Given that consumers may undervalue future fuel costs, the feebate could in fact incentivize consumers to buy vehicles that are in their long-term private interest. While some argue that this effect is generally overstated (Leard, et al, 2017), empirical analysis on US data suggests that consumers may in fact only value approximately 75 per cent of the (discounted) cost of gasoline when they buy vehicles (Allcott and Wozny, 2014). If this were the case in France, feebate-induced consumer surplus would increase sixfold (cf the range estimates in Figure 14.4).

The consumer surplus effects also have distributional implications. Before considering the potential social costs of the fiscal transfer needed to fund the deficit created by the feebate, it was estimated in relation to the French feebate system that people with a higher income would gain more. In fact, in absolute terms, feebate benefits increase monotonically with the income decile (Durrmeyer, 2018). A plausible explanation is that low-income households are less likely to buy a car in the first place. These distributional implications can change depending on how the fiscal deficit is funded in practice.

Figure 14.4 also shows the effects of the feebate on producer surplus, differentiated by domestic and foreign producers. Both gain from the feebate – which makes sense, as the feebate boosted vehicle sales and potentially allowed firms to charge higher margins for clean vehicles (Durrmeyer, 2018).

3.1.5 Comparison of social costs and benefits

Figure 14.5 sums up the results of the preceding analysis.[9] The 2008 feebate does indeed appear to have decreased CO_2 emissions, which is estimated to come with a social benefit of €212 million. However, the additional road use caused negative non-climate externalities. In the baseline model, these are ten times larger than the climate benefits.

The feebate-induced revenue losses amount to €1.5 billion – which is more than six times as large as the estimated value of the climate benefit. Consumer surplus increases by €223 million, but this gain only represents

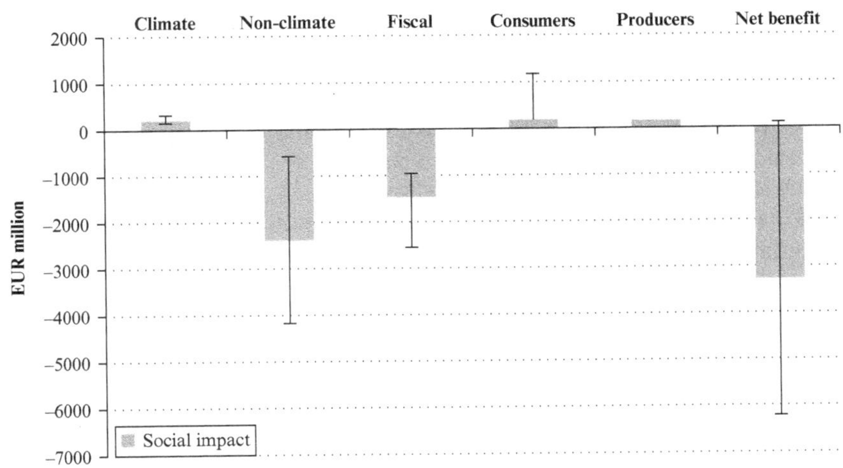

Note: Estimates are based on the analysis presented in Figures 14.1–14.4. Range estimates are the sum of the range estimates presented there.

Figure 14.5 Comparison of social costs and benefits of the 2008 vehicle feebate, in € million

some 15 per cent of the fiscal cost in the baseline specification. However, should consumers fail to internalize 25 per cent of the discounted future fuel cost savings at the time of purchase, the feebate may increase consumer surplus sixfold. Producer surplus increases by €162 million, 12 per cent of the fiscal cost.

The resulting net effect of the 2008 feebate is consequently negative in the baseline specification: it is estimated to decrease social welfare by €3.3 billion. The net effect is, however, quite sensitive to the modelling assumptions. In particular, in a favourable scenario – where climate costs are high (making feebate-induced emission-reductions worth more), non-climate external costs are low, fiscal transfers are costless and consumers undervalue fuel savings – welfare might have increased by some €106 million.

The comparison invites three observations. First, negative non-climate externalities are large in road transport. This suggests that there is a need to supplement vehicle feebate policies with policies that internalize these non-climate externalities. Against this background, it is worth noting that the French government is considering a legislative proposal that would allow cities with more than 100 000 inhabitants to introduce tolls for vehicles entering city centres.

Second, revenue changes from feebate systems can be significant, even when they are designed to be revenue neutral. In particular, this chapter emphasized the need also to consider indirect fiscal effects – and the estimated excise tax revenue losses turned out to be substantially larger than the direct fiscal effects from the feebate. To the extent that raising taxes results in important distortions to economic activities, this can have substantial social costs. It is thus important not to underestimate the extent to which consumers react to tax incentives.

Finally, vehicle feebate systems and related policies may also have substantial benefits for consumers, should they fail to internalize future fuel costs at the time of purchase.

4. CONCLUSIONS

This chapter has illustrated how the results of programme evaluation studies can be used to assess the social costs and benefits of environmentally related tax policies *ex post*. Given that the analysis is only based on the year 2008 – the very first year of the French policy – the results cannot be generalized and do not reflect an evaluation of the French feebate as such, which has now been in place for more than 10 years. If another year been chosen for the analysis, the results may have been different.

Notwithstanding this caveat, this analysis could inform future *ex-post* CBA studies in three main ways.

First, even *ex-post* CBA can involve forward-looking elements. Valuing these elements requires assumptions regarding discount rates and the persistence of behavioural impacts. In the case of the French feebate system, considering lifetime carbon emissions, as opposed to limiting the analysis to quarterly effects, leads to very different conclusions from those drawn in the original study. Whereas the French feebate was originally estimated to have caused a rise in CO_2 emissions, our results suggest that it may in fact have led to a decrease in such emissions. This is reassuring, considering that reducing CO_2 emissions was the objective of the policy.

Second, quantified effects, as well as associated social costs and benefits, are often uncertain. *Ex-post* assessments may thus not deliver authoritative evidence on the true net welfare effects of environmentally related tax policies – or any other policy or project. In the example of the French feebate system, the main uncertainties relate to non-climate external costs, as well as the consumer surplus effects of feebate-induced fuel cost savings. It would therefore appear appropriate to acknowledge this uncertainty upfront and provide decision makers with a range of estimates – as opposed to only reporting net welfare effects that hide the uncertainty.

Uncertainty is not limited to the quantified impacts of the policy; unquantified impacts can equally affect results. Specifically, an important long-run objective of the French feebate is to encourage vehicle manufacturers to develop cleaner cars. Given that decarbonizing transport remains a major challenge, contributing to meeting this objective could in fact represent an important long-run benefit of feebate policies.

NOTES

* Disclaimer: The opinions expressed and arguments employed in this chapter are the sole responsibility of the authors and do not necessarily reflect those of the OECD or of the governments of its member countries.

1. Feebate programmes, often called bonus/malus systems, provide consumers with a rebate or bonus on the purchase price of certain products (a subsidy), whereas the purchase of other products is penalized by a fee (a tax). Rebates and fees may be differentiated by one or several environmentally related criteria, such as grams of CO_2 emissions per kilometre, as in the case of the French feebate.
2. As the name suggests, rebates are feebates without the tax component. Differentiated vehicle purchase taxes typically increase with emission intensity or other environmentally related criteria, providing a general form of tax incentive. Differentiated circulation taxes are similar, but levied recurrently, generally on an annual basis.
3. Non-academic *ex-post* analyses, on the other hand, tend to make more comprehensive assessments of the social costs and benefits – see Becker (2013) for an assessment of the

first five years of the French motor vehicle feebate – but do not identify the causal effects of the policy with the same analytical rigour as academic programme evaluation studies.
4. This is different from the long-run effects reported in D'Haultfœuille, Givord and Boutin (2014), where the authors calculate quarterly effects for the scenario where the entire fleet has been replaced in accordance with the incentives provided by the 2008 version of the feebate.
5. This chapter assumes that local air pollution of the 2008 cohort is identical to the 2008 fleet average. Non-climate effects are thus limited to those resulting from feebate-induced additional road use. Durrmeyer (2018) provides estimates of the feebate on the emission of local pollutants.
6. Durrmeyer (2018) reports €223 million for the same year. This chapter uses the former estimate.
7. The analysis of the fiscal effects disregards tariff revenue from imports of additional cars. The fiscal effects relating to the French annual circulation tax on polluting vehicles are not considered, as the tax was only introduced in 2009 – and this chapter only considers fiscal measures that were already in place in the time period for which the causal effect was estimated. In addition, we do not consider additional corporate tax income that could result from the positive producer surplus effects.
8. In addition to the price effect, feebates may also affect social norms (Hilton, et al, 2014).
9. The analysis assumes that market power is limited to manufacturing, whereas all other industries (in particular, car retailers and gasoline suppliers) are perfectly competitive. Feebate-induced additional profits by the motorway companies are not considered either.

REFERENCES

Alberini, A and Bareit, M, 2017. 'The effect of registration taxes on new car sales and emissions: Evidence from Switzerland', *Resource and Energy Economics*.

Alberini, A, Bareit, M, Filippini, M and Martinez-Cruz, AL, 2018. 'The impact of emissions-based taxes on the retirement of used and inefficient vehicles: The case of Switzerland', *Journal of Environmental Economics and Management,* Volume 88, pp234–258.

Allcott, H and Wozny, N, 2014. 'Gasoline Prices, Fuel Economy, and the Energy Paradox', *Review of Economics and Statistics*, 96(5), pp779–795.

Barrios, S, Pycroft, J and Saveyn, B, 2013. 'The marginal cost of public funds in the EU: the case of labour versus green taxes'.

Becker, E, 2013. *Évaluation économique du dispositif d'écopastille sur la période 2008–2012. Commissariat Général au Développement Durable*.

Dahlby, B, 2008. 'The marginal cost of public funds: theory and applications'. MIT Press.

D'Haultfœuille, X, Durrmeyer, I and Février, P, 2016. 'Disentangling sources of vehicle emissions reduction in France: 2003–2008', *International Journal of Industrial Organization*, Volume 47, pp186–229.

D'Haultfœuille, X, Givord, P and Boutin, X, 2014. 'The environmental effect of green taxation: The case of the French bonus/malus', *Economic Journal*.

Durrmeyer, I, 2018. 'Winners and losers: evaluating distributional effects of the French feebate on the autombile market', sl: sn.

European Commission – Directorate-General for Regional and Urban Policy, 2014. 'Guide to Cost-Benefit Analysis of Investment Projects for Cohesion Policy 2014–2020', sl: sn.

High-Level Commission on Carbon Prices, 2017. 'Report of the High-Level Commission on Carbon Prices', World Bank, Washington, DC.

Hilton, D et al, 2014. 'A tax can nudge: The impact of an environmentally motivated bonus/malus fiscal system on transport preferences', *Journal of Economic Psychology*, Volume 42, pp17–27.

Jacobs, B and de Mooij, RA, 2015. 'Pigou meets Mirrlees: On the irrelevance of tax distortions for the second-best Pigouvian tax', *Journal of Environmental Economics and Management*.

Klier, T and Linn, J, 2015. 'Using Taxes to Reduce Carbon Dioxide Emissions Rates of New Passenger Vehicles: Evidence from France, Germany, and Sweden', *American Economic Journal: Economic Policy*, 7(1), pp212–242.

Kok, R, 2015. 'Six years of CO_2-based tax incentives for new passenger cars in The Netherlands: Impacts on purchasing behavior trends and CO_2 effectiveness', *Transportation Research Part A*, Volume 77, pp137–153.

Konishi, Y and Zhao, M, 2017. 'Can Green Car Taxes Restore Efficiency? Evidence from the Japanese New Car Market', *Journal of the Association of Environmental and Resource Economists*, 4(1), pp51–87.

Leard, B, Linn, J and Zhou, YC, 2017. 'How Much Do Consumers Value Fuel Economy and Performance? Evidence from Technology Adoption', RFF Report.

Mabit, SL, 2014. 'Vehicle type choice under the influence of a tax reform and rising fuel prices', *Transportation Research Part A*, Volume 64, pp32–42.

OECD, 2018a. 'Cost-Benefit Analysis and the Environment: Further Developments and Policy Use', OECD Publishing, Paris.

OECD, 2018b. 'Effective Carbon Rates: Pricing Carbon Emissions through Taxes and Emissions Trading', OECD Publishing, Paris.

Rivers, N and Schaufele, B, 2017. 'New vehicle feebates', *Canadian Journal of Economics*.

Santos, G, 2017. 'Road fuel taxes in Europe: Do they internalize road transport externalities?', *Transport Policy*, Volume 53, pp120–134.

Smith, S and Braathen, NA, 2015. 'Monetary Carbon Values in Policy Appraisal: An Overview of Current Practice and Key Issues', in OECD Environment Working Papers, OECD Publishing, Paris.

Van Dender, K, 2018. 'Taxing vehicles, fuel, and road use: what mix for road transport?', OECD Publishing, Paris.

ANNEX

The cost-benefit analysis is based on the following welfare function:

$$W = CS + PS + (1 + \lambda)T - E$$

where CS stands for consumer surplus, PS is producers' surplus, $1 + \lambda$ is the marginal cost of public funds, T is tax revenue and E is external cost. The chapter then calculates $\Delta W = \Delta CS + \Delta PS + (1 + \lambda)\Delta T - \Delta E$, where $\Delta W \equiv W_1 - W_0$ Here W_1 refers to the social welfare under the 2008 vehicle feebate, whereas W_0 is the counterfactual situation where no feebate was implemented. ΔCS, ΔPS, ΔE and ΔT are defined analogously. The results of the modelling exercise are shown in Table 14A.1.

Changes in external costs, ΔE, that were induced by the 2008 feebate include both climate and non-climate related external costs. With respect to climate costs, this chapter only takes into account the effect of the 2008 feebate on CO_2 emissions, relying on the short-run effects estimated by D'Haultfœuille, Givord and Boutin (2014).

Their estimates are adjusted in four main ways. First, half of the emissions that the original paper considered to be part of the composition effect are reassigned to the manufacturing scale effect. In the original paper, the composition effect also accounts for the fact that manufacturing emissions of feebate-induced cars are lower, given that the models benefiting from the feebate tend to be smaller and lighter. However, as this is a one-off effect that does not persist over vehicles' lifetime, we reassigned this effect to the manufacturing scale effect and renamed the effects fleet composition and manufacturing.

Second, these adjusted quarterly effects are transformed into yearly

Table 14A.1 Modelling results – welfare changes induced by the 2008 vehicle feebate, in € million

	Baseline	Low estimate	High estimate
ΔCS	187	187	1169
ΔPS	162	162	162
(1+λ)ΔT	−1462	−2549	−961
ΔE	2167	263	4023
ΔW	**−3225**	**−6169**	**161**

Note: The low welfare estimate is based on the high external cost estimate, given that the latter enters the welfare equation with a negative sign. Analogously, the high welfare estimate uses the low external cost value.

effects, assuming that vehicle choices are made at the beginning of the year and that quarterly effects scale proportionally.

Third, yearly effects are extrapolated into the future based on the assumption that the 2008 vehicle cohort has a lifetime of 15 years and that composition, rebound and fleet size effects persist unaltered over the lifetime of the vehicle.

Finally, the estimated effects are monetized and discounted to 2008, assuming a social cost of carbon of €60 per tonne of CO_2 and using an annual discount rate of 4 per cent. The sensitivity analysis additionally considers carbon cost values of €30 and €90.

In terms of non-climate effects, only those resulting from additional road use are modelled. The additional road use is derived from the rebound and fleet size climate effects, using sales and mileage information reported in D'Haultfœuille, Givord and Boutin (2014). CO_2 effects are converted into kilometres using the average CO_2 emissions of new vehicles sold over the study period (138 g/km), and then split into vehicle types assuming that 77 per cent (23 per cent) of these kilometres result from diesel (petrol) vehicle use.

The kilometre estimates are monetized by multiplying them with the marginal external cost estimate per kilometre provided by Santos (2017), after converting these into 2008 prices using OECD inflation data. As before, external costs are discounted to 2008 using a 4 per cent discount rate. Based on Van Dender's (2018) meta-analysis, the sensitivity analysis considers the possibility that air pollution and wear and tear might be 50 per cent larger or smaller than estimated by Santos (2017); whereas congestion, accidents and noise estimates could be 80 per cent off.

With respect to the change in government revenue that results from the 2008 feebate – that is, ΔT – three components are modelled. The first is the direct fiscal effect of the feebate – that is, the difference between the sum of the taxes collected and the sum of the subsidies paid out in 2008, or €285 for the whole of 2008 (D'Haultfœuille et al, 2014).

The second is the excise tax effect, which is modelled as the sum of the climate effects resulting from fleet composition, rebound and fleet size effect, multiplied by the effective excise tax rate per tonne of CO_2. Post-2008 effects are discounted.

The third fiscal effect relates to feebate-induced changes to VAT revenue which may come though feebate-induced changes to (1) fuel sales over the lifetime of the vehicles and (2) 2008 car sales. The fuel component of the VAT effect is calculated analogously to the excise tax effect, also using International Energy Agency (IEA) data. The car sales component of the VAT effect is modelled assuming that 13 per cent of 2008 vehicle sales were induced by the feebate, and that the average ex VAT price of these cars was €16 000.

The sum of these fiscal effects is then multiplied with the marginal cost of public funds, $(1+\lambda)$, drawing on France-specific estimates (Barrios et al, 2013).

Estimates for ΔCS and ΔPS are based on Durrmeyer's aggregate welfare analysis (2018).

The sensitivity analysis additionally explores how much larger the consumer surplus effect of the 2008 feebate would be if consumers failed to internalize 25 per cent of discounted future fuel costs when making their purchase decisions (Allcott and Wozny, 2014). Fuel savings are calculated by taking the absolute value of the product of composition effect (in tonnes of CO_2) and total fuel costs as reported by the IEA (after converting these to the CO_2 base). Future fuel savings are discounted using a 4 per cent discount rate.

15. Designing carbon taxes: economic and legal considerations

Claudia Kettner, Daniela Kletzan-Slamanig, Stefan E. Weishaar and Irene J.J. Burgers*

1. INTRODUCTION

Taxes are generally levied by governments to raise revenues for financing public functions (eg, the provision of public goods or support measures for general welfare). This also holds true for taxes relating to the environment – most notably energy taxes, which are a major source of government revenues in many countries.

Nevertheless, taxes can also fulfil another important function: they can be used as a price signal to incentivize changes in behaviour. This idea of using taxes as a corrective measure dates back to the work of AC Pigou in 1920. In recent decades, this approach has increasingly been applied to goods and activities that cause negative environmental effects. Environmental taxes have been implemented to regulate a broad range of externalities, such as water and air pollution, and pesticide use. Since the issue of global warming gained heightened attention at the end of the last century, political and scientific interest in environmentally motivated taxes to mitigate climate change has increased. Since 1989, carbon dioxide (CO_2) taxes have been implemented as a policy instrument to reduce greenhouse gas emissions in a number of countries.

However, while economists are mainly concerned with getting prices right and mitigating market failures – irrespective of the actual instrument used (eg, taxes, levies, fees or emissions trading) – legal scholars are more concerned with such formal criteria and details. Recommendations from both disciplines are not the only aspects to be considered in the real-world design and implementation of environmental taxes, as other political-economic objectives will interfere. In particular, considerations regarding employment, competitiveness and income distribution effects will affect the design of environmental taxes. In this chapter, we provide an overview of the economic and legal perspectives on environmental taxation, with a focus on energy and carbon taxes. Differences between environmental taxation in a theoretical first-best setting and a real-world setting are summarized; as are relevant legal considerations for tax design and the factors which determine its legal form.

This chapter is structured as follows. The economic theory on how to internalize negative external effects is discussed in section 2. Section 3 summarizes the legal theory on energy and carbon taxes, mapping general legal considerations such as distinctions between taxes, fees and levies, and legal design issues of carbon taxes. Section 4 concludes.

2. THE ECONOMIC PERSPECTIVE ON ENVIRONMENTAL TAXES

Since the 1970s, environmental taxes have increasingly been used as a policy instrument to alleviate ecological problems. In contrast to classic command and control regulation, they rely on market forces and offer the advantage of reducing emissions in a cost-effective way while simultaneously providing a source of revenue.[1] As the Organisation for Economic Co-operation and Development (OECD)[2] has stated, 'economic instruments affect costs and benefits of alternative actions open to economic agents, with the effect of influencing behavior in a way that is favorable to the environment'.

Energy in particular is an essential good with relatively inelastic demand. Taxing energy thus provides stable revenue for the government while minimizing the efficiency losses.[3] The revenue raising motive was the predominant driver for introducing energy taxes in the first place. As the need to mitigate the negative environmental effects relating to energy use – in particular, greenhouse gas emissions contributing to global warming – became increasingly obvious, the role of market-based instruments as a lever for altering energy use patterns gained in importance. These included, for instance, the differentiation of tax rates between leaded and unleaded gasoline and, at a later stage, the introduction of carbon taxes and even comprehensive environmental tax reforms in various countries. However, in order to design environmental or carbon taxes that are both environmentally effective and compliant with the basic economic principles of taxation, various theoretical aspects must be considered.

This section provides an overview of the economic perspective on environmental taxation, focusing on energy and carbon taxes. Differences between environmental taxation in a theoretical first-best setting and a real-world setting are summarized. In addition, implications for the actual design and implementation of carbon taxes are discussed.

2.1 Taxing Externalities

Economic theory focuses on the adjustment of prices to reduce environmental externalities while still achieving economically efficient outcomes. The fundamental idea of using a tax to correct negative externalities[4] dates back to 1920, to the work of Pigou.[5] Pigou provided a framework for research on externalities that he referred to as 'uncompensated social services and disservices'. Production activities may have pollution effects which cause costs to society. In the absence of a price signal for pollution, the polluter does not have to pay for these negative external effects. Thus, the marginal private and social interests diverge, which results in a market failure that could be corrected through government intervention. Taxes can therefore be used to internalize the social costs resulting from the production activity – for instance, the damages relating to global warming from the emission of CO_2.[6] To offset the negative effects, the rate of such 'Pigouvian' or corrective taxes should be set to equal the marginal social cost of the pollution damage. As the price of the activity causing the externality is increased by the tax, demand falls.

Pollution taxes are economically efficient: in contrast to command and control instruments prescribing specific technologies or abatement measures for each regulated entity, taxes leave the choice of the preferred abatement option and abatement level to the polluter. In addition, under the strict assumptions used in economic theory, taxes automatically equate marginal abatement costs across firms.

To reduce negative environmental externalities such as CO_2 emissions via a market signal, the policy maker must choose whether to rely on price-based instruments (eg, taxes or levies) or quantity-based instruments (eg, tradable permits). The characteristics of these instruments and their respective advantages have been extensively discussed in economic literature. In a first-best, theoretical setting,[7] price-based instruments and quantity-based instruments achieve the same outcomes. The Pigou tax signals the true social cost to the emitter, who has a financial incentive to reduce emissions up to the point where the value of another unit of emission reduction is equal to the environmental damage.[8] In an emissions trading system, in contrast, the regulator allocates[9] a given quantity of emission permits to polluters. Trading will result in a market price for emissions that again signals damage costs. Given their respective abatement costs and the emission price, polluting firms can decide whether to abate emissions or buy emission permits on the market.

Implemented in the real world, these instruments deliver different results from those in the theoretical first-best setting, as not all of the necessary assumptions are fulfilled. One major difference concerns information about marginal abatement costs and marginal damage from pollution and the effects of uncertainty for determining the optimal tax rate. In contrast to the first-best setting, under uncertainty it is not feasible to reach the socially optimal level of emissions. Instead, the policy should aim to minimize the efficiency losses relating to regulatory intervention in the case of asymmetric information – that is, when polluters know their abatement costs, while regulators do not. Weitzman and White and Wittmann[10] have shown that the optimal choice of policy instrument in terms of efficiency losses depends on the shape of the marginal abatement cost and marginal damage functions. If the marginal cost function is steeper than the marginal damage function, taxes minimize efficiency losses, whereas emission trading schemes are preferable if the damage function is steeper.[11]

In a real-world setting, however, most likely both marginal abatement costs and marginal damages will not be known with sufficient certainty by the regulator, which is at risk of receiving biased information from polluting firms. Under such circumstances, where the optimal solution is not achievable, Baumol and Oates[12] have argued for 'least-cost abatement': instead of the optimal abatement, a predefined emission standard – that is, an acceptable level of pollution – should be targeted in a least-cost approach. Total abatement costs in the economy should be minimized by setting a tax to achieve the desired emission reduction.[13]

Another aspect that was introduced by the OECD[14] is the 'polluter pays' principle, defined as 'the principle according to which the polluter should bear the cost of measures to reduce pollution according to the extent of either the damage done to society or the exceeding of an acceptable level of pollution'. On the one hand, polluters should pay for the environmental damage they cause, to promote economically efficient resource use. On the other hand, such taxes prevent trade distortions from occurring if pollution control measures were subsidized by the government.

Another key challenge in implementing a Pigouvian tax is determining the marginal damage of pollution. Estimates of the social cost of carbon, for instance, show a broad range of between \$10 and several hundred dollars per tonne of CO_2.[15] These differences result, *inter alia*, from the way in which risk and uncertainty regarding the timing and extent of future damages are considered, the assumptions which are made regarding adaptation and technological change and – not least – the choice of discount rates to value impacts in the distant future.[16] This is the main reason why environmental taxes usually are not optimal Pigouvian taxes. Nevertheless, following the least-cost abatement theory and the polluter pays principle, 'second-best' taxes can also deliver positive environmental effects and represent important policy instruments.[17] Thus, carbon taxes – besides other instruments – can also be implemented to meet CO_2 emissions or concentrations targets.[18] The resulting taxes might not comply with the social optimum, but they represent a cost-effective way to achieve the set target (eg, the outcome of international climate negotiations).

2.2 Design Issues from an Economic Perspective

Environmental taxes can play an important role in the policy mix as instruments through which to achieve environmental targets in a cost-efficient way. However, conflicts between policy objectives exist that not only constitute a barrier to the implementation of fiscal instruments but may also result in suboptimal incentive structures when the instrument is applied. Therefore, before implementing environmental taxes or an ecological tax reform, the specific policy objectives should be specified, design criteria should be made transparent and the instrument's costs and benefits should be analysed in an *ex-ante* assessment.

An appraisal of environmental and energy taxes in EU Member States reveals pronounced differences with respect to tax bases and tax rates, as well as redistribution and use of tax revenues.[19] The reason for these differences lies in competing objectives that must be accounted for when introducing an environmental/energy tax or implementing an ecological tax reform. These are:[20]

- ecological effectiveness;
- economic efficiency;
- avoidance of negative effects on distribution;
- avoidance of negative competitiveness effects for energy-intensive firms/sectors;
- compatibility with the existing regulatory framework; and
- administrative feasibility.

A good portion of the economic debate about environmental taxation in recent decades has centred around the theory of a 'double dividend'[21] – that is, on achieving environmental improvements (first dividend) as well as positive macro-economic effects (second dividend). To realize positive economic effects, however, the use of tax revenues is decisive. Recycling offers the opportunity to reduce other distortionary taxes, such as payroll taxes, thus altering relative input prices and contributing to increased labour demand. Potential negative impacts on income distribution and competitiveness may call for the implementation of compensation mechanisms to ease adaptation to the new regulation. However, these compensation measures should be provided only temporarily and not in the form of reductions or exemptions from the environmental tax. By providing specific investment support for energy-efficient technologies or research and development subsidies, the price signal of the tax and the incentive for investments in new technology remain intact.

In summary, regarding environmental taxation economics is mainly concerned with getting the prices right in order to achieve the desired change in behaviour, and with providing consistent incentives to agents in order to reduce the negative externality in question. Compared to other policy instruments (in particular, command and control approaches), taxes are environmentally effective and deliver the intended results at the lowest cost to society (economic efficiency). In contrast legal scholars are more concerned with other details in designing fiscal instruments, as is outlined below.

3. THE LEGAL PERSPECTIVE ON ENVIRONMENTAL TAXES

The preceding section presented the economic approach to energy and carbon taxes. Economic theory can easily be applied in different countries, as it is based on assumptions. The theory can therefore be generalized and applied in other circumstances. The legal approach differs in the sense that it is strongly entrenched in its particular jurisdiction. Insights developed in one jurisdictional context cannot be easily transferred to another. This section examines the legal approach to energy and carbon taxes, which differs from the generalized economic perspective. It first examines the relevant fiscal concepts and what they entail from a legal perspective. Subsequently, relevant fiscal legal design issues are discussed.

3.1 Concepts and Legal Implications

In economic theory, the main dividing line between fiscal instruments lies between taxes and levies, where levies constitute a flexible fiscal component to secure a minimum price. Otherwise, the differences are rather inconsequential. In law, different categories are used and the distinctions are relevant because they give rise to different legal consequences.

Legal scholars have developed their own typology of fiscal measures that are at times specific to a jurisdiction. They therefore often rely on definitions proposed by international organizations when conducting comparative analysis. According to the OECD definition, taxes are characterized as compulsory and unrequited payments to the general government.[22] Taxes serve as a regulatory tool, are a means to foster redistributive equity and – most importantly – raise revenue. Fees 'are compulsory, requited payments to either general government or to bodies outside general government';[23]

thus, money paid should be for services rendered and consequently should also be in proportion with the costs incurred.

From a theoretical perspective, environmental taxes and environmental fees therefore differ in determining the price for pollution. The value of an environmental fee would relate to the value of the benefit received.[24] Benefits for services are an important element in setting the prices of fees. An essential element here is the possibility to accurately determine the price of a service.

Taxes can also reflect benefits that taxpayers receive from the government, given that welfare economics and 'optimal tax policy' theory are based on the benefit principle. This principle may be underlying a specific tax. However, it is not linked to a concrete service, but rather is of a more general and abstract nature. The price of such benefits is difficult to measure, as the market mechanism requiring an equilibrium in what is exchanged cannot be applied. Thus, the level of taxation is determined differently. This is also a point of discussion in economics, as described above in section 2.

Besides taxes and fees, the term 'levy' is also frequently employed in the legal domain. Levies are temporary measures to raise revenue and provide for a social purpose or mitigate a crisis which is generally supported. They are understood as 'soft' charges that usually escape the age-old negative view of taxes. According to Madeleine Taylor, therefore, many 'new' charges are called 'levies' rather than 'taxes'. However, as levies tend to become permanent charges, definitional lines between levies and taxes are blurred.[25] Fees charged by central or local governments can be distinguished from taxes when they are charged as payments for the supply of particular services by the authorities.[26]

The legal classification of a charge as a levy, a fee or a tax has consequences for the democratic procedure that must be legally followed to introduce the charge. The legal competence to introduce it can rest with a central authority or with federal states or municipalities.[27] The power to introduce a particular tax is often fully reserved to one specific level of government but can also lie with concurrent authorities – in this situation the lower-level authority can act insofar as the higher-ranking authority has not acted. This power is often governed by national constitutions and authorities must act within the competencies attributed to them. If they violate their competencies, their actions can be legally challenged. Consequently, the legal form of a measure can be restricted by the particular competency that an authority enjoys. An authority that does not enjoy the competence to introduce a tax may be incentivized to introduce a fee instead to achieve its objective. In the Netherlands, for example, fees have been introduced by the water boards in the area of waste water treatment, water systems and water pollution, and are earmarked for investments and maintenance of the water boards.[28]

Constitutions may also restrict the use of tax proceeds. Milne shows, for example, that the constitution of Oregon stipulates that revenue from taxes on oil and natural gas must be spent on education.[29] In general, the different fiscal concepts limit the way that proceeds can be spent. Revenue derived from fees is earmarked and can be used only for a specific purpose. Tax revenue usually goes to the general budget and can be used for any government expenditure.

Whether the charge is a fee or a tax further has implications for the protection of payers' rights. Generally, the rights of taxpayers are better protected than those of payers of a fee. This also may have consequences for the method of payment, exemptions provided, recovery of payment and legal remedies. Legal principles such as equality, non-discrimination, certainty, reciprocity and good faith may have different implications for fees than for taxes. Moreover, in case of taxation, the same taxable object or event may be taxed twice, giving rise to double taxation. This is unlikely to be the case with regard to fees, as there needs to be a direct relation between the fee and the government service.

3.2 Tax Design Issues and the Law

From a legal perspective, various design issues must be considered as they impact on the object and purpose of the measures by, *inter alia*, affecting their environmental effectiveness and economic efficiency, or requiring compliance with legal principles or rules.

Central to any fiscal measure is to have clarity about its core elements: taxable subject, taxable event and taxable object (the tax base). The 'taxable subject' is the person that is legally obliged to pay the tax if a taxable event occurs. The 'taxable event' is any event or transaction that results in a tax consequence for the party that executes the event; it is the economic object. The economic object may not coincide with the 'legal object'. In the case of environmental taxes, the taxable event is pollution; in the case of carbon taxes, it is the amount of CO_2 that the taxable subject yearly emits. The tax is the price for the emittance. An example where economic object and legal object coincide is the EU carbon tax proposed in 1992 focusing on the carbon content of fuels.[30] An example where economic object and legal object do not coincide is a fiscal measure whereby the taxable event has an environmental nature ('taxing polluting installations'), while the tax base is 'property installed by the installations'.

An environmental tax can take the form of a direct tax or an indirect tax. In the latter case, the taxable subject is not the polluter but, for instance, a gasoline company selling a product whose usage results in the emission of CO_2. Thus, also from a legal perspective, the setting of tax rates is non-trivial and can be guided by the environmental damage or the environmental standard (thus setting the tax rate in a Pigouvian or Baumol-Oats tradition), or by political considerations (ability of willingness to pay of the electorate or the taxpayers), or a combination of these criteria.[31] This is an important nexus between the legal approach and the economic approach to taxation.

Irrespective of whether the fiscal measure focuses on a production process or the use of a pollutant, the taxable event and the tax base must ensure environmental effectiveness. An environmental tax whose tax base is 'property installed by the companies' disregards the actual activity level that is determinative for the actual amount of pollution generated and hence sets wrong incentives.[32] As a consequence, the object and purpose of the measure are oriented towards raising revenue rather than environmental effectiveness. If the overall objective of the legal measure is not satisfied, its legality can be challenged.

Tax exemptions and tax reductions make policy measures more acceptable but undermine their environmental effectiveness. From the economic perspective, such schemes can conflict with the polluter pays principle. From the legal perspective, compliance with European state aid rules is of relevance too.

Environmental taxes, such as carbon taxes, have an environmental purpose. If they are designed as taxes rather than as fees for services rendered, they form part of the general revenue of the state and do not finance specific tasks or objectives.[33] Earmarking environmental tax proceeds to finance specific environmental or social policy objectives may not be possible if constitutional rules prevent this, or if this impairs the rights of the budget legislature and the function of the state budget.[34] It may also be the case that the actual tax legislating body is different from the body that by law is entitled to the revenue. In such a situation, earmarking tax proceeds adds to the level of complexity.[35]

As has already been indicated in the economic section of this chapter, energy and carbon taxes are not only fiscal instruments, but also environmental policy instruments, and thus are subject to environmental law principles. The polluter pays principle has already been mentioned in the economic section, but is equally relevant from a legal perspective.[36] Also from a legal perspective it is recognized that governments rely, *inter alia,* on charges to protect the environment.[37] The OECD introduced this principle in its efforts to introduce measures to reduce pollution and to achieve better allocation of resources by ensuring that the prices of goods reflect the relative scarcity of the environment and natural resources by placing the cost burden on polluters. The polluter pays principle also embodies an anti-subsidy element that reminds public authorities that differences in environmental policies should not lead to the introduction of compensating import levies or export rebates, or measures with an equivalent effect, designed to offset the consequences of these differences on prices.[38]

Other prominent legal principles that must be observed when designing fiscal measures include legality, equality, legal certainty, legitimate expectations, fair play, public trust in tax administration, good faith, transparency, proportionality, non-retroactivity and estoppel.[39] With regard to tax policy in particular, a series of additional guiding principles, known as the OECD Ottawa Taxation Framework Conditions, have been developed. These include neutrality, efficiency, certainty and simplicity, effectiveness and fairness, as well as flexibility.[40]

Substantive EU rules are also relevant for tax design, as they set requirements to be followed and respected by the legislature, since there is supremacy of EU law. For example, fiscal measures relating to energy use or carbon emissions must comply with EU primary law – specifically Articles 110 and 113 of the Treaty on the Functioning of the European Union (TFEU). Article 110 TFEU prohibits a Member State from imposing, directly or indirectly, any internal taxation on the products of other Member States in excess of what is imposed on similar domestic products. Article 113 TFEU stipulates that the Council, acting unanimously in accordance with a special legislative procedure and after consulting the European Parliament and the Economic and Social Committee, can adopt provisions for the harmonization of legislation in the area of turnover taxes, excise duties and other forms of indirect taxation, provided that harmonization is necessary for the internal market and to avoid distortion of competition. Moreover, secondary law must also be observed. The Energy Tax Directive 2003/96/EC provides for minimum tax rates for energy taxes and is applicable to all indirect taxes on energy, with the exception of value added tax. The Excise Directive 2008/118/EC is applicable to indirect taxes on energy products. Jurisprudence of the Court of Justice of the European Union must also be considered, as it gives insight into the application of EU rules. In the *Fondazione Santa Lucia* case, for example, the issue was whether an Italian tax incentive for energy-intensive businesses fell within the ambit of the concept of tax reduction contained in the Energy Tax Directive.[41]

4. CONCLUSIONS

Given the urgency of mitigating anthropogenic climate change, a broad portfolio of instruments must be applied. These include fiscal measures that assign a price to carbon emissions and thus provide an incentive for technological and behavioural changes. This approach has already proved to be successful, especially in relation to other environmental problems. The economic theory regarding taxes for the internalization of negative externalities dates back approximately one century. It focuses primarily on balancing private and social costs of certain detrimental activities by attributing the environmental costs to polluters. However, for real-world implementation, certain adaptations to the ideal theoretical case must be made. This can be assessed by looking at the 26 countries and regions in which carbon taxes have been implemented so far.[42] The legal specifications in particular represent a challenge for implementation.

This chapter has examined the economic and legal approaches to carbon taxes. It has shown that the relevant considerations in both disciplines are quite different. From an economic perspective, the focus is on the ability to raise revenue, as well as the efficiency and environmental effectiveness of the measure. The legal perspective is decisive in deciding whether to design the charge as a tax, a fee or a levy. Ensuring compliance with existing rules – constitutional rules, EU law, international law and general principles of law – further plays a crucial role in the design of such a tax from a legal perspective.

When it comes to actual implementation, the different viewpoints must be taken into account. Besides agreeing on the objective – which is a political issue – a common understanding of the fiscal measure in question must be reached. In practice, the challenge lies in balancing different interests and political objectives while ensuring that the instrument incentivizes emissions abatement and is properly integrated into the existing legal system.

NOTES

* This research is part of the project 'CATs – Carbon Taxes in Austria: Implementation Issues and Impacts' which was funded by Austria's *Klima- und Energiefonds* and carried out within the Austrian Climate Research Programme. We thank Katharina Köberl for her excellent research assistance.

1. Williams RC (2016), 'Environmental Taxation', *Resources for the Future Discussion Paper* 16–24; Milne JE and MS Andersen (2014), 'Introduction to environmental taxation concepts and Research', in Milne JE and MS Andersen (eds), *Handbook of Research on Environmental Taxation*, Edward Elgar, Cheltenham, 15–32.
2. OECD (2001), 'Environmental tax, A guide for policy makers', available at www.oecd.org/env/tools-evaluation/48164926, last accessed 5 May 2019.
3. Harding M, C Martini and A Thomas (2016), 'Taxing Energy Use: Patterns and Incoherencies in Energy Taxation in Europe and the OECD', in Bardazzi et al (eds), *European Energy and Climate Security, Public Policies, Energy Sources and Eastern Partners, Lecture Notes in Energy* 31, Springer, Cham, 233–264. According to the

Ramsey rule, higher tax rates should be imposed on goods for which demand is inelastic in order to raise a given amount of revenue at the lowest cost in terms of market distortions.

4. Externality is usually understood as a situation in which the effect of someone's decision (positively or negatively) influences someone else without a specific contractual agreement (Caldari K and F Masini (2011), 'Pigouvian versus Marshallian tax: market failure, public intervention and the problem of externalities', *The European Journal of the History of Economic Thought* 18 (5), 715–732).
5. Pigou AC (1920), *The Economics of Welfare*, Macmillan and Co, London.
6. A different way of solving the externality problem was put forward by Coase (1960), who argued that under certain conditions, a negotiated settlement between the polluter and the injured party is preferable to a tax on the externality (Coase RH (1960), 'The Problem of Social Cost', *The Journal of Law & Economics* 3, 1–44).
7. It is usually assumed that external costs of emissions from different sources are equal; that there is no uncertainty about costs and benefits; that there are no interaction effects with other policy instruments; and that there is perfect competition in the market. See Norregaard J and V Reppelin-Hill (2000), 'Controlling Pollution Using Taxes and Tradable Permits', *IMF Economic Issues* No 25.
8. See Norregaard J and V Reppelin-Hill (2000), n7 above, for a detailed elaboration.
9. Preferably via auctions, since this allocation procedure generates government revenue.
10. Weitzman M (1974), 'Prices vs. Quantities', *Review of Economic Studies* 41 (4), 477–491. White MJ and D Wittman (1983), 'A Comparison of Taxes, Regulation, and Liability Rules under Imperfect Information', *The Journal of Legal Studies* 12 (2), 413–425.
11. Norregaard J and V Reppelin-Hill (2000), n7 above.
12. Baumol WJ and WE Oates (1971), 'The Use of Standards and Prices for Protection of the Environment', *Swedish Journal of Economics*, 73 (1), 42–54.
13. In such a case emission trading schemes seem to be of advantage as the emission target is built into the policy instrument and no quantity risk is involved. Reaching the same emission level with taxes would probably require adapting the tax rate until the target is met.
14. OECD (1972), Recommendation of the Council on Guiding Principles concerning International Economic Aspects of Environmental Policies, 26 May 1972 – C(72)128, Annex I.
15. Tol (2013) surveyed 75 studies, which included a total of 588 estimates. The mean social cost of carbon was $196 (2010 prices), with a standard deviation of $322. At a real discount rate of 3 per cent, the mean social cost was only $25 (see Tol RSJ (2013), 'Targets for global climate policy: An overview', *Journal of Economic Dynamics and Control* 37 (5), 911–928).
16. Pindyck RS (2013), 'The Climate Policy Dilemma', *Review of Environmental Economics and Policy* 7 (2), 219–237.
17. See Milne JE and MS Andersen (2014), n1 above.
18. Marron DB and EJ Toder (2014), 'Tax Policy Issues in Designing a Carbon Tax', *American Economic Review* 104 (5), 563–568.
19. Kettner C and D Kletzan-Slamanig (2018), 'Energy and Carbon Taxes in the EU: Empirical Evidence with Focus on the Transport Sector', *WIFO Working Paper* 555, www.wifo.ac.at/wwa/pubid/60972, last accessed 5 May 2019.
20. Bach et al (2002), 'The Effects of Environmental Fiscal Reform in Germany – a Simulation Study', *Energy Policy* 30, 803–811.
21. Pearce D (1991), 'The Role of Carbon Taxes in Adjusting to Global Warming', *The Economic Journal* 101(407), 938–948.
22. See OECD ilibrary (2019), www.oecd-ilibrary.org/taxation/tax/indicator-group/english_76e12892-en, last accessed 5 May 2019.
23. OECD (1999), Economic instruments for pollution control and natural resources management in OECD Countries: a survey, Paris; OECD Glossary of Tax Terms, www.oecd.org/ctp/glossaryoftaxterms.htm#T, last accessed 1 February 2017.
24. See Milne JE and MS Andersen (2014), n1 above.

25. Taylor M (2012), 'Is it a levy, or is it a tax, or both?', *Revenue Law Journal* 22 (1), 1–11.
26. See OECD (1999), n23 above.
27. Rodi M and H Ashiabor (2012), 'Legal authority to enact environmental taxes', in Milne JE and M Skou Andersen (eds), *Handbook of Research on Environmental Taxation*, Edward Elgar, Cheltenham, 59–81.
28. See Vollebergh H and JJ Dijk (2017). 'Taxes and fees of regional water authorities in the Netherlands', in *Capacity building for environmental tax reform*: European Commission study (1–12), IEEP. Also, in situations where more money is levied than spent, the earmarking still prevails; see Dutch Supreme Court, Judgment of 17 February 2017, ECLI:NL:HR:2017:253.
29. Milne JE (2017), 'Tax Choices: The Tale of Four States' in Weishaar SE, L Kreiser, JE Milne, H Ashiabor and M Mehling (eds), *The Green Market Transition – Carbon taxes, energy subsidies and smart instrument mixes*, Edward Elgar, Cheltenham, 3–16.
30. See Herrera Molina PM (2012), 'Design options and their rationales', in Milne JE and M Skou Andersen (eds), *Handbook of Research on Environmental Taxation*, Edward Elgar, Cheltenham, 85–101.
31. Herrera Molina (2012), n30 above; and Proposal for a Council Directive introducing a tax on carbon dioxide emissions and energy. COM (92) 226 final, 30 June 1992, Articles 3 and 4.
32. See Herrera Molina (2012), n30 above; and Proposal for a Council Directive introducing a tax on carbon dioxide emissions and energy. COM (92) 226 final, 30 June 1992, Articles 3 and 4.
33. See Rodi and Ashiabor (2012), n27 above.
34. See Rodi and Ashiabor (2012), n27 above.
35. See Rodi and Ashiabor (2012), n27 above.
36. See OECD (2001), n2 above.
37. See OECD (1972), n14 above.
38. See OECD (1972), n14 above.
39. Vanistendael F (2000), 'No European taxation without representation', *EC Tax Review* 200/3. Romano C (2002), 'Advance Tax Rulings and Principles of Law Towards a European Tax Rulings System?', *IBFD,* Amsterdam, 281–384.
40. OECD (2014), 'Fundamental principles of taxation', in *Addressing the Tax Challenges of the Digital Economy*, OECD Publishing, Paris.
41. Case C-189/15 *Istituto di Ricovero e Cura a Carattere Scientifico (IRCCS) – Dondazione Santa Lucia*, of 18 January 2017.
42. Worldbank Group (2018), *State and Trends of Carbon Pricing 2018*, Washington.

16. The use of effective carbon rates as an indicator for climate mitigation policy

Kris Bachus and Ping Gao

1. INTRODUCTION

Effective carbon rates (ECRs) are:

> The total price that applies to CO_2 emissions from energy use as a result of market-based policy instruments. They are the sum of taxes and tradable emission permit prices, and have three components: carbon taxes, specific taxes on energy use and the price of tradable emission permits. (Organisation for Economic Co-operation and Development (OECD), 2016)

ECRs offer an interesting complement to related indicators measuring the use of carbon pricing, such as the implicit tax rate on energy (ITE) (see section 2), and revenue-based indicators and tax rate-based indicators for the use of environmental taxation (Bachus, 2016b). Their novelty mainly lies in the fact that tax rates and Emissions Trading Scheme (ETS) prices are integrated into one indicator.

In this chapter, we first compare the ECR to existing related indicators and evaluate its strengths and weaknesses. Next, we present the general observations from the ECR values calculated by the OECD for 42 countries. We then calculate the national weighted average ECR for a selection of countries – an exercise that the OECD has chosen not to perform, for reasons that will be discussed in sections 3 and 4. Subsequently, we dive into the empirical results by performing a comparative case study of Belgium and China. Although these countries seem to have little in common at first sight, a comparison of their ERCs and concomitant policies raises interesting insights, both for the two countries and for the use of environmentally related taxes (ERT) in general. Finally, we formulate conclusions and recommendations regarding the use of ECRs and the two case studies.

2. THE LINK BETWEEN THE ECR AND OTHER INDICATORS

It is interesting to compare the ECR with two related indicators. The first is the ITE, which is reported on an annual basis for the EU (European Commission and Eurostat, 2016). The ITE is calculated by dividing a country's energy tax revenues by final energy consumption. The second related indicator is the revenues from ERT as a percentage of gross domestic product (GDP).[1] This is the most commonly used indicator in making an international comparison of the use of ERT.

Table 16.1 summarizes the similarities and differences between the ECR and the ITE.

The three indicators have different coverages, which means that they can (and should) be used thoughtfully and for the right purpose. The fact that tax expenditures and free allocation of ETS allowances are not reflected in the ECR is a validity drawback that the other two indicators do not have. On the other hand, the ECR is the only indicator that allows for a distinction to be drawn between renewable (or zero-carbon) energy and fossil-fuel based energy, which is a strong plus. Finally, the ECR, like the ITE, has the advantage that a rise in pollution does not lead to a rise in the indicator.

*Table 16.1 Comparison between ECR and ITE**

	ECR	ITE	Revenues ERT as % of GDP
Coverage	energy tax + carbon tax + ETS	energy tax + carbon tax	energy tax + carbon tax + all other ERTs
Value added tax	excluded	excluded	excluded
Tax expenditures and free allocation of allowances	excluded	included (free allocation n/a)	included (free allocation n/a)
Distinction between zero-carbon and other energy	included	excluded	excluded
Impact of rise of the tax base	no impact	no impact	indicator goes up (validity problem)

Note: * This comparison is an extension of the comparison between different indicators made in Bachus (2016b).

Source: Based on Bachus (2016b), extended by the authors.

3. OECD FINDINGS BASED ON THE ECR

In 2018, the OECD released its second report on the ECR. The 2018 edition covers 42 countries representing 80 per cent of global carbon emissions (OECD, 2018). Hence, the report gives an accurate and comprehensive view of the degree to which carbon emissions are priced around the world.

The OECD uses two benchmark rates: €30 per ton of carbon dioxide (CO_2), which is a low-end estimate of current carbon costs; and €60 per ton of CO_2, a mid-point estimate for 2020. It was found that in 2015, 88 per cent of carbon emissions in the 42 countries were priced below the €30 per ton CO_2 benchmark. 46 per cent of carbon emissions from energy use were unpriced. In 2012, specific energy taxes (mainly excise taxes) represented the bulk of the carbon prices – 93 per cent. Carbon taxes represented only 1.3 per cent of the carbon prices in 2012, while ETS represented 5.6 per cent of the total average ECR.

The OECD developed a new indicator, called the 'carbon pricing gap', that expresses the extent to which emissions are priced at less than €30 per ton. In 2015, the carbon pricing gap was 76.5 per cent for the 42 countries, down from 80.1 per cent in 2012. In the road transport sector, 57 per cent of emissions were priced above €30 per ton, whereas in other sectors this was only 4 per cent. It is fair to say that transport is the only sector that faces high carbon rates; in all other sectors, the effective carbon rates are still very low.

In its 2016 report, the OECD recommended that countries focus on zero and low-priced emissions, as related reforms can often be implemented in a cost-effective way, with limited or no risk of distortionary impacts. The large share of unpriced emissions in sectors other than road transport could be a good place to start.

One observation that can be made when reading the OECD report is that it does not contain a comparison of national average ECRs, which would interest many readers and policy makers alike. We see three reasons for this absence. First, in countries with high road transport taxes (mainly in Europe), the national average ECRs are pushed up by the road transport sector, even though this sector accounts for only 16 per cent of carbon emissions. As a result, many of these countries end up with an average ECR of more than €30 per ton of CO_2 or even €60 per ton of CO_2. This may lead some to conclude that these countries have no need to raise their carbon prices any further. However, carbon rates in most other sectors in those countries tend to be low, and further carbon price increases are therefore required in those sectors. Second, the ECR is an absolute indicator that does not take into account the purchasing power of a country or its level of economic development. As a result, ECRs tend to be much lower in less developed economies, which some may consider to be inaccurate or undesirable. Third, the ECR does not distinguish between freely allocated and auctioned trading permits. As a result, an average ECR could significantly overestimate the effectively paid carbon rate.

In the following section, we calculate the national weighted average ECR for a selection of countries, which we have not yet found in any other publication to date.

4. NATIONAL WEIGHTED AVERAGE ECR

Based on the data provided by the 2016 OECD report, it is possible to calculate an average ECR per country.[2] The carbon prices from specific energy taxes, carbon taxes and ETS are weighted with the shares of the emissions used as weights.[3] The average national ECRs are calculated for a selection of ten countries and for the total of all 41 countries in the OECD study, which were responsible for 80 per cent of worldwide carbon emissions in 2012. The results are shown in Figure 16.1.

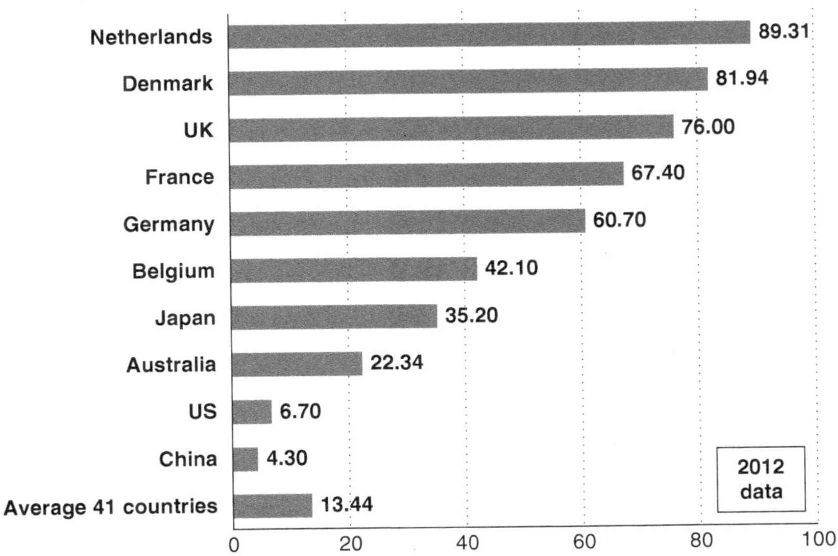

Source: Data from OECD (2016), calculations by the authors.

Figure 16.1 National ECRs for a selection of ten countries and the total for 41 countries (2012 data)

The results reveal big differences from country to country. The 'ranking' of countries from high to low ECR is unsurprising, as other indicators – for example, in relation to ERT – reveal the same 'frontrunners' and 'laggards'; but the significant difference between these two groups is still greater than expected. The highest ECR is for the Netherlands, which is 20 times higher than the lowest ECR, for China. One explanation for the significant differences is the fact that the ECR is an absolute indicator, which leaves countries with lower purchasing power (and GDP) with a lower value. However, the average effective carbon rate charged in the US – the country with the highest purchasing power – is also strikingly low. In this case, only policy and political choices can explain the low carbon price. A second explanation for the very low Chinese ECR is the fact that the OECD data are from 2012; China has since implemented a number of reforms that are likely to boost the national average ECR for more recent data years (see section 8).

Belgium has a low ECR compared to neighbouring countries and other EU countries, but the carbon prices charged in the EU are much higher than in any other part of the world. As the two biggest carbon emitters have such low ECRs, the (weighted) average for the 41 countries is equally low, at €13.44 per ton.

One could argue that this international comparison is inaccurate, as China has significantly lower purchasing power than the US. To correct for purchasing power disparities, the ECR can be calculated in terms of Purchasing Power Parity (PPP), using the (2012) PPP conversion factor and the (2012) exchange rate.[4] The results of that analysis are shown in Figure 16.2.

Readjusting for purchasing power disparities significantly revises the ECRs downwards for Denmark, Japan and Australia, and upwards for China. As a result, the US average ECR is lower than that of China when corrected for such disparities.

5. COMPARING THE ECRS OF CHINA AND BELGIUM

At first sight, China and Belgium appear vastly different countries; China has a population that is 120 times bigger and an area that is 300 times than Belgium's. However, both countries have similar carbon emissions per capita: 7.5 tons per capita in China to 8.3 tons per capita in Belgium.[5] In this and the following sections, we compare the two countries' ECRs up to the level of the underlying sectors and components.

The comparison in Table 16.2 shows that China prices much fewer carbon emissions than Belgium, and those emissions that are priced are

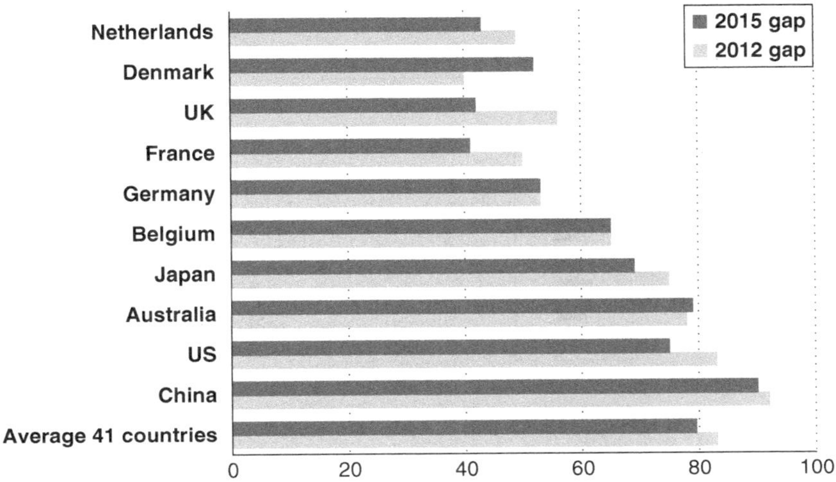

Figure 16.2 *ECR and ECR in PPP terms for a selection of ten countries*

Table 16.2 *Percentage of carbon emissions priced at different levels for China and Belgium*

	China		Belgium	
	2015	2012	2015	2012
% priced at €0	78	82	28	21
% priced at €0.01–30	13	10	49	56
% priced > €30	9	8	23	23
Carbon pricing gap (%)	90	92	65	65

Source: OECD (2018), OECD (2016).

priced at a lower level. China's main challenge is to start pricing the large proportion of carbon emissions that were unpriced in 2012. In Belgium, the primary recommendation could be to deepen rather than broaden carbon rates by increasing some of the existing ECRs to the level of €30 or higher.

6. BEHIND THE CHINESE ECR

Figure 16.3 shows the components of the Chinese ECR and its breakdown by sector.

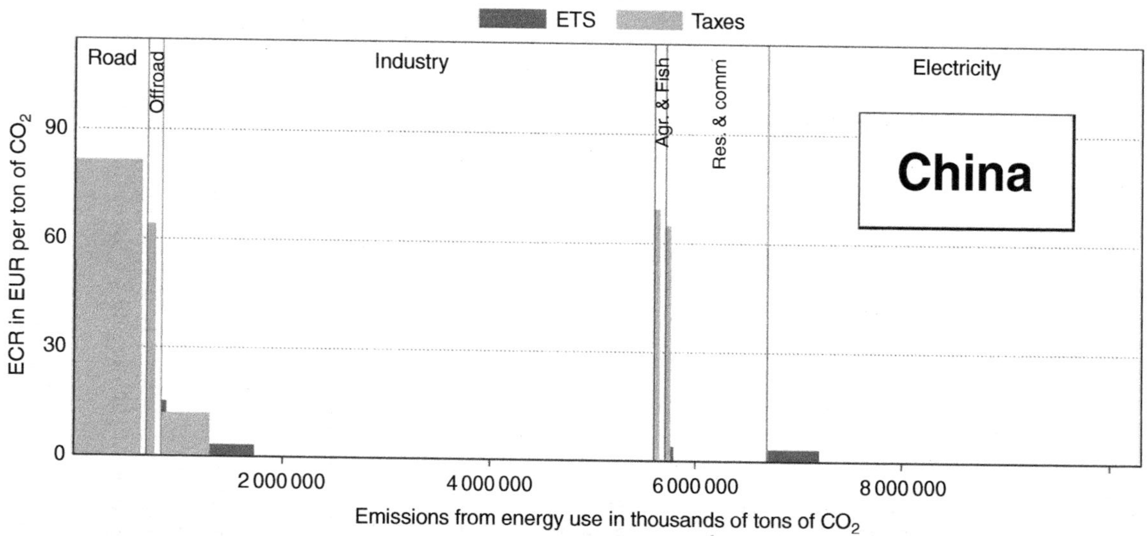

Source: OECD (2018).

Figure 16.3 Average ECRs in China by sector and component in 2015

This breakdown shows again that in 2016, the large majority of Chinese carbon emissions were priced at a zero rate. There is thus still a lot of low-hanging fruit to pick in China: a modest energy (or carbon) tax levied on a broad energy consumption basis would immediately bring down this unpriced emission proportion by a considerable margin.

As in other countries, carbon prices in the (road) transport sector are the highest, but they are still very low compared to the €174 per ton found in Belgium. The biggest difference between China and most other countries is that, outside the transport sector, the use of specific energy taxes in China is low.

For this reason, the seven carbon trading pilot areas (see section 8) have already had a relatively significant impact. Although the geographical area is limited and trading prices are modest, these have immediately accounted for 12 per cent of China's weighted ECR; the remaining 88 per cent are specific energy taxes, primarily in the transport sector. China has no carbon tax.

Other observations are that a proportion of off-road transport and agricultural and fisheries emissions are charged a high carbon rate – over €60 per ton. Both emissions categories are unpriced in Belgium. The residential and commercial sectors pay hardly any effective carbon rates, as 95 per cent of carbon emissions in those sectors are unpriced. Another striking element is that only 13 per cent of carbon emissions from electricity generation plants have a positive carbon price. Again, this is low-hanging fruit and the recently announced national ETS (see section 8) will dramatically reduce the large unpriced proportion of energy generation emissions – possibly even to (close to) zero. The same observation can be made for the industry sector, in which only 12 per cent of carbon emissions have a positive price. Contrary to electricity production, industry will not be a part of the (first phase of) the Chinese national ETS.

7. BEHIND THE BELGIAN ECR

Figure 16.4 shows the components of the Belgian ECR and its breakdown by sector and instrument.

In 2015, Belgium priced 23 per cent of its carbon emissions above €30 per ton of CO_2 – significantly more than the 12 per cent for the 42 countries overall, but less than most other EU countries.

In Belgium, as in most countries, only road transport emissions are taxed at a very high level. In fact, no emissions outside of the transport sector are priced at €30 or higher, which puts the country in the group of laggards in the EU, together with Hungary, Iceland and Luxembourg.

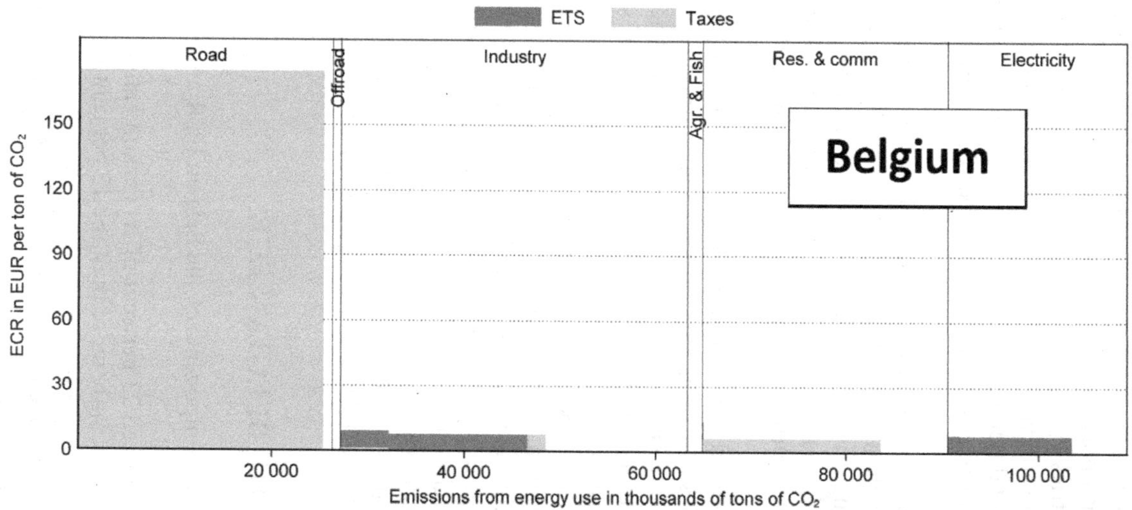

Source: OECD (2018).

Figure 16.4 Average ECRs in Belgium by sector and component in 2015

Other observations for Belgium are that carbon emissions in off-road transport, agriculture and fisheries escape any form of carbon pricing whatsoever. Most of the residential and commercial sector is subject to an ECR of only €6 per ton, while one-quarter of those emissions remain unpriced.

Belgium has no carbon tax; specific energy taxes are the dominant component of the ECR, accounting for 95 per cent of the weighted ECR. The remaining 5 per cent originate from the EU ETS. As in the rest of the EU, in 2015 the EU ETS provided only a relatively weak carbon price signal, as around 30 per cent of Belgian industrial emissions (excluding electricity generation) were unpriced and 100 per cent were priced below €30 per ton. About 18 per cent of Belgian carbon emissions were subject to a combination of specific energy taxes and a permit price in 2012.

8. PROSPECTS FOR THE BELGIAN AND CHINESE ECRS

In this section, we provide an overview of the main changes between 2015–18 (and beyond) which could affect the ECRs of our two case study countries, Belgium and China.

8.1 China

In China, the recent drive for more sustainable economic growth and the battle against air pollution have prompted a greater number of changes than in Belgium. Three reforms relating to carbon and energy pricing stand out. First, the consumption tax rate on refined oil was increased three times in 2014–15. The consumption tax rate on unleaded gasoline rose from RMB 1 per litre in 2009 to RMB 1.52 in 2015; for diesel, it rose from RMB 0.8 to RMB 1.2.[6]

The second reform received more worldwide media attention: in 2013, China started pilot carbon trading in two provinces and five cities. The carbon trading pilots covered 3000 key emission units, with annual emissions of about 14000 tons of CO_2. As of November 2017, the total trading volume of quotas had reached 2 billion tons of CO_2 equivalent – about RMB 4.6 billion. The carbon trading price in 2017 was €2.50 to €5.80 per ton, with transactions totalling €564 million. The quantities and intensity of carbon emissions within the scope of the pilot have shown a downward trend in recent years.

On 19 December 2017, the National Development and Reform Commission launched the national carbon ETS, marking the expansion of carbon trading to the whole country.[7] The national carbon ETS has initially been launched in the power generation industry, which is responsible for about one-third of China's carbon emissions (3 billion tons of carbon per year). Participants are enterprises and other economic organizations in the power sector with annual emissions of at least 26000 tons of CO_2 equivalent.[8] Compared to other international schemes, this threshold is more stringent, which means that power generation enterprises of all sizes will be fully integrated into the carbon market. The first tier of more than 1700 carbon trading enterprises discharge total emissions of more than 3 billion tons of CO_2 equivalent, accounting for about 39 per cent of national carbon emissions. Although the government has announced the launch of the national carbon market, the necessary support systems for testing must still be established. It is estimated that actual trading will start in 2019 or 2020; the initial transaction price will be RMB 50 (€6.40) per ton, and the expected market carbon trading price will be RMB 300 (€38.40) per ton. The national carbon market has chosen the industry baseline method to allocate allowances (for free) to the electricity companies. Although it remains to be seen whether the Chinese national ETS will succeed, the system can be expected to at least substantially reduce the 78 per cent share of 2015 Chinese carbon emissions that were unpriced (see Table 16.2), to 43 per cent or less. With this reform, China has followed the main recommendation of the OECD report, which is to commence policy action by putting a price on unpriced emissions, even if this price is initially low. However, the decision to restrict the ETS coverage to the electricity sector alone means that additional policies will be needed to put a carbon price on industrial emissions, of which 88 per cent had a zero ECR in 2015.

The third reform is the 2016 'fee-to-tax' reform. The Environmental Protection Tax Law was passed by the Standing Committee of the National People's Congress on 25 December 2016, and was formally implemented on 1 January 2018. The environmental protection tax has replaced the existing pollutant discharge fee. Sulphur dioxide (SO_2) and nitrogen oxides (NOx), which are mainly emitted from the consumption of fossil fuels, are covered by the tax. This means that the tax is similar to an energy tax and hence is relevant for the ECR. The conversion of a fee into a tax is important, as the pollutant discharge fee was collected by the local environmental protection agency, and was blamed for promoting local protectionism and providing scope for bargaining in the levy process. The new tax is collected by the local tax bureau, which offers much less room for negotiation. As a result, compliance and the effective levy rate may be expected to be much closer to the nominal tax rate.

The tax rate for air pollutants and water pollutants, which is determined and adjusted by the provincial governments, takes into account the region's environmental capacity, pollution status and economic and social development goals. The upper ceiling of the tax rate is ten times the lower limit. For instance, the environmental tax rate for both SO_2 and NOx emissions is RMB 12 per ton in Beijing, but only RMB 1.2 per ton in rural provinces such as Jiangxi, Xinjiang and Gansu (Sohu, 2017). However, further increases to the level of this tax have already been announced in some provinces, such as Hebei, Shanghai, Shandong, Henan and Jiangsu.

In conclusion, China has been very active over the past five years when it comes to carbon and energy pricing. It remains to be seen what the actual impact of these initiatives will be on China's ECR, as some of the reforms are rather modest and have been hollowed out by inflation. However, given the very low ECR in 2012 and 2015, all of these reforms can be expected to have a tangible impact on the ECR in the near future. Finally, although its success is not guaranteed, the national ETS can be expected to boost China's national average ECR as soon as trading actually starts.

8.2 Belgium

In Belgium, in 2015 the federal government announced the so-called 'tax shift' – a major fiscal reform to be implemented in phases between 2015–18. One measure in this policy package was the gradual equalization of the excise tax rates on diesel and gasoline. This was an ambitious policy goal, as the difference had been as high as €0.28 per litre in 2008 and was still €0.17 at the time the reform was introduced in 2015 (Bachus, 2016a). However, as this equalization – which was finalized by the summer of 2018 – was realized by increasing the diesel tax while reducing the gasoline tax, its impact on the ECR can be expected to be modest (although still tangible).

In Flanders,[9] the Energy Contribution tax on electricity consumption increased suddenly on 1 March 2016 from €3 per year for the average household to a staggering €103. This measure was taken to relieve the high debt burdens of electricity management companies, which had been building up due to the Flemish green certificate system. The new tax measure was very unpopular and led to the resignation of the Flemish energy minister (Bachus, 2016a). At the end of 2017, the Flemish government announced that the tax would be reduced to €9 for the average household. This measure is expected to have a visible impact on Belgium's ECR between March 2016 and the end of 2017; although the fact that this measure was limited to just one of the country's three regions will mitigate its impact.

The ECR includes only taxes that are directly levied on energy. Other taxes that may have an indirect impact on carbon emissions are not included. For instance, in April 2016 the Belgian government[10] introduced road charging for heavy duty vehicles.[11] This measure is expected to have a significant impact on Belgium's environmental taxation indicators (Bachus, 2016a), but not on its ECR, as transport taxes are not included in the ECR.

In conclusion, we expect that Belgium's ECR for the data years 2013–18 will not substantially deviate from the 2012 and 2015 data, except for a temporary surge in 2016–17 due to the changes to the Energy Fund Contribution.

9. CONCLUSIONS

The ECR is an important addition to existing indicators, as it is the only indicator to provide an integrated perspective on carbon price signals from both taxes and ETS. Moreover, the ECR has been calculated for 42 countries accounting for 80 per cent of global carbon emissions, which makes it suitable for comparison and inter-country learning.

The first lesson from the ECR statistics is that in 2015, about half of all carbon emissions remained unpriced. With the exception of the transport sector, a lot of low-hanging fruit remains to be picked in sectors such as electricity generation, industry, residential and commercial, and agriculture and fisheries. There are also important differences between countries, with (mainly northern) European countries having the highest average ECR and the global top two emitters – China and the US – having the lowest average ECR. After correction for purchasing power disparities, we found that China's ECR in PPP terms is slightly higher than that of the US, leaving the US at the bottom of the ranking of the ten countries we selected for our data analysis.

The comparative case study on China and Belgium showed that Belgium has a much higher ECR than China; but in recent years China has taken many policy decisions that should boost its average ECR. The national ETS, which is expected to start trading in 2019 or 2020, will cause a surge in China's average effective carbon prices. However, as industry is not covered in the (first phase of the) national ETS, additional action will be required for that sector; the same can be said for the residential and commercial sector.

In Belgium, fewer carbon pricing reforms have taken place in the recent past, although political discussions on carbon pricing are still ongoing. As Belgium is some way off meeting its binding, EU-imposed 2030 carbon emission targets,[12] we expect that this debate will intensify in the future and may lead to new policy decisions on carbon pricing. Given its position vis-à-vis neighbouring countries, Belgium has scope to impose a carbon tax or higher specific energy taxes on all energy products outside the transport sector. Additionally, although ETS prices hit €20 per ton of CO_2 in 2018, the existing ETS will need further reform at the EU level in order to increase the carbon price for industry and electricity generation.

The ECR indicator is a great complement to existing indicators relating to environmental taxation and emissions trading. There are three areas where work on the ECR could be further refined. First, the national weighted average ECR could be calculated for all 42 countries studied by the OECD, as we did for ten countries. Second, an attempt could be made to differentiate between grandfathered and auctioned tradable allowances – for example, by taking into account government revenues from auctioning. Third, the ECR could be calculated in terms of PPP for all countries, in order to address disparities between countries with different levels of economic development. All in all, the ECR is a valuable addition to the science of measuring the use of economic instruments in climate mitigation policies and should be a fruitful basis for policy learning in the years to come.

NOTES

1. The comparison could also be made with the indicator 'revenues from environmentally related taxes (ERT) as a percentage of total taxation', with similar results.
2. The data year for the 2016 report is 2012 and the data year for the 2018 report is 2015; but due to data restrictions the national ECRs are calculated only for the year 2012.
3. For example, if the carbon rate on gasoline (for transport) is €150 per ton of CO_2 and the share of emissions from gasoline in the total carbon emissions is 8 per cent, then the rate after weighting is 150*0.08 = €12. The summation of all emission shares and carbon rates equals the national weighted average ECR.
4. Data for 2012 from https://data.oecd.org/conversion/exchange-rates.htm#indicator-chart, last accessed 4 January 2018.
5. Data for 2014. Source: World Bank (2017), https://data.worldbank.org/indicator/EN.ATM.CO2E.PC, last accessed 3 January 2018.
6. Data sources: State Administration of Taxation (2015) and State Administration of Taxation (2008). On 3 January 2018, RMB 1 converted into €0.128 or $0.154.
7. Sources: China Electricity Council (2017) and https://sandbag.org.uk/2017/12/19/chinas-national-ets-launches-today/, last accessed 3 January 2018.
8. Which is equivalent to the consumption of about 10000 tons of standard coal per year.
9. Flanders is the northern part of Belgium, home to just over half of the Belgian population.
10. As transport taxation falls under the competence of the three regions and not the federal government, an inter-regional agreement between Flanders, Wallonia and the Brussels-Capital Region was required to make this reform possible.
11. Maximum permissible vehicle mass +3.5 ton.
12. Conclusion made by the authors based on Eurostat data: http://ec.europa.eu/eurostat/en/web/products-press-releases/-/8-04052017-BP, last accessed 4 October 2017.

REFERENCES

Bachus, K (2016a). *Actualisatie indicatoren en uitdiepen studie vergroening van het Vlaams belastingstelsel*, Leuven: Aalst.

Bachus, K (2016b). 'How to tell green from grey? Towards a methodological framework for evaluating the greening of national tax systems', *Ecological Indicators*, 71(Supplement C), 229–238; doi:https://doi.org/10.1016/j.ecolind.2016.04.009.

European Commission and Eurostat (2016). 'Taxation trends in the European Union. Data for Member States, Iceland and Norway', Luxembourg.

OECD. (2016). *Effective Carbon Rates*. Paris: OECD Publishing.

OECD. (2018). *Effective Carbon Rates 2018. Pricing Carbon Emissions through Taxes and Emissions Trading*. Paris: OECD Publishing.

Sohu (2017). 'National provinces announce environmental tax collection standards' (全国各省公布环保税征收标准！差异巨大), available at www.sohu.com/a/210504040_100020209, last accessed 3 January 2018.

State Administration of Taxation (2008). Notice 2008/167 on the increase of the consumption tax rate on oil products (财政部 国家税务总局关于提高成品油消费税税率的通知), http://hd.chinatax.gov.cn/guoshui/action/GetArticleView1.do?id=4732&flag=1, last accessed 3 January 2018.

State Administration of Taxation (2015). Notice 2015/11 on the continuing increase of the consumption tax rate on oil products (关于继续提高成品油消费税的通知), http://hd.chinatax.gov.cn/guoshui/action/GetArticleView1.do?id=484549&flag=1, 28 December 2017, last accessed 3 January 2018.

17. The G20 peer review of fossil fuel subsidies

Aldo Ravazzi Douvan and Gionata Castaldi

1. INTRODUCTION

Fossil fuel subsidies (FFSs) both directly and indirectly encourage congestion in urban areas and unsustainable modes of transport, while increasing greenhouse gas emissions, leading to global warming and climate change. For this reason, the international community has been trying to address this issue for several years.

Since the adoption in 2015 of the Paris Agreement and the UN 2030 Agenda, with its Sustainable Development Goals (SDGs), there have been many policy changes around the world in relation to FFSs. As the Organisation for Economic Co-operation and Development (OECD) (2018) has reported:

> India and Indonesia have made great strides in phasing-out their consumer price supports . . ., a number of fuel tax exemptions have been phased-out in OECD countries, and carbon taxes have been introduced in Mexico and France to internalize the external costs of fossil fuel consumption.

G20 countries are contributing to this attempt through peer reviews of FFSs. The peer review mechanism promotes transparency and accountability in this domain, where environmental, climate and economic issues are at stake. As in traditional OECD peer reviews, best practices are shared, progress is reported to G20 partners and the global community, critical issues are discussed and feedback is received from partners.

FFSs cause excessive consumption of fossil fuels, exacerbate environmental pollution, result in a loss of government income and provoke serious health damages. Moreover, FFSs are inefficient from an environmental and an economic point of view. They may be efficient on social grounds; but experience and analysis have shown that direct subsidies to poor and vulnerable groups are more efficient and avoid under-pricing carbon, sending the wrong price signals to the market in both the short and long term. Extensive policy literature of both intergovernmental organizations and think-tanks supports the need to remove FFSs (eg, Parry et al (2014), Coady et al (2015), Oosterhuis and Ten Brink (2016), Green Budget Europe (2017)).

This is why in 2009, the G20 partners decided to start phasing out FFS 'over the medium term' while emphasizing a major consequence of such fiscal measures: their undermining of 'efforts to deal with the threat of climate change'. G20 peer reviews began in 2016. The first countries to engage in peer review, just after their ratification of the Paris Agreement, were China and the USA, Mexico and Germany followed in 2017, while in 2018 it was the turn of Indonesia and Italy.

Within and beyond this framework, a heterogeneity of approaches among countries as to the definition of 'subsidy' may arise, as well as an attempt to limit analysis of FFSs through ambiguous definitions such as 'inefficient FFSs'. However, common and parallel action by G20 countries may mutually reinforce climate and economic policies.

2. HOW EVERYTHING STARTED: THE G20 PROCESS AND PEER REVIEW OF FFSs

At the third G20 summit (Pittsburgh, September 2009), the G20 leaders had to address global financial and economic criticisms. They decided to adopt a US proposal to phase out 'inefficient' FFSs over the medium term, calling on energy and finance ministers to report their implementation strategies and timeline for action to meet this commitment at the next meeting. The G20 Leaders Statement defined 'subsidies' as 'inefficient fossil fuel subsidies that encourage wasteful consumption, reduce our energy security, impede investment in clean energy sources and undermine efforts to deal with the threat of climate change'.

An International Energy Agency (IEA)/OECD study has estimated that the removal of FFSs by 2020 could reduce global greenhouse gas emissions by 10 per cent by 2050. The G20 Leaders Statement advocated that FFSs be rationalized and phased out, calling on major institutions – the IEA, the Organization of the Petroleum Exporting Countries (OPEC), the OECD and the World Bank – to provide analysis of the scope of energy subsidies and suggestions for their phase-out. This commitment was further confirmed at the Toronto Summit (June 2010).

At the three meetings of finance ministers and central bank governors held in April, June and October 2010, the primary focus was on underlining the G20's willingness and commitment to promote economic recovery in the wake of the financial crisis, and strengthen the global economy through inclusive and sustainable employment, new jobs, greater transparency and reduced market volatility.

Nevertheless, as requested at the Pittsburgh Summit, the IEA, OPEC, the OECD and the World Bank presented a joint report on energy subsidies, entitled 'Analysis of the scope of Energy Subsidies and suggestions for the G-20 Initiative', in which they suggested a roadmap that would allow policy makers to identify, quantify, recognize and estimate the impact of phasing out subsidies. Starting from the assumption that energy is crucial to economic growth and the reduction of poverty, and recognizing the political motivations for their original introduction, the report underlines how energy subsidies often generate market distortions that 'put societies onto inefficient consumption and production paths', encouraging wasteful consumption of natural resources and discouraging a shift towards cleaner fuels. Reform could exert positive effects in this regard by reducing wasteful consumption and contributing to the economy, realigning the financial balance of countries under severe stress – especially at a time of economic crisis – or making available funds for reallocation (eg, supporting industries, income redistributions).

The Pittsburgh and Toronto commitments were confirmed at the Seoul G20 Leaders Summit (November 2010). 'While recognizing the importance of providing targeted support for the poorest', the G20 leaders called for the IEA, the OECD, OPEC and the World Bank to 'further assess and review the progress made in implementing the Pittsburgh and Toronto commitments and report back to the 2011 Summit in France'. At the October 2011 meeting of finance ministers and central bank governors in Paris and the subsequent G20 Summit (Cannes, November 2011), the institutions duly presented an updated study on supporting measures for fossil fuels.

In 2013 the OECD put together for the first time an inventory of support mechanisms for the production and consumption of fossil fuels in 24 of the 35 OECD member countries, identifying 250 mechanisms with an estimated value of US $45–75 billion over the period 2005–10. The IEA identified 37 emerging and developing countries that supported consumption of fossil fuels to a total amount of US $409 billion in 2010 – US $110 billion more than in 2009. OPEC studies estimated that the possible removal of energy subsidies would have a negative impact on the gross domestic product (GDP) of OPEC Member States of around −3.4 per cent on average per year for the first five years, due to a significant increase in inflation and a 2.3 per cent rise in unemployment compared to baseline scenarios.

The 2013 Saint Petersburg G20 Leaders Summit refocused the attention on subsidies, welcoming the development of a methodology for a voluntary peer review process among countries as a valuable way to assure greater transparency and responsibility. In addition, the G20 leaders invited finance ministers, in collaboration with relevant international institutions, to consider strategic options for the design of transition policies.

To this end, the G20 finance ministers requested an *ad hoc* analysis from the World Bank. This analysis focused on the available options that would allow countries to remove FFSs while continuing to ensure that the poorest had access to essential energy services.

Two approaches are outlined in the study: (1) improving the poverty reduction target for existing subsidies; and (2) introducing or strengthening alternative forms of support (whether financial or in kind) for the poor.

From the report's analysis of different countries' experiences and different combinations of the two approaches, it is clear that there is no universal solution; rather, the potential impacts of each measure must be considered in their entirety. For example, in the case of the most widespread cash transfer – the main instrument used to compensate poor households – the direct and indirect impacts of the removal of subsidies and the existence or introduction of an efficient, well-structured social protection system should be considered.

The report further underlines that the effectiveness of any transition policy depends on (1) the accuracy of the cost-benefit evaluation of the reforms, and (2) the direct and indirect impacts of measures on different population segments. As a consequence, the report presents some suggestions on how to prepare for the introduction of reforms, such as the following:

- Timing and planning: if the reduction of subsidies will lead to significant price increases, a gradual transition appears more likely to succeed; while planning is necessary to coordinate the various actors involved in the reform and the implementation of compensatory measures.
- Information and trust: explaining the reasons for the reform, providing information on the resources absorbed by subsidies and clearly describing compensatory measures could facilitate agreement on the need for reform.

During the Brisbane Summit in 2014, the G20 leaders approved the Principles of Energy Collaboration, the sixth of which relates to the rationalization and phase-out of FFSs; while at the Antalya Summit in 2015, the relevance of monitoring and updating on the status of FFSs reform at a global level was also underlined.[1]

The first countries to undergo a peer review were China and the USA in 2016, followed by Mexico and Germany in 2017 and Indonesia and Italy in 2018.

3. G20 PEER REVIEWS OF FFSs: HOW THEY WORK

G20 peer review assessments are a fruitful way to share elements for mutual learning through data collection, methodological procedures and policy actions (Figure 17.1).

The peer review process involves several steps. First, the countries undergoing peer review agree on terms of reference to establish the scope of the measures to be reviewed and a process timeline. The second step is to produce a self-report on existing measures, providing background and information on their implementation, and possibly indicating those which are being phased out in the medium term. This report is then reviewed by a peer review team which provides feedback and questions, generally during an in-person meeting hosted by the countries under review.[2] A final report by the peer review team is finally issued, along with the country's self-report (OECD, 2018).

4. CHINA AND US PEER REVIEWS OF FFSs

4.1 China

In its self-report (G20, 2016a), China identified nine 'inefficient' subsidies with an annual financial effect totalling US $14.5 billion. In particular, these include subsidies to state-owned enterprises (SOEs) for the exploration and extraction of fossil fuels, including a tax rebate on petroleum products used in natural gas and oil extraction, and an exemption from land use tax for SOEs China National Petroleum Company and China National Offshore Oil Corporation. Production is vertically integrated, but there are no subsidies for oil refining and processing, excluding an excise tax rebate on petroleum products used by refining companies themselves.

At the regional level, the peer review team identified subsidies for unemployment in coal-mining companies. There is a perception that local governments exert pressure or divert public expenditure originally earmarked for other uses in order to provide additional financial support to the coal industry. Although there was no estimate of the precise financial effects of these subsidies, their existence was emphasized during the peer review process.

Energy production for domestic heating purposes is subsidized by the central government to keep tariffs below the market level. Three subsidies were identified for utilities engaged in the heating market: two exemptions from land use tax for power stations and one value added tax (VAT) exemption on production, which was introduced to compensate producers for the revenue forgone due to under-pricing.

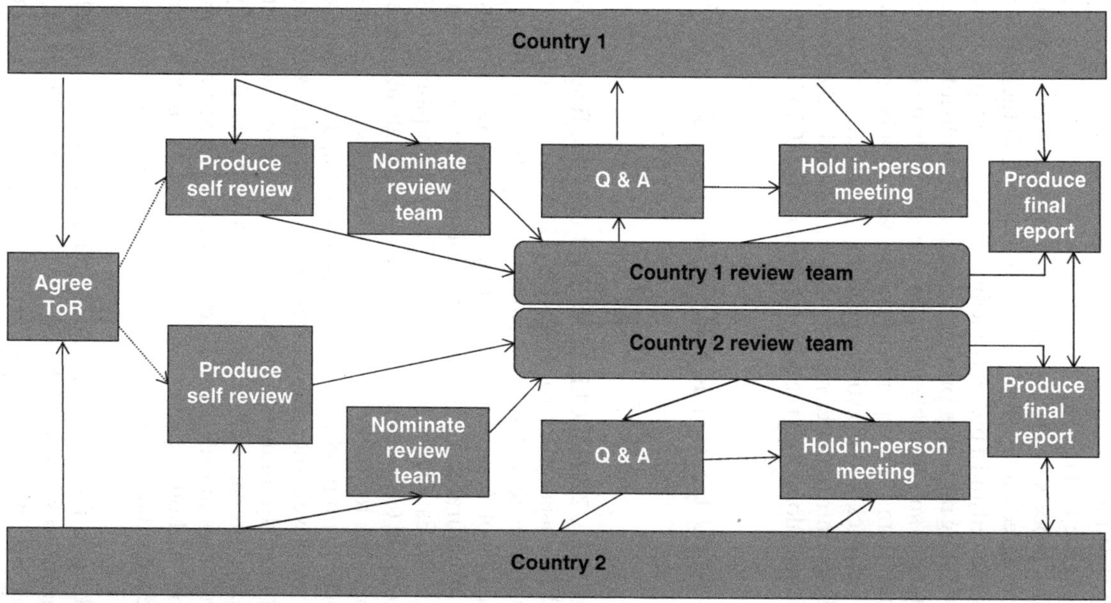

Source: OECD (2018).

Figure 17.1 The mechanism behind the G20 FFSs peer review process

These measures have no quantified financial effect. However, one measure that the government was able to quantify is in the transport sector: a bundle of subsidies for 'professional use' of fossil fuels, such as by taxi drivers, fishermen, forest rangers and public transport companies. This totalled around US $15 billion in 2013.

Finally, in the domestic sector, the government recorded a VAT tax benefit for the consumption of energy products (liquefied petroleum gas (LPG), natural gas, coal and gas for lighting purposes).

The panel of experts (from Germany, the USA and Indonesia) received the Chinese report positively and welcomed the government's intention to reform subsidies in the medium term. Subsidies for SOEs should be reformed, together with the short-term phase-out of the excise duty exemption on fuels used by refining companies and the land use tax exemptions.

Subsidies for energy producers for domestic heating should be reviewed to better reflect market prices. The gradual phase-out of subsidies for 'professional use' is also envisaged. The VAT tax benefit for domestic consumption on energy products has distributional issues, as this might be more beneficial for high-income households. The panel suggested that alternative forms of support to help the most vulnerable consumers be explored.

4.2 The USA

In its self-report (G20, 2016b), the USA described the evolution of the national energy scenario over the last 20 years, emphasizing two opposing trends. First, through advances in fracking and shale energy, the country had entered a new era of energy abundance, increasing oil and gas production levels. Second, more stringent energy standards and emissions control had been approved through the Clean Power Plan.[3]

In this context (quite different from the situation today), the report identified 17 federal FFS labelled as 'inefficient', worth a total amount of US $8.2 billion. Of these, 16 related to the exploration, development and extraction of fossil fuels. Another 'implicit' subsidy was the low excise duty on fossil fuels in the transport sector. The revenue was earmarked for the Highway Trust Fund, which was in deficit. During that period, the government proposed to Congress an additional tariff of US $10.25 per barrel.

The report quoted other subsidies that were not under reform, since they were not considered 'inefficient', such as the Low Income Home Energy Assistance Program – a programme to fight energy poverty that costs around US $3.4 billion.

The panel of experts (from China, Germany and Indonesia) encouraged the US government to take further steps in defining a timeline and action plan for reforming FFSs in the short to medium term.

5. MEXICO AND GERMANY PEER REVIEWS OF FFSs

5.1 Mexico

After outlining the energy context, Mexico's self-report[4] identified 10 FFS worth US $2.5 billion in 2016 – a considerable reduction on the figure for 2013, when they amounted to US $8.9 billion (see Table 17.1).

The Mexican Government identified these based on two main criteria: (1) FFSs that keep prices below opportunity cost in the international markets, as the most direct and relevant form of 'inefficient' subsidies; and (2) tax exemptions and tax differentiations applied to fossil fuels, which it classified as 'inefficient taxes', not inefficiency-inducing subsidies. With this definition, the government restricted the areas of analysis. Within this framework, the government did not consider excise duties to be 'inefficient' FFSs, as the price is not below the full marginal cost of production, so in economic terms there is no loss of revenue.

Among the 10 support measures analysed, two have already been removed (gasoline and diesel subsidies and LPG subsidies – the most substantial in financial terms) as part of a broader reform that the country has undertaken in the last decade.

In the transport sector, after nearly a decade of heavily subsidizing end-user prices of gasoline, diesel and LPG, Mexico began to gradually reduce net subsidies in 2013, due to the fall in the international oil price in 2013, which facilitated implementation of the reform; they resulted in positive net taxes in 2015. In 2015, a maximum reference price was set for administered prices of gasoline, diesel and LPG, preparing the market for liberalization in the form of imports from private companies and the possible arrival of new entrants. In 2016, prices were allowed to fluctuate following international reference prices within a band of +/−3 per cent of the 2015 price.

The energy regulator, the *Comisiòn Reguladora de Energia*, identified those regions that satisfied the requirements for market liberalization and published a timeline for the gradual liberalization of gasoline and diesel prices across the country. Starting from 1 January 2017, the maximum price of gasoline was allowed to rise by as much as 20 per cent, and gasoline and diesel prices began to be fully liberalized in the regions previously identified. By 2018, all regional markets were expected to have full market prices, with exceptions limited to regions where collusion or other anti-competition situations were identified. In addition, the LPG market has been fully open to competition since the beginning of 2017. Thus, LPG is not subject to any excise duty, but only to a carbon tax per litre, applied to the final price (including VAT).

The reform has also transformed SOEs Petròleos Mexicanos (PEMEX) and the Federal Electricity Commission into so-called 'state productive enterprises', with greater autonomy over their management and budget – thus interrupting the historical monopoly in the hydrocarbon and electricity sectors.

The energy sector reform is part of a much broader structural and

Table 17.1 The ten subsidies identified in the Mexican G20 FFSs self-report

No	Full name of the measure	Estimated annual fiscal cost (US $m)	
		2013	2016
Measures for the exploration, development and extraction of fossil fuels			
1	Provisions for producers of hydrocarbons	0	0*
Subsidies and tax benefits for fossil fuels used in transport			
2	Subsidies for excise duty on gasoline and diesel	8245	0
3	Subsidies for excise duty on LPG	373	0
4	Tax benefit for gasoline consumption in the northern border region	81	512
5	Diesel excise tax accreditation to public transport	0	1062
Measures for fossil fuels used in the manufacturing, agricultural and forestry sectors			
6	Support for agricultural and fishing activities	245	127
7	Diesel excise tax accreditation for industrial machinery, other than transportation	0	493
8	Diesel excise tax accreditation for fisheries machinery, including vessels	0	85
9	Diesel excise tax accreditation for farming machinery	0	222
Other tax benefits			
10	Carbon tax exemptions and reductions	n.a.	100.8

Note: * The Mexican government explained that the net fiscal cost of these measures is actually zero, as competitive bidding returns to the state whatever fiscal provisions are given to producers, and as significantly higher taxes are levied on exploration and production than in the rest of the economy.

Source: Elaboration on G20 data (2017a).

institutional reform package called '*Pacto por Mexico*', introduced by President Peña Nieto in 2012. The package targets several sectors – ranging from finance to telecoms, labour and education – with the aim of modernizing the Mexican economy and boosting long-term growth. This reform has generated significant revenue for the Mexican budget, turning a large loss in 2013 (US $8.6 billion) into an additional new source of income (from gasoline and diesel) in 2015 (over US $10 billion), to support the poor.

The G20 peer review team welcomed the recent introduction of a carbon tax – the first to be applied to fuel use outside of road transport – even though the tax rates are substantially below those originally proposed by the government in 2013 and remain below the marginal social cost of carbon emissions. Another limitation is that the tax rates are not determined by the relative carbon content of different fuels. Nevertheless, the peer review team recognized that the carbon tax, together with excise taxes, is a useful instrument to progressively internalize the negative externalities of fossil fuels.[5]

5.2 Germany

After outlining the energy context, Germany's self-report,[6] identified 22 subsidies totalling US $17.6 billion in 2016 (equal to €14.9 billion), in terms of both direct budgetary transfers and tax expenditures (see Table 7.2).

This exercise is not new for Germany: since 1967 the Ministry of Finance has submitted a report on budget transfers and tax expenditures, including FFSs, to Parliament (*Bundestag*) and the Federal Council (*Bundesrat*), together with a draft of the federal budget every two years. At the same time, the Federal Environment Agency (*Umweltbundesamt*) regularly publishes a report entitled *Environmental Harmful Subsidies in Germany*, which includes among these environmentally harmful subsidies all FFSs mentioned in the Ministry of Finance's report, as well as many others not considered in the G20 exercise; these environmentally harmful subsidies were estimated at €57 billion in 2014. In 2018, the Federal Agency for Nature Protection also prepared a specific catalogue on biodiversity harmful subsidies.[7]

Germany's participation in the G20 voluntary peer review process fits within this background of increasing transparency and knowledge of FFS. However, the estimates in the G20 report are approximately half of those of the Federal Environmental Agency.

According to the peer review team, Germany is to be praised for the list of FFSs identified in its self-report and its efforts towards greater transparency in identifying and explaining other measures to support fossil fuel production and consumption. Nevertheless, the team considered the vast

Table 17.2 The 22 subsidies identified in the German G20 FFSs self-report

No	Full name of the measure	Measure identifier	Estimated annual fiscal cost 2016 (€m)
Subsidies for the exploration, development and extraction of fossil fuels			
1	Grants for the sale of German hard coal for electricity generation, for sale to the steel industry and to offset the impact of capacity adjustment	S-1	1288
2	Granting of adjustment benefit to employees in the hard-coal mining industry	S-2	107
Subsidies for the refining and processing of fossil fuels			
3	Tax advantage for energy products used to produce other energy products for the maintenance of operations (producer's privilege)	T-1	350
Subsidies for power and heat generation			
4	Energy tax advantage for electricity generation	T-2	1700
5	Tax advantage for energy products used to power gas turbines and internal combustion engines at advantaged installations in accordance with Section 3 of the German Energy Tax Act (electricity generation, combined heat and power, gas transportation and storage)	T-3	–
Subsidies for fossil fuels used in transport			
6	Tax advantage for energy products used in inland shipping operations	T-4	180
7	Energy tax advantage for local public transport	T-5	72
8	Tax advantage for energy products used in the domestic aviation industry	T-6	570
9	Electricity tax advantage for rail and trolleybus operations	T-7	143
10	Tax advantage for liquefied gas and natural gas used as fuels	T-8	134
Subsidies for fossil fuels used in the manufacturing, agricultural and forestry sectors			
11	Electricity price compensation	T-9	245
12	Energy tax advantage for certain processes and procedures	T-10	553

Table 17.2 (continued)

No	Full name of the measure	Measure identifier	Estimated annual fiscal cost 2016 (€m)
13	Tax advantage for agricultural and forestry businesses (agricultural diesel)	T-11	450
14	Energy tax advantage for companies in the manufacturing sector, and agricultural and forestry businesses	T-12	153
15	Energy tax advantage for companies in the manufacturing sector in special cases (tax cap)	T-13	172
16	Electricity tax advantage for certain processes and procedures	T-14	836
17	Electricity tax advantage for companies in the manufacturing sector, and agricultural and forestry businesses	T-15	1052
18	Electricity tax advantage for companies in the manufacturing sector in special cases (tax cap)	T-16	1614
Miscellaneous tax benefits			
19	Special equalization scheme to reduce the surcharge levied to finance the additional costs of the deployment of renewable energies in electricity generation	T-17	4800
20	Special equalization scheme to reduce the surcharge levied to finance the additional costs of the deployment of combined heat and power plants	T-18	493
21	Relief on grid charges	T-19	No estimate provided
22	*General state measures in the social field*	T-20	No estimate provided

Source: G20 (2017b).

majority of these subsidies to be ‘efficient’ and thus outside the timeline for reform.

In the self-report, this was based on the threat to the international competitiveness of the affected industries and the risk of industry players relocating to ‘pollution havens’ – that is, other countries with less stringent environmental regulations. In a few cases, a tax exemption was justified by the need to avoid double taxation.

The removal of subsidies for the coal mining industry at the end of 2018 marked an important new chapter in the German strategy of subsidy reform, which may be repeatable in other countries as it was designed to be socially and regionally acceptable. The peer review team was particularly interested in professional training and successful labour force relocation, underlining the good work done by the government. The gradual and progressive closure of hard coal mines, with a consequent decline in mining-related jobs, was accompanied by a special support programme for employees and companies to ensure that workers could rapidly find new employment. In addition, a specific support mechanism was designed to target underground workers aged at least 50 and surface workers aged at least 57 who could lose their jobs due to mine closures prior to 1 January 2023: they will receive transitional assistance for up to five years until they are eligible for retirement.

Finally, the peer review team encouraged the German administration to take additional steps to consider alternative measures with less distortive effects in order to meet their objectives of maintaining industry competitiveness, preventing emissions relocation and meeting their global climate goals.

As emphasized in the German self-report, an efficient system of taxation takes into account both positive and negative externalities, and measures them against the induced tax revenue shortfall. To this end, it becomes necessary to quantify the economic effects (i.e., on production volumes, trade and price, and therefore on GDP), and the associated environmental and social costs.

6. ITALY AND INDONESIA PEER REVIEWS OF FFSs

Italy and Indonesia are the two countries in the 2018 peer review process. The in-person meeting for Indonesia was held in Jakarta in December 2017, with a wide participation of reviewing country experts. Italy held its own in-person meeting in Rome in October 2018, expressing willingness to keep up the momentum in phasing out the FFSs that are an obstacle to global climate goals and SDGs (respectively, under the Paris Agreement and the 2030 UN Agenda). Reports are expected in Spring 2019.

Key G20 partners, such as Canada and Argentina, are candidates for peer review in 2019, but more countries may join the process. A key objective of this exercise is to involve as many countries as possible and track the progress of countries already under peer review towards realizing the 2°C goal and the phase-out of FFSs.

7. CONCLUSIONS: THE IMPACT OF THE PHASE-OUT OF FFSs

The removal of FFSs is part of a larger picture of environmental fiscal reform.[8] In this regard, it might be helpful to review the empirical literature – especially on business competitiveness, one of the most sensitive issues on the policy side in different countries.

Studies on the impact of environmental taxes on businesses offer interesting insights. In a comprehensive literature review, Dechezlepretre and Sato (2014) analyse the empirical evidence of the effects of environmental taxes on competitiveness across a wide range of industries in various countries. They conclude that regardless of market conditions and strength, environmental taxes and, more generally, regulation do not have a significant negative effect on competitiveness indicators at company or national level.

In an empirical study on Germany, Flues and Lutz (2015) show that electricity taxes have had no negative effects on business competitiveness indicators such as turnover, exports, value added, investment and employment. Previously, Zhang and Baranzini (2004) reached the same conclusion with respect to potential losses in competitiveness due to the carbon tax – losses that in many cases were insignificant.

Conceptually, increases in energy prices due to the removal of FFSs are directly linked to increases in energy prices due to carbon/energy taxes. However, price increases due to subsidy removal may be particularly significant: in the case of specific subsidies on targeted fuels, reforms have caused energy price increases of 100 per cent and more in the past (Fattouh et al, 2016; Rentschler and Bazilian, 2016). This underlines that a specific case-by-case analysis of FFS reforms is crucial to ensure its effectiveness and efficiency.

Finally, energy subsidies are increasingly causing costly and protracted trade disputes, creating friction between countries. Bougette and Charlier (2015) found that 15 per cent of the trade disputes handled by the World Trade Organization in 2010–13 involved energy subsidies. The study provides a global overview of energy subsidies (mainly, but not exclusively, for fossil fuels and nuclear energy). The work shows that subsidies lead to net costs for society, rather than benefits, in the form of public budget deficits, increased waste, energy fuel shortages, crime associated with the trade in illicit fuels and increased environmental impacts.

NOTES

1. A reconstruction of international and global commitments on FFS is available on request. It is part of the second Italian Catalogue on Environmentally Harmful and Environmentally Friendly Subsidies (Ministry of Environment – TA Sogesid, forthcoming).
2. For Germany and Mexico, a single in-person meeting was held in Berlin in February 2017.
3. Now under review by the current US government; www.epa.gov/energy-independence, last accessed 21 April 2019.
4. G20 (2017a).
5. Indeed, according to the review team (G20, 2017a), 'higher carbon prices across sectors and fuels would likely prompt reductions in GHG emissions, and facilitate a cost-effective fulfilment of Mexico's commitments to its UNFCCC targets'.
6. G20 (2017b).
7. www.bfn.de/fileadmin/BfN/oekonomie/Dokumente/Abbau_naturschaedigender_Subventionen.pdf, last accessed 21 April 2019.
8. See the OECD reports for the G7 in 2017 under the Italian Presidency, 'Towards a G7 Target to phase out Environmentally Harmful Subsidies' and 'Environmental Fiscal Reform – Progress, Prospects and Pitfalls'.

REFERENCES

Bougette P and C Charlier (2015), 'Renewable energy, subsidies, and the WTO: where has the "green gone"?', *Energy Economics*, 51: 407–416.

Coady DP, Parry I, Sears L, Shang B (2015), 'How Large Are Global Energy Subsidies?', IMF WP 15/105.

Dechezlepretre A and M Sato (2014), 'The impacts of environmental regulations on competitiveness', Policy Brief. Grantham Research Institute on Climate Change and Environment, LSE.

Fattouh B, Sen A and T Moerenhout (2016), 'Striking the Right Balance? GCC Energy Pricing Reforms in a Low Price Environment'. *Oxford Energy Comment*.

Flues F and BJ Lutz (2015), 'Competitiveness impacts of the German electricity tax'. OECD Environment Working Paper 88.

G20 (2016a), *China's efforts to phase out and rationalise its inefficient FFSs. A report on the G20 peer-review of inefficient FFSs that encourage wasteful consumption in China*, G20-OECD.

G20 (2016b), *The United States' efforts to phase out and rationalise its inefficient FFSs. A report on the G20 peer-review of inefficient FFSs that encourage wasteful consumption in the United States*, G20-OECD.

G20 (2017a), *Mexico's efforts to phase out and rationalise its FFSs. A report on the G20 peer-review of inefficient FFSs that encourage wasteful consumption in Mexico*, G20-OECD.

G20 (2017b), *Germany's efforts to phase out and rationalise its FFSs. A report on the G20 peer review of inefficient FFSs that encourage wasteful consumption in Germany*, G20-OECD.

Green Budget Europe (2017), 'German inaction in phasing out fossil fuel subsidies causes consternation worldwide', https://green-budget.eu/ accessed on 1 January 2019.

Ministry of Environment – TA Sogesid (forthcoming), 'The Italian Catalogue on

Environmentally Harmful and Environmentally Friendly Subsidies' 2nd edition, www.minambiente.it/pagina/economia-ambientale.
OECD (2017a), 'Towards a G7 Target to phase out Environmentally Harmful Subsidies', a report for the G7 under Italian Presidency, www.minambiente.it/pagina/economia-ambientale accessed on 1 January 2019.
OECD (2017b), 'Environmental Fiscal Reform – Progress, Prospects and Pitfalls', a report for the G7 under Italian Presidency, www.minambiente.it/pagina/economia-ambientale accessed on 1 January 2019.
OECD (2018), OECD Companion to the Inventory of Support Measures for Fossil Fuels 2018, http://dx.doi.org/10.1787/9789264286061-en accessed on 1 January 2019.
Oosterhuis, FH and Ten Brink P (2014), 'Paying the Polluter. Environmental Subsidies and their Reform'. Edward Elgar.
Parry IW, Heine MD, Lis E, Li S (2014), *Getting Energy Prices Right. From Principle to Practice*, IMF.
Rentschler J and M Kornejew (2016), 'Energy subsidy reforms and the impacts on firms: Transmission channels and response measures'. OIES Working Paper.
Zhang Z and A Baranzini (2004), 'What do we know about carbon taxes? An inquiry into their impacts on competitiveness and distribution of income'. *Energy Policy* 32, 507–518.

18. Increasing fiscal transparency in energy policies

Leyla Ates and Sevil Acar*

1. INTRODUCTION

Energy policies are informed by energy supply security, economic development and environmental protection concerns, and energy tax incentives are increasingly employed as a key policy tool. The call to phase out inefficient fossil fuel subsidies in the form of direct or indirect transfers (eg, tax expenditures) has come to the forefront of the political agenda, as a result of international efforts (G20 2009; EC 2011). It is clear that accessible, timely and reliable fiscal data is crucial to the effective and efficient monitoring of government policies on tax expenditures in general, and on energy tax expenditures in particular.

In this regard, European Council Directive 2011/85/EU, obliging Member States to introduce domestic provisions for the publication of detailed information on the impact of tax expenditures on revenues by 31 December 2013 at the latest, ensures the regular public availability of tax expenditure data to monitor the energy tax incentive policies of all 28 countries. It is already possible to access data on some EU member states' fossil fuel subsidies in the Organisation for Economic Co-operation and Development (OECD) Inventory of Estimated Budgetary Support and Tax Expenditures for Fossil Fuels (OECD 2018). However, this data is limited to fossil fuels and hence does not cover tax incentives for renewables or energy efficiency. More importantly, the OECD does not impose a legal transparency obligation on member countries to provide tax expenditure reporting. The EU Directive does not make clear the scope of the legal transparency obligations on tax expenditures, which has led to different implementation practices among Member States (Kalyva 2015). Furthermore, uniform tax expenditure reporting practices are not currently possible, because of difficulties in defining and measuring tax expenditures (Oosterhuis et al 2014). Nonetheless, the basic level of transparency underwritten by the Directive enables tax policy to be scrutinized by academics and civil society across the 28 nations, which in turn enhances the quality of the data available. To exemplify this, we present in this chapter a case study of Turkey.

Turkey began publishing detailed tax expenditure reports in 2016. This publicly accessible data has enabled us for the first time to measure how and to what extent the government supports the energy sector through tax incentives. To this end, section 2 of this chapter explains the legal basis for tax expenditure reporting in Turkey and outlines the shortcomings of the Turkish tax expenditure reports, with a particular focus on energy tax policies. Section 3 attempts to estimate Turkey's energy tax expenditures for the years 2015 and 2016, as well as expenditures for the next four years, taking into account the previous technical shortcomings. Lastly, section 4 summarizes and discusses the findings.

2. TAX EXPENDITURE REPORTING IN TURKEY

2.1 The Legal Framework of Tax Expenditure Reporting

Tax expenditures are laws, rules or regulations that lead to a loss of revenue by allowing certain taxpayers to pay lower taxes or no taxes at all, in order to achieve certain social and economic goals. Tax concessions such as tax deductions, exceptions and exemptions that cause deviations from normal tax liabilities are called 'tax expenditures' in the literature. These expenditures have direct influences, such as reducing public revenues, as well as other indirect effects. The focus of this chapter is on tax incentives for energy in Turkey, which can be grouped under three headings: fossil fuels, renewable energy and energy efficiency tax expenditures (Sherlock and Stupak 2015). Just like direct transfers, tax expenditures for energy can have a significant restraining role for state budgets via their public revenue reducing effects (OECD 2015). Considering this, US Assistant Secretary of the Treasury Stanley Surrey functionally equated tax expenditures with spending and coined the term 'tax expenditure' for the first time in 1967 (Altshuler and Dietz 2008). He argued that tax expenditures should be made more transparent and be subject to regular scrutiny by legislatures in the same way as direct spending. Otherwise, Congress could not effectively exercise its budgetary control and manage its tax policy (Roberts 2016).

Since the beginning of the Republican era, all Turkish constitutions (1924, 1961 and 1982) have enshrined the general budgetary principle of unity, albeit in a limited manner. The principle of unity requires all public revenues and expenditures to be entered in the budget (CVCE 2016); but the Turkish constitutions mention only expenditures to be determined in budgetary law, not revenue. Article 161, paragraph 1 of the current

Turkish Constitution of 1982 states that: 'The expenditure of the State and of public corporations, other than state economic enterprises, shall be determined by annual budgets.' Meanwhile, Article 161, paragraph 2 designates the Parliament's legislative responsibility for 'the preparation, implementation, and control of the central government budget'. In this regard, public finance laws always clearly spelled out not only expenditures, but also revenues to be determined in the budget (Ates 2017). The budgetary principle of unity has broadly informed the Turkish Parliament's amendments of public finance legislation and integration of tax expenditures into the budget. However, it was the World Bank's support of public finance management reform (World Bank 1995) which prompted the introduction of the current public finance legislation, Law 5018 on Public Finance Management and Control Law, in 2003. Law 5018 acknowledges fiscal transparency as a basic principle of budgeting in Article 7 and details the scope of the budget law in Article 15, paragraph 2, as follows:

> Central Government Budget Law shall include revenue and expenditure estimations for the first year and the following two years; the budget deficit or surplus amount, if any, and how the deficit will be covered or where the surplus will be used, if any; tax revenues renounced due to tax exemptions, exceptions, reductions and similar practices; borrowing and warranty limits; authorities to be granted for the implementation of budgets; attached schedules; provisions pertaining to the revenues and the expenditures to be implemented during the fiscal year.

Thus, with this Law, the Turkish Parliament integrated tax expenditures for the first time in the budgetary process (Ates 2017). In doing so, it recognized tax expenditures as '(indirect) spending programs delivered through the tax system' (cf Ruggeri 2005).

This understanding also coincides with the principle of legality of taxation. When the government uses indirect spending to deliver its programme, it in fact grants tax concessions through tax laws to achieve policy goals. According to the legality principle, which has its initial roots in the Magna Carta, taxes are prescribed by law (Cagan 1982). This principle is reflected in Article 73, paragraph 3 of the 1982 Turkish Constitution, entitled 'Tax duty': 'Taxes, fees, duties, and other such financial obligations shall be imposed, amended, or revoked by law.' This principle not only requires a legal basis for the imposition of taxes, but also grants tax concessions to qualified taxpayers, thus abrogating – fully or partially – tax duties by law (Gunes 2000). The Turkish Constitutional Court acknowledged this in its first tax incentive decision on the law granting investment allowances along with custom duty exemptions,[1] stating:

> As investment allowance ultimately means reducing tax rates – that were imposed by laws – via an amendment for taxpayers who will benefit from this allowance; even the refund of customs duties represents the exemption of taxpayers fully or partly from those duties. Indeed, several Constitutional Court rulings to date have stated that the elements of taxes and other duties such as taxpayers, the tax base, rates, assessment, accrual, and payment procedures as well as penalties imposed and the statute of limitation shall be regulated by law under Article 61[2] of the Constitution. While these rulings do not mention the elements of tax exemption or exception, these are undeniably as important as the aspects of taxation law mentioned above. For this reason, those elements must also be determined by law as a result of the rule in the referred Constitutional article. (Ates, 2017)

Just as the legality principle promotes the transparency of tax systems, regular reporting on tax expenditures works in the same way.

Consequently, the principles of fiscal transparency and legality both require sound tax expenditure reporting. To this end, since 2005 the General Directorate for Revenue Regulation (formerly the General Directorate for Tax Policy) at the Ministry of Finance has produced tax expenditure inventories that list items of tax expenditure and total estimates of those items as an annex to annual budgets (BUMKO 2018). The General Directorate has also produced more detailed tax expenditure reports – first for the year 2007 and then, after a nine-year interval, for 2016 and 2017. Nonetheless, current Turkish reporting practice does not fully reflect these principles. The following sub-section discusses these shortcomings in detail.

2.2 Shortcomings of Current Reporting Practice in Turkey

In the US, the direction of energy tax policy can be ascertained by examining tax expenditure reports. Such an analysis indicates that although the revenue losses arising from energy tax incentives in the 1970s–80s are similar to revenue losses in the 2000s, the composition of energy tax incentives has changed significantly (Sherlock 2011). Until the 2000s, most revenue losses associated with energy tax expenditures were the result of fossil fuel tax incentives. This trend has now been reversed: today, there are more energy tax incentives in favour of renewable energy. The sum total of US energy sector tax incentives was estimated at $23.3 billion in 2013. Of this, 20.4 per cent relates to fossil fuels, 57.4 per cent to renewable energy and the remaining 22.2 per cent to energy efficiency (Sherlock and Stupak 2015).[3] For several reasons, however, the Turkish tax expenditure reports do not allow for trends in revenue losses associated with energy tax incentives to be examined in sufficient depth to provide insight into the direction of Turkish energy tax policy (cf Sherlock 2011).

First, while one section of the Turkish tax expenditure reports is entitled 'Infrastructure, Energy and Transportation', it is not clear which items of expenditure relate only to energy, and not to infrastructure or transportation. Moreover, a wider examination of the enumerated tax incentives reveals that some important tax expenditure provisions relating to energy – such as investment incentive schemes for energy producers – are listed under an entirely different function: that of 'improving business and boosting investment' (Ates 2017). A specific inventory of energy tax incentives is thus required to determine the extent to which these incentives are used and how this support is distributed among different energy sources.

Second, as Batirel previously revealed (2013), the Turkish tax expenditure reports do not include all tax incentives. We have identified 56 energy-related tax incentives in the Turkish tax system. However, the most recent Turkish expenditure report, from 2017, only enumerates 24 of these (Ministry of Finance 2017). Even if the enumerated energy tax expenditure items give rise to most of the revenue losses, this incomplete information makes a conclusive review of energy tax incentives in Turkey impossible.

The next section presents a framework for an alternative calculation of energy tax expenditures in order to combat the shortcomings of the current reporting practice.

3. AN ALTERNATIVE CALCULATION OF ENERGY TAX EXPENDITURES IN TURKEY

In this section, we examine whether and to what extent the energy sector is supported by tax incentives from the state budget. In other words, we attempt to produce an inventory by examining various energy tax expenditures enumerated in the Turkish tax expenditure reports of 2016 and 2017. Our calculations differ from the OECD inventory of tax expenditures, as we include a few more tax expenditure items on energy and do not restrict our coverage to fossil fuel subsidies only.

Below, we take the tax expenditure reports of 2016 and 2017, which provide the tax expenditure amounts for 2015 and 2016 respectively, as the basis for our calculations and projections. Next, we define the various assumptions made in order to explain our calculations of energy tax expenditures for each item. Finally, we add up the numbers for each year to arrive at the total tax expenditure amount for the energy sector. Table 18A.1 in the Appendix summarizes the findings.

3.1 Tax Incentives for Investments with Incentive Certificates

Energy projects are subsidized under the New Investment Incentive System, which was introduced in April 2012. This comprises four schemes: (1) the General Investment Incentive Scheme, (2) the Regional Investment Incentive Scheme, (3) the Large-Scale Investment Incentive Scheme, and (4) the Strategic Investment Incentive Scheme. Coal exploration, production and investments in coal-fired power plants are subsidized through the Regional Investment Incentive Scheme, and are included as 'priority investments' which receive more generous investment incentives. This programme categorizes Turkish regions and cities according to their development levels and aims to support relevant industries in those cities in line with their development potential. In general, the scheme offers subsidies in the form of a customs duty exemption, value added tax (VAT) exemption, tax reduction, social security premium support (employer's share), land allocation and interest support, with the terms and rates of support depending on the region (Regions 1 to 6, with Region 6 attracting the highest levels of support).

In addition, renewable energy investments are subsidized within the General Investment Incentive Scheme, which grants such projects a VAT exemption, customs duty exemption, and income tax withholding support, provided that the investment is made in Region 6.

A few energy investments have also been supported under the Large-Scale Investment Incentive Scheme and the Strategic Investment Incentive Scheme.

3.1.1 Article 32/A of the Corporate Income Tax Law: corporate income tax rate reduction

The tax expenditures realized through the corporate income tax (CIT) rate reduction for 2015 totalled TL 2 174 681 000. This was multiplied by 0.36, which is the percentage of fixed investments in energy for 2015, according to the New Investment Incentive System. Similarly, the total amount realized for 2016 was TL 2 344 934 000. This was multiplied by 0.34, which is the percentage of fixed investments in energy for 2016. The energy tax expenditures stemming from the CIT rate reduction corresponded to TL 782 885 000 and TL 797 278 000 respectively for 2015 and 2016. The percentage of fixed investments in energy within the New Investment Incentive Scheme increased to 0.57 in 2017. As Turkey invests heavily in energy projects each year, we assumed that this percentage would persist until 2020; we therefore multiplied the tax expenditure forecasts for 2017–20 by this rate to arrive at the energy tax expenditure projections.

3.1.2 Provisional Article 80 of the Personal Income Tax Law: personal income withholding tax support

The New Investment Incentive System statistics were again taken as the basis for our calculations regarding personal income withholding tax support. The total tax expenditures realized through personal income withholding tax support in 2015 and 2016 were TL 8 628 000 and TL 17 108 000 respectively. The same percentage of fixed investments in energy applied, as above. Hence, the energy tax expenditures stemming from personal income withholding tax support corresponded to TL 3 106 000 and TL 5 817 000 respectively for 2015 and 2016. The projections from the 2017 tax expenditure report were multiplied by 0.57 to arrive at the 2017–20 forecasts for the energy sector.

3.1.3 Article 13/d of the VAT Law: VAT exemption for imported and/or locally provided investment machinery and equipment and the sale or rental of intangible rights and software

The same methodology was applied to the VAT exemption for investment machinery and equipment. For 2015, TL 1 792 247 000 was multiplied by 0.36, and for 2016, TL 1 034 193 000 was multiplied by 0.34 in order to arrive at the total energy tax expenditures stemming from this exemption in the relevant years. 0.57 is the assumed percentage of fixed investments in energy from 2017 onwards.

3.1.4 Provisional Article 30 of the VAT Law: VAT refund for building and construction expenses

Similarly, the total tax expenditures realized through the VAT refund for building and construction expenses for investments with incentive certificates were calculated using the 2015 and 2016 percentages of fixed investments in energy. The results were as follows: TL 8 065 000 x 0.36 = TL 2 903 000 in 2015; and TL13 718 000 x 0.34 = TL 4664 000 in 2016. 0.57 is the assumed percentage of fixed investments in energy from 2017 onwards.

3.2 Tax Incentives for Electricity Production Investments within the Scope of Build-Operate and Build-Operate-Transfer Projects

Build-operate and build-operate-transfer contracts that include take-or-pay clauses and Treasury guarantees are models of public-private partnership (PPP) that aim to attract private sector investment (Atiyas, Cetin and Gulen 2012). Turkey introduced these models for the first time in 1984 by allowing the government to authorize domestic and foreign companies subject to private law provisions to participate in electricity generation, transmission, distribution and trading.

3.2.1 Provisional Article 29 of the VAT Law: VAT exemption for the supply of goods and services

The total tax expenditures realized through the VAT exemption for the supply of goods and services for projects realized under build-operate or build-operate-transfer contracts were calculated based on the sectoral investment percentages of the PPP projects reported by the Ministry of Development (2018). Accordingly, energy investments accounted for \$9 166 253 529 out of a total \$61 657 554 041 in PPP investments, which corresponds to a percentage of 0.15. This percentage was assumed to remain constant throughout the years 2015–20 in our calculations.

3.2.2 Provisional Article 5 of the Special Consumption Tax (SCT) Law: exemption for fuel oil and diesel oil to be used in electricity generation

The actual amounts and forecasts for this item were directly reported in the tax expenditure reports (2016, 2017) for the years 2015–20.

3.3 Tax Incentives for Energy R&D Investment

3.3.1 Provisional Article 75 of the Personal Income Tax (PIT) Law: personal income withholding tax support

According to TurkStat (2018a), the energy sector (eg, electricity, gas, steam, water supply, sewerage) accounted for 257 000 of all 26 621 000 jobs filled in 2015, and 257 000 of all 27 205 000 jobs filled in 2016. These figures were used to calculate the actual energy tax expenditure due to personal income withholding tax support in 2015 and 2016. The projected expenditure figures for 2017–20 were multiplied by 0.01 from 2017 onwards, as the percentage of total employment filled by the energy sector was assumed to be constant, based on the 2015–17 figures.

3.3.2 Article 3/1 of the Research and Development Law: tax credits

TurkStat (2018b) has reported central government budget appropriations and outlay on research and development (R&D) in accordance with socio-economic objectives for the years 2008–17. Accordingly, energy R&D as a percentage of total R&D expenditures corresponded to 0.03 in 2015 and 0.02 in 2016. These ratios were multiplied by the tax expenditures realized for energy in the stated years. For the forecasts for the 2017–20 period, 0.02 was assumed as the total annual percentage of energy R&D.

3.3.3 Article 3/A of the R&D Law: tax credits

The same methodology as above was applied here.

3.4 Other Tax Incentives for Energy Production and Consumption

3.4.1 Article 23/3 of the PIT Law: exemption for underground workers

The percentages of workers that are employed by mining companies TTK and TKI in total mining and quarrying employment were used in order to estimate expenditures on workers employed in the energy sector. Court of Accounts (2018) and TurkStat (2018a) data were used for this purpose. The assumed percentage of mine workers was taken as 0.18 from 2017 onwards.

3.4.2 Article 13/c of the VAT Law: exemption for petroleum and precious metal explorations

The actual amounts and forecasts for this item were directly reported in the tax expenditure reports (2016, 2017) for the years 2015–20.

3.4.3 Article 7/1-b of the SCT Law: exemption for petroleum exploration and production activities

The actual amounts and forecasts for this item were directly reported in the tax expenditure reports (2016, 2017) for the years 2015–20.

3.4.4 Article 7/3-c of the SCT Law: exemption for vehicles to be used in petroleum exploration activities

The actual amounts and forecasts for this item were directly reported in the tax expenditure reports (2016, 2017) for the years 2015–20.

3.4.5 Article 7A of the SCT Law: exemption for fuel oil used by vehicles carrying export goods

The actual amounts and forecasts for this item were directly reported in the tax expenditure reports (2016, 2017) for the years 2015–20.

3.4.6 Article 12 of the SCT Law – Governmental Decree 2002/4482: exemption for fuels used in air transport

The actual amounts and forecasts for this item were directly reported in the tax expenditure reports (2016, 2017) for the years 2015–20.

3.4.7 Article 12 of the SCT Law – Governmental Decree 2003/5868: exemption for fuels used in maritime transport

The actual amounts and forecasts for this item were directly reported in the tax expenditure reports (2016, 2017) for the years 2015–20.

3.4.8 Article 12 of the SCT Law – Governmental Decree 2005/8704: exemption for bioethanol used as input in gasoline production

The actual amounts and forecasts for this item were directly reported in the tax expenditure reports (2016, 2017) for the years 2015–20.

3.4.9 Article 12 of the SCT Law – Governmental Decree 2008/14061: exemption for liquefied petroleum gas (LPG) used as input in ethylene production

The actual amounts and forecasts for this item were directly reported in the tax expenditure reports (2016, 2017) for the years 2015–20.

3.4.10 Article 12 of the SCT Law – Governmental Decree 2011/1435: exemption for products such as naphtha, petroleum coke and petroleum bitumen

The actual amounts and forecasts for this item were directly reported in the tax expenditure reports (2016, 2017) for the years 2015–20.

3.4.11 Article 12 of the SCT Law – Governmental Decree 2013/5595: exemption for diesel oil produced by blending with biodiesel

The actual amounts and forecasts for this item were directly reported in the tax expenditure reports (2016, 2017) for the years 2015–20.

3.4.12 Article 12 of the SCT Law – Governmental Decree 2014/6881: exemption for LPG used in aerosol production

The actual amounts and forecasts for this item were directly reported in the tax expenditure reports (2016, 2017) for the years 2015–20.

4. SUMMARY AND DISCUSSION OF FINDINGS

The sum of each column in Table 18A.1 in the Appendix sets out the annual tax expenditure amounts for energy from 2015–20. Accordingly, in 2015 the energy sector benefited from TL 11 021 741 000 of tax expenditure. In 2016 this amount increased to TL 11 846 500 000. As a result of the projections in the tax expenditure report for 2017 and our assumptions regarding the percentage of tax expenditure attributable to the energy sector, projected tax expenditures amount to TL 15 993 845 000 in 2017; TL 18 204 454 000 in 2018; TL 18 750 413 000 in 2019; and TL 20 929 021 000 in 2020.

While the energy sector accounts for only a small share of Turkish gross domestic product (GDP), these figures are nonetheless highly significant. For instance, electricity, gas, steam and air conditioning supply contributed just 1.3 per cent to GDP in 2016. According to TurkStat (2018c) data, the sector's share of GDP never exceeded 1.6 per cent between 1998–2016, although it did increase during this period. On the other hand, energy tax expenditures corresponded to 0.5 per cent of Turkish GDP in both 2015 and 2016.

Furthermore, the available data suggest that energy tax expenditures weigh heavily on total tax revenues in Turkey. The country's total tax revenue – referring to compulsory transfers to the central government for public purposes – amounted to TL 427 billion in 2015 and TL 478 billion in 2016 (World Bank 2018). As such, energy tax expenditures as a percentage of total tax revenue corresponded to 2.6 per cent in 2015 and 2.5 per cent in 2016.

According to the OECD, TL 9971410000 of tax expenditures in Turkey went towards fossil fuels in 2015 and TL 10935292000 in 2016 (OECD 2018). It should also be noted that the OECD counts rebates for diesel used in agriculture as a tax expenditure item. If that is excluded from the OECD figure, the 2016 value of energy tax expenditures falls to TL 10218292000. The estimates presented in this chapter are far above the OECD tax expenditure numbers for Turkey (eg, our calculation for 2016 exceeds the OECD estimate by TL 1.6 billion), given that we have also included tax expenditures for renewable energy in our analysis.

5. CONCLUSON

The estimates for energy tax expenditures in Turkey remain unreliable, due to difficulties in estimating some future elements (eg, projections for 2017–20) and assumptions regarding the percentage of related expenditure attributable to the energy sector. Further examination of these incentives would be helpful in informing the debate on energy subsidies in Turkey. This would help to illuminate the true cost to the government budget by determining the extent of the revenue lost through energy tax expenditures. In future, we intend to determine how energy tax incentives are used and distributed among different energy sources. However, this case study provides clear evidence that the transparency of fiscal data on tax expenditures depends on the regular publication of such data. Transparent tax expenditure reporting will ensure that researchers can further improve the quality of data available on this vital area of tax policy.

NOTES

* This research has been supported by the Horizon 2020 program of the European Union through the project COFFERS (Combating Fiscal Fraud and Empowering Regulators) (grant agreement No 727145) and Altinbas University Scientific Research Projects Unit (PB2017-BAHAR-HUKUK-1). We would like to thank the participants in the 19th Global Conference on Environmental Taxation at the University of San Pablo, Madrid and the Altinbas University Workshop on "Increasing Fiscal Transparency in Energy Policy" for their helpful comments, and Aylin Armagan for research assistance.

1. Investment allowance or credits are a form of tax subsidy that enable the investor to write off an amount that is greater than the cost of the investment (Zolt 2014).
2. This article is from the former Turkish Constitution of 1961 and equivalent of Article 73 of the current Turkish Constitution of 1982.
3. Nonetheless, although the amount of renewable energy tax expenditures is considerably higher than the amount of fossil fuel tax incentives, fossil fuels dominate energy production in the USA with a share of 78.5 per cent (Sherlock and Stupak 2015).

REFERENCES

Altshuler R and Dietz R (2008). 'Tax Expenditure Estimation and Reporting: A Critical Review', www.nber.org/papers/w14263, last accessed 2 January 2019.

Ates L (2017). 'Transparency as a Key Prerequisite for the Success of Energy Subsidy Reform: A Case Study of Tax Subsidies in Turkey', in Boix RS (ed), *Aspectos Constitucionales Controvertidos De La Tributación Ambiental*. Cordoba: Universidad Nacional de Córdoba.

Atiyas I, Cetin T and Gulen G (2012). *Reforming Turkish Energy Markets: Political Economy*. New York: Springer.

Batirel OF (2013). Vergi Harcamaları, Mali Saydamlık İlkesi ve Anayasaya Uygunluk. *Istanbul Ticaret Universitesi Sosyal Bilimler Dergisi* Vol 12: 24.

Butce ve Mali Kontrol Genel Mudurlugu (BUMKO) (2018). *Merkezi Yonetim Butce Kanunu ve Ekleri;* www.bumko.gov.tr/TR,61/merkezi-yonetim-butce-kanunu-ve-ekleri.html, last accessed 30 December 2018.

Cagan N (1982). *Vergilendirme Yetkisi*. Istanbul: Kazanci Hukuk Yayınlari.

Court of Accounts (2018). Kamu Isletmeleri Genel Raporlari; https://www.sayistay.gov.tr/tr/?p=2&CategoryId=101, last accessed 25 December 2018.

Group of 20 (G20) (2009). G20 Leaders Statment: The Pittsburgh Summit; www.g20.utoronto.ca/2009/2009communique0925.html, last accessed 2 January 2019.

CVCE (2016). Budgetary Principles; www.cvce.eu/obj/budgetary_principles-en-3f6aa90a-486a-40c7-9a50-76ea3decdabb.html, last accessed 25 December 2018.

European Commission (EC) (2011). Roadmap to a Resource Efficient Europe. COM(2011) 571; http://eurlex.europa.eu/LexUriServ/LexUriServ.do?uri=COM:2011:0571:FIN:EN:PDF, last accessed 2 January 2019.

Gunes G (2000). '*Butce Hakki ve Butce Uygulamalari*' In *Anayasal Mali Duzen*; www.maliyesempozyumu.sakarya.edu.tr/sites/maliyesempozyumu/file/1372373051-13-turkiye-maliye-sempozyumu-pdf.pdf, last accessed 30 December 2018.

Kalyva A (2015). Political Economy of Tax Expenditures. http://ec.europa.eu/economy_finance/events/2015/20151019-workshop/documents/7._kalyva_-_tax_expenditures_en.pdf, last accessed 2 January 2019.

Ministry of Development (2018). *TC Cumhurbaskanligi Strateji ve Butce Baskanligi*

Kamu-Ozel Işbirligi ile Yurutulen Projeler; https://koi.kalkinma.gov.tr/, last accessed 25 December 2018.
Ministry of Finance (2006). Tax Expenditure Report of 2006. Ankara.
Ministry of Finance (2012). Public Financial Management and Control Law No 5018; www.sgb.gov.tr/Mevzuat/01.Kanun/Public%20Financial%20Management%20and%20Control%20Law%20No.%205018.pdf, last accessed 15 December 2018.
Ministry of Finance (2016). Tax Expenditure Report of 2016. Ankara.
Ministry of Finance (2017). Tax Expenditure Report of 2017. Ankara.
OECD (2015). *OECD Companion to the Inventory of Support Measures for Fossil Fuels 2015*. Paris: OECD Publishing.
OECD (2018). *Inventory of Estimated Budgetary Support and Tax Expenditures for Fossil Fuels 2018*. Paris: OECD; www.oecd.org/site/tadffss/data, last accessed 2 January 2019.
Oosterhuis F, Ding H, Franckx L and Razzini P (2014). 'Enhancing comparability of data on estimated budgetary support and tax expenditures for fossil fuels'; http://ec.europa.eu/environment/enveco/taxation/pdf/201412ffs_final_report.pdf, last accessed 2 January 2019.
Roberts TM (2016). 'Picking Winners and Losers: A Structural Examination of Tax Subsidies to Energy Industry', *Columbia Journal of Environmental Law* Vol 41: 1.
Ruggeri G (2005). 'Public Expenditure Incidence Analysis' in Shah A (ed), *Public Expenditure Analysis*. Washington, DC: The World Bank Publication.
Sherlock MF (2011). 'Energy Tax Policy: Historical Perspectives on and Current Status of Energy Tax Expenditures'; www.leahy.senate.gov/imo/media/doc/R41227EnergyLegReport.pdf, last accessed 15 December 2018.
Sherlock MF and Stupak JM (2015). 'Energy Tax Incentives: Measuring Value Across Different Types of Energy Resources'; https://fas.org/sgp/crs/misc/R41953.pdf, last accessed 25 December 2018.
TurkStat (2018a). *İktisadi faaliyet kollarına göre istihdam* (NACE Rev 2) *istatistikleri;* www.turkstat.gov.tr/, last accessed 10 December 2018.
TurkStat (2018b). *Ar-Ge İstatistikleri, Sosyo-Ekonomik Hedeflere Göre Merkezi Yönetim Bütçesinden AR-GE Faaliyetleri için Ayrılan Ödenek ve Harcamalar*; www.tuik.gov.tr/PreIstatistikTablo.do?istab_id=2030, last accessed 12 December 2018.
TurkStat (2018c). *İktisadi faaliyet kollarına göre cari fiyatlarla gayrisafi yurtiçi hasıla istatistikleri*; www.turkstat.gov.tr/, last accessed 12 December 2018.
World Bank (1995). 'Turkey-Public Finance Management Project: Main Report', Washington, DC: World Bank; http://documents.worldbank.org/curated/en/241921468778233891/Main-report, last accessed 5 December 2018.
World Bank (2018). 'World Development Indicators, World Bank Data on Tax Revenue'; http://databank.worldbank.org/data/reports.aspx?source=2&series=NY.ADJ.SVNG.GN.ZS&country=#, last accessed 5 December 2018.
Zolt EM (2014). 'Tax Incentives and Tax Base Protection Issues'; www.un.org/esa/ffd/wp-content/uploads/2014/10/20140604_Paper3_Zolt.pdf, last accessed 2 January 2019.

APPENDIX

Table 18A.1 Energy tax expenditures in Turkey (in thousand TL)

CORRESPONDING LAW	ARTICLE NUMBER	DESCRIPTION	2015	2016	2017	2018	2019	2020
Corporate Income Tax Law (CIT Law)	Article 32/A	CIT rate reduction	782885	797278	2891040	3281908	1983811	2214310
Personal Income Tax Law (PIT Law)	Provisional Article 80	Personal income withholding tax support for investments with incentive certificates	3106	5817	11348	12881	14473	16155
Value Added Tax Law (VAT Law)	Article 13/d	VAT exemption for imported and/or locally provided investment machinery and equipment as well as selling and renting of intangible rights and software within the scope of incentive certificates	645209	351626	685969	778699	874926	976584
Value Added Tax Law (VAT Law)	Provisional Article 30	VAT refund for building and construction expenses for the investments to be realized within the scope of investment incentive certificate	2903	4664	9099	10329	11606	12954
Value Added Tax Law (VAT Law)	Provisional Article 29	VAT exemption for the supply of goods and services for projects to be realized within the scope of build-operate or build-operate-transfer projects	48864	229980	271110	307759	345791	385968
Special Consumption Tax Law (SCT Law)	Provisional Article 5	SCT exception introduced for fuel oil and diesel oil to be used in electricity generation	202902	229042	266528	302557	339946	379444
Personal Income Tax Law (PIT Law)	Provisional Article 75	Personal income withholding tax support for R&D personnel	3348	4264	5161	5962	6699	7477

CORRESPONDING LAW	ARTICLE NUMBER	DESCRIPTION	2015	2016	2017	2018	2019	2020
Law No 5746 on Supporting Research and Development Activities (R&D Law)	Article 3/1	R&D tax credits in Law No 5746 (VHR 2016 sayfa: 249)	18143	15334	22523	19969	22437	25044
Law No 5746 on Supporting Research and Development Activities (R&D Law)	Article 3/A	R&D tax credits in Law No 5746	750	2600	3933	3435	3859	4307
Personal Income Tax Law	Article 23/3	PIT exemption for underground workers	24302	27069	30865	35037	39367	43941
Value Added Tax Law (VAT Law)	Article 13/c	VAT exemption for petroleum and precious metal exploration	327195	524038	609805	692238	777782	868152
Special Consumption Tax Law (SCT Law)	Article 7-1/b	SCT exemption for petroleum exploration and production activities	74329	46287	5386	61144	68700	76682
Special Consumption Tax Law (SCT Law)	Article 7-3/c	SCT exemption for vehicles to be used in petroleum exploration activities	38	0	0	0	0	0
Special Consumption Tax Law (SCT Law)	Article 7/A	SCT exemption for fuel oil used by vehicles carrying export goods	257592	351414	408928	464207	521571	582173
Special Consumption Tax Law (SCT Law)	Article 12, Governmental Decree 2002/4482	SCT exemption for fuels used in air transport	3344591	3511584	4086307	4638694	5211921	5817494

Table 18A.1 (continued)

CORRESPONDING LAW	ARTICLE NUMBER	DESCRIPTION	2015	2016	2017	2018	2019	2020
Special Consumption Tax Law (SCT Law)	Article 12, Governmental Decree 2003/5868	SCT exemption for fuels used in maritime transport	609,202	696 120	810 050	919 553	1 033 187	1 153 233
Special Consumption Tax Law (SCT Law)	Article 12, Governmental Decree 2005/8704	SCT exemption for bioethanol to be used as input in gasoline production	105 248	125,262	145,763	165,467	185,915	207,516
Special Consumption Tax Law (SCT Law)	Article 12, Governmental Decree 2008/14061	SCT exemption for LPG used as input in ethylene production	54 893	17 429	20 282	23 023	25 868	28 874
Special Consumption Tax Law (SCT Law)	Article 12, Governmental Decree 2011/1435	SCT exemption for such products as naphtha, petroleum coke and petroleum bitumen	4 217 188	4 594 402	5 346 345	6 069 064	6 819 048	7 611 353
Special Consumption Tax Law (SCT Law)	Article 12, Governmental Decree 2013/5595	SCT exemption for diesel oil produced by blending with biodiesel	211 072	204 335	237 777	269 920	303 276	338 513
Special Consumption Tax Law (SCT Law)	Article 12, Governmental Decree 2014/6881	SCT exception for LPG to be used in aerosol production	87 980	107 957	125 626	142 608	160 231	178 848

Index